BRUEGEL

Although philosophers, physicians, and others have long pondered the meanings and experiences of growing older, gerontology did not emerge as a scientific field of inquiry in the United States until the twentieth century. The study of aging borrows from a variety of other disciplines, including medicine, psychology, sociology, and anthropology, but its own scientific basis is still developing. Despite dozens of aging-related journals, and a notable increase in state, regional, national, and international networks, there are no widely shared techniques or distinctive methods. Theories of aging remain partial and tentative.

Crossing Frontiers is the first book-length study of the history of gerontology. By tracing intellectual networks and analyzing institutional patterns, W. Andrew Achenbaum explores how old age became a "problem" worth investigating and how a multidisciplinary orientation took shape. Gerontology is a marginal intellectual enterprise but its very strengths and weaknesses illuminate the politics of specialization and academic turf-fighting in U.S. higher education

Crossing frontiers

Crossing frontiers

Gerontology emerges as a science

W. ANDREW ACHENBAUM

Department of History
University of Michigan

CAMBRIDGE
UNIVERSITY PRESS

Published by the Press Syndicate of the University of Cambridge
The Pitt Building, Trumpington Street, Cambridge CB2 1RP
40 West 20th Street, New York, NY 10011–4211, USA
10 Stamford Road, Oakleigh, Melbourne 3166, Australia

© Cambridge University Press 1995

First published 1995

Printed in the United States of America

Library of Congress Cataloging-in-Publication Data
Achenbaum, W. Andrew.
Crossing frontiers : gerontology emerges as a science / W. Andrew
Achenbaum.
p.   cm.
ISBN 0–521–48194–5–ISBN 0–521–55880–8 (pbk.)
1. Gerontology – United States – History.   I. Title.
HQ1064.U5A625   1995
305.26 – dc20
94–47972
CIP

A catalog record for this book is available from the British Library.

ISBN 0–521–48194–5 Hardback
ISBN 0–521–55880–8 Paperback

To all my friends, and especially
William Kelly and Jan Lewis

The essence of friendship is entireness,
a total magnanimity and trust.
                    Ralph Waldo Emerson

Contents

Part II: Gerontology takes shape in the era of Big Science

Acknowledgments

I thank the Spencer Foundation, particularly Marion Faldet, for the support that resulted in this book. For four years they made it possible for me to spend a quarter of my time reading and reflecting on the history of gerontology. Conversations with Jane Barney, Bob and Gene Berkhofer, Ed Berkowitz, Jay Devine, David Hollinger, Gail Kara, Jane Ketchin, Peter Laslett, John Modell, Michel Philibert, Dan Resneck, Lu Schaefer, and especially with a long-time mentor, Peter N. Stearns, proved quite helpful at the formative stages of the project. Rick Moody gave me shrewd advice on how to make cross-disciplinary comparisons.

Colleagues and friends in the aging-research community offered many useful insights. I am especially grateful to Jack Cornman, who not only obtained travel funds so that I could interview several leaders in the Gerontological Society, but who also offered helpful comments on several manuscript chapters. Scott Bass served as a terrific sounding board. I learned much from talking to Marjorie Adler, Bob Atchley, George Baker, Vern Bengtson, Jim and Betty Birren, Dan Blazer, Butch Blumenthal, Elaine and Steve Brody, Harold Brody, Bud Busse, Vince Cristofalo, Tuck Finch, the late Jo Freeman, Linda George, the late Raymond Harris, Len Hayflick, Rosalie Kane, Oscar Kaplan, Ed Kaskowitz, Al Lansing, Powell Lawton, Bernice Neugarten, Harold Orbach, Matilda and Jack Riley, Carol Schutz, Jim Schulz, the late Millie Seltzer, Ethel Shanas, and the late Nathan Shock. Bruce Craig, Fernando Torres-Gil, Manuel Miranda, and Bill Oriol supplied valuable information about federal involvement in research on aging.

In the course of writing this book, I also worked on two other projects that I hope will form a trilogy as the fiftieth anniversary of the founding of the Gerontological Society of America is observed. Jeanne Bader originally proposed the idea of compiling biographical sketches of several hundred gerontologists, past and present, who had been active in the field. I finished *A Biographical Dictionary of Gerontology* for Greenwood Press with one of my graduate students, Daniel M. Albert. Both helped me as *Crossing Frontiers* took form: Jeanne constantly supplied clippings and historical documents she came across; Dan read an early draft of this manuscript with the sensibilities of a historian of science. On *Keywords of Gerontology*, a collection to be released by Springer Publishing Company, I worked with Carole Haber and Steve Weiland, who over the years supplied a stream of citations on disciplinarity. These two books cover in greater detail some people and themes discussed much too briefly here.

Colleagues at the Institute of Gerontology (IoG) have been a treasured resource for more than twenty years. Willie Edwards gave me run of the library when I was in graduate school; Mary O'Brien, Dorothy Coons, Carol Hollenshead, Harold Johnson, and John Tropman involved me in IoG activities during the late 1970s. For roughly a decade, I have been working closely with the Institute's current director, Richard C. Adelman. Dick has been very supportive of my professional endeavors, and he is a wonderful collaborator. In the latter stages of this project, he also gave me savvy critiques of the strengths and weaknesses of my history from his perspective as a biochemist and gerontological maven. I also have benefitted from Fred Bookstein's tough goading; from seriously playful brown-bag lunches and conversations with the late Ben Cohen and Wilma Donahue, Brant Fries, Tom Hickey, Dorrie Rosenblatt, and Lois Verbrugge; and from timely bibliographic assistance from John Faulkner, Jeff Halter, and Rich Miller. Exchanges with colleagues and speakers at weekly IoG seminars have been a rich source of ideas. Having produced more versions of this manuscript than either of us cares to count, Pat Blackman proves that an administrative assistant with a healthy sense of the absurd is indispensable in this age of word processors and modems. Others at the University of Michigan facilitated my work. The University's libraries are superb. Leif Backman and his staff cheerfully tracked down books and articles for me, and obtained through Inter-Library Loan those publications we did not have. Fran Blouin and his associates at the Bentley Historical Collections made it possible for me to enrich the university's holdings in the history of gerontology and to gain access to its archives. Colleagues and associates elsewhere on campus, especially Ruth Dunkle, Rose Gibson, Harvey Guthrie, John Hagen, John Holland, Joel Howell, Peg Kusnerz, Susan Lipschutz, John Lundin, Howard Markel, Tom Morson, Ginny Peacock, Marion Perlmutter, Larry Root, Johnnie Spraggins, and Mayer Zald suggested ideas to pursue. Two historians-in-the-making, Greg Raynor and Hajj Womack, helped during summers; former graduate students and post-docs, notably Keith Arbour and Lucinda Orwoll, pointed me in new directions; working with Avram Mack on his senior essay was instructive.

I also thank many who have listened to excerpts of this book when it still was a work-in-progress. Students in the Ph.D. programs in gerontology at the University of Massachusetts–Boston and the University of Southern California provided good feedback. I learned much from friends abroad, including Andrew Blaikie, Malcolm Johnson, Paul Johnson, Stephen Katz, Victor Marshall, and Alan Walker.

Frank Smith is the prime reason why I like to publish books with Cambridge University Press. He knows what it takes to produce good history. I thank Frank for letting my friend, Thomas R. Cole, read the manuscript for the Press. Tom listened critically over the years as I wrestled with ideas; he made good recommendations in the margins in every chapter, which I duly incorporated and gratefully acknowledge. David Van Tassel, who also served as a reader, offered as incisive a set of suggestions for revisions for this book as he had for my first monograph. More than any other person, David has created opportunities for insinuating voices from the humanities into gerontologic discourse. With others in my cohort of researchers on aging, I owe tremendous debt to this master historian. I also thank Herbert Gilbert and Mary Hogan for overseeing the final stages of production.

Having dedicated my first three books to my wife, to my parents, and to my daughters, respectively, it seems fitting that I should acknowledge my friends in a monograph that focuses on networks. Mine has been a rich life, thanks in large measure to words and experiences shared with some terrific human beings. So, in addition to those who are friends as well as colleagues mentioned above, here's to Aggie, Art, Barbara, Barry, Betsy, Cathy, Cece, Charlie, Chris, Chuck, Dan, David, Donny, Eric, Ginna, Hannah, Jackie, Jim, JoAnn, John, Jude, Karl, Louisa, Lydia, Malcolm, Mary Ann (in several forms), Marg, Mark, Martha, Mary, Michael, all the Mujicas, Pam, Peg, Rob, Sarah, Seth, Teich, and Valerie. I dedicate this book to Bill, my college roommate, and to Jan, already a soul mate in graduate school. Over the years we have crossed many frontiers (intellectual and otherwise) together in our respective journeys of life; I treasure the memories and look forward to the next vistas.

Abbreviations

AARP	American Association of Retired Persons
AAUP	American Association of University Professors
ACS	American Cancer Society
AGHE	Association for Gerontology in Higher Education
AGS	American Geriatrics Society
AHA	American Heart Association
AMA	American Medical Association
AoA	Administration on Aging
APA	American Psychological Association
APS	American Psychological Society
ASA	American Society on Aging
BLSA	Baltimore Longitudinal Study of Aging
CCD	Committee on Child Development, University of Chicago
CES	Committee on Economic Security
CHD	Committee on Human Development, University of Chicago
CHGD	Center for Human Growth and Development, University of Michigan
DVA	U.S. Department of Veterans Affairs
FSA	Federal Security Agency
GAR	Grand Army of the Republic
GEU	Geriatric Evaluation Unit
GRC	Gerontology Research Center, Baltimore
GRECC	Geriatric Research, Education, and Clinical Center
GSA	Gerontological Society (of America)
HEW	U.S. Department of Health, Education, and Welfare
HHS	U.S. Department of Health and Human Services
IAG	International Association of Gerontology
IHA	Institute of Human Adjustment, University of Michigan

IoG	Institute of Gerontology, University of Michigan
ISMRRD	Institute for the Study of Mental Retardation and Related Disabilities, University of Michigan
ISR	Institute for Social Research, University of Michigan
JoG	*Journal(s) of Gerontology*
LSRM	Laura Spelman Rockefeller Memorial
NCI	National Cancer Institute
NCOA	National Council on the Aging, Inc.
NEH	National Endowment for the Humanities
NHDVS	National Home for Disabled Volunteer Soldiers
NIA	National Institute on Aging
NICHD	National Institute on Child Health and Human Development
NIH	National Institute(s) of Health
NIMH	National Institute on Mental Health
NORC	National Opinion Research Center, University of Chicago
NRPB	National Resource Planning Board
NRTA	National Retired Teachers Association
NSF	National Science Foundation
RF	Rockefeller Foundation
SRC	Survey Research Center, University of Michigan
SSRC	Social Science Research Center
TG	*The Gerontologist*
U-M	University of Michigan
USC	University of Southern California
VA	Veterans Administration
VAMC	Veterans Administration Medical Center
VHS&RA	Veterans Health Services and Research Administration
WHCoA	White House Conference on Aging
WPA	Works Progress Administration

Introduction

Crossing Frontiers argues that gerontology did not emerge as a scientific field of inquiry in the United States until the twentieth century. The field's subject matter – "the study of aging from the broadest perspective"[1] – has deep, variegated roots. Scripture and classical literature attest to the "crown of glory" and other blessings that might be attained by older people. These same sources also describe "days of sorrow" often endured by unfortunate elders who lived too long. Writers from the fourth through nineteenth centuries added to the treasure-trove of positive, negative, ambiguous, ambivalent, and conflicting images of the bio-medico-psycho-social dimensions of the last stage of life. Many "facts" that scientists report in the current gerontology literature correspond to age-old descriptions of old age.[2]

By the same token, gerontologists lately have disclosed other aspects of aging that are truly novel. According to demographers, at least two-thirds of the improvement in human longevity has occurred since 1900. During this century, gains in life expectancy at birth and in adulthood have altered relationships: for the first time in our history, most middle-aged Americans have more living grandparents than children; senior citizens outnumber teenagers. There is an increasing incidence of five-generation families.[3]

1 This is the definition of "gerontology" that appears in the glossary of *Age Words* issued by the National Institute on Aging in 1986. For more on other definitions, see W. Andrew Achenbaum and Jeffrey S. Levin, "What Does Gerontology Mean?" *The Gerontologist*, vol. 29 (June 1989): 393–400.
2 Gerald Gruman, *A History of Ideas About the Prolongation of Life* (Philadelphia: American Philosophical Society, 1966); W. Andrew Achenbaum, "Societal Perceptions of Aging and the Aged," in Robert H. Binstock and Ethel Shanas, eds., *Handbook of Aging and the Social Sciences*, 2d ed. (New York: Van Nostrand Reinhold, 1985), pp. 129–48; Thomas R. Cole, David D. Van Tassel, and Robert Kastenbaum, eds., *Handbook of the Humanities and Aging* (New York: Springer, 1992).
3 Samuel H. Preston, "Children and Elderly in the U.S.," *Scientific American*, vol. 251 (1984):

Thanks to breakthroughs in biotechnology, we are on the verge of modifying processes of senescence at the cellular level. New medications, sophisticated prosthetic devices, and a better understanding of diet and nutrition have dramatically improved the quality of late life. Such advances have largely resulted from fresh ways of thinking about senescence, more precise methods of measuring phenomena, and new networks and organizations designed to disseminate information and evaluate results. As the twentieth century draws to a close, a sound scientific basis for studying old age is taking shape. That said, it must be quickly added that gerontology has not yet emerged as a science, a discipline, or a profession.

So old age is one thing, gerontology another. Histories of old age cover much of the material in this history of gerontology, but the foci are not identical.[4] An interpretation of historical old age might begin, for instance, with Seneca's dictum, *senectus morbidus est,* and then trace how linking age and disease influenced generations of philosophers, physicians, and ordinary people who gazed at senescence, often distorting their perception of its pathological features. Like other historians of aging, I indicate that most present-day researchers on aging do not consider old age a disease. No "magic bullet" retards senescence. There is much to learn about how and why people age as they do.[5]

A somewhat different set of questions underlies this book, however. Why did twentieth-century Americans who claim(ed) expertise as researchers on aging want to call themselves (and be recognized as) "scientists?" How has the field's relationship to other disciplines and professions changed over time? Has gerontology always aspired to be multidisciplinary? What factors have facilitated and constrained institution building? In addressing these and other questions, *Crossing Frontiers* explores why a growing number of investigators, often working at the margins of a science, have made it a major priority to do research on what they call "normal," "successful," and "productive" aging, and to leave it to geriatricians, pathologists, and other specialists to cure and alleviate diseases prevalent in late life.

Crossing Frontiers focuses on recent U.S. developments, but it begins with gerontologic motifs expressed in the Age of Discovery. Ideas and myths prevalent on both sides of the Atlantic during the sixteenth- and

---

435; Vern L. Bengtson and W. Andrew Achenbaum, eds., *The Changing Contract Between Generations* (Hawthorne, NY: Aldine, 1993).

4 An analysis of footnotes in *Crossing Frontiers* would indicate more citations to works by such historians of aging as Thomas R. Cole, Brian Gratton, Gerald Gruman, and Carole Haber in Chapter 1, where the topics overlap, than elsewhere.

5 The best contemporary guides to the literature on biogerontology are Leonard Hayflick, *How and Why We Age* (New York: Ballantine, 1994); Caleb E. Finch, *Longevity, Senescence, and the Genome* (Chicago: University of Chicago Press, 1990); and Michael Rose, *Evolutionary Biology of Aging* (New York: Oxford University Press, 1991). Dated, but still instructive, is Alex Comfort, *Ageing: The Biology of Senescence,* 2d ed. (New York: Holt, Rinehart & Winston, 1964).

seventeenth-centuries, which still affect the science of gerontology, arose out of changes in science that transformed human thinking about the natural order. "Traditionally, knowledge had been based on faith and insight, on reason and revolution," observes I. Bernard Cohen. "The new science discarded all of these as ways of understanding nature and set up experience – experiment and critical observation – as the foundation and ultimate test of knowledge."[6] Gerontologists, as heirs to that tradition, worry about research design, sampling, controls, measurements, and validity. Sometimes investigators try to appear more scientific than their work justifies so as to counter specters haunting the field. Charlatans used to promise to postpone debility, old age, and death. Many gerontologists also fear that they may be belittled as impostors. This book's cover illustrates another image. David Teniers the Younger portrays "The Alchemist" (1649) as an elderly, bearded man in tabard and fur cap. Aided by a junior associate, he works in a room cluttered with vials, pots, skulls, and musty books. An hourglass and an owl – symbols of longevity and age – bracket the painting. But viewers see that the alchemist's work ends in smoke and dust.[7] This impression lingers in faculty committees, government agencies, and other quarters where the current status of research on aging and the future of gerontology are discussed.

Two Precursors

A Spaniard began exploring frontiers of aging in the New World a century before the Pilgrims arrived. Juan Ponce de Leon (1460–1521), a page in the royal court of Aragon, joined Christopher Columbus on his second expedition in 1493. Fifteen years later, as governor of Puerto Rico, he sought new lands and riches. Intrigued by natives' tales of a Fountain of Youth, which were circulating in the Spanish court, the conquistador launched a series of expeditions. He eventually colonized Florida in 1513. Francisco Lopez de Gomara, a contemporary, observed that Ponce de Leon was "intent on finding out the spring of Bimini and a river in Florida, the Indians of Cuba and Hispaniola affirming that old people themselves in them became young again."[8] Although he suspected that the spring he had found in St. Augustine was not really the fountain, Ponce de Leon never

---

6 I. Bernard Cohen, *Revolution in Science* (Cambridge, MA: Harvard University Press, 1985), p. 79.

7 Peter C. Sutton, *The Age of Rubens* (Boston: Museum of Fine Arts, 1993), pp. 420–2.

8 Quoted in Charles B. Reynolds, *The Landing of Ponce de Leon: A Historical Review* (Mountain Lakes, NJ: author, 1934), p. 10. Biographical details on Ponce de Leon taken from the *Encyclopaedia Britannica*. See also T. Frederick Davis, "Juan Ponce de Leon's Voyages to Florida, *The Quarterly Periodical of the Florida Historical Society*, vol. 14 (July 1935): 1–62.

doubted that he would discover "the river, whose water rejuvenated the aged."[9]

Such exploits serve to introduce several gerontologic themes that recur throughout this book. Subsequent researchers on aging were not necessarily driven by the conquistador's desire for wealth and glory, but like him, many have tried to conquer frontiers in the name of Science. When Ponce de Leon took risks, he incorporated the best "scientific" information and social intelligence available. The idea that bathing in vital springs restored youth could be traced back to the Hindu legend of Cyavana (ca. 700 B.C.) and, independently, to biblical references (Gen. 2:10; Ps. 36:9; Rev.22:2). Aristotle had proposed that immersion in magical streams restored vitality to the aged's cold, dry skin. Alexander the Great searched for the Fountain of Youth. Sixteenth-century cognoscenti knew about Herodotus's report concerning a Persian emperor who had sought an Ethiopian spring with water oilier and lighter than was to be found elsewhere. Fountain-of-youth motifs figured prominently in fifteenth- and sixteenth-century art and literature. Furthermore, twentieth-century scientists can appreciate actions Ponce de Leon took to maximize his chances of success.[10] Far from a solitary odyssey, his venture was supported by church and crown; he took account of conflicting reports from Spanish observers and Indian experts. Like any seasoned investigator, Ponce de Leon remained open to the possibility of making a serendipitous discovery. The explorer was a skeptical optimist who based his doubts and hopes on what he and his peers deemed to be "empirical" data.

Ponce de Leon may have been the first Spaniard to spark the gerontologic imagination in the New World, but he was not the only European to advance research on aging during the Age of Discovery. Roughly a century after the conquistador's death, Francis Bacon (1561–1626), lawyer, philosopher, and Lord Chancellor under James I, composed his *New Atlantis*. Bacon's utopian fable, which was inspired in part by New World discoveries, recounts the adventures of British and Spanish explorers who sailed westward from Peru, lost their bearings, and eventually came ashore on terra incognita. The place had extensive orchards and botanical gardens; zoos, where reptiles and birds and insects were dissected in order to comprehend the workings of the human anatomy; and buildings in which scientists tested the properties of light, sound, and smell.

At the center of Bacon's fictional outpost was the House of Salomon [*sic*], or College of Six Days Works, a self-perpetuating scientific institute said to have been established in 300 B.C. In "the finding out of the true

9 The phrase is from Herrera y Tordesilla's *Historia General de las Indias* (1605), which is quoted in Leonard Olschki, "Ponce de Leon's Fountain of Youth," *The Hispanic American Historical Review*, vol. 21 (August 1941): 365.

10 Olschki, "Ponce de Leon's Fountain of Youth," p. 384.

nature of all things," Bacon's scholars assessed each other's work critically, but they did not presume to have a sense of "aperspectival" objectivity. (Theirs was not a "knowledge without a knower"; such a scientific orientation did not arise until the nineteenth century.[11]) Insights were put to practical use: The College's novices and masters, experimenters and collectors, abstracters and compilers gave the Europeans "knowledge of the affairs and state of those countries to which they were designed, and especially of the sciences, arts, manufactures, and inventions of all the world; and withal to bring unto us books, instruments, and patterns in every kind."[12] The "public interest" warranted the college's activities; public goods were the expected outcome.

Science, according to Bacon, was advanced by an autonomous, secure cadre of creative minds, by specialists who subscribed to the mission and methods of the College. Their agenda was open-ended, but Bacon's characters, like Ponce de Leon, had a burning desire to become masters of exploration: "The knowledge we now possess will not teach a man even what to *wish*."[13] Like Ponce de Leon, Bacon's ideal scientists took risks, seeking wisdom in unfamiliar places. They often ended up "in the midst of the greater wilderness of waters in the world." Bacon envisioned that these latter-day Jonahs would find themselves "between death and life; for we are beyond both the old world and the new."[14] For all the incumbent dangers, the gamble promised extraordinary payoffs. In the New Atlantis, European sailors no longer were at Nature's mercy. With God's help, they were free to create new ideas based on the objects of their perceptions.[15]

Bacon believed that the utopian goals of the *New Atlantis* were attainable through basic and applied research. "Human knowledge and human power meet in one," he declared in *Novum Organum* (1620), "truth . . . and utility are here the very same things." Because the convergence of knowledge and power depended on how Nature was to be understood, Bacon urged

---

11 For more on the history of objectivity, see Evelyn Fox Keller, "The Paradox of Scientific Objectivity," *Annals of Scholarship*, vol. 9 (1992): 135–53; and Lorraine Daston and Peter Galison, "The Image of Objectivity," *Representations*, vol. 40 (1992).

12 Francis Bacon, *The Advancement of Learning and New Atlantis*, ed. Arthur Johnston (Oxford: Clarendon Press, 1974), p. 230. See also Adi Ophir and Stephen Shapin, "The Place of Knowledge," *Science in Context*, vol. 4 (1991): 11.

13 From the preface to Bacon's *De Interpretatione Naturae* (1603), quoted in Johnston, p. x. See also, Jean Overton Fuller, *Sir Francis Bacon* (London: East-West Publications, 1981), ch. 69; Judah Bierman, "Social and Society in the New Atlantis and Other Renaissance Utopias," *Publications of the Modern Language Association of America*, vol. 78 (1963): 492–500; Theodore K. Rabb, "Francis Bacon," *Encyclopedia of Social Sciences* (New York: Macmillan and Free Press, 1968), I: 496.

14 Bacon, *The New Atlantis*, ed. Johnston, pp. 217, 219.

15 For more on this, see J. Weinberger, "Science and Rule in Bacon's Utopia: An Introduction to the Reading of the *New Atlantis*," *American Political Science Review*, vol. 70 (1976): 865–85.

readers to forsake the Idols of the Tribe, the Cave, the Market-place and the Theatre. "I reject all forms of fiction and imposture; nor do I think it matters," he added, "whether the new world be that island of Atlantis, with which the ancients were acquainted, or now discovered for the first time." The pursuit of knowledge required "firmness of mind . . . a fresh examination of particulars." Bacon implored researchers to fashion tools for "dissecting and anatomizing the world most diligently," just as architects considered "not only the architecture of the whole frame of a work, but also the several beams thereof," and physicians did experiments on human subjects to understand the body.[16]

Inhabiting a remote outpost of Science delighted the citizens of New Atlantis. There, in contrast to Europe, scientists enjoyed both the means of attaining a good old age as well as the simple, abundantly available necessities for making longevity pleasant.[17] Bacon himself relied on practical hints for longevity that had accumulated over the centuries. His *History of Life and Death* (1622–3) offered "recommendations [that] may seem a little commonplace but it would hardly be believed with how much care they have been studied."[18] To underscore Bacon's hopes for future science, literary executors attached a "wish list" to the 1625 edition of *The New Atlantis*. The title said it all: *Magnalia Naturae, praecipue quoad usus humanos* cited those wonderful works of Nature that would benefit humankind. The first four items – the prolongation of life, the restitution of

---

16 Quotations from and references to *Novum Organum* come respectively from Rabb, "Francis Bacon," I: 495; "The Idols of Human Understanding," reprinted in Ryan D. Tweney, Michael E. Doherty, and Clifford R. Mynatt, *On Scientific Thinking* (New York: Columbia University Press, 1981), pp. 31–2; J. Fuller, *Bacon*, p. 273; and Hanbury Brown, *The Wisdom of Science* (New York: Cambridge University Press, 1986), p. 83. See also P. B. Medawar, *The Art of the Soluble* (London: Methuen & Co., 1967), pp. 121, 134; Evelyn Fox Keller, "Fractured Images of Science, Language, and Power," *Poetics Today*, vol. 12 (Summer 1991): 227. The architecture analogy comes from *The Advancement of Learning*, ed. Johnston, p. 137. For Bacon's influence on "modern" science, see P. Rossi, "Baconianism," in P. Wiener, *Dictionary of the History of Ideas* (New York: Scribner, 1968), I: 172–9; Thomas S. Kuhn, *The Essential Tension* (Chicago: University of Chicago Press, 1977), pp. 44–7. On the lack of mathematics, see H. Butterfield, *The Origins of Modern Science* (London: G. Bell and Sons, 1950), p. 75; Lisa Jardine, *Francis Bacon: Discovery and the Art of Discourse* (New York: Cambridge University Press, 1974), p. 79.

17 It is no coincidence that seventeen of the fifty-one Europeans in the fable were sick when they reached land. Bacon knew that seventeen, an unlucky number, stood for nature in Pythagorean symbolism. The contrast with Europe was clear. See Howard B. White, *Peace Among the Willows* (The Hague: Nijhoff, 1968), pp. 191–230.

18 Bacon's recommendations included moderate exercise, a glass of water before bed, and whey in bath water. The passage from *History of Life and Death* is quoted in J. Fuller, *Bacon*, p. 305. *Magnalia naturae* is reprinted in Johnston, p. 249. The manner of promoting healthful longevity on New Atlantis has relevance to current aging-related investigations. Confirming earlier hypotheses may not be the most glamorous research task, but it remains an essential component of the gerontologic enterprise.

youth in some degree, the retardation of age, and the control of incurable diseases – remain priorities among researchers on aging to this day.

Ponce de Leon and Bacon also prefigure twentieth-century style of research on aging in the manner that their gerontologic inquiries missed the mark. Ponce de Leon did not find his Fountain; his quest has been dismissed as quixotic by nearly everybody except those who wish to capitalize on its Romance.[19] After the U.S. Civil War, an English florist opened the Paradise Groves and Rose Gardens in St. Augustine, where the Fountain of Youth was supposed to exist. Others sold "special" oranges at the site. "Ponce got it wrong," wrote Charles Tenney Jackson in *The Fountain of Youth* (1904). "Why, all Florida is jammed with hotels, and the hotels with people who haven't a decent stomach to bless 'em."[20] In 1932, R. James Gale and associates began promoting a salve known as "Ponce de Leon Cream," which promised to restore sexual vitality after users locally applied "certain rare roots, leaves, and berries." A fraud order was issued when authorities determined that the cream was simply a red pepper salve.[21] Nonetheless, the myth that someday, somehow, the conquistador's search will be vindicated continues to allure. "Ponce de Leon was looking in all the wrong places," opined a 1990 *Newsweek* feature. "With the benefit of time, brainstorms, and biochemistry, scientists are on the verge of finding the true fountain of youth."[22] Perhaps *Newsweek*'s writers are correct. Even if they are wrong, their argument shows how Bacon's legacy can be conjoined with Ponce de Leon's quest.

Preconceived ideas – what Bacon decried as the Idols to which individuals, the masses, the scientific community, and the marketplace clung – do thwart gerontologic innovation.[23] But Bacon failed to appreciate that research on aging done at the frontiers of knowledge languishes unless integrated into mainstream science. In addition, accomplishing Bacon's aging

---

19 Charles Gibson, *Spain in America* (New York: Harper Torchbook, 1966), pp. 182–3; Edward Gaylord Bourne, *Spain in America* (New York: Harper & Brothers, 1904), pp. 159–68.

20 Charles Tenney Jackson, *The Fountain of Youth* (New York: Outing Publishing Company, 1904), p. 14. See also Carita Doggett Corse, *The Fountain of Youth* (St. Augustine, FL: n.p., 1936).

21 Arthur J. Cramp, *Nostrums and Quackery and Pseudo-Medicine*, vol. 3 (Chicago: American Medical Association, 1936), p. 102.

22 Sharon Begley, Mary Hager, and Andrew Murr, "The Search for the Fountain of Youth," *Newsweek*, March 5, 1990: 44.

23 Kuhn, *Essential Tension*, p. 48; Sidney Ross, "Scientist: The Story of a Word," *Annals of Science*, vol. 18 (June 1962): 67; Bernard Barber, "Resistance by Scientists to Scientific Discovery," *Science*, vol. 134 (1 September 1961): 596–602; Giles Gunn, *Thinking Across the American Grain* (Chicago: University of Chicago Press, 1992). I recognize that the logic of this paragraph suggests that Gregor Mendel, not Charles Darwin, may someday be considered a patron saint of gerontology!

agenda may have been frustrated by the very process institutionalized to facilitate science. Bacon's fictional College helped to inspire British scientists to found the Royal Society in 1662, but detractors sniff that only a lord chancellor would propose that science be organized in a top-down manner. Critics of the budgetary power that federal agencies exercise on aging-related investigations see parallels today in the control of inquiry occasioned through "research-by-administration."[24]

So in calling Ponce de Leon and Francis Bacon precursors of gerontology, I propose that contemporary U.S. researchers on aging are still wrestling with a central paradox that existed centuries ago. Gerontologists prove to be most successful in their efforts to yield new insights about aging when they try in unconventional ways to rediscover time-tested ways of investigating processes of senescence. Ponce de Leon was not a reckless conquistador. The Spaniard's search for the fountain of youth "fit" both beliefs and misconceptions that had been transmitted across continents over the centuries. Similarly, New Atlantis was a scientific commonwealth that had been thriving for nearly two millennia before Europeans reached its shore. Bacon ironically portrayed its venerable mores, with deliberate allusions to Aristotle's *Rhetoric*,[25] as more progressive than those prevailing in the established order of seventeenth-century Britain.

Gerontologists need to reclaim their past, not for its own sake, but so they can use it as they envision their collective future. The historical record shows that twentieth-century researchers on aging made progress not by slavishly accepting the wisdom of their elders but by building critically upon it, applying the latest techniques and methods. The overriding goal of gerontologic biological, medical, behavioral, and social science since at least the 1930s has been to understand fundamental processes and mechanisms of aging.[26] This quest is still considered unrewarding by many scientific gatekeepers and funding agencies. Gerontology is not a titan of Big Science. Nevertheless, by focusing on basics, gerontologists have staked a field. With enough imagination and solid results, they may yet persuade other scientists that "age" and "aging" explain much about human development. In the process, as more and more practitioners accept the insights

---

24 Brown, *The Wisdom of Science*, p. 6. See also Derek J. de Solla Price, *Little Science, Big Science . . . and Beyond* (New York: Columbia University Press, 1986), p. viii; Antonio Perez-Ramos, *Francis Bacon's Idea of Science* (Oxford: Oxford University Press, 1988), p. 33; V. J. McGill, "Pragmatism Reconsidered," *Science and Society*, vol. 3 (1939): 296, 318.

25 Jerry Weinberger, *Science, Faith, and Politics* (Ithaca, NY: Cornell University Press, 1985), p. 77.

26 I am not excluding the arts and humanities from "gerontology," as I trust will be evident throughout the book. But I do not consider the arts and humanities to be "sciences," even though epistemologically and methodologically they have things in common. Indeed, as I suggest in this paragraph, even when gerontology more fully emerges as a science, there will be a vital role for the arts and humanities to play.

and critical input of scholars from the humanities, arts, and other domains, gerontology might attain a degree of self-reflexivity that will move discourse beyond positivist critiques of methods to include scientifically grounded reflections on aging, death, and finitude of life.

Keywords

Throughout the narrative of *Crossing Frontiers: Gerontology Emerges as a Science* there is a historical analysis of ideas that are embedded in the book's title. These *keywords* provide "particular formations of meaning – ways not only of discussing but of seeing many of the central experiences."[27] They serve metaphorical functions, which are as evocative as they can be seductive. "It has been well said that analogies may help one into the saddle, but are encumbrances on a long journey," observed economist Alfred Marshall in 1897. "It is well to know when to introduce them, it is even better to know when to stop them off."[28]

Crossing Frontiers sets the stage for introducing a mixed cast of characters into play. Those who have blazed gerontology's terra incognita have been a motley group – entrepreneurs, social workers, nurses and physicians, demographers and economists, teachers, students, policy analysts, bench scientists, behaviorists, humanists, bureaucrats – as diverse as the explorers, miners, traders, outlaws, poachers, farmers, herders, loggers, merchants, and tourists who settled the West. Twentieth-century gerontologists have had to adapt their professional training and tribal customs in ways analogous to the accommodations made by Native Americans, African Americans, Spanish Americans, Asian Americans, first- and second-generation Europeans, and other immigrants. Resembling border patrols, vigilantes, and government agents, latter-day agents (members of peer review panels, deans, and federal contractors) try to maintain a semblance of order.[29] The dramatis personae of the gerontologic community, like pioneers in the West, have been as eager for success as they were mindful of the risks.

There have been power struggles among competing interests. Some hope to make a reputation by exploiting recently opened domains, "new areas of ignorance." Conversely, subfields can "develop when jurisdictions become vacant."[30] Others stay in place, investigating problems in senescence

27 Raymond Williams, *Keywords* (New York: Oxford University Press, 1976), p. 13.
28 "The Old Generation of Economists and the New," in *Memorials of Alfred Marshall*, ed. A. C. Pigou (New York: Keeley & Millman, 1956), p. 314.
29 Patricia Nelson Limerick, *The Legacy of Conquest* (New York: Norton, 1987), pp. 21, 27; Jennifer Milliken, "Travelling Across Borders," *Social Epistemology*, vol. 4 (1990): 317–21; The metaphors come from Mattei Dogan and Robert Pahre, *Creative Marginality* (Boulder, CO: Westview, 1990), p. 172.
30 Andrew Abbott, *The System of Professions* (Chicago: University of Chicago Press, 1988), p. 3. See also Pierre Bourdieu, "The Field of Cultural Production, or the Economic World

within the confines of their own area of specialization. Self-styled gerontologists, after all, are not the only specialists who have advanced research
on aging.[31] Lines separating academic disciplines and scientific tribes are
no more and no less ambiguous than those on frontier maps. Discoveries
inevitably call existing contiguous boundaries into question. New patterns
of interaction necessitate realignments. Clashes arise as different sets of
experts assert their autonomy, expand their authority, or challenge other
groups who seek the same rewards or clients.[32]

All these scenarios are possible on the *frontier*, a word that can mean
several things in describing relationships between those in the center(s) and
people on the periphery. Originally the French used the term to refer to a
"facade" of a building; then it meant "border." Over time, frontier also
came to mean a strip of land, a demarcation line, and a defensive barrier.[33]
Ambiguities inherent in this keyword permit many scripts. Researchers on
aging often protect and defend their borders as if they were boundaries of
a suzerainty. But frontiers of aging may also be depicted as oases that are
transforming and being transformed by scientific work conducted elsewhere. Because rules for redrawing lines depend on historical circumstances, multidisciplinarity flourishes in gerontology's liminality.[34]

Reversed," *Poetics*, vol. 12 (November 1983): 324; Suzanne Gearhart, *The Open Boundary of History and Fiction* (Princeton, NJ: Princeton University Press, 1984), pp. 4–5.

31 The same can be said of other fields, of course, including the writing of U.S. Western
history. See John W. Caughey, "The American West," *Arizona and the West* (1959): 8–
9; Alan Taylor, *Liberty Men and Great Proprietors* (Chapel Hill: University of North
Carolina Press, 1990), p. 3; Gerald L. Geison, "Scientific Change, Emerging Specialties,
and Research Schools," *History of Science*, vol. 19 (1981): 29; Paul K. Hoch, "Migration
and the Generation of New Scientific Ideas," *Minerva*, vol. 28 (1987): 209–37; Tony
Becher, *Academic Tribes and Territories*, (Manchester: The Society for Research into
Higher Education & Open University Press, 1989), p. 104.

32 Donald Fisher, "Boundary Work and Science," in *Theories of Science in Society*, ed. Susan
E. Cozzens and Thomas F. Gieryn (Bloomington: Indiana University Press, 1990), pp. 98–
101; Thomas F. Gieryn, "Boundary-work and the Demarcation of Science from Non-
Science," *American Sociological Review*, vol. 48 (1983): 791–2.

33 There are parallels in English according to the *Oxford English Dictionary*, which also adds
that "frontier" can mean part of a country that touches another, a fortress, a frontlet, or
the front line of an army. Similar variations occur in Spanish, Italian, and German. See
Peter Burke, *A New Kind of History from the Writings of Febvre* (London: Routledge &
Kegan Paul, 1973), pp. 209–17; *Oxford English Dictionary*, compact edition, vol. 1, p.
1,086.

34 Michael Kearney, "Borders and Boundaries of State and Self at the End of the Empire,"
Journal of Historical Sociology, vol. 4 (March 1991): 52–74; Peter Sahlins, "Natural Frontiers Revisited," *American Historical Review*, vol. 95 (1990): 1,423–51; John Higham,
"Finding Centers Among the Margins," *American Literary History*, vol. 3 (Winter 1991):
745–6; David J. Weber, *The Spanish Frontier in North America* (New Haven, CT: Yale
University Press, 1992); Cozzens and Gieryn, *Theories of Science*, p. 60; Stephen Green-
blatt and Giles Gunn, *Redrawing the Boundaries* (New York: Modern Language Association of America, 1992).

Crossing Frontiers offers three hypotheses about the history of gerontology based on this metaphorical foray. First, despite their preoccupation with defining boundaries, most researchers on aging in fact do not share "an intensified collective consciousness."[35] Frontier conditions favor mavericks, upstarts who sometimes get ahead through cunning or charm, confident that the loose criteria for measuring success will enable them to "pass."[36] Meanwhile, those with proprietary interests in the field have difficulty imposing order among competitors. So although researchers on aging take pride in trailblazing, many crave a sense of approval and legitimacy that eludes them if they tarry too long on the frontier.

Second, because senescence remains a secondary "problem" in most disciplines and professions, Big Science rarely takes notice of what seems exciting in aging-research circles. Gerontologists feel obliged to publish one set of handbooks on aging after another in order to keep up with the exponential growth of information, but their work does not always impress those who survey the field from afar. Incommensurability of research traditions, of standards for evaluation, and of canons for dissemination create an ironic conundrum. "Distance lends enchantment" to gerontology from some vantage points, but it also can diminish overall appreciation for research on aging.[37]

Third, turf questions exacerbate differences in strategies deployed in conquering frontiers, especially when pioneers (re)discover that choice "space is already disciplined and contained."[38] Here is where the central power of disciplinary traditions is most keenly felt. Gerontology thrives when scientists take risks, but investigators can only survive if their scientific work is sustained. Hence successful researchers on aging generally lead split lives; they must satisfy their own discipline's standards for tenure and annual raises while interacting with gerontologic scholars from divergent backgrounds. The contested territory is usually not assessed by gerontologists the same way: What matters to policymakers in Washington does not invariably excite psychologists in Los Angeles or physicians in the Little Rock

---

35 Robert Merton, "Insiders and Outsiders," *American Journal of Sociology*, vol. 78 (1972): 11.; Stephen Cole, "The Hierarchy of Sciences?" ibid., vol. 89 (1983): 111.

36 The phrase "incursive nomadism" comes from Victor Turner, *Dreams, Fields, Metaphors* (Ithaca, NY: Cornell University Press, 1974), p. 17; Joel Arthur Barker, *Discovering the Future* (St. Paul, MN: ILI Press, 1988), pp. 25–6; A. A. Abrahamsen, "Bridging Boundaries Versus Breaking Boundaries," *Synthese*, vol. 72 (1980): 365–78.

37 The phrase comes from H. M. Collins, *Changing Order* (Newbury, Pk., CA: Sage, 1985), p. 145. See also, Donald Fisher, "Boundary Work and Science," in *Theories of Science in Society*, ed. Susan E. Cozzens and Thomas F. Gieryn (Bloomington: Indiana University Press, 1990), p. 98.

38 Milliken, "Travelling Across Borders," p. 318. For the frontier analogy, see Taylor, *Liberty Men and Great Proprietors*, pp. 57, 83, 148; and Earl Pomeroy, "Toward a Reorientation of Western History," *Mississippi Valley Historical Review*, vol. 41 (March 1955): 579–600.

VA hospital. Hence *Crossing Frontiers*'s comparative approach: No single institution or cluster of investigators reveals how certain keywords, centers, societies, and subfields developed in an ongoing, multifaceted historical process.[39]

I use the verb *emerge* to signify gerontology's transitory, uneven stages of growth. "It would be an error to suppose that the great discoverer seizes at once upon the truth, or has any unerring method of divining it," declared economist William S. Jevons in *The Principles of Science* (1877). "Fertility of imagination of abundance of guesses at truth are among the first requisites of discovery; but the erroneous guesses must be many times as numerous as those that prove well found."[40] Gerontology's development has been slow. Theories that on first hearing impressed researchers, lay audiences, and rival professional groups were soon forgotten if they did not live up to expectations.[41] Serendipity has sometimes bestowed more success on investigators than they deserved. Paradigm shifts, rare in most fields, have not transformed research on aging.[42]

How does gerontology compare to other fields at similar points of development? It is tempting to appropriate Poincare's description of sociology in 1900 – "the science with the most methods and the fewest discoveries" – to characterize postwar research on aging.[43] Albert Rosenfeld, a science

39 Opting for a comparative approach guarantees a certain arbitrariness and limitation in coverage. For more, see Becher, *Academic Tribes and Territories*, pp. 79 ff. Edward A. Tiryakian, "The Significance of Schools in the Development of Sociology," in *Contemporary Issues in Theory and Research*, ed. William E. Snizek, Ellsworth R. Fuhrman, and Michael K. Miller (Westport, CT: Greenwood, 1979), pp. 211–18; Stephen Fuller, *Social Epistemology* (Bloomington: Indiana University Press, 1988), p. 191; Victor Weiskopf, "Frontiers and Limits of Science," *American Scientist*, vol. 65 (July 1977): 406; Burton R. Clark, *The Higher Education System* (Berkeley and Los Angeles: University of California Press, 1983), p. 15.

40 Quoted in D. K. Simonton, "Chance-Configuration Theory of Scientific Certainty," in *Psychology of Science*, ed. Barry Gholson et al. (New York: Cambridge University Press, 1989), p. 185. See also Michael Alan Schwartz and Osborne Wiggins, "Science, Humanism, and the Nature of Medical Practice," *Perspectives in Biology and Medicine*, vol. 28 (Spring 1985): 339; Augustine Brannigan, *The Social Basis of Scientific Discoveries* (New York: Cambridge University Press, 1981), p. ix; Donald E. Polkinghorne, *Narrative Knowing and the Human Sciences* (Albany, NY: State University of New York, 1988), pp. 2–3.

41 Fritz Ringer, "The Intellectual Field, Intellectual History, and the Sociology of Knowledge," *Theory and Society*, vol. 19 (1990): 273. For a complementary view, just as gerontology was emerging, see Stephen Pepper, "Emergence," *Journal of Philosophy*, vol. 23 (1926): 241–5.

42 See Gerald Holton, *The Scientific Imagination* (New York: Cambridge University Press, 1978), p. 10; H. M. Collins, "The Place of the 'Core Set' in Modern Science," *History of Science*, vol. 19 (1981): 13; Stephan Fuchs and Jonathan H. Turner, "What Makes a Science 'Mature?' " *Sociological Theory*, vol. 4 (Fall 1986): 143–50; Everett Mendelsohn, ed., *Transformation and Tradition in the Sciences* (New York: Cambridge University Press, 1984).

43 Quoted in Herbert J. Gans, "Sociology in America: The Discipline and the Public," *American Sociological Review*, vol. 54 (1989): 10. Yet, the development of gerontology, I be-

editor for *Life* and the *Saturday Review* in the 1960s and 1970s, welcomed the field's emergence. "Gerontology, the scientific study of the aging process, is one of the most important frontier areas in current biomedical research," Rosenfeld declared in *Prolongevity* (1976). "Each sortie into the frontier areas of aging research provides a reminder of how totally in flux those frontiers are."[44] Rosenfeld's survey highlighted W. Donner Denckla's theory of a brain-based hormonal clock of aging and Roy Walford's work on immunology, but omitted the work being done at the Gerontology Research Center in Baltimore; he did not visit investigators at Duke or Michigan. Rosenfeld acknowledged that "entire areas of conventional, old-fashioned gerontology have been given short-shrift in order to allow a full account of some of the more recent avant garde developments."[45] *Crossing Frontiers* highlights different vistas.

Gerontology remains a field very much in the formative stages of emergence. It has acquired some disciplinary features. Students can earn B.A.s, M.A.s, and Ph.D.s through gerontology programs. There are dozens of aging-related journals, and a notable increase in state, regional, national, and international networks. But there are no widely shared techniques or distinctive methods. Theories of aging remain partial, tentative.[46] Nor does gerontology extend the rights, rites, and privileges of a profession. It claims no monopoly on knowledge or skills.[47] *Crossing Frontiers* does not predict

lieve, thus far more closely resembles psychology than sociology. Both have grown by dividing into small, discrete islands of knowledge and applied research. But researchers on aging have not yet endured the debates and schisms that have marked the maturation of various educational, research, and clinical subfields of contemporary psychology. Because this theme will be elaborated in *Crossing Frontiers*, it suffices to cite Arthur W. Staats, "Paradigmatic Behaviorism, Unified Theory Construction Methods, and the Zeitgeist of Separatism," *American Psychologist*, vol. 36 (March 1981): 239–56.

44 Albert Rosenfeld, *Prolongevity* (New York: Avon, 1976), pp. vii, 198.

45 Ibid., p. 197. The references to GRC, Michigan, and Duke appear on p. 204. This book refers to very few of the scientists Rosenfeld grouped together as "the gerontologist as Captain Ahab," treats GRC and Duke in ch. 3, and takes Michigan as an interesting example of how university-based research centers have changed over time.

46 Robert Kastenbaum, "Theories of Human Aging," *Journal of Social Issues*, vol. 21 (1965): 13–36; Paul B. Baltes, "Theoretical Propositions of Life-Span Developmental Psychology," *Developmental Psychology*, vol. 23 (1987): 611–26; Leonard Hayflick, "Theories of Biological Aging," in *Principles of Geriatric Medicine*, ed. Reubin Andres, Edwin L. Bierman, and William R. Hazzard (New York: McGraw-Hill, 1985), pp. 9–40; Edward L. Schneider, "Theories of Aging," in *Modern Biological Theories of Aging*, ed. Huber R. Warner et al. (New York: Raven, 1987), pp. 1–4. The literature on disciplines is vast, but I found especially helpful Burton R. Clark, *Faculty Culture* (Berkeley: Center for the Study of Higher Education, 1962); Sheldon Wolin, "Political Theory as Vocation," *American Political Science Review*, vol. 69 (1969): 1,062–82; Frederick Suppe, *The Structure of Scientific Theories*, 2d ed. (Urbana: University of Illinois Press, 1977); Steve Fuller, *Philosophy of Science and Its Discontents* (Boulder, CO: Westview, 1989); Ben Agger, *Socio(onto)logy* (Urbana: University of Illinois Press, 1989).

47 Terence J. Johnson, *Professions and Power* (New York: Macmillan, 1972); Magali Sarfatti Larson, *The Rise of Professionalism* (Berkeley and Los Angeles: University of California

if or when researchers on aging will form a discipline or profession, for the field's future is uncertain. Information scientists report that "much of science and social science is interconnected within and across disciplines" through more than 8,500 fields.[48] One of the issues girding this book is the question of whether *gerontology*, in contrast to *geriatrics*, may already have outlived its influence and its usefulness as a self-contained endeavor.

To preclude confusion in terminology, I define geriatrics as "the study of the medical aspects of old age and the application of knowledge related to the biological, biomedical, behavioral, and social aspects of aging to prevention, diagnosis, treatment, and care of older persons." Gerontology, philosopher H. R. Moody observes, "is a multidisciplinary assembly of explanatory themes, each involving theoretical forms that simply do not move in the same conceptual universe."[49] The two groups have interests that overlap without converging. Geriatrics is a medical subspecialty: Physicians now can be certified as geriatricians by passing examinations administered by medical boards in internal medicine, family practice, and psychiatry. That gerontology's boundaries are more jagged attests to both the messiness and singularity of how fields emerge.

"The field of research only opens wider and wider as we advance," declared Henry A. Rowland in "A Plea for Pure Science" (1883), "and our minds are lost in wonder and astonishment at the grandeur and beauty unfolded before us."[50] Rowland's poetic image of a "scientific field" differs from major intellectual figures, such as Albert Einstein, Kurt Lewin, and

Press, 1977); Gerald L. Geison, ed., *Professions and Professional Ideologies in America* (Chapel Hill: University of North Carolina Press, 1983); Robert Stevens, *Law School* (Chapel Hill: University of North Carolina Press, 1983); Renee C. Fox, *The Sociology of Medicine: A Participant Observer's View* (Englewood Cliffs, NJ: Prentice-Hall, 1989), ch. 2; Rolf Torstendahl and Michael Burrage, eds., *The Formation of Professions* (Newbury Pk., CA: Sage Publications, 1990); JoAnne Brown, "The Semantics of Professions," Ph.D. diss., University of Wisconsin, 1985.

48 The statistic on fields comes from Diana Crane and Henry Small, "American Sociology Since the Seventies," in *Sociology and Its Publics*, ed. Terence C. Halliday and Morris Janowitz (Chicago: University of Chicago Press, 1987), p. 197. For the present, it suffices to note that my interpretation differs in varying degrees from the cogent arguments found in R. D. Bramwell, "Gerontology as a Discipline," *Educational Gerontology*, vol. 11 (1985): 201–5; Pamela F. Wendt and David A. Peterson, "Gerontology: A Case Study in the Evolution of Professional Education," in ibid., vol. 16 (1993): 181–98; and the proceedings of a 1990 symposium on "Generations of Gerontology," published in *International Journal of Aging & Human Development*, vol. 35 (1992): 1–82.

49 Robert N. Butler, "Geriatrics," in *The Encyclopedia of Aging*, ed. George L. Maddox *et al.* (New York: Springer, 1987), p. 284; DeWitt C. Baldwin and Ruth Ann Williamson Tsukuda, "Interdisciplinary Teams," in *Geriatric Medicine*, ed. Christine K. Cassel and John R. Walsh (New York: Springer-Verlag, 1984), vol. 2, 430. For this definition of gerontology, see Harry R. Moody, "Toward a Critical Gerontology," in *Emergent Theories of Aging*, ed. James E. Birren and Vern L. Bengtson (New York: Springer, 1988).

50 Quoted in Burton R. Clark, *The Academic Life* (Princeton, NJ: Carnegie Foundation for the Advancement of Teaching, 1987), p. 25.

Quincy Wright, who respectively enunciated specific field theories in physics, social psychology, and international relations.[51] My use of the keyword *field* as a way to situate gerontology in the scientific realm is influenced primarily by Pierre Bourdieu, who contends that "science is a social field of forces, struggles, and relationships that is defined by the relations of powers among the protagonists."[52] Bourdieu's field works like a magnet, with power lines in which various elements interact dialectically in intellectual and institutional terms bounded by the field's own fluid logic and mechanisms. To this, I incorporate Michel Foucault's observation that "the formation of discourses and genealogy of knowledge need to be analyzed, not in terms of types of consciousness, modes of perception and forms of ideology, but in terms of tactics and strategies of power."[53] Fields vary in

51 The word actually entered the vocabulary of physics in the 1850s and 1860s; Lords Kelvin and Maxwell used it to highlight aspects of their electromagnetic theories. Neoclassical economists appropriated theoretical insights from nineteenth-century physical notions of fields. Paul F. Kress, *Social Science and the Idea of Process* (Urbana: University of Illinois Press, 1970), pp. 133–4; Albert Lepawsky, Edward H. Buehring, and Harold D. Lasswell, *The Search for World Order* (New York: Meredith Corporation, 1971), p. 371. There were, according to historians of sciences, precedents that date back to at least the eighteenth century in mathematics and natural philosophy. See G. N. Cantor and M. J. S. Hodge, eds., *Conceptions of Ether* (Cambridge: The University Press, 1981), pp. 37–41; Philip Morawski, *Against Mechanism* (Totowa, NJ: Rowman & Littlefield, 1988), pp. 6, 30; Sheldon S. Wolin, *Politics and Vision* (Boston: Little, Brown, 1960), pp. 282–3. Thomas Hobbes (1588–1679) imagined society to be a "field" of forces.

52 Pierre Bourdieu, "The Peculiar History of Scientific Reason," *Sociological Forum*, vol. 5 (Spring 1991): 3; "The Specificity of the Scientific Field and the Social Conditions of the Progress of Reason," *Sociology of Science*, vol. 14 (1975): 19–47; *Homo Academicus* (Cambridge: Polity Press, 1988); and Bourdieu and Loïc J. D. Wacquant, *An Invitation to Reflexive Sociology* (Chicago: University of Chicago Press, 1992). In "Intellectual Field and Creative Project," *Social Science Information*, vol. 8 (1969): 89, Bourdieu takes a line from Proust for his epigraph: "Theories and schools, like microbes and globules, devour each other and by their struggle ensure the continuing of life." Pierre Bourdieu and James S. Coleman, *Social Theory for a Changing Society* (Boulder, CO: Westview, 1991), p. 384. Bourdieu, "The Genesis of the Concepts of Habitus and of Field," *Sociocriticism*, no. 2 (1985): 11–24. See also Dudley Shapere, *Reason and the Search for Knowledge* (Dordrecht: Reidel, 1984), ch. 14.

53 Quotation from Michel Foucault, *Power/Knowledge: Selected Interviews and Other Writings*, ed. Colin Gordon (New York: Pantheon, 1980), p. 77. See also Foucault, *The Archeology of Knowledge* (New York: Pantheon, 1972), p. 37. See also Harry Redner, *The Ends of Science* (Boulder, CO: Westview, 1987); and Fritz Ringer, *Fields of Knowledge* (New York: Cambridge University Press, 1992); Earl Hunt, "Cognitive Science," *Annual Review of Psychology*, vol. 40 (1989): 603–29; Seymour B. Sarason, *The Creation of Settings and the Future Societies* (San Francisco: Jossey-Bass, 1972); M. J. Mulkay, G. N. Gilbert, and S. Woolgar, "Problem Areas and Research Networks in Science," *Sociology*, vol. 9 (1975): 187–203. The term "intertraditional" was coined by Stanley Cavell and appears in Peter Brooks, "How Humanists Can Make Productive Use of the Contemporary Battle of Books," *Chronicle of Higher Education* (December 9, 1992): B1–B2; David Bloor, *Knowledge and Social Imagery* (London: Routledge & Kegan Paul, 1976), pp. 141–3; Aron Gurswitch, *The Field of Consciousness* (Pittsburgh: Duquesne University Press, 1964), pp.

terms of access to other domains. They differ in their capacity for bridging views across "disciplinary subcultures," "networks," "communities," "hybrid fields," and "interfields."[54]

For consistency's sake, in *Crossing Frontiers*, cross-disciplinary refers to interactions that incorporate ideas, methods, or themes from two sources. Multidisciplinary ventures involve at least three disciplines. Only those scientific projects or scholarly endeavors that integrate at least two different perspectives into a blended product qualify as interdisciplinary. Such work is rare; it requires considerable institutional support and cooperation. But interdisciplinarity yields significant results: From such initiatives, according to Karl Deutsch and associates, came nearly half of all major social science advances from 1900 to 1929 and two-thirds from 1930 to 1965.[55] Gerontology began as a multidisciplinary endeavor. Little research in aging to date truly deserves to be called interdisciplinary. Most projects tend to be short-lived and noniterative.[56]

Given the explosion of knowledge and changes in the structure of its production, defining *science* in any domain is hard nowadays. Most analysts agree that it is a matter of attitude, "a principled openness toward . . . new and temporarily valid knowledge in a universe of constant change."[57] A spirit of skepticism and attention to detail are valued in pur-

319–20; and Seymour H. Mauskopf, *The Reception of Unconventional Science* (Washington, DC: AAAS Symposium, 1979).

54 Burton R. Clark, ed., *Perspectives on Higher Education* (Berkeley and Los Angeles: University of California Press, 1984), pp. 181–4; Mattei Dogan and Robert Pahre, *Creative Marginality* (Boulder, CO: Westview, 1990); Tony Becher, "Toward a Definition of Disciplinary Cultures," *Studies in Higher Education*, vol. 6 (1981): 109–22; Lindley Darden and Nancy Maull, "Interfield Theories," *Philosophy of Science*, vol. 44 (1977): 43–64; Iskender Gokalp, "The Interrelating of Scientific Fields," *Studies in the History and Philosophy of Science*, vol. 21 (1990): 413–29; Quincy Wright, *The Study of International Relations* (New York: Appleton-Century Crofts, 1955), pp. 524–6.

55 R. Jurkovich and J. H. P. Paelinck, *Problems in Interdisciplinary Studies* (Brookfield CT: Gower, 1984); Paul K. Hoch, "Institutional Versus Intellectual Migrations in the Nucleation of New Scientific Specialties," *Studies in the History and Philosophy of Science*, vol. 18 (1987): 481–500. The survey of interdisciplinarity in Karl W. Deutsch, John Platt, and Dieter Senghass, "Conditions Favoring Major Advances in Social Science," *Science*, vol. 171 (5 February 1971): 459.

56 To switch metaphors, James Birren compares gerontology to "islands of knowledge." If it were an interdisciplinary field, he probably would compare it to an archipelago. See Julie Thompson Klein, *Interdisciplinarity* (Detroit: Wayne State University, 1990); see also David O. Sears, "Political Psychology," *Annual Review of Psychology*, vol. 38 (1987): 229–55; Jerry G. Gaff and Robert C. Wilson, "Faculty Cultures and Interdisciplinary Studies," *Journal of Higher Education*, vol. 42 (1971): 186–201; Steven Weiland, *Intellectual Craftsmen* (New Brunswick: Transaction Publishers, 1991); Peter H. Rossi, "Researchers, Scholars and Policy Makers," *Daedalus*, vol. 98 (1964): 1,142–61; JoAnne Brown and David K. van Keuren, *The Estate of Social Knowledge* (Baltimore: Johns Hopkins University Press, 1991).

57 The phrasing is that of an intellectual historian, David Hollinger, quoted in *The Estate of*

suing three of science's prime aims – comprehension, explanation, and prediction.[58] Philosophers disagree about the sources of authority and hegemony in scientific inquiry,[59] but most acknowledge that scientific *methods* diverge from practices in other spheres of everyday life. Reductionism governs laboratory procedures in the natural sciences.[60] More sophisticated instrumentation yields better measurements. The mathematical expression of relationships facilitates the standardization of results and theory building.[61]

In recent years, critics of earlier schools of the sociology of knowledge have undermined many claims about the superiority and distinctiveness of Science. "The hallmark of modern consciousness is its enormous multiplicity," writes Clifford Geertz.[62] Scientists increasingly understand the world in terms of ever more specialized, noncumulative theories. If "science is a human rather than a social activity," then all types of data, methods, and

Social Knowledge ed. Brown and van Keuren, p. xix. See also Vivian Gornick, *Women in Science* (New York: Simon & Schuster, 1983), pp. 15–19; Philip J. Holts, *Scientific Temperaments* (New York: Simon & Schuster, 1988). "The scientific spirit is of more value than its products," declared T. H. Huxley in his *Life and Letters*, ed. Leonard Huxley (New York: D. Appleton, 1904), vol. 2, p. 13.

58 The trinity of aims comes from Victor Weisskopf, "The Frontiers and Limits of Science," *Daedalus*, vol. 113 (1984): 187. Talcott Parsons agreed. He felt that clarity fostered "the elimination of vagueness and ambiguity, increasing integration and consistency, and the development of complex interrelations among concepts [that] make inferences to new empirical insights possible." Parsons is quoted in *The Nationalization of the Social Sciences*, ed. Samuel Z. Klausner and Victor M. Lidz (Philadelphia: University of Pennsylvania Press, 1986), pp. 46–7.

59 Jurgen Habermas, *Knowledge and Human Interests* (Cambridge: Polity Press, 1987), p. 317; Michel de Certeau, *The Practice of Everyday Life* (Berkeley and Los Angeles: University of California Press, 1984), pp. 6–8.

60 J. Bronowski, *Science and Human Values* (New York: Julian Messner, 1956), p. 27; Redner, *Ends of Science*, p. 43; Stuart S. Blume, *Perspectives in the Sociology of Science* (New York: Wiley, 1968), p. 28; Barry Barnes, *T. S. Kuhn and Social Science* (London: Macmillan Press, 1982), p. 121; Bernard Barber, *Social Studies of Science* (New Brunswick: Transaction, 1990), p. 84; William H. Jeffreys and James O. Berger, "Ockham's Razor and Bayesian Analysis," *American Scientist*, vol. 80 (January–February, 1982): 64–80; Francisco Jose Ayala and Theodorius Dobyansky, *Studies in the Philosophy of Biology* (New York: Macmillan, 1974), pp. viii–x; J. G. Kemeny and P. Oppenheim, "On Reduction," *Philosophical Studies*, vol. 7 (1956): 6–19.

61 Kuhn, *Essential Tension*, pp. 44, 220; Abraham Kaplan, *The Conduct of Inquiry* (San Francisco: Chandler Publishing Company, 1964), p. 27; Robert John Ackermann, *Data, Instruments, and Theory* (Princeton, NJ: Princeton University Press, 1985); John Ziman, *Reliable Knowledge* (New York: Cambridge University Press, 1978), p. 13.

62 Clifford Geertz, *Local Knowledge* (New York: Basic, 1983), p. 167. See also Stanley Aronowitz, *Science as Power* (Minneapolis: University of Minnesota Press, 1988), p. viii. See also Andrew Pickering, ed., *Science as Practice and Culture* (Chicago: University of Chicago Press, 1992); Harold Himsworth, *Scientific Knowledge and Philosophic Thought* (Baltimore: Johns Hopkins University Press, 1986); and Patrick Suppes, *Probabilistic Metaphysics* (Oxford: Blackwell Publisher, 1984).

interpretations are potentially relevant to gerontology.⁶³ Paradoxically, to codify information about aging requires greater compartmentalization of knowledge. "Specialization has brought us to the point we have reached," Abraham Flexner wrote in 1930, "and more highly specialized intelligence will alone carry us further."⁶⁴

Big Science increasingly determines how gerontology emerges. Since the Great Depression, the United States has been a world pacesetter in terms of investment in scientific projects and training scientists. Americans have produced roughly 30 percent of all papers in chemistry and physics. By the 1970s, U.S. scholars dominated the international gerontological community.⁶⁵ Money is a major factor, but so are the striking cross-national differences in the perceptions and operations of scientific organizations. A century ago, the London *Daily News* characterized the word "scientist" as an "ignoble Americanism," the "cheap and vulgar product of trans-Atlantic slang." Now, U.S. scientific expertise is well respected everywhere. Insights from North American research on aging spread abroad, though investigators in other countries usually adapt materials to their own cultural and scientific traditions. "If a subject does not exist," a French dictum has it, "found a chair." In the United States scholars lay out a field.⁶⁶ Adminis-

63 The phrase comes from Larry Laudan, "The Pseudo-Science of Science?" *Philosophy and Social Criticism*, vol. 11 (1981): 194. See also Robert M. Rosenzweig with Barbara Turlington, *The Research Universities and Their Patrons* (Berkeley and Los Angeles: University of California Press, 1982); Charles Taylor, "Understanding in Human Science," *Review of Metaphysics*, vol. 34 (1980): 25-38; Burton R. Clark, ed., *The Academic Profession* (Berkeley and Los Angeles: University of California Press, 1987); Bill McKelvey, *Organizational Systematics* (Berkeley and Los Angeles: University of California Press, 1982); Alexandra Oleson and John Voss, *The Organization of Knowledge in Modern America, 1860–1920* (Baltimore: Johns Hopkins University Press, 1979); Ian Hacking, *Representing and Intervening* (Cambridge: Cambridge University Press, 1983).

64 Quoted in Robert S. Morison, ed., *The Contemporary University, USA* (Cambridge, MA: Houghton Mifflin, 1966), p. 6. For three different perspectives on this, see Alan Walker, "Aging and the Social Sciences: The North American Way," *Ageing and Society*, vol. 7 (1987): 235–41; W. Andrew Achenbaum, "One United States Approach to Gerontological Theory Building," ibid., vol. 9 (1989): 179–98; and George L. Maddox, "Social and Behavioral Research on Ageing: An Agenda for the United States," ibid., vol. 14 (1994): 97–108.

65 de Solla Price, *Little Science*, pp. 8–9; Brown, *Wisdom of Science*, p. 33; David Dickson, *The New Politics of Science* (New York: Pantheon Books, 1984), p. 19; Joseph Ben-David, *Fundamental Research and the Universities* (Paris: Organization for Economic Cooperation and Development, 1968). For more on common bonds cross-nationally, see Kenneth R. Hoover, *The Elements of Social Scientific Thinking*, 4th ed. (New York: St. Martin's Press, 1988); Burton R. Clark, *The Higher Education System* (Berkeley: University of California Press, 1983); Fritz Ringer, *Fields of Knowledge* (New York: Cambridge University Press, 1992). If, as experts contend, the number of scientists doubles every fourteen years, then 90 percent of all scientists are still alive.

66 Whereas an Italian university might list in its curricula experts in forty different fields, its U.S. counterparts would have twice as many specialties. See Clive Church, "Disciplinary Dynamics," *Studies in Higher Education*, vol 1. (October 1976): 104; Clark Kerr et al.,

trative policies also matter. Until recently, Moscow set the agenda for Russia's renowned research institutes. French bureaucrats influence academic appointments. In comparison, U.S. science during the twentieth century seems fairly decentralized, despite the influence major public and private institutions exercise on research priorities here.[67]

Crossing Frontiers thus highlights continuities, changes, breakthroughs, and detours in gerontology as it has emerged in twentieth-century America. The case studies presented here are representative not exhaustive. They were selected to underscore historical variations in the field as well as the struggles and negotiations that took place between gerontologists and other scientists, policymakers, and academics. To the extent that this "comparison and analysis" illuminates how gerontology took shape, then my book may help researchers on aging to look hard at their options as they chart future directions. "Chronicling the intellectual history of a field is tricky business, especially for insiders," observed gerontologist Joe Hendricks. "For one thing, insiders are immersed in playing the field; for another, history is as much a matter of consensus as is any other 'truth.' "[68]

12 *Systems of Higher Education* (New York: International Council for Educational Development, 1978); Sidney Ross, "Scientist," *Annals of Science*, vol. 18 (1962): 79; Gerard Radnitzky, *Anglo-Saxon Schools of Metascience* (Goteborg: Akademiforlaget, 1983) Stephen Brooks and Alain-G. Gagnon, *Social Scientists, Policy, and the State* (New York: Praeger, 1990), p. 124; Mattei Dogan and Robert Pahre, *Creative Marginality* (Boulder, CO: Westview, 1990), p. 9; Centre for Educational Research and Innovation, *Interdisciplinarity* (Paris: Organization for Economic Co-operation and Development, 1972); Martin Bulmer, *Social Science Research and Government* (New York: Cambridge University Press, 1987). On the "singularity" of traditions, see James Clifford, *The Predicament of Culture* (Cambridge, MA: Harvard University Press, 1988); Michael McGerr, "The Price of Transnational History," *American Historical Review*, vol. 96 (1991): 1,056–72; Michael Kammen, "The Problem of American Exceptionalism," *American Quarterly*, vol. 45 (March 1993): 1–43.

67 Industrialists and entrepreneurs have invested heavily in university-based science. Andrew Carnegie gave his own money and William Walker used industrial funds to establish institutes in Pittsburgh, Pennsylvania, and Cambridge, Massachusetts, that would generate patents and new technologies. Academic leaders responded in kind: In 1913, the American Association for the Advancement of Science formed the Committee of 100 to foster better industry–university cooperation. Terry Nichols Clark, *Prophets and Patrons* (Cambridge, MA: Harvard University Press, 1973); Dogan and Pahre, *Creative Marginality*, p. 229; Daniel S. Greenberg, *The Politics of Pure Science* (New York: The New American Library, 1967), p. 67; Simon Rottenberg, "The Role of Government in the Growth of Science," *Minerva*, vol. 19 (Spring, 1981): 43–70; Dorothy Nelkin, *Science as Intellectual Property* (New York: Macmillan, 1984), pp. 16–17.

68 Jon Hendricks, "Generations and the Generation of Theory in Social Gerontology," *International Journal of Aging and Human Development*, vol. 35 (1992): 35. It was T. S. Eliot who claimed that "comparison and analysis are the chief tools of the critic." See his "The Function of Criticism," in *Selected Essays* (New York: Harcourt, Brace & World, 1961), p. 21. See also Tony Becher, "Toward a Definition of Disciplinary Cultures," *Studies in Higher Education*, vol. 6 (1981): 109–22; and Charles Rosenberg, "Wood or Trees," *Isis*, vol. 79 (1988): 565–70.

I consider myself a nomad in these frontiers: I am a historian and gerontologist, but I am not a scientist. I have not staked a consensus position. Rather, I have tried to show the penetrability of institutional boundaries, the contingent nature of scientific inquiry, and the ironies that inhere in developing a field of research in the human sciences: "Always the same tribe, never the same multiplicity, always the same process, never a stable state, always a single event, never a predictable outcome."[69] If *Crossing Frontiers* prompts critical thinking, this history of gerontology will have served my purpose.

69 The use of the term *nomad* comes from Gilles Deleuze and Felix Guattari, *A Thousand Plateaus* (Minneapolis: University of Minnesota Press, 1987), pp. xii, 380. The quoted material is from Ronald Bogue, *Deleuze and Guattari* (London: Routledge, 1989), p. 11.

Part I

Old age becomes a "problem" worth investigating scientifically

IN 1874 GEORGE M. BEARD, M.D. read a paper before the Medico-Legal Society of New York on "Legal Responsibility in Old Age, Based on Researches into the Relation of Age to Work." "It would be easy to ascertain the law of the relation of age to work by the mere expression of an opinion," he noted, "and thousands of opinions have been expressed upon it." It would be "comparatively easy" to determine whether gifted people did their best work at younger or older ages, Beard elaborated, "but partial statistics, prepared to form a theory, can never settle these questions – cannot satisfy the inquirer, nor relieve the doubter; nor have any convincing power whatever." Beard had great faith in Science, but he knew that appropriate methods were not yet available to illuminate processes of human aging:

> If physiology alone could solve these problems – if it were possible for the microscope to so reveal the complex mechanism of the brain, and if chemistry could so analyze its intricate and manifold constituents as to make it a human possibility to determine, from the brain itself, both the general and special functions of which it is capable, and the modifications which these functions undergo by age, by disease, and external conditions – then, by a sufficient number of post-mortem examinations, these hard questions could be scientifically answered; but, unfortunately for these methods of investigation, physiology and pathology are just born, and neither our children nor our children's children can expect to see them exact and complete sciences.[1]

Beard's prose was infelicitous, but his observations prescient. Gerontology did not emerge as a science in the United States until the twentieth century. Research done by physiologists, biologists, and pathologists initially shaped

1 George M. Beard, *Legal Responsibility in Old Age* (1874), p. 4. The edition I used was reprinted in *The "Fixed Period" Controversy*, ed. Gerald J. Gruman (New York: Arno Press, 1979).

the field. Scientists' major challenge from the outset was to disentangle the cumulative effects of aging, of disease, and of environmental assaults on human capacities over the life course. They also needed to determine whether declining bodily functions were associated with "general or specific" modifications that occurred with age. To solve "these problems" required a multidisciplinary approach.

Part I traces the origins of "modern" gerontology in the United States from the colonial era through the first decades of the twentieth century. Because scientists generally choose to focus on problems that are "intellectually interesting and 'do-able,' "[2] this section of *Crossing Frontiers* traces how and when certain problems of aging and old age were framed by successive waves of investigators. Articulating a research agenda was the first step, operationalizing a strategy, the second. "In any . . . variety of practical or scientific problems, the task set by the problem is to find a method or technique for doing something, whether it be to launch a boat or bombard helium atoms with X-rays," observed Lawrence K. Frank, a foundation officer who played a critical role in advancing research programs in both child development and gerontology between the world wars. "Each new generation seemingly builds up its habits of behavior around the tools and techniques which science provides."[3]

The production and publication of Edmund Vincent Cowdry's highly respected handbook, *Problems of Ageing* (1939), heralds the emergence of gerontology as a field of scientific inquiry in the United States. Thereafter, researchers interested in pursuing various biomedical, behavioral, and social problems of human aging began to develop networks that cut across formal disciplinary and professional boundaries. They established centers dedicated to research on aging, which enabled experts to participate on major multidisciplinary projects. Ironically, despite these promising developments, gerontology for most of this century remained a peripheral scientific enterprise. The specter of Ponce de Leon, quacks, and alchemists dogged investigators. Some of gerontology's founders called for uniformity of purpose; others tried to "prove" the scientific merits of their efforts by showing how it was grounded in Baconian principles or Darwinian theory. It is the diversity of strands in the historical narrative and the plurality of viewpoints expressed, however, that commands attention here.[4]

2 Joan H. Fujimura, "Constructing 'Do-able' Problems in Cancer Research: Articulating Alignment," *Social Studies of Science*, vol. 17 (1987): 257.

3 Lawrence K. Frank, "Social Problems," *American Journal of Sociology*, vol. 30 (1925): 464, 471. See also Willard Waller, "Social Problems and the Mores," *American Sociological Review*, vol. 1 (December 1936): 922–33.

4 Gerontology is hardly unique in this regard. This theme is also evident in Allan Megill, "Fragmentation and the Future of Historiography," *American Historical Review*, vol. 96 (June 1991); 693–8; and M. J. Mulkay, G. N. Gilbert, and S. Woolgar, "Problem Areas and Research Networks in Science," *Sociology*, vol. 9 (1975): 187–203.

1

Surveying the frontiers of aging

"HOW CAN WE TRY TO TRANSFORM to a normal and physiological condition old age, at present utterly pathological, unless we first understand the most intimate details of its mechanism?" asked Elie Metchnikoff in *The Nature of Man: Studies in Optimistic Philosophy* (1908). "I think it is extremely probable that the scientific study of old age and of death, two branches of science that may be called *gerontology* and *thanatology*, will bring about great modifications in the course of the last period of life."[1] In these two sentences, the world-renowned director of the Pasteur Institute not only invited his contemporaries to engage in scientific research on aging, but he also coined a name for such a field of inquiry. Once investigators better understood basic structures, mechanisms, and processes, Metchnikoff hoped, the "utterly pathological" features of senescence could be modified. Scientific progress would be slow because there was so much to learn, but "faith must be in the power of science," Metchnikoff acknowledged. "Our generation has no chance of attaining physiological old age and normal death; but it may take real consolation from the thought that those who are now young may advance several steps in that direction. It may reflect that each succeeding generation will get closer

---

1 Elie Metchnikoff, *The Nature of Man: Studies in Optimistic Philosophy* (New York: G. P. Putnam's Sons, 1908 [1st French ed., 1903]), pp. 289, 297–8. Other historians of aging have interpreted Metchnikoff's place in the evolution of theories of the biology of aging differently than I. Thomas R. Cole, for instance, emphasized Metchnikoff's patriarchal voice in expressing optimism and not the promise of prolongevity amid fin de siècle malaise. See Cole's *The Journey of Life* (New York: Cambridge University Press, 1992), pp. 185–90. Other analysts pay scant attention to Metchnikoff's gerontologic interests, seeing them as part of his contributions to immunology. Alfred I. Tauber and Leon Chernyak, *Metchnikoff and the Origins of Immunology* (New York: Oxford University Press, 1991).

and closer to the solution and that true happiness one day will be reached by mankind."[2]

Elie Metchnikoff (1845–1916) was "the foremost of French medical men," according to Edwin E. Slosson, a leading U.S. commentator of scientific developments in the early twentieth century. "Like Pasteur . . . [he] entered the realm of medicine by crossing the frontier of another science."[3] What *was* the cross-disciplinary journey that led Metchnikoff to *gerontology?* Actually, it was unplanned: Metchnikoff crossed several scientific frontiers during the course of his distinguished career. Far from his intent at the outset, Metchnikoff's last major project was an attempt to modify old age so as to allow a "natural death" instinct, analogous to sleep, to end human life.[4] In all of his work, Metchnikoff evinced certain attitudes that sociologists of science associate with pioneering efforts to create new scientific fields of inquiry. Well trained in biology and respectful of scientific methods, Metchnikoff was a specialist who was open to different ways of pursuing knowledge. He had an ability to combine chance observations and eclectic notions into testable hypotheses. Metchnikoff's willingness to challenge scientific orthodoxy led him at the beginning of the century to formulate an imaginative theory of aging.[5]

It is important, however, not to exaggerate the significance of the man who named gerontology in this account. Elie Metchnikoff was not the Father of Gerontology. The field has many origins. Some of its progenitors would be surprised that later generations of scientists and historians would make connections between their contributions and subsequent developments. Metchnikoff had a clearer sense than most of what he hoped to accomplish in gerontology. He had faith that scientific approach could prolong human life. But Metchnikoff's accomplishments fell short of "revolutionary" achievements, whether judged by the testimony of his contemporary witnesses, later documentary histories, assessments by historians of aging, or his current place in "the living scientific tradition."[6]

---

2 Metchnikoff, *Nature*, pp. 302 ("faith") and 299–300.

3 Edwin E. Slosson, *Major Prophets of To-Day* (Boston: Little, Brown, and Company, 1914), p. 150.

4 Elie Metchnikoff, "Studies of Natural Death," *Harper Magazine*, vol. 114 (January 1907): 273.

5 For more on the importance of attitudes in advancing science, see *The Estate of Social Knowledge*, ed. Jo Anne Brown and David K. van Keuren (Baltimore: Johns Hopkins University Press, 1991), p. xix.

6 The four tests came from I. Bernard Cohen, *Revolution in Science* (Cambridge, MA: Harvard University Press, 1985), pp. 41–4. See also Bernard Barber, *Social Studies in Science* (New Brunswick, NJ: Transaction Publishers, 1990), pp. 3–4. Among the "assessments" in histories of aging I consulted were, in addition to those in note 1, essays and books by James Birren, Robert Butler, Joseph Freeman, Gerald Gruman, Carole Haber, Leonard Hayflick, and Nathan Shock. (Full citations to these authors appear at places in the text where

So why start this chapter with Metchnikoff? There are three reasons. First, at a time in which U.S. gerontology is better endowed than anywhere else in the world, it is important to remember that North American scientists did not always enjoy such a comparative advantage. At the beginning of the twentieth century, most U.S. scientists lacked adequate laboratory facilities. They could not do the large-scale experimentation possible in major European universities and institutes. Second, tracing the impact of Metchnikoff's gerontologic ideas in the U.S. research reveals the state of scientific knowledge among researchers on aging on this side of the Atlantic before 1900. "A field is all the more scientific," Pierre Bourdieu notes, "the more it is capable of channeling, of converting as a variable motives into scientifically proper behavior."[7] Did Metchnikoff's peers agree that science someday might unlock the mysteries of aging? What other questions were they investigating, what other theories were they evaluating? If they did not or could not channel Metchnikoff's ideas into their activities, what does this tell us about their priorities? These questions lead to a third reason for beginning with Metchnikoff: Reactions to his ideas serve to gauge popular ideas about senescence at the turn of the century. Were his opinions about prolongevity quickly accepted? Did the socioeconomic dimensions of later years attract as much attention to its physical capacity and clerical features? Did ordinary people disentangle *physiological* and *pathological* images of old age as sharply as did Metchnikoff? Or was that cast of mind more readily associated with physicians and those who conducted biological experiments?

Elie Metchnikoff: "The Ponce de Leon of our day"[8]

Elie Metchnikoff, born in the steppes of Russia, was the youngest of five children. His father, a general in the Imperial Army, was a modest landowner; his mother, a Jew, was the daughter of a writer. One brother was a distinguished geographer, a radical who served as Garibaldi's adjutant. Another, president of the Kiev House of Justice, became the subject of Tolstoy's *Death of Ivan Ilych*. Elie was a precocious, sickly child with a mercurial temper. Dissuaded by his mother from pursuing medicine, he plunged into zoology. By the age of twenty, "Quicksilver" (his family nickname) had already published his first scientific articles, written several combative book reviews, withstood the criticism of a prominent German

---

I relied on their insights.) In several instances, I was surprised to discover *no* reference to Metchnikoff.

7 Pierre Bourdieu and Loïc J. D. Wacquant, *An Invitation to Reflexive Sociology* (Chicago: University of Chicago Press, 1992), p. 177.

8 Dr. Henry Smith Williams, "Metchnikoff: Seeker After Eternal Youth," *Cosmopolitan*, vol. 53 (September 1912): 440.

physiologist, and accused a senior professor of stealing some of his ideas.[9] In 1865 Metchnikoff began to collaborate with another Russian zoologist on a study of what we would call germ layers in invertebrate embryos. By comparing the growth to maturity of two closely related flatworms, he demonstrated that recapitulations of particular developmental patterns in lower forms of life occur in radically different ways. Thus, early on, relationships among growth, development, and maturity interested him.

Metchnikoff's experiments in the 1860s and 1870s showed his classical training. "Makers of generalizations should proceed very slowly," he wrote, "passing only by the smallest stages from particular facts . . . to attain principles neither vague nor ambiguous, but clear and exact and that would not be denied by nature herself."[10] Although this observation resembles one of Bacon's aphorisms, Metchnikoff's views, as Thomas Cole has noted, were rooted in Romantic assumptions. Whereas the scientific views of his peers were being transformed by Darwin's ideas, Metchnikoff initially had reservations about the theory of natural selection. He insisted that embryological research should not get ensnared in evolutionary problematics. In the first stage of his career, Metchnikoff systematically investigated particular variations in development *within* species (such as medusas and sponges) in order to discover "disharmonies" both among parts of an organism and between a species and its environment. His studies of digestion revealed no underlying unity; disharmonies presented themselves over the life course. "Development," Metchnikoff wrote, "appears to be a more general phenomenon than progress."[11] Hence he wanted to learn about "harmony" in developmental processes.

The second stage of Metchnikoff's career began in 1882, when he moved to Messina, Italy, to escape political turmoil in Russia and to recuperate from an illness. "A new thought suddenly flashed across my brain." In the course of his research, Metchnikoff noticed that a splinter introduced into starfish larvae would provoke reactions between parasites and phagocytes (i.e., devouring cells) similar to what occurred in humans. "Thus it was in Messina that the great event of my scientific life took place," Metchnikoff recalled decades later. "A zoologist until then, I suddenly became a pathologist. I entered a new road in which my later activity was to be ex-

---

9 Biographical details in Slosson, *Major Prophets*, p. 153; Gert H. Brieger, "Introduction," to Elie Metchnikoff, *Immunity in Infective Diseases* (New York: Johnson Reprint Company, 1968), pp. xvi–xvii; Daniel P. Todes, *Darwin Without Malthus* (New York: Oxford University Press, 1989), p. 83; Tauber and Chernyak, *Metchnikoff*, pp. 5–7. Metchnikoff's health problems would persist in early adulthood. He suffered from failing eyesight and depression. Metchnikoff twice tried to commit suicide, once after the death of his first wife.

10 Metchnikoff, *Nature*, p. 204; Cole, *Journey of Life*, pp. 187, 190. I also benefited from Cole's comments on an earlier version of this chapter.

11 This 1871 statement is quoted in Tauber and Chernyak, *Metchnikoff*, p. 85; Leon Chernyak and Alfred I. Tauber, "The Idea of Immunity," *Journal of the History of Biology*, vol. 23 (Summer 1990): 220–32, 239n116.

erted."[12] For the next twenty-five years Metchnikoff refined and defended his theory that phagocytes (leukocytes, or white corpuscles as they are known in humans) were the first line of defense against acute infection.

Expertise he had acquired through studies of embryology, parasitology, and digestion prepared Metchnikoff well to cross frontiers into the domains of comparative pathology and medicine. In 1884 he declared that blood congested at a wound site as a result of white blood cells' efforts tried to overcome the invading microbes. That same year he wrote a paper reporting parallels between the digestive activities of amoeboid cells and changes in embryologic development. Both phenomena, Metchnikoff suggested in accordance with his phagocytic theory, were manifestations of the sometimes conflicted, sometimes harmonious interactions between cells of the same body.[13] Rudolph Virchow, whose cell theories transformed studies of pathology in the nineteenth century, and Louis Pasteur, the eminent chemist and microbiologist, immediately heralded Metchnikoff's discoveries. Other contemporaries recognized that the phagocytic theory had implications for work in microbiology, pathology, embryology, evolutionary biology, and biological chemistry. Barely forty years old, Metchnikoff was considered by his peers to be a pathfinder, someone who succeeded at blazing new frontiers of knowledge.

In 1888 Metchnikoff relocated to the newly founded Pasteur Institute, where he worked for the rest of his life. "In Paris I succeeded at last in practicing pure Science apart from all politics or any public function." He enjoyed interacting with his colleagues, who did not necessarily agree with his theories, and teaching a course in microbiology with Wilhelm Roux. There, Metchnikoff could pursue his multidisciplinary predilections with freedom to take risks, knowing that his colleagues would not tolerate recklessness. "Working by your side and drawing largely from your vast and varied stores of knowledge, I felt myself safe from those divagations into which a zoologist, who had wandered into the domain of biological chemistry and of medical science, is likely to stray."[14] The Pasteur Institute provided Metchnikoff with a haven for research and a refuge from attacks by scientists who vociferously criticized his views.

Metchnikoff's phagocytic theory was opposed on several fronts. Some

---

12 Quoted in Olga Metchnikoff, *Life of Elie Metchnikoff* (Boston: Houghton Mifflin, 1921), pp. 115–17. See also, James G. Hirsch, "Immunity to Infectious Diseases: Review of Some of the Concepts of Metchnikoff," *Bacteriological Review*, vol. 23 (1959): 48–60.

13 Chernyak and Tauber, "Idea of Immunity," p. 244n124; Todes, *Darwin*, p. 85; Brieger, "Introduction" to Metchnikoff, *Immunity*, pp. xix–xxi; Slosson, *Prophets*, p. 154; Tauber and Chernyak, *Metchnikoff*, p. xv.

14 First quotation in Olga Metchnikoff, *Life*, p. 136; the second comes from the preface of Metchnikoff's *Immunity in Infective Diseases* (1901). See also Paul Weirdling, "Scientific Elites and Laboratory Organisations in fin de siècle Paris and Berlin," in *The Laboratory Revolution in Medicine*, ed. Andrew Cunningham and Perry Williams (New York: Cambridge University Press, 1992), p. 179.

investigators argued that inflammations were due to lesions in the walls of blood vessels that permitted the passive leakage of "humors" around the injured area. Even those who shared Metchnikoff's belief in a cellular as opposed to a humoral theory of inflammation did not wholly subscribe to his notion that the body had the innate capacity to produce cells that actively fought diseases. Some critics, having shown that phagocytes failed to ingest certain types of pathogens, set forth an alternative model of *acquired* immune processes. As opposition mounted, Metchnikoff became more rigid in defending his theory, more extravagant in making his claims. New research findings, however, undermined the appeal of Metchnikoff's position. The discovery of antibodies in 1890 prompted scientific interest in humoral theories of immunity. Paul Ehrlich's 1897 paper outlining a side-chain theory of antibody formation inspired countless quantitative studies of antigen–antibody reactions. Thereafter, molecular chemists, rather than biologists or pathologists, were judged to be at the vanguard of immunological research. Thus, Metchnikoff's phagocytic theory was already in eclipse by 1905, when he attempted to rebut critics by publishing his 591-page book, *Immunity in Infective Diseases.*[15] (Scientists did not return to the phagocytic theory until the 1960s, when studies of cellular immunity again came into favor.)

Although his contemporaries were questioning the utility of his phagocytic theory in immunology, Metchnikoff believed that his conceptual framework still had wider relevance across several domains of biology and medicine. Metchnikoff used the opening paragraphs of his *magnum opus* to signal his readiness to cross new frontiers at this juncture in his scientific career:

> The problem of immunity in relation to infective diseases is one that not merely concerns general pathology but has a very important bearing on all branches of practical medicine, such as hygiene, surgery and the veterinary art. . . . The question of immunity is, however, apart from its practical aspect intimately connected with pure theory. The immunization of animals useful to man is likewise a question of such great importance to agriculture and to industry as to have now become the object of legislation.[16]

In my opinion, these lines illuminate Metchnikoff's sense of the scope and operation of scientific inquiry. First, he was intrigued by a big "problem," like the connection between immunity and infectious diseases, whose intellectual boundaries are not confined to a single discipline but bear on "all

15 For more on this, see Arthur M. Silverstein, *A History of Immunology* (San Diego: Academic Press, 1989), esp. pp. 38–55, 94; Tauber and Chernyak, *Metchnikoff*, pp. 136–8, 172; Hirsch, "Immunity," p. 59. As if to show their impartiality, the 1908 Nobel prize was shared by Elie Metchnikoff and Ehrlich "in recognition for their work on immunity."

16 Metchnikoff, *Immunity*, p. 1. I have reversed the order of the second and third sentences of the text for present purposes; it does not distort the author's argument.

branches." Second, he was interested in the relationship between theory and practice. This led him, third, to a concern for applying basic research to "legislative" matters. Metchnikoff, portraying himself an advocate of "practical medicine," worried about agricultural and industrial issues – a stance not often found among bench scientists. These themes became quite evident in his next major project. Metchnikoff's studies into the prolongation of life extended his work in immunology and embellished his "optimistic" philosophical visions.

"The scientific study of old age is therefore indispensable," Metchnikoff observed, because "our knowledge [is] so limited that the subject may be dealt with in a few lines."[17] A desire to go in new directions inspired Metchnikoff's interest, but his attraction to the problem of senescence was at least partly a personal affair. Metchnikoff, fully recuperated at age fifty-three from a major illness, "felt an ardent desire to live." Keenly aware that members of his immediate family were short-lived, he worried about dying. Eleven years later, despite maintaining a strict regimen of diet and exercise, he feared that "I look much older than I really am."[18] Metchnikoff also was aware that old men in Russia (though, fortunately not in France) generally had to give up productive careers. No wonder, then, that Metchnikoff considered old age "the epoch of our existence which is full of the greatest contradictions."[19] Some of the features of late life disgusted him: "Old age is repulsive at present, because it is an old age devoid of its true meaning, full of egoism, narrowness of view, incapacity, and malignancy." Nevertheless, given the intellectual and social contributions some elders made to society, "there is no reason to be pessimistic on the subject of old age."[20]

Having earlier blazed the frontiers of immunology to pursue research leads prompted by his studies of zoology and embryology, now Metchnikoff's investigations in immunity fed his research in aging. "A veritable battle rages in the innermost recesses of our body."[21] Phagocytes, he posited, turned hair white; "senile atrophy" resulted from disappearing nerve

17 The first half of the quotation comes from Elie Metchnikoff, "Old Age," in *Annual Report of the Smithsonian Institution for the Year Ending June 30, 1904* (Washington, DC: n.p., 1903–4), p. 549. The second part of the quotation comes from his *Nature*, p. 229.

18 Olga Metchnikoff, *Life*, p. 182. His physical appearance is described in Herman Bernstein, *With Master Minds* (New York: Universal Series Publishing Co., 1913), p. 61; retirement, in Metchnikoff, "Old Age," p. 534. Columnists who interviewed Metchnikoff toward the end of his life invariably commented on his youthful face and gait.

19 Metchnikoff, "Old Age," 536; for the contributions of the old-old, see p. 550.

20 Metchnikoff, *Nature*, pp. 294–5. On optimism, see p. 261. Again, see Cole, *Journey of Life*, for a less benign interpretation of Metchnikoff's attempts to resurrect patriarchical authority in pursuing his search for longevity.

21 Metchnikoff, *Nature*, p. 239; Alfred I. Tauber and Leon Chernyak, "Metchnikoff and a Theory of Medicine, *Journal of the Royal Society of Medicine*, vol. 82 (December 1989): 699–701.

cells. Building upon and extending the logic of earlier inquiries, Metchnikoff attributed the "principal phenomena of old age" to the action of macrophages, microbes that collected in the digestive system. As he put it in 1904:

> The theory of old age and the hypotheses which are connected with it may be summarized in a few words: the senile degeneration of our organism is entirely similar to the lesions induced by certain maladies of a microbic origin. Old age, then, is an infectious chronic disease which is manifested by a degeneration, or an enfeebling of the noble elements, and by the excessive activity of the macrophages. These modifications cause a disturbance of the equilibrium of the cells composing our body and set up a struggle within our organism which ends in a precocious aging and in premature death, contrary to nature.[22]

"Disharmonies," according to Metchnikoff, did not afflict just the aged. Citing medical studies, anthropological reports, and his own embryological investigations, he opted for a developmental paradigm: "Human life is subject from its very beginning to the pernicious disharmonies in the constitution." But the "greatest disharmony" was manifest in the "morbid nature of old age."[23]

Metchnikoff's theory of aging, at first glance, has some parallels to various homeostatic, degenerative, and wear-and-tear theories of aging that have been formulated in gerontological circles during the twentieth century. And it is fascinating to note, especially in light of subsequent developments, the extent to which Metchnikoff's construction of biological old age was medicalized. Ahead of his time, he appreciated the power of infectious diseases on the health status of elderly persons. Yet many of Metchnikoff's hypotheses do not mesh with contemporary gerontologic thinking. Medical scientists nowadays distinguish far more sharply than he did between chronic and infectious diseases. Unlike latter-day gerontologists, Metchnikoff often made direct comparisons between human aging and other forms of plant and animal senescence. Not hesitating to draw analogies between child growth and late-life development, he opted for a life-course approach to the study of aging. The idiosyncratic features of Metchnikoff's phagocytic theory of aging limited its appeal to contemporaries and later scientists. Not surprisingly, it did not deter him from attacking other people's ideas.

Metchnikoff did not hide his contempt for old-age remedies promoted by journalists, quacks, and charlatans. He treated scholarly publications harshly, too. Metchnikoff rejected works that went beyond their evidence and posited that tissues and organs invariably degenerated in old age. On the basis of his own studies, he demolished various studies of comparative

---

22 Metchnikoff, "Old Age," p. 548. Earlier material from idem, *Nature*, pp. 238–43.
23 Metchnikoff, *Nature*, pp. 283, 285. See also, Todes, *Darwin*, p. 84; Tauber and Chernyak, *Metchnikoff*, p. 24.

longevity and "natural death" in reptiles, birds, mammals, and humans. He challenged August Weismann's theory that the proliferation of certain cells culminates in a given organism's death.[24] Rather than concede the inevitability of decay and degeneration with advancing years, Metchnikoff thought that someday a "normal," "physiological old age" ideally could be attained by humans. The ravages of age, he felt certain, could be reversed: Metchnikoff cited evidence that phagocytes devouring blood corpuscles in a clot could undo the effects of paralysis in cases of apoplexy. The strategy, then, was to find ways to prolong life by eliminating the pathological manifestations of old age in accordance with his theory to ward off infectious diseases in late life. Metchnikoff looked forward to the day when pathologists, embryologists, cytologists, and clinicians could explain how and why people grew weaker as they aged.

"The power of science" had not yet advanced far enough to guarantee success in people's efforts to attain a healthful old age. Nonetheless, on the basis of his own research, Metchnikoff offered an "elixir of life" that promised some benefits. Eating yoghurt, claimed Metchnikoff, killed noxious "macrophages." In both *The Nature of Man* (1903) and *The Prolongation of Life* (1908), he offered biochemical and cross-cultural evidence to corroborate his claims about the powers of sour milk for prolonging life. He noted the extreme longevity enjoyed by yoghurt-loving Bulgarians. That he himself had reached age seventy (despite his family's predisposition to die prematurely) demonstrated the importance of hygiene, plain living, and daily ingestion of yoghurt. Metchnikoff was tapping into a tradition of relying on good personal hygiene and proper diet as a way of promoting healthful longevity. (A century later, geriatricians and gerontologists would also be invoking health promotion as a way to maintain vigor in later years.) Not all of Metchnikoff's peers were impressed. Some physicians and scientists derided the old man as "the modern Ponce de Leon searching for the Fountain of Immortal Youth and finding it in the Milky Whey."[25] To them, Metchnikoff seemed more like a conquistador than someone applying Baconian logic to the problem of old age.

Once again, however, it should be Metchnikoff's prescience, not the failure of his quixotic speculations and remedies, that attracts our attention. On both sides of the Atlantic, people around the turn of the century were deploring and bemoaning the obsolescence of old age. Accustomed to playing the role of contrarian, Metchnikoff affirmed that "it is useful to prolong

---

24 Elie Metchnikoff, *The Prolongation of Life: Optimistic Studies* (New York: Putnam, 1908), pp. 36, 53, 118; *idem,* "Old Age," p. 538.
25 Slosson, *Major Prophets,* p. 175. For more on yoghurt, see Metchnikoff, *Prolongation,* pp. 168–78; idem, *Nature,* pp. 248–57; Olga Metchnikoff, *Life,* p. 251; Sir Ray Lankester, *Science from an Easy Chair* (New York: Macmillan Company, 1911), p. 43. For a contemporary interpretation, see Debra Jan Bibel, "Elie Metchnikoff's Bacillus of Long Life, *ASM News,* vol. 54 (1988): 661–5.

human life."[26] Despite the pessimism about the prospects for finding a cure for the vicissitudes of age that pervaded scientific and popular circles, he dared to offer hope that life expectancy even in adulthood might be extended through proper hygiene as well as scientific advances. Long before others would come to share his vision, Metchnikoff called for a science of gerontology, grounded in existing disciplines and specialties, as a way to advance human well-being: "Science, which has already done so much to fight diseases, would also find means of struggling against *premature* old age and *precocious* death, thus leading us to the normal, vital cycle, *orthobiosis*."[27] Whereas Metchnikoff had as a young scientist minimized the chances of humans ever attaining the ideal of orthobiosis – a ripe old age at the end of a healthful and fulfilling life – he now felt that it was theoretically possible to bend the laws of nature. Humans, through sound applications of science, which was revealing patterns of development and senesecence, could "modify human nature and transform its disharmonies into harmonies."[28]

Not only did Metchnikoff change his outlook as a result of his work on prolongevity, but he also revised earlier assessment of other scientists' ideas. Toward the end of his life, Metchnikoff endorsed the very principles of Darwinism that he once had repudiated. "The phagocytic doctrine developed entirely on the basis of Darwin's evolutionary theory," he declared in 1895. Fourteen years later, in a keynote address at Cambridge University at a celebration of the fiftieth anniversary of the publication of *Origins of Species*, Metchnikoff argued that Darwin's theory influenced a wide range of studies, including his work on prolongevity.[29] Ironically, by grounding his ideas in Darwinism at the very time that his phagocytic model was being undermined by scientific rivals, Metchnikoff may have managed to enhance his theory's credibility. Metchnikoff also used Darwinian language mingled with Baconian principles and Hegelian logic in presenting his philosophy of science and in recounting his *Forty Years' Search for a Rational Conception of Life*; it supported his belief that societal progress depended on faith in science and human agency:

> The ethical problem reduces itself to this: to allow the majority of human beings to reach life's goal, that is, to accomplish the whole cycle

26 Metchnikoff, *Prolongation*, p. 135. Anticipating an argument made by G. Stanley Hall in *Senescence*, Metchnikoff emphasized the mental vitality manifest in the very old.

27 This is how Olga Metchnikoff put it in her *Life*, p. 281. See also Metchnikoff, *Prolongation*, pp. 325ff.

28 Metchnikoff, quoted in Olga Metchnikoff, *Life*, p. 282. Unlike Cole, who emphasized the Enlightenment foundations of Metchnikoff's framework, I prefer here to suggest ways that Metchnikoff prefigures the goal of those who would lay the scientific foundations of U.S. gerontology after World War I.

29 Quotation (1895) in Todes, *Darwin*, p. 82; Lankester, *Easy Chair*, pp. 39–40. See also Metchnikoff, *Nature*, ch. 3; idem, *Prolongation*, p. 184.

of a rational existence to its natural end. We are still very far from that. . . . Its final realization will demand more scientific researches, which must be allowed the widest and freest scope. It is to be foreseen that existence will have to be modified in many ways.[30]

Many of Metchnikoff's hypotheses may have subsequently been proven erroneous, and some of his hopes have not been realized. But they could not be dismissed as the eccentric views of a stereotypical old man. By framing his ideas in metaphors understood by orthodox scientists and the lay public alike, he made new ideas accessible. This tack furthered Metchnikoff's hopes that gerontology would become a science that "allowed the widest and freest scope" in theory and in practice.

Where Metchnikoff's gerontologic vision fits in the context of U.S. science

Elie Metchnikoff's work on longevity was well disseminated in the United States. He prepared a long essay on "old age" for the 1904–5 Smithsonian Annual Report. An American journalist hailed Metchnikoff as one of the *Major Prophets of To-Day* (1914). Popularized accounts of his research appeared in *McClure's* and *Cosmopolitan*. "This 'vulgarization' not only . . . appeased his pride in his work, but also, as he was aware, enabled the man in the street to form a juster estimate of his value to society."[31]

The press treated this "broad humanitarian" in generally laudatory terms. Many who compared him to a latter-day Ponce de Leon did not do so to ridicule him. Metchnikoff's work "surely suggests that the scientific search for a fountain of youth has proved a less futile and visionary quest than it once seemed."[32] Like their European counterparts, some U.S. writers questioned both the scientific and philosophical bases of Metchnikoff's "optimistic" vision. Albion W. Small, the nation's foremost sociologist, dismissed *The Nature of Man* as "unscientific science. . . . The serious element in the book is set forth with just enough stage business to charm the galleries. It will not be surprising if the flights of Metchnikoff's fancy presently pass into the bric-a-brac of popular science, but really there is no

---

30 From Elie Metchnikoff's *Flora of the Human Body* (1901), quoted in Olga Metchnikoff, *Life*, p. 224. I could not obtain a copy of Metchnikoff, *Forty Years' Search*.

31 Charles Darbarn, "Metchnikoff: The Savant and the Man," *Fortnightly*, vol. 107 (February 1917): 287. Metchnikoff, "Old Age"; Arthur E. McFarlane, "Prolonging the Prime of Life," *McClure*, vol. 25 (September 1905): 541–51; Professor Metchnikoff and Dr. Henry Smith Williams, "Why Not Live Forever?" *Cosmopolitan*, vol. 53 (September 1912): 436–9; Slosson, *Major Prophets*, ch. 4 (of six).

32 First quotation from "Elie Metchnikoff," *Outlook*, vol. 113 (July 26, 1926): 687; second from Henry Smith Williams, "Metchnikoff." See also, P. Chalmers Mitchell, "The Straight Way of Life," *World's Work*, vol. 15 (November 1907): 9,540–4; Walter B. Cannon, "Metchnikoff," *The New Republic*, vol. 8 (August 12, 1916): 37–9.

immediate occasion for a new cult."[33] Others felt that it was precisely his ability to communicate the excitement of science to a lay audience that was so refreshing: "Among the dry-as-dust specialists, M. Metchnikoff is as a pioneer in an untried country, and perhaps a bit of an adventurer."[34]

Researchers in the United States cautioned that the supposed therapeutic benefits to be derived from "the fermented milk known as lacto-bactilline" remained unproven. "To obtain the necessary scientific data will require elaborate and very laborious experiments covering long periods of time," declared C. A. Herter, M.D., a professor of pharmacology at Columbia University. "With the aid of such experiments I have no doubt that the usefulness of soured milk in health and in disease will be definitely and discriminatingly established. The limitations of utility will become equally plain, and I predict that they will prove to be many."[35] Perhaps even more striking than Herter's equivocation was his confidence in extensive, elaborate laboratory tests performed in the United States at the beginning of the twentieth century. Either way, the results of basic research were useful, for Metchnikoff's theory, even if disproven, might spur research on aging. Would that have been the case a century or two earlier?

Interest in physical aspects of old age in the New World predates the twentieth century, but it would unduly stretch the meaning of science to claim that the research on aging that was done actually matched Metchnikoff's in terms of theoretical or methodological rigor.[36] The earliest "scientific" catalog of the ailments and attitudes of older people was Cotton Mather's *The Angel of Bethesda* (1724), which linked the sacred and the profane. Others studied Nature for political ends. During the early years of the republic it was generally believed that "tables of longevity may everywhere be considered touchstones of government, the scale on which may

33 A. W. Small, "Review of *The Nature of Man*," *American Journal of Sociology*, vol. 9 (January 1904): 580, 582. See also, "Elie Metchnikoff," *Nation*, vol. 103 (July 20, 1916): 53–4; F. Carrel, "The Optimum of Metchnikoff," *Fortnightly*, vol. 89 (May 1908): 851–9.

34 Sketch, *Critic*, vol. 43 (November 1903): 391–2.

35 C. A. Herter, "On the Therapeutic Action of Fermented Milk," *Popular Science Monthly*, vol. 74 (1904): 46.

36 To compose the rest of this chapter, I revisited the materials I had collected to write *Old Age in the New Land: The American Experience Since 1790* (Baltimore: Johns Hopkins University Press, 1978). I supplemented these data with my subsequent research and the findings of others in the field. In particular, see David Hackett Fischer, *Growing Old in America*, exp. ed. (New York: Oxford University Press, 1977); essays by John Demos, Daniel Scott Smith, and Maris Vinovskis in *Aging and the Elderly*, ed. David D. Van Tassel, Stuart Spicker, and Kathleen M. Woodward (Atlantic Highlands, NJ: Humanities Press, 1983); Carole Haber, *Beyond Sixty-Five* (New York: Cambridge University Press, 1983); Cole, *Journey of Life*; and essays by Carole Haber and Brian Gratton, David Troyansky, and Peter Stearns in the *Handbook of Aging and the Humanities*, ed. Thomas R. Cole, David D. Van Tassel, and Robert Kastenbaum (New York: Springer Publishing, 1992).

be measured their excellencies and their defects, the perfection or degradation of the human species."[37] Treatises by William Godwin, Antoine-Nicholas de Condorcet, and Thomas R. Malthus published in the 1790s stimulated decades of speculation about the possibility and desirability of prolonging life in a "proper" political economy. William Barton constructed life expectancy tables for his *Observations on the Progress of Population and the Probabilities of the Duration of Human Life, in the United States of America* (1791). Almanacs regularly featured items about Americans living to advanced ages. Hezekiah Niles, editor of the country's most widely read antebellum magazine, claimed that such evidence confirmed the New Republic's superiority over the Old World in terms of longevity. Jeremy Belknap and Dr. Benjamin Rush credited the environment with sustaining mental and physical vitality; the very elderly, they noted, generally succumbed only to the "gradual decay of nature."[38] Enlightenment science served political ends in the early American republic.

Commentators expressed an interest in aging and longevity for its own sake. Some documented variations in human longevity. In *The New Encyclopedia* (1797), William H. Hall reiterated the centuries-old opinion that "longevity is in great measure hereditary."[39] Dr. John Bell, a member of the American Philosophical Society and the College of Physicians and Surgeons, was one of the first to verify Benjamin Franklin's observation that women's chances for long life exceeded men's. Dr. Charles Caldwell in *Thoughts on the Effects of Age on the Human Constitution* (1846) noted racial differences in longevity. In addition to noting exceptional cases of longevity, nineteenth-century commentators talked in terms of "averages." They often followed the lead of Adolphe Quetelet, who advanced the proposition that measuring human development was analogous to studying phenomena in physics. "Man is born, grows up, and dies, according to certain laws that have never been properly investigated." The task of *social physics*, Quetelet declared in 1842, was to determine "the average man, amongst different nations, both physical and moral."[40] Quetelet provided his Eur-

---

37 Quoted in James H. Cassedy, *Demography in Early America* (Cambridge, MA: Harvard University Press, 1969), p. 263. For more on this theme, see Gerald J. Gruman, *A History of Prolongation* (Philadelphia: American Philosophical Society, 1966).

38 Jeremy Belknap, *History of New Hampshire*, 3 vols. (Boston: Bradford and Read, 1813) vol. 3: 171–3.

39 See the articles on "longevity" in Hall's *The New Encyclopedia* (London: William H. Hall, 1797) and in the First American edition of the *Encyclopaedia Brittanica*: see also, Frederick Marryat, *A Diary in America* (1839; reprint ed., Bloomington: Indiana University Press, 1960), pp. 120–1; Daniel Harrison Jacques, *Hints Toward Physical Perfection* (New York: Fowler and Wells, 1859), pp. 209–14.

40 L. Adolphe J. Quetelet, *A Treatise on Man and the Development of His Faculties* (Gainesville, FL: Scholars Facsimilies and Reprints, 1969), p. 9. For more on Quetelet's influence on gerontology, see James E. Birren, "The Process of Aging," in *Our Aging Society*, eds. Alan Pifer and Lydia Bronte (New York: Norton, 1986), p. 265; Fred L. Bookstein and

opean contemporaries and future U.S. scientists a way to compare data about "l'homme moyen" derived from "natural" processes with those obtained in "social" settings. As we shall see, twentieth-century gerontologists would be greatly influenced by such ideas, even if they did not know Quetelet was their source.

One reason why many European ideas about the human life course failed initially to take root in the United States was that prevailing scientific thought and practices limited the ability of antebellum students of old age and longevity to make much headway. Medicine on this side of the Atlantic was rudimentary. Unlike Europe, where pathology was developing as a specialty, diseases here were classified, explained, and treated in terms of simple pathogenic conditions, an imbalance in humors, or a loss of vital forces. Sanitary reform in the United States got underway later than in Europe. Compared to European accomplishments, the fruits of basic research in North America were modest. Similarly, age-specific responses to social needs of any sort were slow to develop. The U.S. reformers hesitated to propose costly institutional measures to help orphans and needy children, who constituted a large segment of the "deserving" population. American pediatrics did not come into being until the 1880s. Once in place, these initiatives did not spur much medical or philanthropic concern about the problems of the elderly.[41] Furthermore, before orthodox practitioners achieved much success in improving people's health in the United States, they had to demonstrate to the public that their education and therapies guaranteed better results than remedies offered by their competition. Many Americans judged physicians' cures no more effective – and no less illusory – in curing illnesses and restoring health than home remedies and herbs. In the absence of any magic drug or arcane technique to ward off debilities in later years, adhering to "general principles" of healthy living – such as eating and drinking in moderation – appeared the surest method of remaining vital in old age.

As a result of biological theory and medical research, however, the stage was set to alter scientific ideas about old age during the last third of the nineteenth century. Biological studies became less descriptive and more experimental. The U.S. researchers began to follow the example of such European physiologists as Hermann von Helmboltz (1821–94), Claude Bernard (1813–78) and J. S. Haldane (1860–1936), who were studying the

W. Andrew Achenbaum, "Aging as Explanation," in *Voices and Visions*, ed. Thomas R. Cole et al. (New York: Springer Publishing Company, 1992).

41 Sydney A. Halpern, *American Pediatrics* (Berkeley and Los Angeles: University of California Press, 1988); N. Ray Hiner and Joseph M. Hawes, *Growing Up in America* (Urbana: University of Illinois Press, 1985); Rosemary Stevens, "The Changing Idea of a Medical Specialty," *Transactions & Studies of the College of Physicians of Philadelphia*, vol. 2 (September 1980): 159–77; Walter I. Trattner, *From Poor Law to Welfare State*, 3rd ed. (New York: Free Press, 1984).

changes, or lack of change, in the constitution of body fluids and the interactions in the function of many organs and systems. With the discovery of X rays (1895), biologists here and abroad not only gained a new research tool, but they found that the physical sciences, themselves transformed by this invention and other theories, offered an ever more fruitful lode of ideas to explore.[42] Medical research, in turn, was enriched by new ideas in the biological and physical sciences. Early nineteenth-century images of old age being a period of natural decay were called into question. More and more experts concluded that the debilities associated with late life were a cause, not just a result, of decline in old age. On the basis of new etiological paradigms and more precise instruments, bench scientists and clinicians started to show empirically the pathological dimensions of senescence.

The most influential work of the period was produced in Europe. In *Leçons cliniques sur les maladies des vieillards et les maladies chroniques* (1867), Jean-Martin Charcot systematically studied the relationship between old age and illness. His analysis was based on case histories of elderly women confined in a large public hospital in Paris. Charcot divided diseases into three categories: (1) ones that arose from general physiological changes, (2) those that existed at earlier stages of life but presented special characteristics and dangers in old age, and (3) diseases from which the aged seemed immune. Charcot stressed the importance of identifying localized structural lesions: "In old age, the organs seem, as it were, to become independent of one another: they suffer separately, and the various lesions to which they may become subject are scarcely echoed by the anatomy as a whole."[43] Charcot's work did not radically depart from existing ideas about diseases in old age. George Cheyne (1671–1743), Giovanni Battista Morgagni (1681–1771), Albrecht von Haller (1707–77), Christian Wilhelm Hufeland (1762–1836), and Sir Anthony Carlisle (1768–1840) all anticipated his emphasis on the localized pathological manifestations of late life. French and German physicians had published compendia before him. Nonetheless, Charcot's treatise, the first of its genre translated into English, appeared at a time in which U.S. physicians were acquiring the concepts, methods, and instruments necessary to do structural pathology.

"American Medicine," declared Harvard's Edward H. Clarke in 1876,

---

42 Garland E. Allen, *Life Science in the Twentieth Century* (New York: Cambridge University Press, 1979).

43 Jean-Martin Charcot, *Clinical Lectures on the Diseases of Old Age*, trans. Leigh Hunt (New York: William Wood, 1881), pp. 4, 26. See also, Joseph T. Freeman, "Medical Perspectives in Aging," *Gerontologist*, vol. 5 (March 1965), pt. 2, pp. 21–2; M. D. Grmek, *On Ageing and Old Age* (Den Haag: Uitgevereig Dr. W. Junk, 1958), pp. 71–2, 78. Here, again, my interpretation of Charcot differs somewhat from that of other historians of aging. See Cole, *Journey of Life*, pp. 200–1 and Carole Haber, "Geriatrics: A Specialty in Search of Specialists" in *Old Age in a Bureaucratic Society*, ed. David D. Van Tassel and Peter N. Stearns (Westport, CT: Greenwood, 1982), pp. 74–5.

"has been enfranchised from superstition, quasi-charlatanism, bald empiricism, and speculation, affiliated with the natural sciences, studied by the same methods and the same appliances as they are and, like them, has been placed upon the solid basis of fact and demonstration."[44] Medical schools were established at Harvard, Pennsylvania, Columbia, Johns Hopkins, and Michigan. Hospitals in major metropolises underwrote basic research, trained health specialists, and built expensive laboratories for their staff. The training and credibility and thus authority of a select (and self-selecting) cadre of researchers were affirmed by formal examinations and accreditation boards. Thanks to these developments, U.S. medical research was advancing, but it still lagged behind developments in Germany, France, and Britain. Hybrid specialties, such as biological chemistry and experimental physiology, were flourishing in Europe, but around the turn of the century they still had few advocates in the United States. Indeed, a fissure, if not yet a chasm, was widening in the United States between those who pursued research in laboratories and those who made their careers in clinics.[45] This gradation within the ranks of professionals – wherein successful investigators enjoyed much prestige, but clinicians on average earned more money – was to affect the rewards system of gerontology in its formative years. (The pendulum continues to swing back and forth. Nowadays, health-outcomes researchers battle specialists in molecular medicine for power.)

Caring for the elderly hardly promised much professional opportunity for an ambitious young physician. It was a remote outpost, not a challenging frontier. As late as 1900, most U.S. doctors and journalists continued to recommend traditional ways of dealing with the aches and pains of old age; few explored their causes. Whatever advances could be expected in treating old people were likely through therapeutic interventions, not as a result of medical research.[46] Nevertheless, new ways of conceptualizing, researching, and treating diseases in old age were emerging on this side of the Atlantic. During the same period that Metchnikoff began his studies of longevity, some of the country's leading biomedical researchers were exploring biological aspects of senescence. Often they cited European au-

44 Edward H. Clarke, M.D., et al., *A Century of American Medicine* (Philadelphia: Henry C. Lea, 1876), pp. 10–11. See also John Harley Warner, "Science in Medicine," *Osiris*, vol. 1 (1985): 37–58; Thomas L. Haskell, ed., *The Authority of Experts* (Bloomington: Indiana University Press, 1984).

45 Russell C. Maulitz, "Physician Versus Bacteriologist," in *The Therapeutic Revolution*, ed. Morris J. Vogel and Charles E. Rosenberg (Philadelphia: University of Pennsylvania Press, 1979), p. 104. See also George Rosen, "Changing Attitudes of the Medical Profession to Specialization," *Bulletin of the History of Medicine*, vol. 12 (1942): 343–54; Robert E. Kohler, *From Medical Chemistry to Biological Chemistry* (New York: Cambridge University Press, 1982).

46 *Scientific Colonialism* ed. Nathan Reingold and Marc Rothenberg (Washington, DC: Smithsonian Institution, 1987).

thorities to bolster their opinions. *Senility*, once simply a synonym for *old age*, now referred specifically to the "weaknesses and decrepitude characteristic of old age."[47] Harvard Medical School anatomist Charles Sedgwick Minot chose to "follow Charcot closely" in defining senility for the *Reference Handbook of Medical Science* (1885). Like Metchnikoff, Minot focused on the lives of the cell. "Old age is the period of slowest decline – a strange, paradoxical statement," he argued in *Age, Growth, and Disease* (1908). Pursuing a hypothesis that Metchnikoff would not have endorsed, Minot went on to suggest that biologists and psychologists alike should entertain studying its manifestations in light of a "theory of permanent mental fatigue, in connection with the theory of gradual decline."[48] Others investigated senile gangrene, senile bronchitis, senile pneumonia, and senile chorea.[49]

Biologists in the United States very often developed hypotheses about the pathological and physiological aspects of senescence that diverged from their European peers because the North Americans organized themselves and their research along different lines. Students were encouraged early in their careers to specialize in either botany or zoology. Greater specialization caused interests appropriately considered biological to range from paleontology to pharmacology. "It seems to me that the biologists are far more diversified in their interests than are the chemists and that it would be correspondingly more difficult to organize them satisfactorily into a single society."[50] Indeed, a federation of biological societies was not formed until 1923, decades after the founding of the American Chemical Society.

Given the fragmentation of interests among biologists, there really were not schools of thought among these researchers investigating issues of senescence. Most efforts were fairly idiosyncratic. For instance, Charles Manning Child, a zoologist at the University of Chicago, spent more than fifteen years looking for connections between individuation and reproduction with age. "Some of these ventures with other fields have been attended by the feeling that discretion would perhaps have been the better part of valor, for any venture very far outside one's own little garden plot of scientific thought is likely to be attended by a very decided feeling of strangeness," Child acknowledged in *Senescence and Rejuvenescence* (1915). "Neverthe-

47 For more on this, see Achenbaum, *Old Age in the New Land*, pp. 43–4.
48 Charles Sedgwick Minot, "Senility" in *Reference Handbook of Medical Science*, ed. Albert H. Buck, 7 vols. (New York: William Wood, 1885), 6:388. See also idem, *The Problem of Age, Growth and Death* (New York: Putman, 1908, pp. 5, 245.
49 Richard Quain, *A Dictionary of Medicine* (New York: D. Appelton & Co., 1883), p. 1,416; George M. Gould, *Illustrated Dictionary of Medicine, Biology and Applied Science*, 5th ed. (Philadelphia: P. Blakiston & Co. 1903), p. 1,315; Christian A. Herter, *Biological Aspects of Human Problems* (New York: Macmillan, 1911), pp. 112–19.
50 Bradley M. Davis, quoted in *The American Development of Biology*, ed. Ronald Rainger, Keith R. Benson, and Jane Maienschein (New Brunswick, NJ: Rutgers University Press, 1991), p. 110.

less such ventures are necessary if different lines of investigation and thought are to be connected and synthesized into a harmonious whole."[51] Child's fundamental conclusion, that progression and regression occur during all phases of an organism's development, has been confirmed by others. But few tried to replicate his study of genetic reproduction in plants and animals.

Biologist Edmund B. Wilson, like Child, attempted to build bridges between subfields in his research on aging. As an undergraduate at Yale, he learned about both Darwin's theory of evolution and Weismann's theory of germ plasm continuity and the noninheritance of acquired characters. In seeking to reconcile the perspectives of evolutionists and cytologists, Wilson analyzed processes of cell mitosis and conjugation. In his classic study, *The Cell in Development and Inheritance* (1896), Wilson hypothesized that "the processes of growth and division sooner or later came to an end, undergoing a process of natural 'senescence.' "[52] Wilson's theories remain in circulation. During the first two-thirds of the century, according to zoologist Hermann T. Muller, undergraduates and graduate students would be taught this fundamental principle of the biology of aging, without being told "the main source from which it was issued."[53]

Metchnikoff's phagocytic theory of aging thus was only one of many competing perspectives on senescence. No single theory every attracted a critical mass of supporters during the first decades of the twentieth century; few biologists were interested in investigating "problems" related to gerontology. Those who did attract attention did not necessarily advance the field. Some studies of aging proved so controversial as to cast doubts among ordinary citizens about the efficacy of any work on senescence. Dr. Charles E. Brown-Sequard reasoned, for example, that injecting semen into the blood stream of old men might restore lost vigor. (He proposed but did not test the possibility that similar endocrinal interventions would help women.) Within months of his report, Brown-Sequard's formula appeared on the market as "Pohl's Spermine Preparations." Other products substituted monkey testicular extracts for semen. Interest waned, however, after high expectations were not met. "The sooner the general public, and especially septuagenarian readers of the latest sensation understand that . . . there is no elixir of life, the better," pontificated the *Boston Medical and Surgical Journal*.[54]

51 Charles Manning Child, *Senescence and Rejuvenescence* (Chicago: University of Chicago Press, 1915), pp. vi, 459.

52 Edmund B. Wilson, *The Cell in Development and Inheritance* (1896; New York: Jolenson Reprint Corporation, 1966), p. 130.

53 Hermann J. Muller, "Introduction" to Wilson, *The Cell*, p. x. Vincent J. Cristofalo, who recommended that I read this classic, confirmed Muller's sense of its importance.

54 "Is There an Elixir of Life," *Boston Medical and Surgical Journal*, vol. 121 (August 15, 1889): 167–8. See also, Newell Dunbar, ed., *Dr. Brown-Sequard's Own Account of the*

Neither Brown-Sequard's failure nor Metchnikoff's deterred other bench scientists from seeking practical remedies based on theories about aging. On both sides of the Atlantic, several well-known investigators attempted during the first decades of the twentieth century to eradicate toxic disturbances that they claimed were located in various part of the body. The efforts were part of a fin de siècle positivist impulse, although scientists and quacks had proposed plant remedies and cellular therapies as rejuvenation schemes centuries earlier.[55] Sir Victor Hursley concentrated on the degeneration of the thyroid glands. Arnold Lorand focused on ductless glands. Serge Veronoff and Eugene Steinach independently attempted to refine Brown-Sequard's experiments by grafting the glands of young animals to older ones. Pierre Delbet prescribed magnesium chloride to patients. William Bailey proposed ionizing the elderly's endocrine system with radioactive elements.[56] None of these remedies worked. The risk takers faced ridicule by pursuing unorthodox theories about senescence. The string of failures made physicians and other professionals wonder if any cure to the problems of late life could be discovered.

Middle-class Americans were not as discouraged as the experts. The lure of "scientific" remedies to old age greatly appealed to the public. Advertisements for hair dyes and pills to restore vitality, sexual and otherwise, filled journals and newspapers. Hygienists, reminding readers that they were as old as their arteries or glands, promoted "physical culture rejuvenation" programs. San Francisco businessman Sanford Bennett swore that special exercises and diet illuminated *Old Age, Its Cause and Prevention: The Story of an Old Body and Face Made Young*. The book featured photographs of Bennett's impressive physique. *The Secret of a Much Longer Life* (1906), according to Captain G. E. D. Diamond, who claimed to be

"Elixir of Life" (Boston: J. G. Cupples Co., 1889), pp. 22–8; William Hammond, "The Elixir of Life," *North American Review*, vol. 394 (September 1889): 257– 64; John M. Hoberman and Charles E. Yesalis, "The History of Synthetic Testosterone," *Scientific American* (February 1995): 77–81.

55 Gerald J. Gruman, "Cultural Origins of Present-Day 'Age-ism,' " in *Aging and the Elderly*, ed. Stuart F. Spicker, Kathleen M. Woodward, and David D. Van Tassel (Atlantic Highlands, NJ: Humanistic Press, 1978), pp. 370–5. See also Eric J. Trimmer, *Rejuvenation* (New York: A.S. Barnes, 1967), chs. 2, 7.

56 Charles G. Stockton, "The Delay of Old Age and the Alleviation of Senility," *Journal of the American Medical Association*, vol. 45 (July 15, 1905): 169; Arnold Lorand, *Old Age Deferred* (1910; reprint ed., Philadelphia: Davis, 1912); Marshall Langton Price, "Ancient and Modern Theories of Old Age," *Maryland Medical Journal*, vol. 49 (February 1906): 45–61; Genevieve Grandcourt, "Eternal Youth as Scientific Theory," *Scientific American*, vol. 121 (November 15, 1919): 482; Serge Voronoff, *Life* (New York: Dutton Co., 1920); Paul Kammerer, *Rejuvenation and Prolongation of Human Efficiency* (New York: Boni & Liveright, 1923); Henry Rubin, "Youth by Radiation," *Forum*, vol. 72 (November 1924): 653–5; Henry S. Simms and Abraham Stolman, "Changes in Human Tissue Electrolytes in Senescence," *Science*, vol. 86 (September 17, 1937): 270; "The Salt of Old Age," *Literary Digest*, vol. 106 (September 20, 1930): 26.

110, was exercise and rubbing olive oil into body parts in pain or "ailing from rheumatic tinges."[57]

Although few present-day experts in aging consider rubbing olive oil on joints the next best thing to finding the Fountain of Youth, nearly everybody in the health-promotion business agrees that regular, moderate exercise is essential to promoting a healthful life style. So is a balanced diet, temperance in drinking, and abstinence from tobacco. Guides to healthful longevity have circulated for milennia, starting with Galen, the second-century Roman physician who emphasized the importance of individual lifestyle in preventing disease. The genre flourished thereafter.

Around the turn of this century, big business joined physicians and popular writers in urging individuals to take stock of their health. In 1908, Theodore Roosevelt appointed a "Committee of 100" to assess the conservation of human resources. Irving Fisher, a political economist at Yale, headed the blue-ribbon panel. Significantly, Fisher deemed the conservation of human life to be part of his mandate: He claimed that disability and sickness cost the nation $1.5 billion per year. A year later, Harold Ley approached Fisher with his idea for a health examination service. If insurance companies knew potential subscribers' medical history and physical status, they could better assess the risks of coverage. Consumers, in turn, would have a "scientific" basis for understanding causes of illness and death. Using his network from the Committee of 100, Fisher and Ley launched the Life Extension Institute in 1914. Over the next two decades, the Institute conducted more than 1.5 million examinations. Insurance companies reported that policyholders who took advantage of these exams were in better health. No one asserted, however, that the ravages of age had been eliminated.[58]

Old age "is a disease, that is to say, it is essentially a pathological condition," concluded a columnist. "But for it there exists no therapy, no cure."[59] Little wonder, then, that few expressed great optimism about the prospects of finding a scientific remedy for the problems of senescence. Those who were sanguine about something positive emerging out of ger-

57 Achenbaum, *Old Age*, p. 62; Cole, *Journey of Life*, pp. 184–5. These health-promotion books resemble other works of this genre. See, for instance, Harold Begbie, *Twice-Born Men: A Clinic in Regeneration* (New York: Fleming H. Revell, 1909), which offers inspiring stories of the way men's lives were changed by working in the Salvation Army.

58 Patricia Daniels, *Life Extension Institute at 75* (New York: Life Extension Institute, 1988). Professor Fisher's multidisciplinary predilections merit note. He wrote his dissertation on "Mathematical Investigations in the Theory of Value and Price" under J. Willard Gibbs, then the nation's foremost physicist. There, he expressed keen interest in "mechanical analysis" between physics and economics, which then was applied to laws of longevity. See Fisher's early work in *Reports of Economic Classics* (New York: Augustus M. Kelley, 1961), pp. 85ff.

59 Carl Snyder, "The Quest for Prolonged Youth," *Living Age*, vol. 251 (November 10, 1906): 323.

ontology in the future were in a minority, at the margins of the scientific community.

Two alternatives: Toward medical and psychosocial models for gerontology

Elie Metchnikoff, this chapter suggests, was probably the best-known proponent around the turn of the century of what he characterized as the "optimistic philosophy of senescence." Metchnikoff hoped that science could someday alleviate, if not eradicate, the ravages of age. A few other visionaries expressed a similar confidence. I. L. Nascher, a physician, and G. Stanley Hall, a psychologist, independently produced prophetic works designed to persuade their contemporaries that old age could be salvaged. Nascher wrote *Geriatrics: The Diseases of Old Age and Their Treatment, Including Physiological Old Age, Home and Institutional Care, and Medico-Legal Relations* (1914). The subtitle was unwieldy, but it clearly underscores Nascher's cross-disciplinary breadth. G. Stanley Hall, who achieved international fame for his two-volume study of *Adolescence* (1904), was seventy-eight when he published *Senescence: The Last Half of Life* (1922). Hall used historical, medical, literary, biological, physiological, and behavioral evidence to prove that older people had resources hitherto unappreciated. Basically, these texts offered alternatives to the Russian's pathological model of aging. Nascher and Hall shared Metchnikoff's enthusiasm for the prospects of future research on aging. But *Geriatrics* and *Senescence* differed from one another in focus; they were not grounded in the same disciplinary traditions. The works set the stage for a set of important debates over gerontology's boundaries during its formative years. Was research on aging primarily the province of biomedical scientists or were its behavioral and social aspects equally important? Were frailty and disease concomitants of the aging process, or was senescence a natural phenomenon in a normal course of human life?

Ignatz Leo Nascher, born in Vienna in 1863, was brought to the United States as an infant. He entered City College and then transferred to Columbia where he earned a pharmacy degree (1882) and his M.D. (1885). He published his first article on "A Young Living Fetus" four years later in the *Medical Record of New York*. The early years of Nascher's career were mainly spent practicing medicine.[60] Then, in 1909, Nascher published in *The New York Medical Journal* an article he entitled "Geriatrics." Not only did he coin the name for a new medical subspecialty, but in the process he made two assertions about old age that he would reiterate over and again in his writings. First, Nascher claimed that "senility is a distinct period of

60 Joseph T. Freeman, "Nascher: Excerpts from His Life, Letters, and Works," *The Gerontologist*, vol. 1 (March 1961): 17–26.

life . . . a physiological entity as much so as the period of childhood." And if pediatrics deserved to receive "special attention," then, second, it followed that geriatrics should be considered as a "special branch of medicine."[61]

Nascher acknowledged his debts to those who had investigated pathological and physiological aspects of late life. *Geriatrics*, he claimed, was conceived as an update to the 1881 English translation of Charcot's *Lessons on the Diseases of Old Age*. He also cited the work of eighteenth- and nineteenth-century French, German, British, and (the few) North American medical investigators who reported their case studies of elderly patients. Nascher's claim that "all anatomical and physiological standards are based upon averages" manifestly harked back to Quetelet. Like Metchnikoff, he was fascinated with "problems that are intimately bound up in the grand mystery of life and death."[62] Nascher accepted some of the underlying assumptions of the Nobel Laureate's phagocytic theory, but he did not accept Metchnikoff's contention that microbes were responsible for death in old age. "A radical theory," he noted, "should have a more substantial basis than plausible argument."[63] Nascher's views on senescence appear closer to embryologist Charles Sedgwick Minot and cytologist Charles Manning Child to the extent that he hypothesized that "in the evolution of tissue cells the late cells differ from the earlier ones."[64] Nascher reckoned that his new medical specialty had a better chance of garnering support if it was grounded in theories that were current but not too unorthodox.

Nascher eschewed monocausal theories of senescence. "There is undoubtedly a determining factor which is the subject of the various theories that have been advanced, but there are in addition contributing factors, causative and resultant, which hasten the senile processes."[65] Nor did he look upon old age as a malady, as did many of his contemporaries. Nascher claimed that disease in late life was a "pathological process in a normally degenerating body." Most of *Geriatrics* is devoted to identifying symptoms

---

61 I. L. Nascher, "Geriatrics," *New York Medical Journal*, vol. 90 (1909): 358. Virtually the same themes are elaborated in his "Practical Geriatrics," *Medical Council*, vol. 22 (1917): 33–6.

62 I. L. Nascher, *Geriatrics*, (Philadelphia: P. Blakiston's Son & Co., 1916 [1914]), p. v (2d ed., preface) and pp. vii–x (1st ed., preface). See also Henning Kirk, "Geriatric Medicine and the Categorisation of Old Age," *Ageing and Society*, vol. 12 (1992): 499–514.

63 I. L. Nascher, "Tissue Cell Evolution," *New York Medical Journal*, vol. 92 (1910): 918.

64 I. L. Nascher, "Why Old Age Ends in Death," *Medical Review of Reviews*, vol. 25 (1919): 291. Child and Manning from different perspectives held that old age resulted from cumulative changes in the properties of cells and tissues as an organism matured. See Minot, *Problem of Age*, p. 249; and Charles Manning Child, *Senescence and Rejuvenescence*, pp. 58, 271, 301, 309, 459, 465. Although Nascher does not say so, his views of the lives of cells also differed from his contemporary, Alexis Carrel. See introduction to Part II.

65 Nascher, *Geriatrics*, pp. 47–8.

of thirty-seven primary senile diseases, twenty-one secondary senile diseases, thirty-three "preferential" diseases (not including eighteen different forms of carcinoma), twenty-seven modified diseases, and fifty-six diseases uninfluenced by advancing years. Nascher emphasized the contrast between "senility" and "senile pathology." Old age, in his opinion, was not a pathological state of maturity, but a distinct, normal physiological stage of life. Caring for the aged required a distinctive approach: "My object . . . is to call attention to the primary indications in diseases in senility, which should be not to cure the disease but to prevent death. In maturity incidental complications and the questions of diet are secondary to the treatment of the pathological condition. In senility they are of primary importance."[66] Traditional empiricism and a good bedside manner, Nascher believed, were as valuable in distinguishing pathological and physiological processes of aging as the scalpel and microscope.

Nascher's description of a geriatrician may seem old-fashioned, but his proscription for the specialty was truly forward-looking. "As interest in the dependent child led to the scientific study of child welfare," he reasoned, "so might an interest in the dependent aged lead to the scientific study of senility, of the needs and wants, the peculiarities and infirmities, the happiness and welfare of the aged."[67] Nascher realized that a new medical specialty like geriatrics needed to be organized along lines that had proven successful in launching other domains. Mindful of age-specific parallels, he invited A. Jacobi, M.D., the father of American pediatrics, to write the Introduction to *Geriatrics*. (Drawing an analogy between pediatrics and geriatrics was not altogether persuasive intellectually. As Nascher fully acknowledged, the welfare of children aroused sympathy. "The idea of economic worthlessness," he reasoned, "instills a spirit of irritability if not positive enmity against the helplessness of the aged."[68] But the pediatric precedent, he figured, was the best available to him.) In 1915, Nascher founded the New York Geriatrics Society. Two years later, he inaugurated a feature in the *Medical Review of Reviews*. In the department's heading Nascher was called "the Father of Geriatrics."[69] Figuring that geriatrics had a better chance of taking off if it were perceived primarily as a medical specialty, Nascher targeted his features primarily to fellow physicians. Yet he did not limit his appeals to the medical community. To understand patients' conditions in late life, Nascher insisted that relevant social statis-

---

66 I. L. Nascher, "The Treatment of Disease in Senility," *Medical Record of New York*, vol. 76 (1909): 990.

67 I. L. Nascher, "The Neglect of the Aged," *Medical Record, New York*, vol. 86 (1914): 457.

68 Quotation in Haber, "Geriatrics: A Specialty in Search of Specialists," in Van Tassel and Stearns, p. 77.

69 I. L. Nascher, "Salutatory," *Medical Review of Reviews*, vol. 23 (1917): 29.

tics had to be gathered. Nascher thus investigated social aspects of aging and, in the process, probed topics that more rightly belonged to the field of gerontology than geriatrics.

Nascher's interest in medical sociology actually predated his commitment to geriatrics. His second publication (1908) was an article on prostitution. A year later he published *The Wretches of Povertyville: A Sociological Study of the Bowery* in which he made passing reference to characters such as "Duddy Ward" and "Old Shakespeare." The analysis contrasted the living conditions and lifestyles of the poor with "a rational ideal in the sociological aspect of our city." Indeed, Nascher's analysis showed his affinity to other reformers who were bolstering their critiques of social ills with statistics and sociological generalizations. He espoused the Progressive hope that "scientific philanthropy and rational laws will take the place of the useless and pseudo-charities and inconsistent discretionary statutes now dealing with the wretches."[70] Because of his interest in reform issues, Nascher was unwilling to limit his focus to clinical studies of the elderly. He embarked on a social survey of old-age poverty. "There is probably no class of dependents where welfare has been more completely neglected, who have received less scientific study and care, than the aged," Nascher told a National Conference of Social Work in 1917. "The child dependent has the world for its guardian; the aged dependent is disowned by his own."[71] Nascher's call to study and remedy the causes of old-age dependency was one of the first made in America, although landmark investigations of old-age poverty and social insurance legislation in Britain had preceded U.S. initiatives by a quarter of a century. Indeed, before the 1920s, Lee Welling Squier's *Old Age Dependency in the United States* (1912) and a 1915 Massachusetts *Report on Old Age Pensions, Annuities, and Insurance* were the only studies that matched in scope and detail Charles Booth's 1894 classic, *The Aged Poor in England and Wales*. "In the United States," declared social reformer William Dwight Bliss Porter, "the old-age problem is not yet so serious."[72]

Initially, Nascher's advocacy of geriatrics had limited impact despite his efforts to mobilize interest in a variety of circles. Some colleagues accepted the distinction he made between pathological and physiological causes of

70 I. L. Nascher, *The Wretches of Povertyville* (Chicago: Jos. J. Lanzit, 1909), pp. 298–9. See ch. 4 for some of his characterizations of the old.

71 I. L. Nascher, "The Institutional Care of the Aged," *Proceedings of the National Conference of Social Work* (Chicago: The Conference, 1917), pp. 350–6.

72 William Dwight Porter Bliss, "Old Age Pensions," *The Encyclopedia of Social Reform* (New York: Funk & Wagnalls, 1897), pp. 952–4. See also William Graebner, *A History of Retirement* (New Haven, CT: Yale University Press, 1980); and Brian Gratton, *Urban Elders* (Philadelphia: Temple University Press, 1985). For more on British trends, see Martin Bulmer, *Social Science and Social Policy* (London: Allen & Unwin, 1986), pp. 224–6.

death in late life.[73] A few clinicians shared some of his concern for integrating basic science, social research, and advocacy, but none so fully combined these interests in their own careers. Nascher's contributions, honored by other pioneering geriatricians such as Malford W. Thewlis, are duly recorded in U.S. histories of old age and of geriatrics. Still, an important part of the legacy is that Nascher's pioneering ideas and organizations met with considerable resistance. He had had difficulty finding a firm willing to publish *Geriatrics*. Things did not get easier over time. Nascher admitted that he was the only full-time geriatrician as late as 1926.[74] Like many other prophets, Nascher's message fell mainly on deaf ears.

The prevailing culture of medicoscientific professionalism thwarted Nascher's efforts to disseminate his ideas and to create a new field in paradoxical ways. Any attempt to create a medical specialty at the beginning of the century was bound to be more difficult than it had been a few decades earlier. Most specialists and practitioners hoped their boundaries were "impenetrable," sociologist James R. Angell noted in 1920. "The actual fact, of course, is that the dividing lines of science are like the hedgerows, in large measure arbitrary and practical, and consequently subject to persistent modification."[75] The most efficacious way to modify the status quo, Nascher thought, was to make the case for innovation and boundary crossing as conservatively as possible. Nascher may have undermined his own campaign by suggesting that physicians interested in the diseases of old age pay attention to the social sciences. To make the focus of geriatrics appealing to physicians, Nascher had to emphasize the biomedical aspects of aging, often at the expense of its social components. Conversely, too much stress on the basic sciences would please the physicians and bench scientists that Nascher needed to attract, but it would not rally the social science community. Ironically, what seemed most appealing about Nascher's orientation – its holistic, multidisciplinary approach – seemed to deter those specialists who had been taught to hew to rigorous (and familiar) standards. Breadth, too often, resulted in diffuseness. "Lack of specificity in aim affects seriously the problem of training," declared Abraham Flexner, whose 1910 report, *Medical Education in the United States and Canada*, to the Carnegie Corporation transformed the professional training of

---

73 Thus, according to one eulogist, Metchnikoff did not die of old age: "He probably would not have died for a good many years if it had not been for heart trouble hereditary in his family." Arno Dosch-Fleurot, "Why Metchnikoff Died," *World's Work*, vol. 32 (1916): 614.

74 I. L. Nascher, "A History of Geriatrics," *Medical Review of Reviews*, vol. 32 (1926): 283; Barclay Moon Newman, "Geriatrics," *Scientific American*, vol. 163 (1940): 190. This pattern would recur later in the century, as we shall see: Leonard Hayflick initially had difficulty getting his radical ideas disseminated in well-known journals.

75 James R. Angell, "Organization of Research," *Scientific Monthly*, vol. 11 (1920): 33.

physicians. "A profession needs in these days a form of expression and record that is scientific rather than journalist in character."[76] As one person working alone, Nascher simply could not provide the basic theories, data, or peer review necessary to launch a medical specialty.

While Nascher was trying to illuminate the distinctive biomedical features of senescence and to highlight social aspects of the last stage of life, an eminent U.S. psychologist gathered data to show his fellow septuagenarians that their intellectual and moral gifts were desperately in need. "Intelligent and well-conserved senectitude has very important social and anthropological functions in the world, not hitherto utilized or even recognized," G. Stanley Hall speculated in *Senescence*, "the chief of which is most comprehensively designated as in our very complex age of distracting specialization."[77] On first reading, it seems that Hall grossly exaggerated the originality of his proposal. Older people's capacity for offering practical advice and wisdom based on experiences accrued over the years, after all, was considered one of the constructive functions of age prior to the Civil War. Hall, unlike earlier writers, did not idealize the virtues of age over the assets of youth: "While old age is not at all venerable *per se* we have a mandate to make it ever more so by new orientation, especially in a land and age that puts a premium upon its splendid youth."[78]

The significance of Hall's *Senescence* is that it set a standard to psychosocial studies for aging that parallels what Nascher endeavored to do for *Geriatrics*. Both books were explicitly multidisciplinary in approach. Both, starting from the assumption that "successive stages of life in man differ from each other," tried to persuade skeptical readers and potential critics that there were exciting things to learn about the last stage of life. Some important behavioral research, in part prompted by these works, was underway by the end of the 1920s. Much of it, however, reaffirmed (now with scientific evidence) earlier fears about growing older. Edward L. Thorndike and his associates in *Adult Learning* (1928) confirmed the curvilinearity in learning patterns by age advanced half a century earlier by Sir Francis Galton and George M. Beard.[79] In a similar vein, Harry L.

---

76 Abraham Flexner, "Is Social Work a Profession," *School and Society*, vol. 1 (1915): 901, 908, 911.

77 G. Stanley Hall, "Old Age," *Atlantic*, vol. 127 (January 1921): 29–30; Hall, *Senescence* (New York: D. Appleton, 1922), pp. v, ix, 133, 405–7. For more on this theme, see William Lyon Phelps, *Happiness* (New York: Dutton, 1927), p. 40; Gerald W. Johnson, "What an Old Girl Should Know," *Harper's Magazine*, vol. 168 (April 1934): 608.

78 Hall, *Senescence*, p. 407. For more on antebellum views, see Achenbaum, *Old Age*, ch. 1–2; for more on Hall, see Cole, *Journey of Life*, ch. 10.

79 Edward L. Thorndike et al., *Adult Learning* (New York: Macmillan, 1928). See also Francis Galton, *Hereditary Genius* (London: Henry King, 1869); idem., *Inquiries into the Human Faculty* (London: Macmillan, 1883); George M. Beard, *Legal Responsibilities in Old Age* (New York: Russell's, 1874); idem., *American Nervousness* (New York: Putnam, 1881).

Hollingworth presented data in *Mental Growth and Decline* (1927) that seemed to confirm the prevailing notion that a "forward-looking interest" is "less characteristic of age than of youth." Irving Lorge attempted to qualify some of these findings by suggesting that older people did not necessarily decline mentally. Lorge admitted that the aged did respond to questions more slowly.[80]

Note the irony: Calls for quantitatively and qualitatively more social scientific approaches to gerontology did not necessarily corroborate the case for optimistic images of old age desired by Metchnikoff, Nascher, and Hall. As historians of aging Thomas Cole, Gerald Gruman, and Carole Haber have shown, all three men defined late life in dualistic terms; they distinguished between normal and pathological old age. This dualistic conception was grounded as much in Victorian morality as it was in empirical reality. The trio believed that scientific advances in senescence would pave the way for more positive assessments of growing older; they expected science someday to make it possible for people to affix constructive meanings and purposes to later years. For the moment, however, most scientific and popular writing focused on the vicissitudes associated with finitude of human life. Debilities and decrements were considered a product of basic processes and mechanisms of senescence itself.[81]

What optimists and pessimists, basic and applied investigators, and biomedical and social scientists alike shared was their common use of the language of mathematics. "My sole purpose," declared D'Arcy Wentworth Thompson in his classic study, *On Growth and Form* (1917), "is to correlate with mathematical statement and physical law certain of the simple outward phenomena of organic growth and structure or form, while all the while regarding, *ex hypothesis*, for the purposes of this correlation, the fabric of the organism as a material and mechanical configuration."[82] At the next stage of gerontology's development, a new generation of scholars would take Thompson's statement of purpose to heart. For them, method would take precedence over teleology. But researchers on aging after 1920 still were bedeviled by a challenge that investigators earlier in the century had not resolved. They hoped to create a field of inquiry that rested ultimately on no single, much less comprehensive, view of human aging. Nor did they want gerontology to violate the canons and methodologies of the several dissimilar disciplines that had a stake in the enterprise. As a consequence, there was no obvious strategy for success.

80 Harry L. Hollingworth, *Mental Growth and Decline* (New York: D. Appleton, 1927); Irving Lorge, "Never Too Old to Learn," *Vital Speeches*, vol. 3 (1937): 364.
81 Achenbaum, *Old Age*, chs. 3, 6.
82 D'Arcy Wentworth Thompson, *On Growth and Form* (Cambridge: Cambridge University Press, 1917), p. 10.

Several generalizations emerge from this all too cursory survey of the frontiers of aging, intended mainly to establish a contrast between "premodern" and "modern" gerontology. Each of the explorations cited in this chapter was basically an *individual* venture. Elie Metchnikoff counted on staff support from assistants and colleagues at the Pasteur Institute, but he conducted his own course in his lab. I. L. Nascher was a solitary figure. So was G. Stanley Hall. Over time, research findings were disseminated more widely, but gerontology was not yet a collective enterprise. Hence, first there was no network in place. Second, the *social* aspects of human aging attracted less scientific interest than its physiological, pathological, or biological aspects. In part, this attests to the relative backwardness of "scientific" social research in the United States until the first decades of the twentieth century.[83] In part, this reflects a centuries-old interest among all groups to use science to restore vitality in later years or to prolong life. Third, the research on aging that was done before the 1930s probably had little impact on postwar U.S. gerontologic science.

So although the words *gerontology* and *geriatrics* were both coined in the first decade of the twentieth century, neither field attracted much interest or excitement among scientific investigators. Based on developments in science and society at large, a small but growing number of experts felt that the maladies of late life would be "cured." Nevertheless, there was yet no panacea, and many researchers doubted that one would ever be found. The quest for the scientific equivalent of the Fountain of Youth seemed as tantalizing and illusory as it had in Ponce de Leon's day.

Research on aging entailed risks, more than most scientists at the beginning of the century were prepared to take. Inherent in both gerontology and geriatrics was a sense that investigators must be willing and able to cross intellectual frontiers in order to appreciate the complex interconnectedness of a multifaceted "problem" like human senescence. Such a presumption was hard to reconcile with the premium placed on specialization that animated most scientific endeavors in the early 1900s. As the fate of the hero of Sinclair Lewis's *Arrowsmith* made clear, researchers who chose to pursue the objects of their own intellectual curiosity paid a price for resisting peer pressures. Real-life problems embraced by gerontology and thanatology were important to researchers only to the extent to which they had been framed as "scientific problems" deemed worthy to investigate. Within the U.S. scientific community, there were few alliances between investigators in the clinic and practitioners at the bedside; basic and applied researchers in the social sciences rarely interacted.

Thus research on aging at the start of the century was increasingly be-

---

83 See Dorothy Ross, *The Origins of American Social Science* (New York: Cambridge University Press, 1991); and Roger L. Geiger, *To Advance Knowledge* (New York: Oxford University Press, 1986).

coming multifaceted in scope, but it remained fragmented. No one had formulated *the* theory of senescence that appealed to most researchers on aging. Most scientists working in different disciplines on the same fundamental issues tended to talk past one another. This nascent pluralist tradition put investigators at cross-purposes as much as it promoted multidisciplinarity. Tensions between basic and applied science, and between biomedical and sociobehavioral research, were to influence the scientific orientation of the gerontologic enterprise as the field began to assume a collective identity in the 1930s.

2

Setting boundaries for disciplined discoveries

ON OCTOBER 1, 1928, Aldred Scott Warthin, presented an influential lecture on "the pathology of the aging process" to the New York Academy of Medicine. The University of Michigan professor of pathology claimed that there were three stages (evolution, maturity, and involution) to the human "tragicomedy."[1] Next he detailed pathological conditions associated with growing older, especially those presenting themselves in the central nervous and cardiovascular systems. Warthin then assessed the wide array of theories about senescence competing for support in the 1920s. Some accentuated monocausal changes in pH or the accumulation of toxic wastes. Other models focused on the loss of function or decline in growth at the cellular level. According to Warthin, aging was primarily a physiological, not a pathological, process. Specific patterns of change varied from system to system, species to species. "Senescence is due primarily to the gradually weakening energy-charge set in action by the moment of fertilization."[2] Based on current evidence, Warthin doubted that bodily "decline" could be deferred much past age seventy-five. Contrary to the optimistic hopes of an earlier generation of scientists, chances for rejuvenescence thus far were impossible. The biological reality of enfeeblement presaged difficulties for society because the percentage of older people in the population was increasing.

Warthin's keynote lecture for the Academy's program on "the problem

---

1 Warthin was the first to deliver a Wesley M. Carpenter Lecture. His text "The Pathology of the Aging Process," was printed in the *Bulletin of the New York Academy of Medicine*, vol. 4, 2d ser. (October 1928): 1,006–46 and reprinted in the *New York State Journal of Medicine*, vol. 28 (November 15, 1928): 1,349–61. Warthin considered the lecture to be the "nucleus" of his monograph, *Old Age – The Major Involution: The Physiology and Pathology of the Aging Process* (New York: Paul B. Hoeber, 1929), pp. vii–ix.
2 Warthin, "Pathology of the Aging Process," p. 1,045.

of aging and of old age" was billed as "an experiment in graduate medical service," a venture planned "without previous experience."[3] George E. Vincent, president of the Rockefeller Foundation (RF), told an audience consisting largely of physicians that "this conference of prospective experts is long overdue. It is high time that we should learn more about old age. . . . Your profession can do much by telling the truth about . . . modern substitutes for Ponce de Leon's spring."[4] Warthin was only one in an impressive group of invited speakers, which included Sir Farquhar Buzzard, Regius Professor of Medicine at Oxford; Louis Dublin, a statistician at Metropolitan Life Insurance Company; and two luminaries from the Rockefeller Institute for Medical Research, Alfred E. Cohn and Nobel laureate Alexis Carrel. Once the symposium papers were published, however, the New York Academy of Medicine felt that it had done its part to stimulate research on aging. To the best of my knowledge, no scientific careers in gerontology or geriatrics resulted from these proceedings. No professional networks were forged. Investigators apparently returned to their labs and clinics, attending to business as usual. Doing research on aging was not yet a collective, structured enterprise in the United States.

In contrast, the publication of Edmund Vincent Cowdry's *Problems of Ageing* under the aegis of the Josiah Macy, Jr. Foundation a decade later *did* signal the emergence of gerontology as a field of scientific inquiry in this country. As we have seen, some research into the basic mechanisms of aging and into diseases of old age predated the 1930s. Not until the second third of this century, however, did U.S. scientists begin to collaborate in developing theories and discovering facts about senescence. Some contributors to Cowdry's volume went on to set boundaries for future multidisciplinary investigations into aging: They helped to establish professional organizations and research institutes that remain in operation to this day. Subsequent researchers paid attention to the same sorts of questions the Cowdry group had identified, adopted the methodologies they had utilized, and pursued the research priorities they had enunciated. The framework and standards established by this first cohort of gerontologists took advantage of the resources (fiscal and technical) at their disposal. Their work reflected the environment (intellectual and institutional) in which the participants had matured. As we shall see, subsequent researchers on aging sometimes have been too loyal – and, at other times, not faithful enough – to the founders' breadth of vision and penchant for risk taking. It is critical, then, to examine the social and ideological milieu of the 1930s, in which researchers curious about processes of aging embarked on cross-

3 Samuel W. Lambert, "Annual Graduate Fortnight," *Bulletin of the New York Academy of Medicine*, vol. 4 (November 1928): 1,063.

4 George E. Vincent, "The Doctor – Trainer or Healer," *Bulletin of the New York Academy of Medicine*, vol 4 (November 1928): 1,064, 1,067.

disciplinary ventures that conjoined basic and applied research, training, and practice in the biomedical, behavioral, and social sciences.

Reconstructing the early years of gerontology as a collective, scholarly enterprise in the United States requires: (1) identifying who supplied the financial support for advancing knowledge and training students; (2) tracing the personal and professional bonds that were forged among a cadre of bright, distinguished, energetic researchers who were predisposed to design a multidisciplinary agenda and prescribe suitable methods for inquiry; and (3) analyzing the formal networks and vehicles that took shape by the end of the 1930s for communicating ideas. It is the details that give the story of gerontology's emergence as a science its specificity.

Who would have guessed in 1933, after all, that a grant of $3,250 to enable an anatomist at Washington University to investigate arteriosclerosis would spur a venturesome foundation shortly thereafter to earmark larger sums of money for assessing the state of scientific work on aging? The chain of events recounted here did not take shape serendipitously. It was hardly preordained that developments should unfold as they did. Many other domains of the U.S. scientific enterprise before World War II, after all, remained self-consciously anti-institutional and individualistic.[5] This is why historical context matters so much: Much of the sense of "community" nurtured by researchers on aging depended on the particular mix of personalities and politics, of challenges and constraints that enveloped intellectual exchanges during certain proceedings. Some scientists and administrators mentioned in this chapter made the fateful choice to do research on aging through happenstance. Others reached the decision to pursue options in gerontology more deliberately. Their sense of how to advance their careers dovetailed with ideas about how to advance knowledge about senescence that were beginning to circulate in major foundation headquarters and in laboratories in U.S. academic centers.

Establishing the network

Nowadays, the federal government underwrites most of the research on aging in the United States. In 1987, for instance, the National Institute on Aging alone awarded nearly $146 million for basic research in gerontology and geriatrics; the U.S. Administration on Aging allocated $25 million for training and research. These figures do not include research underwritten by the departments of Education, Health and Human Services, Labor, Commerce, Veterans Affairs, the other National Institutes of Health, or independent federal agencies. In contrast, private U.S. foundations gave

5 David Hollinger, "Free Enterprise and Free Inquiry," *New Literary History*, vol. 21 (1990): 898.

only $30.6 million for research and evaluation grants; this sum represented about a fifth of their total giving for aging-related activities that year.[6]

Prior to World War II, Washington played a far more modest role in setting priorities and paying for biomedical and social scientific research. Members of the National Academy of Science (established in 1863) and the National Research Council (chartered in 1918) were expected to do little more than speak for the interests of scientific experts in the Capitol. Scientists based in universities and corporations did not want central agencies playing more than an advisory role in shaping research activities where they worked. Congress only appropriated $750,000 "for construction and equipment of additional buildings" when it established a National Institute on Health (NIH) in 1930. Funds for research fellowships and other activities were to be raised through private donations.[7]

Although North American charitable endeavors started in the seventeenth century, U.S. philanthropic foundations only began to realize their potential during the early twentieth century. Americans were unwilling at the time to rely on Washington to be the center of reformist activities; most federal legislators were chary to intervene too far into domestic affairs. Foundations thus were in a position to take on major responsibility for achieving goals unmet in the Progressive political and social agenda. Large sums of money for "improving the welfare of mankind" became available through the Milbank Memorial Fund (1905); the Russell Sage Foundation (1907); the Carnegie Corporation of New York (1911); the RF (1913); the first of the community trusts, the Cleveland Foundation (1914); the Commonwealth Fund (1918); the John and Mary R. Markle Foundation (1927); and the W. K. Kellogg Foundation (1930).[8] Keen to create a distinctive

---

6 Federal statistics come from U.S. Senate, Special Committee on Ageing, *Developments on Aging: 1987*, vol. 2 (Washington, DC: Government Printing Office, 1988), pp. 144, 384; for foundation trends, see Barbara R. Greenberg et al., *Aging: The Burden Study of Foundation Grantmaking Trends* (New York: The Foundation Center, 1991), p. 11. I use data so that the figures are comparable. After 1987, the NIA budget more than doubled, so recent dollar amounts would have made the contrast more vivid.

7 Victoria A. Harden, *Inventing the NIH* (Baltimore: Johns Hopkins University Press, 1986), p. 197; Robert Kargon and Elizabeth Hodes, "Karl Compton, Isaiah Bowman, and the Politics of Science in the Great Depression," *Isis*, vol. 76 (1985): 301–18; Lewis Auerbach, "Scientists in the New Deal," *Minerva*, vol. 3 (1965): 457–82; Carroll Pursell, "Anatomy of a Failure," *Proceedings of the American Philosophical Society*, vol. 109 (December 1965): 342–51.

8 Barry Karl and Stanley Katz, "The American Private Philanthropic Foundation and the Public Sphere," *Minerva*, vol. 19 (1981): 236–71. For statistics, see Warren Weaver, *Philanthropic Foundations* (New York: Harper & Row, 1967), pp. 21–38; John Z. Bowers and Elizabeth F. Purcell, eds., *Advances in American Medicine*, vol. 1 (New York: Josiah Macy, Jr. Foundation, 1976), pp. 32–3; Howard S. Berliner, *A System of Scientific Medicine* (New York: Tavistock Publications, 1985). As many foundations (18) were established in the first decade of this century as were chartered before 1900. Numbers grew thereafter: in the 1950s alone another 2,839 foundations came into existence. For a broad historical view of

societal niche for themselves and to operate in a prudent, efficient manner, foundations put great faith in experts and in scientific management. "This is an age of science," declared RF's Wickliffe Rose in 1923. "All important fields of activity, from the breeding of bees to the administration of an empire, call for an understanding of the spirit and technique of science. . . . Promotion of the development of science in a country is germinal; it affects the entire system of education and carries with it the remaking of a civilization."[9]

Most foundation leaders agreed that science was *the* "method of knowledge," but they acknowledged that science had many branches. To promulgate appropriate standards for "scientific approaches" to problem solving was a daunting challenge. During the Progressive era, men such as Wickliffe Rose and Simon Flexner spoke grandly of the "advancement of human knowledge" through the creation of national and regional scientific communities. In this spirit, the Carnegie Foundation for the Advancement of Teaching commissioned Abraham Flexner's *Medical Education in the United States and Canada* (1910), which prompted the most radical curricular reforms for teaching physicians in this century. Philanthropic officers after World War I chose to create cross-disciplinary specialties, develop new research tools, and identify "problems" that would engage both bench scientists and social reformers. Throughout the period, foundations sought to realize their objectives through the priorities they enunciated and the grant proposals they solicited. In so doing, they felt that they were making research "the organized technique of science itself for its own propagation. It is, so to speak, the reproductive process of science."[10]

Philanthropies like the RF took an increasingly aggressive proactive stance in managing new directions in science. Staff hoped to transform the physical sciences as successfully as they had reformed medical education. The Foundation was unabashedly elitist in devising a strategy. "Begin with physics, chemistry, and biology," Rose urged, "locate the inspiring productive men." A decade later, his successor, Warren Weaver, stressed that RF "has the opportunity to choose only the very best men, the very best

the significance of these foundations, see Peter Dobkin Hall, *Inventing the Nonprofit School* (Baltimore: Johns Hopkins University Press, 1992).

9 Quoted in Robert E. Kohler, *Partners in Science* (Chicago: University of Chicago Press, 1991), pp. 137–8. I relied heavily on this book for understanding philanthropic and scientific activities in this period.

10 This was James R. Angell's view expressed to the National Research Council in 1919. Quoted in Ellen Condliffe Lagemann, *The Politics of Knowledge* (Middletown, CT: Wesleyan University Press), p. 31. I do not mean to suggest that foundations were the only catalyst for multidisciplinary research, particularly in the study of human development. The Iowa Child Welfare Research Station, established in 1917, was already renowned for its "investigation of the best scientific methods" before its program was underwritten by foundations. See Therese R. Richardson, *The Century of the Child* (Albany: State University of New York Press, 1989), p. 132.

special facilities, and only those researches which most significantly key together."[11] Weaver rewarded scientific risk takers who disregarded disciplinary boundaries *and* seemed likely to produce excellent results. His "project-grants in biochemistry-biophysics" went to those who used isotopes and the latest equipment, especially when combining insights from organic chemistry and physiology. Nor did he hesitate to advance his own hobby horses. (Weaver himself had the right credentials and contacts: He was a rising mathematician with an interest in physics at the University of Wisconsin when a mentor invited him to come to the RF. Weaver's apprenticeship exposed him to turf battles beyond his expertise: He learned to resolve conflicts between medical researchers and physical scientists, poachers and careerists.) Weaver wanted to develop a research program on "vital processes."

The future, Weaver sensed, lay in the biological sciences, which after the 1920s were expanding into a "big" science. Believing that scientists should pursue elusive problems of "disorganized complexity," he hoped to translate to new domains of knowledge the principle of "complementarity" enunciated by Niels Bohr in 1928. It really does not matter that Weaver failed to attract many university-based scientists to the study of vital processes. The key thing to note is how his vision meshed with RF's watchwords: "restriction within fields and co-operation between fields."[12] This orientation colored foundation officers' perceptions of the status of work in the social sciences. Their sense of the value of cross-disciplinary work affected their willingness to support those fields with some connections to the biological sciences, such as the emerging area of human development.

Many philosophers, psychologists, and sociologists after World War I tried to enhance their reputations in the academic community by emulating principles and methods in vogue in the natural sciences. Those who advanced social science research in the foundation world followed suit. Not surprisingly, physicists and biologists pressed for greater support (because their labs and equipment were more expensive), but there actually was considerable parity in allocating resources across disciplines during the 1920s. The RF's General Education Board, for instance, appropriated more than $14 million on natural science projects at just fourteen sites between 1923 and 1931. The Laura Spelman Rockefeller Memorial (LSRM) bestowed grants totaling more than $20 million for social science research between 1923 and 1928. The Memorial chose projects that emphasized scientific methodology in their design. It wanted investigators to apply findings to remedy "real-life" problems, such as to improve the welfare of

11 The Rose quotation in Kohler, *Partners*, p. 137; Weaver quoted on p.401. See also idem, "A Policy for the Advancement of Science," *Minerva*, vol. 10 (1980): 480–515.
12 Warren Weaver, *Science and Imagination* (New York: Basic, 1967), pp. 28–33; idem, *Scene of Change* (New York: Scribner, 1970), pp. 59–60, 174; RF watchwords quoted in Kohler, *Partners*, p. 267.

mothers and children.[13] Nor was RF alone in its support of promising ventures. The Carnegie Corporation gave a distinguished psychologist, Edward L. Thorndike, $325,000 in grants between 1922 and 1938 to study cognitive differences in individuals. The Social Science Research Council (started in 1923) and the American Council of Learned Societies (chartered in 1924) provided new sources of support; the John Simon Guggenheim Foundation (established in 1925) supported work by behaviorists and humanists at levels almost as generous as that garnered by physicists and biologists.[14] As a result of the largesse of a few foundations, large-scale social science projects become feasible.

A common raison d'être and strategic instinct appears to have guided philanthropic pacesetters. The commitments that RF and LSRM made to the social sciences were led by Beardsley Ruml and Lawrence K. Frank, intellectual-managers who proved as disinterested and astute in brokering grants as their colleagues Rose and Weaver. Ruml, a Chicago Ph.D. who studied with Charles Merriam, assisted the president of the Carnegie Corporation before becoming head of LSRM at age twenty-seven. After graduating from Columbia in 1912, Frank honed his skills as an institutional economist through positions at the New York Telephone Company, War Industries Board, and New School for Social Research. Frank's first task at LSRM was to conduct a survey of the social sciences (1923). He concluded that "the growth of science is conditioned by the availability of scientists," particularly those who explored "concrete situations."[15]

Foundations could play an instrumental role in fostering excellence in the social sciences, Ruml believed, by "planning over a period of years to attack really fundamental situations and to reach relatively remote ends." Among other things, this strategy gave philanthropies license to risk endowments to nurture universities' capacity for generating knowledge in new

13 Richardson, *Century of the Child*, p. 129; Hamilton Cravens, *Before Head Start* (Chapel Hill: University of North Carolina Press, 1993), pp. 45–6.

14 Martin Bulmer and Joan Bulmer, "Philanthropy and Social Science in the 1920s," *Government and Opposition*, vol. 18 (Winter 1982): 347–407; Kohler, *Partners*, p. 202; Robert F. Arnove, ed., *Philanthropy and Cultural Imperialism* (Boston: G.K. Hall, 1980), p. 89; Lawrence J. Rhoades, *A History of the American Sociological Association* (Washington, DC: American Sociological Association, 1981), pp. 7–8; Jean Alonzo Curran, *Founders of the Harvard School of Public Health* (New York: Josiah Macy, Jr. Foundation, 1970), p. 24.

15 Stanley Coben, "Foundation Officials and Fellowships," *Minerva*, vol. 14 (1976): 225–40; Bulmer and Bulmer, "Philanthropy and Social Science," p. 371; Franz Samuelson, "Organizing for the Kingdom of Behavior," *Journal of the History of the Behavioral Sciences*, vol. 21 (January 1985): 33–47. See also Frank's memorandum, dated April 26, 1924, in the LSRM files, ser. 2, box 2 in the Rockefeller Archives: "One of the ways in which social science will probably be developed is through study of the way people live and work actually."

frontiers. (That said, there were limits to this commitment: No one proposed creating a social science counterpart to the Rockefeller Institute for Medical Research.) High priority was placed on underwriting fellowships for promising, young scholars and on establishing support for "men of competence in a spirit of objectivity and thoroughness with freedom of inquiry and expression."[16] In the late 1920s, Lawrence Frank was convinced that scientific progress required older ideas to be superseded by "newer conceptions more congruous with the actual evidence." Frank believed that future success in the social sciences lay with junior investigators, who were better trained. Accordingly, he felt that grantsmakers must be prepared to foment "conflict between the younger generations and the older." Foundations had to be venturesome in challenging orthodoxy. "The development of a social science, with emphasis upon the real science," asserted Frank, "is waiting upon the emancipation of some of the younger generation from the domination of social theories over their thinking and anything which would help to encourage originality to venture out from the beaten paths."[17]

Lawrence Frank's views at the time on how the study of child development should proceed along organizational lines conformed with RF's ideology:

> The scientific significance of the study of child development resides, I think, in the fact it is a study of the total organism in as many different methods as possible.... It follows from this that if the child is to be parcelled out for the study of specific problems of the cooperating departments, the research then loses its major significance and becomes a plan for furthering the research interests of the different sciences rather than the promotion of research on child development.... Experience has shown, too, that someone from the outside who comes in with a clean slate is apt to be more successful in dealing with the various departments than a person who has been identified with a particular department in the university.[18]

16 Quotes from Bulmer and Bulmer, "Philanthropy and Social Science," pp. 367, 380. See also, George W. Corner, *A History of the Rockefeller Institute* (New York: Rockefeller Institute Press, 1964).

17 Lawrence K. Frank, "Social Science Research Council," unpublished report, undated but ca. 1927. Laura Spelman Rockefeller Memorial Files, ser. 3, folder 684. This idea recurs in other people's work. James B. Conant called the pursuit of new fields a "young man's game" in *Science and Common Sense* (New Haven, CT: Yale University Press, 1951), p. 77. See also David L. Hull et al., "Planck's Principle," *Science*, vol. 202 (17 November 1978): 717-23; and *infra*, "Chapter 8."

18 Letter from Lawrence K. Frank to Dr. George W. Stratton of the University of California, Berkeley, dated April 13, 1927. I am indebted to Alice Boardman Smuts for sharing this letter that is in the Rockefeller Archive Center. Frank dated his own interest in child development back to 1923. See Milton J. E. Senn, "Insights on the Child Development

Frank stressed multidisciplinary perspectives. He wanted to develop institutions that would directly observe children using the latest technologies and insights from the human sciences. A positivist, Frank believed that science, properly applied, could improve society.[19] His pattern of making grants reflected these beliefs. Impressed by the pioneering work done at the Iowa Child Welfare Research Station that had opened in 1917, Frank invested substantial funds in establishing a network of Institutes of Child Welfare at Columbia (1924), Minnesota and Toronto (1925), Yale (1926), and Berkeley (1927). He gave a series of grants to rising stars such as Case Western's T. Wingate Todd, who used X-rays to study patterns of adolescent growth. The National Research Council received $10,000 between 1926 and 1930 to support its committee on Child Development. Frank also was generous in considering requests from schools and practitioners who ran child welfare agencies.

Besides facilitating the production of basic and applied research, Frank insinuated his own notions into the field. He wrote the chapter on "Child and Youth" for the Hoover administration under the aegis of the President's Research Committee on Social Trends. Frank's involvement in the problem of human growth and development grew during the 1930s. With his support, RF funds were made available to found the Society for Research in Child Development (1933), thus enabling the professional group to start its own quarterly journal and monograph series. In 1934, Frank invited scholars from a variety of disciplines to spend a month at Dartmouth's Hanover Inn to figure out how to teach youth what was known about human behavior. "I learned that this was Larry's way," recalls Margaret Mead, one of the participants, "to create situations, pose problems, and then let those whom he had involved become gradually more involved with the problems he posed, and with working with each other."[20]

Thanks to their staffs' vision and organizing abilities, as well as their vast wealth and prestige, foundations by the 1930s had emerged as major architects of research programs and institutional networks in the medical, natural, and social sciences. For all of LSRM's interest in child development, the philanthropy was not interested in sponsoring programmatic research on aging. Creating a science of gerontology simply was not a high priority at RF, despite the attention that old-age pensions and other social

Movement in the United States," *Monographs of the Society for Research in Child Development*, vol. 40 (August 1975): 14.

19 Cravens, *Before Head Start*, pp. 47–9; Joseph M. Haines and N. Ray Hiner, eds., *American Childhood* (Westport, CT: Greenwood, 1985), pp. 440–1.

20 Mead quotation from Senn, "Insights on the Child Development Movement," p. 9. See also John E. Anderson, "Child Development: An Historical Perspective," *Child Development*, vol. 27 (June 1956): 181–96; Dorothy McLean, "Child Development," ibid., vol. 25 (March 1954): 3–8; Mary Catherine Bateson, *Our Own Metaphor* (New York: Knopf, 1972), pp. 7–8.

problems of the elderly were attracting in the popular press and policy-making circles during the 1930s. Rather than explore problems of senescence, Weaver wanted to invest in psychobiology, biophysics and biochemistry, genetics, physiology, and embryology; he hoped to encourage the study of the biology of sex, internal secretions, nutrition, and radiation effects.[21] Similarly, prior to 1936, Frank was more interested in problems of childhood and youth than those of maturity and old age. Even the largest foundations had to cut back in the depths of the Great Depression, which made funds for aging research harder to obtain. Into this vacuum, a new philanthropy decided to make its mark by underwriting investigations of diseases in old age and basic inquiries into processes of senescence.

In 1930, the same year that the NIH was created, Kate Macy Ladd gave $5 million to establish the Josiah Macy, Jr. Foundation, in memory of her father. Mrs. Ladd's venturesome turn of mind is manifest in her Letter of Gift:

> It is my desire that the Foundation in the use of this gift should concentrate on a few problems rather than the support of many undertakings, and that it should primarily devote its interest to the fundamental aspects of health, of sickness, and of methods for the relief of suffering; in particular to such special problems in medical sciences, medical arts and medical education as require for their solution studies and efforts in correlated fields as well, such as biology and the social sciences. To these ends the Foundation might give preference in the use of this fund to integrating functions in medical science and medical education for which there seems to be particular need in our age of specialization and technical complexities. . . . I hope, therefore, that the Foundation will take more interest in the architecture of ideas than in the architecture of buildings and laboratories.[22]

The Macy Foundation boldly aspired to promote a healthfulness that, in Mrs. Ladd's words, "resides in the wholesome unity of mind and body." Rather than follow wealthier foundations' lead in supporting biochemical and physiological research, the board chose to invest in psychological and sociological studies, "to synthesize old and new data derived from the highly specialized researchers and new techniques."[23] It valued cross-disciplinary, integrative research that promised practical payoffs.

From the start, Ludwig Kast, the first president of the Macy Foundation, was "concerned with the processes of aging and with degenerative

21 This was Weaver's proposed agenda in December 1933. See Kohler, *Partners*, p. 283.
22 Quoted in Josiah Macy, Jr. Foundation, *A Review by the President of Activities for the Six Years Ended December 31, 1936* (New York: Josiah Macy, Jr. Foundation, 1937), pp. 14–15. Mrs. Ladd gave additional gifts, but the Macy Foundation remained small. In 1955, its endowments were around $28 million. Thirty years later, the market value was less than $72 million. Rockefeller Foundation assets that year exceeded $1.6 billion.
23 The Josiah Macy, Jr. Foundation, *A Review of Activities, 1930–1955* (New York: Josiah Macy; Jr. Foundation, 1955), p. 5.

changes."[24] He intended the small foundation to take sensible risks with its limited resources. Early in 1931, the Macy Foundation sought the advice of the Division of Medical Sciences of the National Research Council, chaired by Dr. Edmund Vincent Cowdry. It was a fortuitous consultation, ultimately benefiting from Cowdry's diverse experiences and international contacts. Born in Alberta in 1888, Cowdry was trained at the universities of Toronto and Chicago. He held appointments in anatomy and zoology at Chicago, Johns Hopkins, the Peking (China) Medical Union College, and the Rockefeller Institute for Medical Research prior to becoming a professor of cytology at Washington University in 1928. Cowdry held leadership positions in such organizations as the American Association of Anatomists, the Society of Experimental Biologists, the Academy of Tropical Medicine, and the Bermuda Biological Station. He was an editor of *Endocrinology* and the *American Journal of Physical Anthropology*, chaired RF task forces on yellow fever and infantile paralysis, and led eight scientific expeditions to the Pacific and Africa.[25] After canvassing U.S. and European scientists, Macy executives and Cowdry were persuaded that they should begin to probe the mysteries of late life by examining arteriosclerosis, which afflicted many older people (including Mrs. Ladd). Research on the disease to date was scattered.

Cowdry agreed to help the Macy Foundation to systematize information about arteriosclerosis, "formulate the principal problems," and devise a plan for "attacking" them. "This decision to make haste slowly and by securing the cooperation of specialists to thoroughly explore the possibilities for research strongly appealed to [me]," declared Cowdry. "It brings to bear upon a chronic disease that kind of team work which has proved such an effective instrument in the investigation of acute infections."[26] Half of the specialists Cowdry consulted were pathologists or histologists, many from Europe. Professor Ludwig Aschoff, "the Nestor of arteriosclerosis research" who headed a pathology institute in Freiburg, sounded the project's theme by distinguishing, as Warthin had done a few years earlier, between pathological and physiological aspects of aging. Arteriosclerosis, he contended, was a "malady" and "affliction" of old age that should not be counted "among the changes attending the process of aging."[27]

24 Ludwig Kast, "Foreword," *Arteriosclerosis*, ed. Edmund Vincent Cowdry (New York: Macmillan, 1933), p. v; see also *Twentieth Anniversary Review of the Josiah Macy, Jr. Foundation* (1950), pp. 30–2.

25 Biographical data from J. McKeen Cattell and Jaques Cattell, eds., *American Men of Science*, 6th ed. (New York: Science Press, 1938), p. 299; see also Joseph T. Freeman, "Edmund Vincent Cowdry: Creative Gerontologist" *The Gerontologist* vol. 24 (1984): 641–5 (henceforth this journal will be abbreviated *TG*); George W. Corner, *The Seven Ages of a Medical Scientist* (Philadelphia: University of Pennsylvania Press, 1981, p. 99.

26 Edmund Vincent Cowdry, "Preface," in *Arteriosclerosis*, p. ix.

27 Ludwig Aschoff, "Introduction," *Arteriosclerosis*, ed. Edmund Vincent Cowdry (New York: Macmillan, 1933) p. 5. Kast calls Aschoff the "Nestor" of the field in his "Fore-

Rather than issue a single-authored summary report, Cowdry asked twenty-three experts to give in-depth, disciplinary-specific analyses of arteriosclerosis. In bulk and tone, Cowdry's edited volume resembled a *handbook,* a genre that is "one of the few generalizing influences in a world of overspecialization."[28] Cowdry's decision to publish a handbook reflected his own professional style and his conviction that this was the best way to advance science. In 1924, the same year that Edmund B. Wilson published the third edition of his path-breaking volume, *The Cell in Development and Heredity,* Cowdry had edited a multiauthored text, *General Cytology.* He had commissioned articles that focused on cellular chemistry, cellular physiology, cellular structure and cellular function as well as chapters on descriptive methods and experimental techniques for doing tissue cultures and microdissection. Wilson's feat was praised, but single authors could no longer expect to survey the whole field. Cowdry's *General Cytology,* in contrast, was praised by reviewers for its "comprehensiveness," "extensiveness," and "exhaustiveness."[29]

Arteriosclerosis, Cowdry's second handbook, looked like other technical, "insider" compendia published during the 1930s. Unlike specialized monographs or textbooks popularizing academic specialities, handbooks mapped out what P. W. Bridgman in *The Logic of Modern Physics* (1927) called "operational concepts" – ideas and methods fundamental for advancing knowledge. Hence the first *Handbook of Child Psychology* was issued in 1931. "Problems, techniques, and results cannot be sharply differentiated. A problem, however stated, does not become a scientific problem until a method of attack can be set up," observed John E. Anderson in the volume's introduction. "Results, in their turn, depend upon technique, and other problems put in their appearance only as technique and results move forward."[30] Scholars in other emerging fields followed suit. Twenty-four scholars contributed to *A Handbook of Social Psychology* (1935) "to organize a representative cross-section of serious methods of

---

word," p. vii. Note how from the start Macy made an effort to bring the senior people together to delineate where work should be done.

28 "Encyclopedias," *Encyclopedia Brittanica,* 15th ed. (1985), vol. 18: 368.

29 Keith R. Benson, Jane Maienschein, and Ronald Rainger, eds., *The Expansion of American Biology* (New Brunswick, NJ: Rutgers University Press, 1991), pp. 8, 24, 46.

30 John E. Anderson, "The Methods of Child Psychology," in *A Handbook of Child Psychology,* ed. Carl Murchison (Worcester, MA: Clark University Press, 1931), p. 1. Fulfilling Anderson's prophecy, a radically revised edition of the *Handbook of Child Psychology* was issued two years later. Bridgman quoted in Laurence D. Smith, *Behaviorism and Logical Positivism* (Stanford, CA: Stanford University Press, 1986), p. 55; see also Percy W. Bridgman, "The Logic of Modern Physics," reprinted in *Readings in the Philosophy of Science,* ed. Herbert Feigl and May Broderick (East Norwalk, CT: Appleton-Century-Crofts, 1953), pp. 34–6; Bruce Kuklick, *The Rise of American Philosophy* (Cambridge: Harvard University Press, 1977), p. 461.

investigating social mechanisms."[31] Cowdry's decision to prepare the *Arteriosclerosis* handbook made sense.

Besides supporting Cowdry's assessment of the state of research on arteriosclerosis, the Macy Foundation between 1931 and 1934 made grants to ten universities and research agencies to "foster cooperation among clinical, experimental, and morphological investigators."[32] Most of the studies were small-scale: They tracked cholesterol and calcium metabolism, tissue growth and changes, and the relation of blood supply to vessels. Ludwig Kast indicated that he was receptive to underwriting a bolder venture. In October 1935, Cowdry suggested to Macy's president that a wider approach be taken in order to understand the problems of aging. The Foundation agreed: "Here was virgin territory with broad implications for many of the biological, medical, and social sciences. Here was an opportunity for a foundation to assist in the development of a new field of science which, by its nature, demanded the integration of data, methods, and concepts from many special branches – a coordinated, multi-professional approach."[33] Cowdry was invited to orchestrate the next stage of activities.

How the Macy Foundation, E. V. Cowdry, and John Dewey defined the problems of aging

Cowdry relied on institutional connections and personal ties in planning a conference at Woods Hole, Massachusetts, in 1937 to survey current work in aging. He understood the importance of recruiting topflight scientists who ideally would form a social group coherent enough to communicate with one another and to reach out to a broader audience. Cowdry also knew that, since the turn of the century, Woods Hole had been "the center of the unified science of biology," a place were chemists, psychologists, and medical researchers could interact and relax with biologists in a genteel resort that had up-to-date research facilities.[34] So he first recruited from the ranks of the Union of American Biological Societies, of which he happened to be president. "The common feature of all member societies is that they are concerned in the investigation of living things," Cowdry pointed out. "The problems of growth, the upswing of the curve of vital processes, are being energetically attacked with adequate financial support. Those of aging, the downswing of the curve resulting inevitably in death, are on the contrary shamefully neglected."[35] He got support for his project from the

31 Carl Murchison, ed., *A Handbook of Social Psychology* (Worcester, MA: Clark University Press, 1935), p. ix.
32 Macy Foundation, *Twentieth Anniversary Review*, p. 32.
33 Ibid., pp. 32–3.
34 Philip J. Pauly, "Woods Hole, 1882–1925," in *American Development of Biology*, ed. Rainger *et al.*, pp. 136–42.
35 Edmund Vincent Cowdry, "Woods Hole Conference on the Problems of Aging," *Scientific*

divisions of Medical Sciences, Biology, Agriculture, Anthropology, and Psychology of the National Research Council. Cowdry also solicited the advice of Lawrence Frank, who joined Macy's staff in 1936.

If, as Harvard's S. S. Stevens observed, "the scientist has always been proud of his hard head and his tough mind,"[36] then Cowdry had reason to admire the people he selected to contribute to his *Problems of Ageing* (1939), the first U.S. handbook of gerontology. All but four of the twenty-five authors were eventually listed in *Who's Who* or another Marquis publication (such as *Who Was Who in American History–Science and Technology*); detailed biographical material is missing for only one contributor, Macdonald Critchley, a Canadian neurologist. There was a wide age spread: Five were still active past the age of seventy, including Nobel laureate Karl Landsteiner, and Johns Hopkins clinician Llewellys Barker, who over the course of his career had been president of five scientific societies and a vice president of the American Medical Association. Six men were in their sixties, nine in their fifties, and four in their forties. At thirty-nine, Clive McCay was the "kid"; experiments he was conducting at the time, on the effects of dietary restriction in prolonging the lives of mature rats, before too long secured for the Cornell nutritionist a place in the gerontologic pantheon.[37]

Indicative of the eminence of the contributors to Cowdry's *Problems of Ageing* was the respect with which they were held by their scientific peers. With support initially from the Carnegie Institution of Washington, J. McKeen Cattell, a professor of psychology at Columbia University, began to compile a biographical directory "to make men of science acquainted with one another and with one another's work." In the 1906 edition, which included 4,000 entries, he invited ten luminaries in twelve "principal sciences" to identify those in the top quartile; by the sixth edition (1938), Cattell's *American Men of Science* had grown to 28,000 entries, of whom 2,250 had earned "stars."[38] Five of Cowdry's authors were designated as leaders in the first edition; three more received stars in the second edition, six in the fourth, and two each in the fifth and sixth editions. Seven were

Monthly, vol. 45 (August 1937): 189–91. For a broader statement on the significance of recruiting talent, see Belver C. Griffith and Nicholas C. Mullins, "Coherent Social Groups in Scientific Change," *Science*, vol. 177 (15 September 1972): 959–64.

36 S. S. Stevens, "Psychology and the Science of Science," *Psychological Bulletin*, vol. 36 (April 1939): 221. Stevens's gendered imagery merits brief comment. His ideal scientist resembles a soldier armed for combat.

37 For more on McCay, see Franklin C. Bing, "Old Salvelinus Fontinalis," *Perspectives of Biological Medicine*, vol. 13 (1970): 563–81. Not everybody who attended the 1937 Woods Hole Conference contributed to Cowdry's 1939 volume, or vice versa. I have therefore focused on the twenty-eight authors, not the participants.

38 Information on the 1903 volume and survey appear in J. McKeen Cattell and Jaques Cattell, eds., *American Men of Science*, 5th ed. (New York: Science Press, 1933), pp. v, 1276, 1278; other data in this paragraph from the 6th ed. (1938).

listed but not starred. Although many presumed at the time that there was an inverse relationship between age and productivity, none of those contributors who had achieved fame earlier in the century were considered to be past their prime in the late 1930s. Llewellys Barker, Harvard physiologist Walter B. Cannon, and John Dewey received high rankings in a 1903 survey for reshaping their respective fields; in a 1946 questionnaire, two authors (Cannon and Chicago physiologist A. J. Carlson) were among the scientists most frequently cited as outstanding mentors. Besides the fact that their scientific achievements were recognized by their peers, these individuals' careers have two other characteristics in common.

First, most of the contributors to Cowdry's volume were pathfinders but not necessarily adventurers. Based on his analysis of *American Men in Science*, Stephen Sargent Visher concluded that "the scientist who within any of the recognized sciences opens up new fields, or contributes notably to fields recently opened is more likely to be starred than he who contributes to aspects already fairly well known."[39] (Other factors, such as place of birth or education, were said to count. Warren Weaver's "tremendous respect for the vigor of the young people who are not too far removed from the pioneering spirit" comes to mind when counting how many of Cowdry's authors were born in the Midwest and/or trained at universities of Chicago, Michigan or Wisconsin.[40]) Such parochial biases notwithstanding, scientific honors before World War II went mainly to those trailblazers who broke new ground *within* specialties, not those who crossed disciplinary frontiers: "A man who worked between well-recognized fields, in biochemistry, geophysics, or astrophysics, for example, or whose work overlapped two or more sciences, as does that of many ecologists and biologists, was rarely starred unless highly distinguished."[41]

Many contributors to *Problems of Ageing* earned stars, not because their best-known work was deemed cross-disciplinary, but because they excelled in more than one mainline field. "To him who observes them from afar, it appears as though they are scattering and dissipating their energies," declared Nobel laureate Santiago Ramon y Cajàl, a neuroanatomist, "while in reality they are channeling and strengthening them."[42] Cowdry himself

39 Stephen Sargent Visher, *Scientists Starred in "American Men of Science," 1903–1943* (Baltimore: Johns Hopkins Press, 1947), p. 2.

40 Warren Weaver, "Science and the World of Scholarship," *The Robert A. Welch Foundation Research Bulletin*, vol. 6 (January 1960): 12. Visher, a geographer, also takes careful note of luminaries' place of birth, education, and advancement.

41 Stephen Sargent Visher, "J. McKeen Cattell and American Science," *Science and Society*, vol. 66 (December 13, 1947): 451. For more on resistance to interdisciplinarity, see Stephen Toulmin, "From Form to Function," *Daedalus*, vol. 106 (1977): 143.

42 Santiago Ramon y Cajàl, *Recollections of My Life* (Cambridge, MA: MIT Press, 1937), p. 171. I am indebted to Robert S. Root-Bernstein for this reference. In a forthcoming essay, "Correlations Between Avocations, Scientific Style, Work Habits, and Professional Impact of Scientists," Root-Bernstein and colleagues Maurine Bernstein and Helen Garnier

was respected as an anatomist, cytologist, and zoologist. A. E. Cohn was a pathologist and internist; William Crocker, a botanist and scientific administrator; Stacy Guild, an anatomist and otologist; L. O. Howard, an entomologist and museum director; H. S. Jennings, a zoologist and geneticist; Edward Krumbhaar, a pathologist and internist; Karl Landsteiner, a pathologist and immunologist; Clive McCay, a physiological chemist and nutritionist; William MacNider, a pharmacologist and pathologist; Walter R. Miles, a psychologist and physiologist; Frederick Weidman, a dermatologist and pathologist; and Clark Wissler, an anthropologist and psychologist. "Persons with mediocre talent," it was claimed in the 1930s, "should not attempt to master a broad, comprehensive field." This is why Cowdry picked exceptional people. He sought polymaths capable of bringing to a multifaceted problem an understanding of how things worked that was honed in several scientific fields of endeavor.[43]

Second, although they were trained in diverse specialties and disciplines, many authors were familiar with one another's work prior to contributing to *Problems on Ageing*. Lawrence Frank's publications abound with references to John Dewey (a Macy director and his teacher at Columbia), Walter B. Cannon, and T. Wingate Todd.[44] Anton J. Carlson had been testing Cannon's hypotheses for more than two decades. Alfred E. Cohn and Jonas S. Friedenwald had written articles for *Arteriosclerosis*. In 1934, Cannon, Todd, and Wissler served together on the National Research Council's Committee for Research in Problems of Sex.[45] Furthermore, an examination of references in the 1939 volume indicates that many contributors cited the same texts. Not only did they refer to one another's work

argue that many contemporary polymathic scientists "developed non-functional networks of enterprise," which heighten their self-understanding and facilitate their efforts to make scientific connections.

43 Quotation about mediocrity in Oliver H. Lowry, "How to Succeed in Research Without Being a Genius," *Annual Review of Biochemistry*, vol. 59 (1990): 3. Professional identifications all taken from the scientists' biographical entries in the fifth edition of *American Men of Science* (1933).

44 In general, see Stephen Schlossman, "Philanthropy and the Gospel of Child Development," *History of Education Quarterly*, vol. 21 (Fall 1981): 275–99. For typical uses of Dewey, see Lawrence K. Frank, "Development of Science," *Journal of Philosophy*, vol. 21 (1924): 15; idem, "Time Perspectives," *Journal of Social Philosophy*, vol. 4 (1939): 311. For Cannon, see idem, "The Problem of Child Development," *Child Development*, vol. 6 (1935): 8; idem, *Society as the Patient* (New Brunswick, NJ: Rutgers University Press, 1949), p. 361. For Todd, see idem., *Individual Development* (New York: Doubleday, 1955), p. 7; idem, "The Beginnings of Child Development and Family Life Education in the Twentieth Century," *Merrill-Palmer Quarterly*, vol. 8 (1962): 212.

45 Leo Postman, ed., *Psychology in the Making* (New York: Knopf, 1962), p. 110; Corner, *Seven Ages*, p. 267. Although Cannon did not contribute to *Problems of Ageing*, ed. Edmund Vincent Cowdry (Baltimore: Williams & Wilkins, 1942), 2d ed., he did attend the 1937 Woods Hole Conference. See Walter Bradford Cannon, "Homeostasis in Senescence," *Journal of Mt. Sinai Hospital*, vol. 5 (1939): 599.

with greater frequency than their successors would do in the 1990s, but they also gleaned valuable information from past masters: six authors wrote about Raymond Pearl's work on longevity, five invoked Alexis Carrel's hypotheses concerning the lives of the cell, and four mentioned ideas about involution set forth by Aldred Scott Warthin.[46]

Two more prosopographical details about the authors of Cowdry's *Problems of Ageing* should be noted by way of contrast to the contributors of the *Handbook of Child Psychology*. On the one hand, no woman wrote a chapter for the aging volume. This doubtless reflects the editor's solicitation of stars in the biomedical sciences. As S. S. Stevens intimated, "tough" scientists were mostly men; few eminent female natural scientists were interested in late-life development. (Had Cowdry drawn more heavily from the behavioral sciences, the gender balance might have shifted. Ten of the two dozen contributors to the second edition of the *Handbook of Child Psychology* were women, including Charlotte Bühler, Mary Cover Jones, and Margaret Mead. Psychology offered more opportunities than the "hard" sciences for women, especially those who studied children.) On the other hand, whereas physicians and clinicians were conspicuously absent from various handbooks of psychology, Frank and Cowdry invited several medical scientists to write about aging from the perspective of their specialty. "Medicine is and must be regarded as an applied science," declared Alfred E. Cohn.[47] Because it was a "discouragingly difficult field," geriatrics, no less than gerontology, needed to be firmly grounded in sound, scientific data.[48]

Lawrence K. Frank set the tone for his colleagues in his preface. Three sets of questions he posed suggest his sensitivity to balancing disciplinary interests and to enveloping new approaches within traditional canons of research. First, what were the prevailing concepts of senescence in the 1930s? Did old age result from "degenerative diseases," the natural outcome of "the process of ageing," or both? Second, what were the characteristics of the gerontologic "problem?" Did criteria for gauging its

---

46 W. Andrew Achenbaum, "The State of the Handbooks on Aging in 1990," *TG*, vol. 31 (February 1991): 132–4.

47 Alfred E. Cohn, "Medicine and Science," *Journal of Philosophy*, vol. 25 (July 19, 1928): 405. Other Cowdry contributors agreed. Barker, who was William Osler's successor at Hopkins, insisted that his clinicians do bench science. Earl T. Engle, a professor of anatomy at Columbia, was a generation younger than Barker, but he too agreed that the vitality of any clinical specialty depended on the quality of its laboratory research.

48 Barclay Moon Newman, "Geriatrics," *Scientific American*, vol. 163 (October 1940): 192. For more on relation of clinicians to scientists, see Alan Gregg, "A Critique of Medical Research," *Proceedings of the American Philosophical Society*, vol. 87 (January 1944): 317; A. McGehee Harvey, *Science at the Bedside* (Baltimore: Johns Hopkins University Press, 1981), pp. 64–6; Howard C. Taylor, Jr., *The Recruitment of Talent for a Medical Specialty* (St. Louis, MO: Mosby, 1961), p. 10; A. Baird Hastings, *Crossing Boundaries* (Grand Rapids, MI: Four Corners Press, 1989), pp. 36–8.

scientific scope also illuminate its social dimensions? Third, what incentives and obstacles influenced how people used "scientific" knowledge in dealing with "social" issues perceived to have wide-ranging societal ramifications? Could strategies for solving analogous types of problems be transferred to this domain? Mindful of the scientific risks, Frank advocated taking as broad a perspective as possible in grappling with these issues. "Senescence must for the present be regarded as a distinct problem, within the larger biological question," he asserted. Yet the problem was "not a purely biological question, but has large cultural, social, and psychological implications."[49]

Echoing both Warthin and Aschoff, Frank acknowledged that there were two conflicting models of aging in the 1930s. The first approach "interprets the changes found in aged organs as due to infections, toxins, traumas, and nutritional disturbances or inadequacies which have forced cells, tissues and fluids to respond with degenerative changes and impairments."[50] Aging demonstrably brought decline and debility, which is why many scientists linked images of old age and disease in the 1930s. "Pathology is the fundamental branch of medicine," declared Simon Flexner, president of the Rockefeller Institute for Medical Research.[51] A pathological model of senescence highlighted the elderly's age-specific decrements. Probing the etiology of lesions might ultimately lead to a cure, or at least relief, for some late-life maladies. If they better understood the causes and manifestations of diseases in old people, clinicians could develop appropriate therapeutic interventions.

The second approach, in contrast, stressed age-related changes in basic processes. An organism's capacities and functions often diminished with the sheer passage of time. Very often, diseases weakened the body's regulatory mechanisms. Such pathological causes of decline, however, should not be confused with the effects of normal aging. Putting primary focus on disease, it was felt, missed an opportunity for increasing scientific knowledge about fundamental processes of growth and human development over the life course. Senescence represented the normal culmination of natural developmental processes. Those who embraced this position, following Nascher's lead, thought that geriatrics should become a medical specialty analogous to pediatrics.

Contributors to *Problems of Ageing* debated the merits of pathological and normal models of senescence along lines that still prompt arguments today. Alfred Cohn, a Rockefeller Institute cardiologist, felt that "ageing is either disease or not disease," but shared Western Reserve anatomist T.

---

49 Lawrence K. Frank, "Introduction" to *Problems of Ageing*, 1st ed., ed. Edmund Vincent Cowdry (Baltimore: Williams & Wilkins, 1989), p. xv.
50 Ibid., p. xiii.
51 Quoted in Corner, *A History of the Rockefeller Institute*, p. 187.

Wingate Todd's opinion that "age changes and age infirmities are so inter-woven that it is not easy to segregate the former from the latter."[52] A. C. Ivy, a physiologist and pharmacologist at Northwestern, reported that al-though half of the forms of lethal cancers arise in tissues or organs of the digestive system, most elderly people died with functioning systems. Based on their respective studies, neurologist Macdonald Critchley and Johns Hopkins ophthalmologist Jonas S. Friedenwald took a middle position, hy-pothesizing that "ageing is not entirely a simple physiological process nor yet an exclusively pathological state."[53]

Some contributors' dubiety reflected their cautiousness in the face of tre-mendous variations in data. Frank pointed out in his preface that aging could not be attributed to a single structural or functional change or error. People matured at different rates; so did various parts of their bodies. Sex- and gender-specific differentials were salient. Sample size and biases may have distorted ideas about girls and development. Other researchers elab-orated this theme. University of Pennsylvania pathologist Edward Bell Krumbhaar documented morphologic variations in lymphatic tissue. Yale psychologist Walter R. Miles argued that individual personality, not chron-ological age, was a good predictor of productivity, wisdom, and intelligence in later maturity. Anatomist Edgar Allen reminded readers that menopause occurs when other systems were in their prime. Dermatologist Fred Weid-man wrote that study of the skin, "supplying the most unequivocal signs of ageing,"[54] manifested some progressive alterations, though rarely enough to counterbalance "retrograde processes."

Given such variations in processes of aging, researchers disagreed about what chronological boundaries to place on their studies. Cornell's Clive McCay argued that biochemical patterns "should be investigated long be-fore the final alterations of the declining years have taken place. . . . Here alone lies some hope of reversing reactions which day by day introduce the changes that finally result in senility." Based on his experiments with aging rats, McCay believed that intervention was most efficacious the earlier it occurred. Anton J. Carlson, a physiologist at the University of Chicago, conceded that "the problem of ageing embraces the entire life span," but went on to argue that pursuing such a hypothesis was "not very useful at this stage of biology." Carlson recommended that attention be focused on late-life developments where there were "both data and methods of testing their interpretation."[55]

---

52 Alfred E. Cohn, "Cardiovascular System and Blood," in *Problems*, p. 120; T. Wingate Todd, "Skeleton, Locomotor System and Teeth," ibid., p. 278.

53 Jonas S. Friedenwald, "The Eye," in *Problems*, p. 496.

54 F. D. Weidman, "Ageing of the Skin," in *Problems*, p. 358. Note that Weidman talked in terms of "signs," not "symptoms."

55 Clive M. McCay, "Chemical Aspects of Ageing," in *Problems*, p. 372; Anton J. Carlson, "The Thyroid, Pancreatic Islets, Parathyroids, Adrenals, Thymus and Pituitary," in ibid.,

Divergent conceptions of the relationship between aging and maturing underscored the importance of determining how the parts fit together. William deB. MacNider, dean of North Carolina's medical school, stressed that any analysis of aging tissues and organs be viewed as a local expression of biological phenomena that influenced the whole organism. To study the process of aging thus presupposed knowledge beyond one's area of specialization. Walter B. Cannon echoed this sentiment when he reported a progressive impairment of regulatory devices controlling temperature, glucose concentrations, and osmotic pressures in individuals over forty. But the eminent Harvard physiologist doubted that alterations in homeostatic mechanisms could be fully appreciated until more basic research was done in nearly every area. Clinician Llewellys Barker urged that primary attention be placed on "determining biological factors" – a view shared by authors of articles that dealt with plants, protozoa, insects, and vertebrates. In his own chapter, Cowdry opined that "the problem . . . is one of great complexity." He hoped scientists would find "clues as to the nature of the processes of ageing by balancing local alterations in cells and fibers against changes in fluid environment."[56]

One way to try to make sense of such disparate viewpoints was to delineate at the outset the conceptual and methodological conundrums associated with "problems" of aging. John Dewey, renowned philosopher, educator, psychologist, and Macy board member who was himself approaching eighty, seemed ideally suited to perform this task. Scholars and ordinary citizens respected Dewey's originality. "The genesis of all new developments is in the critical, reflective and creative thinking of the gifted individuals who are able to free themselves, in part at least, from their coercive traditions and to make new assumptions and develop new methods and techniques of inquiry," observed Lawrence Frank. "John Dewey exemplifies the foregoing as few others have ever done."[57] Dewey himself believed that philosophers could serve as a "liaison officer between the conclusions of science and the modes of social and personal action." Philosophers, if versed in scientific methods, were well suited as critical thinkers to "resolve the modern crisis."[58]

p. 361. See also Alexis Carrel, "Physiological Time," *Science*, vol. 74 (December 18, 1931): 618.

56 Llewellys F. Barker, "Ageing from the Point of View of the Clinician," in *Problems*, p. 740; E. V. Cowdry, "Ageing of Tissue Fluids," ibid., pp. 686, 690; Cannon, "Homeostasis," pp. 598–606.

57 Lawrence K. Frank, "Culture and Personality," in *John Dewey: Philosopher of Science and Freedom*, ed. Sidney Hook (New York: The Dial Press, 1950), p. 88.

58 Quoted in Daniel J. Wilson, "Science and the Crisis of Confidence in American Philosophy," *Transactions of the Charles S. Perice Society*, vol. 23 (1987): 235–59. For more on this theme, see J. S. Haldane's Gifford Lectures, published as *The Sciences and Philosophy* (London: Hodder & Stoughton Ltd., 1929), p. 183; and Charles Hartshorne, "The Parallel Development of Method in Physics and Psychology," *Philosophy of Science*, vol. 1 (1934):

Dewey's introduction to *Problems of Ageing* bears the marks of a prolific writer still capable of dashing off 8,000 words one day and discarding them the next. Privately, he confided that his critics thought "that if I have ever had two ideas that hung together it was a piece of good luck."[59] Dewey's analysis of the gerontologic problem, hastily written, merits careful scrutiny. The essay builds on Dewey's lifetime quest to integrate iconoclastic thinking and Progressive action in scientific ways. "There has never been a time since philosophy began when it was not defined either as a comprehensive synthesis of all science, or as a criticism, rectification, and extension of the partial and hence distorted conceptions of the special sciences, or as an analysis of these conceptions and of the methods that attended them with a view to discovering the ultimate traits of existence," Dewey wrote in 1902. "The philosophy of a period always is in the science of the time."[60]

True to the scientific, philosophical, and pragmatic modes of Progressive discourse, Dewey affirmed that "ageing" was indeed a dynamic, interactive, multifaceted "problem":

> There is a problem and one of scope having no precedent in human history. Biological processes are at the roots of the problems and of the methods of solving them, but the biological processes take place in economic, political, and cultural contexts. They are inextricably interwoven with these contexts so that one reacts upon the other in all sorts of intricate ways. We need to know the ways in which social contexts react back into biological processes as well as to know the ways in which the biological processes condition social life. This is the problem to which attention is invited.[61]

In order to put the old-age problem into context, Dewey invoked a wide range of concurrent developments. He referred to the concatenation of falling infant mortality rates, longer life expectancies, new ways of organizing industry and providing welfare, the rise of political groups that demanded (often conflicting) rights for the young and the aged, and the pervasive ignorance concerning the psychology and sociology of growing old. As was his style, Dewey presupposed that all aspects of the problem under inquiry were interrelated, though he understood that the connections would not be evident until further analysis and synthesis.[62] This meant that gerontology

455ff. Bridgman stressed this theme in a revised edition of *The Logic of Modern Physics* (New York: Macmillan, 1938).

59 Dewey quoted in Robert B. Westbrook, *John Dewey and American Democracy* (Ithaca, NY: Cornell University Press, 1991), p. 496. For other details, see Max Eastman, "John Dewey," *Atlantic* (December 1941): 671–85; Sidney Hook, *John Dewey: An Intellectual Portrait* (New York: John Day Co., 1939), p. 20.

60 John Dewey, "Some Connections of Science and Philosophy" (1902), first published in *Encounter*, vol. 49 (August 1977): 77–82.

61 John Dewey, "Introduction," in *Problems*, p. xxvi.

62 James Gouinlock, *John Dewey's Philosophy of Value* (Atlantic Highlands, NJ: Humanities 1972), p. 131; J.E. Tiles, *Dewey* (London: Routledge, 1988), pp. 22, 115.

required theories and data that explicated the interaction of "the relation of the biological and the cultural"[63] forces that affected all aspects of growing older. Because the "foundation of any serious consideration" was provided by "biological and related chemical knowledge," Dewey recommended probing first the structural and functional dynamics that take place at the cellular, molecular, organic and systemic levels. Once basic processes of human aging were better understood, the dynamics of these developments had to be connected with the fluid interplay that occurred among psychological, social, cultural, and environmental factors. Linking different types of data was possible, Dewey felt, as long as one shared his assumption that "the subject-matter of social problems is existential. In the broad sense of 'natural,' social sciences are, therefore, branches of natural science."[64]

Dewey thus confirmed the importance of taking a multidisciplinary approach to understand the problems of aging. In the execution phase, he extolled the merits of employing modes of analysis that dared to cross disciplinary boundaries in order to take in the "big picture." In *Experience and Education* (1938), he declared that "problems are the stimulus to thinking,"[65] a way of getting closure on critical intellectual issues. Contemporaries agreed. "An important part of a scientific investigation often lies in the recognition and the formulation of the problem and in the working out of a definite plan of attack," observed Nobel laureate Irving Langmuir.[66] Grappling with new problems required flexibility, because key questions rarely fit into existing ways of apprehending experience. Progress in every endeavor depended on adhering to scientific logic, observing research canons, analyzing data statistically, and subjecting findings to impartial, peer review. The most efficacious strategy for nurturing new lines of inquiry, in Dewey's opinion, did not entail reducing all insight to mathematical equations, or treating physics as the paradigmatic science. "A new larger field is formed, in which new energies are released, and to which new qualities appertain." No wonder Dewey seemed to delight more in the way the process unfolds than in how it actually reaches closure. "Regulation, conscious direction and science imply ability to smooth over the rough junctures, and to form by translation and substitution a homogenous medium."[67] Scientific methods provided such a medium.

63 Dewey, "Introduction," in *Problems*, p. xxii.
64 John Dewey, *Logic* (New York: Holt, 1938), p. 487. There are many parallels between ideas Dewey elaborated in this book and those that appear in his introduction to Cowdry's *Problems of Ageing*. They were composed contemporaneously. See, for example, his discussion of how a "problem" emerges, pp. 25–33, 104–7.
65 John Dewey, *Experience and Education* (New York: Macmillan, 1938), p. 96.
66 Irving Langmuir, "Science as a Guide to Life," *Sigma Xi Quarterly*, vol. 22 (March 1934): 82. Sociology was established as a problem-solving discipline. See Albion W. Small, "The Methodology of the Social Problem," *American Journal of Sociology*, vol. 4 (1899): 113–44.
67 John Dewey, *Experience and Nature* (Chicago: Open Court Publishing Company, 1926),

Dewey believed that choosing the right mix of methods would ensure researchers on aging intellectual breadth without sacrificing rigor. "The special technical problems of ageing are all connected with processes of growth," he asserted. "Science and philosophy meet on common ground in their joint interest in discovering the processes of normal growth and in the institution of conditions which will favor and support ever continued growth."[68] Scientific method was "the only authentic means" of coming to grips with "everyday experiences" such as growing older. A certain ambiguity lurks beneath Dewey's statements. Adherence to the canons of scientific method was indispensable, but the application of science required a measure of self-reflexivity. Hence philosophy and science not only could be fused in the process of discovery, but in Dewey's opinion, they *had* to be joined. Philosophy would become more analytically rigorous, science less linear. Gerontologists, generally committed to developing a science along positivist lines, only recently have begun to take a "critical" stance toward science, which Dewey considered so indispensable at the outset.

Science as a path to discovery, according to Dewey, transformed both means and ends in the process: "The problem of knowledge is the problem of discovery of methods for carrying on this enterprise of redirection. It is a problem never ended, always in process."[69] Dewey's emphasis on method's central role in scientific inquiry was widely shared. "The edifice of science is built of materials which must be drawn from sources," declared Dean William Welch of the Johns Hopkins medical school in 1907. "The deeper we can lay the foundations and penetrate into the nature of things, the closer are the workers drawn together, the clearer their community of purpose and the more significant to the welfare of mankind the upbuilding of natural knowledge."[70] As researchers and practitioners tried to gauge gerontology's cross-disciplinary promise and to strike a proper balance between scientific complexity and practical relevance, it made sense not to delineate the field's perimeters too hastily. Despite his penchant for taking bold risks, Dewey realized that a "field of knowledge can not be attacked

---

p. 272. Reference to physics on p. 139. As we shall see in the next section, not all scientists and philosophers agreed with Dewey on these points. He himself changed his views on the place of mathematics in scientific inquiry. Compare Dewey's "Galton's Statistical Methods," *Publications of the American Statistical Association*, vol. 1 (September 1889): 331–4, with *The Philosophy of John Dewey*, ed. Paul Arthur Schilpp (Evanston, IL: Northwestern University, 1939), pp. 239, 342.

68 Dewey, "Introduction," in *Problems*, pp. xxvi–xxvii.

69 John Dewey, *The Quest for Certainty* (1929) reprinted in *John Dewey: The Later Works*, ed. Jo Ann Boydston (Carbondale: Southern Illinois University Press, 1984), 4: 236. See also, idem, *Experience and Education*, p. 111; idem, "Science as Subject-Matter and as Method," *Science*, vol. 31 (January 28, 1910): 121–7; Daniel J. Wilson, *Science, Community, and the Transformation of American Philosophy, 1860–1930* (Chicago: University of Chicago Press, 1984), pp. 2–6, 175.

70 Quoted in Hastings, *Crossing Boundaries*, p. 233.

en masse. . . . Detailed aspects and phases of these problems must be discriminated into still lesser elements. A degree of specialization is a necessity of scientific advance."[71]

Scientific method not only explicated how parts fit together but, to Dewey's mind, it also enabled social engineers to apply their knowledge in real-life situations. Knowing that "many perplexing problems now attendant upon human old age have a psychological-social origin" rendered artificial distinctions between "basic" and "applied" research or between a scientist's "personal" or "professional" commitments. "Recognition of the seriousness of the problem as well as application of the knowledge that is already in our possession is impeded by traditional ideas, intellectual habits and institutional customs," Dewey warned. Reifying outmoded principles and methods would impede research on aging. "There is urgent need for a philosophy of personal and institutional life that is consequent with present knowledge."[72] John Dewey at eighty saw scientists' nascent interest in gerontology as part of a broader movement to make "scientific insight . . . an indispensable instrument of free and active participation in modern social life."[73] Problem solving was a social act that shaped and transformed to promote individuals' moral growth in an ever-changing world.

The quest for a unified gerontologic science proves elusive at the outset

Cowdry, Dewey, and Frank deserve much credit for their efforts to seek common ground, a "homogenous medium" for the diverse viewpoints about *Problems of Ageing* expressed by their colleagues. In the process, they self-consciously laid the foundations for creating a *multidisciplinary* gerontologic venture. To understand basic processes of aging, it was not enough to assemble experts from different disciplines. They had to create a shared vocabulary and to translate ideas from one domain to another. As Lawrence Frank expressed it,

> simple cause and effect relationships can scarcely be considered in such total organic interactions; they must be supplemented, or perhaps replaced, by a broader conceptual picture of the functioning organism as

71 John Dewey, "The Supreme Intellectual Obligation," *Science*, vol. 79 (March 16, 1934): 240–1. "The real function of a specialty was essentially to facilitate intensive study of the subject and to perfect technique," declared Humphrey Rolleston in "The Treatment of Venereal Diseases," *Lancet*, vol. 1 (February 12, 1927), p. 356.

72 Dewey, "Introduction" in *Problems*, p. xxvi.

73 John Dewey, *The School and Society* (Chicago: University of Chicago Press, 1900), p. 21; idem, *The Public and Its Problems* (New York: Holt, 1927), p. 174. See also, Alfonso J. Damico, *Individuality and Community* (Gainesville: University Presses of Florida, 1978), p. 31; Timothy V. Kaufman-Osburn, "John Dewey and the Liberal Science of Community," *Journal of Politics*, vol. 46 (1984): 1,163.

a "field" (to borrow the term from physics) in which the totality and the parts are dynamically interrelated and therefore are continuously reacting to each other and to the environment. The already demonstrated fruitfulness of the "field" concept in embryology indicates its probable future service in the study of ageing.[74]

Frank elaborated on this point in the second edition of *Problems of Ageing* (1942): "The problem is multi-dimensional and will require for its solution not only a multidisciplinary approach but also a synoptic correlation of diverse findings and viewpoints."[75]

The challenge of gerontologic inquiry from the very beginning, as Lawrence Frank and his colleagues keenly understood, was to attract an excellent cohort of investigators who were willing and able to cross intellectual frontiers. In a field so open and unexplored, plenty of room was envisioned for both narrow scientific specialization and for bold experimentation in designing programs for the elderly. But in order to show how parts fit together and to detect holes in the whole, there was a need to recruit and train experts who, having mastered the theories and techniques of at least one discipline, could grapple with the intrinsic and extrinsic dimensions of aging in scientific and practical terms. In retrospect, thanks to a fortuitous set of historical circumstances and the shrewd negotiation of a scientific opportunity, scientists and administrators maximized in at least three ways the likelihood that research on aging would succeed.

First, the quality of *Problems of Ageing* made gerontology appealing to "stars" and intellectuals, not charlatans and second-rate minds. Scientists communicated with one another after the first edition of the volume went out of print. Enough contributors maintained an interest in the biomedical puzzles of aging to form a "subfield" of biomedical specialists in gerontology. Only four social scientists attended the 1937 Woods Hole Conference, but sociologists, anthropologists, and especially psychologists quickly joined the small band of researchers of aging. Three of the five charter members of the Gerontology Society had contributed articles to Cowdry's volume, as had half of the members of the Society's first Council.[76] Because productive scholars literally in their prime did much of the spadework, gerontologic interests immediately branched out, as new possibilities were explored. By continuing to assess and cite each other's work and by teaching students ideas and techniques pertinent to the field, a "critical mass"

---

74 Frank, "Foreword," in *Problems*, p. xvi. See also, F. S. C. Northrop, "The Method and Theories of Physical Science in Their Bearings upon Biological Organization," *Growth*, 2d suppl. (1940): 127–54; and *infra.*, Introduction.

75 Lawrence K. Frank, "Foreword to the Second Edition," in *Problems of Ageing*, 2d ed., Edmund Vincent Cowdry (Baltimore: Williams & Wilkins, 1942), p. xv.

76 Organization Section, *Journal of Gerontology*, vol. 1 (1946): 134–6. For more on this, see Chapter 4.

of first-rate minds existed that was sufficient to create the institutional fabric necessary to sustain progress.[77]

Second, gerontology's architects tried to craft a language that would facilitate the search for unifying themes. Consider, for instance, the provocative, often metaphoric, uses made of the term *homeostasis*. Although the concept was anticipated by Claude Bernard, a nineteenth-century physiologist, it was popularized in scientific circles by Walter Cannon, who investigated self-regulatory processes in the digestive system, then in adrenals and sympathetic systems, and then in discussing the body's autonomic features in general. When he revised his influential study, *The Wisdom of the Body*, Cannon added a chapter on "the aging of homeostatic mechanisms," which incorporated ideas refined through interactions with Cowdry's group.[78] Social scientists at the University of Chicago and elsewhere began to follow Cannon's lead and invoke homeostasis as a way of linking changes across biological, psychological, and cultural domains. Like the "field" of aging itself, the term's allusiveness permitted users to refer to complex, dynamic processes simultaneously occurring at several levels in different systems.[79]

Third, as Cowdry and Macy officials organized the Woods Hole Conference and designed *Problems of Ageing*, they did not formulaically follow a set script. They tried neither to anticipate nor to control all contingencies.

77 On the initial predominance of biomedical interest, see Cowdry, "Woods Hole Conference," *Scientific Monthly*, vol. 45 (August 1937): 189–91; "Puzzle of Old Age Gets Brand New Answer," *Newsweek*, vol. 10 (October 25, 1937): 41. For current ideas about how social-intellectual traits of founding members affect organizational growth, see Michael Mulkay, "Three Models of Scientific Development," *Sociological Review*, vol. 28 (1975): 509–26; Daryl E. Chubin, "Conceptualization of Scientific Specialties," *Sociological Quarterly*, vol. 17 (Autumn 1976): 448–76; Alan Bayer and Jeffrey Dutton, "Career Age and Research-Professional Activities of Academic Scientists," *Journal of Higher Education*, vol. 43 (May/June 1977): 259–82; Stephen Cole, "Age and Scientific Performance," *American Journal of Sociology*, vol. 84 (1979): 958–77.

78 Walter Bradford Cannon, *The Wisdom of the Body* (1932; New York: Norton, 1939), pp. xviii, 203, 287; idem, "The Body Physiologic and the Body Politic," *Science*, vol. 93 (January 3, 1941): 1–10; idem, *The Way of an Investigator* (New York: Hafner Publishing, 1965), pp. 219–22; Donald Fleming, "Walter B. Cannon and Homeostasis," *Social Research*, vol. 51 (Autumn 1984): 309–40.

79 For the way that terms such as "homeostasis" bridge cultures, creating "interfields," see Henrika Kuklick, "A 'Scientific Revolution,'" *Sociological Inquiry*, vol. 43 (1973): 3–22; Hamilton Cravens, *The Triumph of Evolution* (Philadelphia: University of Pennsylvania Press, 1978), pp. 218–22; and Nancy L. Maull, "Unifying Science Without Reduction," *Studies in History and Philosophy of Science*, vol. 8 (1977): 144–62. Parallels might also be noted between Cannon's term and Talcott Parson's notion of "functionalism," a concept that influenced social scientific definitions of gerontology. See infra, Chapter 3. Yet not everyone was enthusiastic. Cowdry, for instance, did not like the term "homeostasis," noting local "disequilibria" in groups of cells and tissues. See James E. Birren, "History of the Psychology of Aging," *TG*, vol. 1 (June 1961): 75.

That said, there were striking similarities between what U.S. pioneers' advancing research on aging tried to accomplish and what pathfinders in other domains of the sociology of knowledge were doing in Europe at the time. On both sides of the Atlantic, those who had achieved eminence in traditional fields were often receptive to advancing multidisciplinary work.[80] There are instructive parallels in the process leading to the publication of Cowdry's *Problems of Ageing* and the new empirical connections made in Ludwik Fleck's *Genesis and Development of a Scientific Fact* (1935). Fleck's account of how Germans tried to conceptualize and eradicate syphilis offered "from the grab bag of laboratory life ... insights that are not always logically compatible and that frequently scrape only the surface of historical and contemporary evidence, but they are nonetheless redolent of these links that tie our time to his."[81] In both instances, teams of scientists reviewed classic theories and past experiments to determine their value as "guidelines." Rather than rely on journals to give scientific direction, these self-appointed members of a scholarly vanguard designed a vademecum, a handbook to reflect their collective wisdom and to serve as the basis for future work. From their "proto-ideas" the Germans organized what they called a "thought collective," that is, "a community of persons exchanging ideas or maintaining intellectual interaction."[82] Fleck (like Cowdry, Frank, and Dewey) underscored the importance of facilitating a scientific group's deliberations in order to reach consensus about boundaries and to agree about where they disagreed. Individual differences of opinion mattered, as they do in all stages of scientific development, but for a field to emerge, some basis for consensus had to be laid.

Some of gerontology's founders envisioned that the basis for consensus in research on aging would rest on high standards of scientific excellence. They expected gerontology to evolve into a unified field of inquiry with a common set of methodologies. Few, however, went so far as to participate in a more ambitious German–U.S. project, the "unity of science movement." Otto Neurath first started talking to colleagues such as Nils Bohr, Rudolph Carnap, and Albert Einstein about compiling an *International Encyclopedia of Unified Science* in the 1920s. Dewey wrote an essay with a theme as generic as its title – "Unity of Science as a Social Problem" – for volume I (1938), but his contribution to the next volume ("A Theory

80 A study of British scholars, for instance, indicates that distinguished physicists and chemists were most likely to succeed in migrating to new areas of expertise prior to World War I. Roy M. Macleod and E. Kay Andrews, "Scientific Careers of 1851 Exhibition Scholars," *Nature*, vol. 218 (June 15, 1968): 1,011–16.

81 From a review of a 1979 reprint of Ludwick Fleck's *Genesis and Development of a Scientific Fact*, quoted in Daryl E. Chubin, *Sociology of Sciences* (New York: Garland Publishing, 1983), p. 24.

82 Ludwik Fleck, *Genesis and Development of a Scientific Fact* (1935; Chicago: University of Chicago Press, 1979), p. 39.

of Valuation"), as well as private notes, indicate that *his* program for unifying science at the time diverged considerably from Neurath's and from schemes circulating among members of the Vienna Circle.[83] Indeed, a decade after the publication of Cowdry's *Problems of Ageing*, Dewey acknowledged that "scientific inquiry is still so recent as to be immature and inchoate." Similarly, he conceded that the clusters of ideas and allusions that he and Lawrence Frank attributed to the term *field* were in flux: "The physicist's uses . . . are undergoing reconstructions, and the definite correspondence needed for behavioral application can not be established."[84]

Dewey told friends gathered for his ninetieth birthday that "only in the last two years have I come to see the real drift and hang of the various positions I have taken."[85] The admission was as disingenuous as it was disarming, for Dewey had been battling critics for decades. Not all friends shared his faith in progress, in the efficacy of accumulating scientific knowledge. Some found his conception of human interaction reductionist. Dewey's support of intellectuals-as-activists disturbed CCNY colleagues like philosopher Morris Cohen: "Ardor for social reform is admirable in any one, but detachment and a critical attitude are the special duties of those who as scientists or philosophers have to maintain the canons of scientific integrity."[86] Aspects of Dewey's philosophy were subject to fierce attack by

83 Otto Neurath, Rudolph Carnap, and Charles Morris, eds., *Foundations of the Unity of Science* (1938; Chicago: University of Chicago Press, 1969), I: ix–xi, 29–38. For Dewey, see R. W. Sleeper, *The Necessity of Pragmatism* (New Haven: Yale University Press, 1986), pp. 168–9; Ronald C. Tobey, *The American Ideology of National Science, 1919–1930* (Pittsburgh: University of Pittsburgh Press, 1971), p. 90; C.H. Hockett, "Biophysics, Linguistics, and the Unity of Science," *American Scientist*, vol. 36 (1948): 558–72.

84 First quotation in John Dewey, "Philosophy's Future in Our Scientific Age," *Commentary* (October 1949): 391; second in John Dewey and Arthur F. Bentley, *Knowing and the Known* (1949; Great Barrington, MA: Behavioral Research Council, 1973), p. 176. For a similar odyssey, see Hans Reichenbach, *Experience and Predictions* (Chicago: University of Chicago Press, 1938). Reichenbach is interesting for three reasons. While at the University of Berlin, he was instrumental in establishing the Unity of Science movement. Second, after a stint in Istanbul, he migrated to the University of Chicago. Third, his ideas influenced a seminal piece by Maria Reichenbach and Ruth Anna Mathers, "The Place of Time and Aging in the Natural Sciences and Scientific Philosophy," which James E. Birren solicited for *The Handbook of Aging and the Individual* (Chicago: University of Chicago Press, 1959), pp. 43–80. See *infra*, Chapter 3, and Charles Morris, "On the History of the International Encyclopedia of Unified Science," *Synthese*, vol. 12. (1960): 517–21.

85 Quoted in *Dewey and His Critics*, ed. Sidney Morgenbesser (New York: Journal of Philosophy, Inc., 1977), p. 9.

86 Morris R. Cohen, "Some Difficulties in Dewey's Anthropocentric Naturalism," *The Philosophical Review*, vol. 49 (1940): 228. See also, S. N. Eisenstadt, "The Classic Sociology of Knowledge and Beyond," *Minerva*, vol. 25 (Spring 1987): 81; David Hollinger, "The Knower and the Artificer," *American Quarterly*, vol. 39 (1987): 37, 45. And had Johns Hopkins followed through on a plan to close its Department of Psychology in the Depression, then a tradition started by G. Stanley Hall and elaborated by his student Dewey might have been extinguished at the very moment it was giving shape to the gerontologic

even friendly critics on many grounds. Little wonder, then, that gerontology's founders found it difficult to incorporate Dewey's recommendations as they tried to impose coherence on their fledgling field.

To unify research on aging would entail negotiating differences in individual scholars' interests, dealing with data incommensurability, and counterbalancing departmental rivalries. It was a formidable challenge in light of multiplying disciplinary traditions and loyalties. Pressures to compartmentalize information in the 1930s competed with the scientists' urge to pursue knowledge for its own sake, much less the desire of some activists to remake the world through the synthesis of generalizable knowledge. This conflict pervaded all scholarly communities. The virtues of basic research were pitted against the payoffs of applied research. Irving Langmuir, who won a Nobel prize in chemistry while working in the labs of General Electric, believed that "pure" research yield greater payoffs than research designed to produce results. Other colleagues focused on the tension between generalists and specialists. They stressed the advantages of putting biologists in physics labs, of firing imagination by capitalizing on the plurality of sciences.[87] This line of argument aroused antipathy. Sociologist William F. Ogburn posited that sciences grew only through differentiation. Science, which represented "a revolt against the apparent wholeness of things," perforce was at "loggerheads with common sense" and cooperative ventures doomed to fail in the face of ignorance. "No progress can be made by observation or experiment," Abraham Flexner asserted, "unless one's field is circumscribed."[88] Still others opted for the via media, proposing (apparently with no sense of irony) that the politics of science resembled the League of Nations or, invoking the theory of natural selection, that specialization could be pushed to the limits.[89] Everyone agreed that links were needed; the disagreements centered on how many and of what type.

imagination. See Stewart H. Hulse and Bert F. Green, Jr., eds., *One Hundred Years of Psychological Research in America* (Baltimore: Johns Hopkins University Press, 1986), p. 42.

87 Irving Langmuir, "Fundamental Research and Its Human Value," *Scientific Monthly*, vol. 46 (April 1938): 358–65; idem, "Unforeseeable Results of Research," in *The Scientists Speak*, ed. Warren Weaver (New York: Boni & Gaer, 1947), pp. 338–41; Austin L. Porterfield, *Creative Factors in Scientific Research* (Durham, NC: Duke University Press, 1941); T.H. Morgan, "The Relation of Biology to Physics," *Science*, vol. 65 (March 4, 1927): 213.

88 William F. Ogburn, "The Folkways of a Scientific Sociology," *Proceedings of the American Sociological Society*, vol. 24 (1930): 1–11; Abraham Flexner, *Universities* (New York: Oxford University Press, 1930), p. 114; Harold J. Laski, *The Dangers of Obedience and Other Essays* (New York: Harper & Brothers, 1930), pp. 154–7; H. Levy, "What Is Science?" in *Science in the Changing World*, ed. Mary Adams (New York: The Century Company, 1933), pp. 51–3.

89 E. E. Slosson, "The Philosophy of General Science," *School and Society*, vol. 20 (December 27, 1924): 799; H. G. Wells, Julian S. Huxley, and G. P. Wells, *The Science of Life* (New

Rationality and careful measurement, Dewey believed, were enough to bridge the natural and social sciences. Recent methodological developments lent credibility to his views on the philosophy of science. Scientists in the 1930s were hopeful that the promising advances in probability theory would lend to breakthroughs in theory building. New techniques and modern equipment enhanced both the capacity and the reliability of scientific observation. "In Nature is actualized the ideal of mathematical simplicity," declared Albert Einstein.[90] But many who wrote about methodological issues took a contrary position, contending that methods were domain-specific. What was quantifiable in one field did not count in another. Experimental methods appropriate in a biological lab could not be replicated, certainly not experientially, in a hospital or old-age home. "A method is not scientific just because it has been successful in one field," physicist F. S. C. Northrop noted. "It is scientific only for a given type of problem."[91] Devising new scales and scoring devices or elaborate experiments with more sophisticated equipment did not invariably lead to conceptual breakthroughs.

Methodological skirmishes thus revealed deeper schisms that belied collegial claims that all faculty enjoyed equal standing within the community of scholars. Before 1940 doing research in the natural sciences clearly was more prestigious than working in the social sciences. Physics reigned supreme. Sociology and psychology still were considered immature theoretically and methodologically.[92] Consequently, fealty to scientific canons

York: Doubleday, Doran, 1931), vol. 2: 634–635; Herbert Blumer, "Science without Concepts," *American Journal of Sociology, vol.* 36 (1931): 515–33.

90 Albert Einstein, "On the Method of Theoretical Physics," *Philosophy of Science*, vol. 1 (1934): 167. See also, Percy W. Bridgman, "New Vision of Science," *Harper's*, vol. 158 (March 1929): 444–6; Stuart A. Rice, ed., *Methods in Social Science* (Chicago: University of Chicago Press, 1931); Max Planck, *Where is Science Going?* (New York: Norton, 1932), p. 63; Michael Oakeshott, *Experience and Its Mode* (1933; New York: Cambridge University Press, 1966), p. 245; T. Swann Harding, "All Science Is One," *American Journal of Sociology*, vol. 41 (June 1936): 492–503; Alexis Carrel and Charles A. Lindbergh, *The Culture of Organs* (New York: Paul B. Hoeber, 1938); Harold Jeffreys, *Theory of Probability* (Oxford: Clarendon Press, 1939); Joseph Mayer, *Social Science Principles in Light of Scientific Method* (Durham, NC: Duke University Press, 1941); Smith, *Behaviorism*, p. 308.

91 Quoted in *Eleven Twenty-Six*, ed. Louis Wirth (1940; New York: Arno Press, 1974), p. 271. See also Herbert Blumer, "The Problem of the Concept in Social Psychology," *American Journal of Sociology*, vol. 45 (1940): 708; F. Stuart Chapin, "The Experimental Method and Sociology," *Scientific Monthly*, vol. 4 (1919): 133; idem, "The Meaning of Measurement in Sociology," *Proceedings of the American Sociological Society*, vol. 24 (1930): 83, 89, 94; Robert MacIver, "Is Sociology a Natural Science?" ibid., 25 (1931): 25–35.

92 On physics as queen, see J. F. Brown, "Freud and the Scientific Method," *Philosophy of Science*, vol. 1 (1934): 324; Howard Becker, "Limits of Sociological Positivism," *Journal of Social Philosophy*, vol. 6 (1941): 362; J. G. Morawski, "Organizing Knowledge and Behavior at Yale's Institute of Human Relations," *Isis*, vol. 77 (1986): 236. On the social

would not guarantee comity in gerontology. As a president of the American Psychological Association (APA) put it in 1940, "Methodism as the sole requirement of science means that all the faithful crowd onto a carpet of prayer, and with their logical shears cut more and more inches of the rug, permitting fewer and fewer aspirants to enjoy status."[93]

There were other sources of contention besides disagreements over methods and the jockeying for power that occurred between biomedical scientists and other investigators. The founding cohort of researchers on aging debated whether applied research should be a component of gerontology. Lawrence Frank felt that scientists had a special responsibility to help the general public understand the meaning of human life. Since his days at LSRM, he had stressed the need to study the "values" that guided day-to-day interactions. Dewey shared Frank's interest in applying science to everyday situations. In fact, Dewey's concern with "the problem of the relation of psychology to the social sciences—and through them to social practice, to life itself" dated back at least to his 1899 APA presidential address.[94] Two contributors to *Problems of Ageing*, Carlson and Ivy, were sponsors of the American Association of Scientific Workers, which mobilized reform-minded scientists during the New Deal. Nevertheless, many scientists in the 1930s were disturbed by such declarations of scientists' responsibility for the public good. "Science and action are two entirely different processes," William Fielding Ogburn contended, stipulating that social researchers should be concerned with discovering, not doing something with, new knowledge. Positions like Ogburn's impelled Robert S. Lynd to ask his colleagues to reconsider their goals in *Knowledge for What?* (1939).[95] Still, some investigators must have legitimately pondered what an immature field like gerontology yet had to offer policymakers by way of basic information and policy recommendations.

sciences, see Henrika Kuklick, "Boundary Maintenance in American Sociology," *Journal of the History of the Behavioral Sciences*, vol. 16 (1980): 201–19; William Fielding Ogburn, and Alexander Goldensweiser, eds., *The Social Sciences and Their Interrelations* (Boston: Houghton Mifflin, 1927); Ernest Becker, *The Lost Science of Man* (New York: George Braziller, 1971), pp. 26, 60, 108.

93 Gordon Allport, "The Psychologist's Frame of Reference," *Psychological Bulletin*, vol. 37 (1940): 1–28.

94 Frank quoted in Benjamin C. Gruenberg, *Science and the Public Mind* (New York: McGraw-Hill, 1935); Dewey in *American Psychology in Historical Perspective*, ed. Ernest R. Hilgard (Washington, DC: American Psychological Association, 1978), p. 65.

95 Peter J. Kuznick, *Beyond the Laboratory* (Chicago: University of Chicago Press, 1987); Ogburn, quoted in Wirth, *Eleven Twenty-Six*, p. 293; Alfred E. Cohn, *Medicine, Science, and Art* (Chicago: University of Chicago Press, 1931); David E. Leary, "Wundt and After," *Journal of the History of the Behavioral Sciences*, vol. 13 (1979): 231–41; Don S. Kirschner, *The Paradox of Professionalism* (Westport, CT: Greenwood Press, 1986), pp. 63, 150; Martin Bulmer, "Support for Sociology in the 1920s" *American Sociologist*, vol. 17 (1982): 190.

The institutional founders of gerontology, in short, had to make some tough choices. Did issues surrounding the aging and/or the aged truly constitute a distinct, bounded "problem?" Could investigators accommodate competing theories and utilize methods across the biomedical and social sciences? Would those who wanted to do applied research be viewed as different from, and probably deemed inferior to, more traditional scholars? Or should scholars who pursued fundamental questions about the finitude of life and death try to translate ideas into action in the social arena?

Debating such issues quickly become a major activity in gerontologic circles. Similar exercises of disciplinary narcissism took place in nearly every academic unit before World War II. Sociologists worried that the Lynds' *Middletown* (1929) and *Recent Social Trends* (1933) diluted the discipline's credibility by bifurcating its academic and popular audiences. Similarly, gatekeepers of political science, the history of science, and international studies stopped welcoming everybody to their ranks as they steadily enclosed their respective specialties. Heated debates over theory and praxis occurred in literature, history, and biochemistry.[96] Secular trends within psychology concurrently featured intramural disputes over the uses of biological, physical and behavioral paradigms; recurring boundary disputes with philosophers and clinicians; and anxiety over what quacks, popularists and faddishness did to the field. Such conflicts soon bedeviled research on aging.

Gerontology began auspiciously. First-rate minds and savvy foundation leaders grappled with big issues at its creation. The popular media picked up on the significance of *Problems of Ageing*. But, as Cowdry himself noted, "There purely physical, chemical and biologic mechanisms of aging are just beginning to be studied. There are vast fields as yet totally unexplored. Nearly equal is our ignorance of the psychiatric, emotional and sociological aspects of aging."[97] To attract the interest of the scientific community in understanding the basic processes of aging, the field had to offer more than big questions and professional challenges. Historians of science remind us that seminal ideas necessary for discipline building are found in many places over a prolonged period of time; few, however, get off the ground.

96 Arnold Thackray and Robert K. Merton, "On Discipline Building," *Isis*, vol. 63 (December 1972): 473–94; Robert E. Kohler, *From Medical Chemistry to Biological Chemistry* (New York: Cambridge University Press, 1982); David M. Ricci, *The Tragedy of Political Science* (New Haven, CT: Yale University Press, 1984); Robert A. McCaughey, *International Studies and Academic Enterprise* (New York: Columbia University Press, 1984); Gerald Graf, *Professing Literature* (Chicago: University Press, 1987); Peter Novick, *That Noble Dream* (New York: Cambridge University Press, 1987).

97 Edmund Vincent Cowdry, "We Grow Old," *Scientific Monthly*, vol. 50 (January 1940): 53. See also Roy Helton, "Old People," *Harper's Magazine* (October 1939): 454; F. R. Moulton, "New Plans for Related Articles," *Scientific Monthly*, vol. 50 (January 1940): 95–6; "Attack on Old Age Problems," *Science News Letter*, vol. 38 (December 1940): 356.

The schism between humanistic and scientific scholarship that took place in the 1920s, moreover, had lasting repercussions for conceptual and methodological advances in "science" in the United States.[98] Among other things it made multidisciplinary collaborations difficult to sustain intellectually and organizationally. For gerontology to grow, institutions needed to be formed, ones that enabled scientists to take advantage of local resources and were deemed consonant – but not slavishly so – with the spirit of the times.

98 Joseph Ben-David and Randall Collins, "Social Factors in the Origins of a New Science," *American Sociological Review*, vol. 31 (August 1966): 451–66; John Higham, "The Schism in American Scholarship," *American Historical Review*, vol. 72 (October 1966): 1–21.

3

Establishing outposts for multidisciplinary research on aging

REFLECTING ON *The Way of the Investigator*, Walter Bradford Cannon identified certain intellectual qualities and technical competencies that every medical researcher should possess. "The investigator in biological science should have, besides a knowledge of electrical apparatus and its uses, a good grounding in other aspects of physics and also chemistry."[1] In addition to this, complex statistical methods were "a valuable adjunct to the biologist's mental equipment" in order to measure phenomena as accurately as possible. Cannon felt that "serendipity" made multidisciplinary approaches efficacious in the biological and physical sciences. Solutions to "urgent, difficult and apparently baffling social problems are likely to be made by minds characterized by learning and liberality," the Harvard physiologist, who was one of gerontology's architects, noted. "Quite unforeseen possibilities will unexpectedly spring forth."

Cannon's own career as a researcher, teacher, and philosopher of science attests to the importance of intellectual curiosity, dedication and "unforeseen possibilities" in the life of an investigator. Family friends and neighbors in St. Paul, Minnesota, made it financially possible for Cannon to attend Harvard; he graduated summa cum laude in 1896. Upon receiving his M.D. four years later, he was appointed an instructor of physiology at Harvard Medical School; from 1906 until his retirement in 1942, he served as George Higginson Professor of Physiology. Cannon presented his first research papers while in medical school: Using primitive X-ray equipment, he was the first person to study the motor activity of the alimentary tract

---

[1] Walter Bradford Cannon, M.D., *The Way of an Investigator: A Scientist's Experiences in Medical Research* (New York: Hafner Publishing Company, 1965), p. 38; Walter Bradford Cannon, "The Role of Change in Discovery," *Scientific Monthly*, vol. 50 (1940): 204-9. Cf. Arthur Kornberg, *For Love of Enzymes* (Cambridge: Harvard University Press, 1989), pp. 34, 267, 285.

uncomplicated by anesthesia. The physiologist subsequently extended his inquiries to gastroenterology, endocrinology, and studies of muscle, nerves, the nervous system, and emotional behavior. He later developed assays for adrenal secretion. Equally important, as we learned in Chapter 2, were the postulates that Cannon formulated about homeostasis – ideas that he refined as he studied processes of senescence toward the end of his career.[2]

Many of gerontology's other pioneers shared Cannon's conviction that formidable intelligence, methodological sophistication, and prior success in collaborative ventures were necessary to launch a new cross-disciplinary field. They too recognized serendipity's role in advancing knowledge, but having an agenda was also vital. Successful inquiries had to be carefully structured and constantly refined in accordance with scientific canons if they were to flourish. Rather than try to impose a single vision for gerontology, researchers on aging at the outset acknowledged the plurality of ideas and methods that existed. Thus, in 1941, two years after the publication of E. V. Cowdry's *Problems of Ageing*, five contributors to that volume (Cannon, Cowdry, A. Baird Hastings, Clive McCay, and Jean Oliver) endorsed a proposal by Dr. Edward J. Stieglitz, a clinician with the U.S. Public Health Service, that the field conceptually be divided into three areas: the biology of senescence, geriatric medicine, and the sociology of an aging population. "These three facets, which might be likened to the application of three perspectives to a single problem or entity, are so intimately related that they cannot actually be separated."[3] But Stieglitz's three-part division did not generate the smoothly multidisciplinary operation that he and his colleagues envisioned. Gerontology was not, and probably never would be, a unified science. To secure diverse perspectives on aging, promoters tried to attract scientists from many disciplines and professions.

Intellectual as well as organizational considerations prompted the quest

2 Jean Mayer, "Walter Bradford Cannon," *Journal of Nutrition*, vol. 87 (1965): 1-8; *Walter Bradford Cannon, 1871-1945*, A Memorial Exercise held at the Harvard Medical School, November 5, 1945; Chandler McC. Brooks, Kiyomi Koizumi, and James O. Pinkeston, eds., *The Life and Contributions of Walter Bradford Cannon* (Albany: State University of New York, Downstate Medical Center, 1975); and Saul B. Benson, A. Clifford Berger, and Elin L. Wolfe, eds., *Walter B. Cannon* (Cambridge: Harvard University Press, 1987). Omitted here is any reference to Cannon's international service, editorships, consultationships, and textbook writing. References to his relationship in gerontology appear passim.

3 Edward J. Stieglitz, "The Relation of Gerontology to Clinical Medicine," in *Transactions of the Twelfth* (1950) *Conference on Problems of Aging* (New York: Josiah Macy, Jr. Foundation, 1951), p. 113. The tripartite division appears in a series of Stieglitz's papers. See idem, "Aiding Aging," *Technology Review*, vol. 43 (June 1941): 390. For more on the practical, see idem, "Wise Investment of Leisure," *Scientific Monthly*, vol. 51 (August 1940): 149; for two other early statements on "normal" aging, see idem, "Problems of Aging," *Pennsylvania Medical Journal*, vol. 45 (December 1941): 215; and idem, "Aging as an Industrial Health Problem," *Journal of the American Medical Association*, vol. 116 (March 29, 1941): 1,384.

for complementarity, not uniformity, in gerontology's formative years. Research on aging, as Stieglitz realized, "crosses the lines of all divisions of thought and thus applies all the many methods of science as instruments for its advance."[4] A truly scientific synthesis of senescence had to wait until researchers did empirical studies that analyzed "problems" clustered around common issues. If properly conducted, Stieglitz contended in 1943, "the observations and conclusions derived from such investigations will fit into the broad pattern and thus amplify the whole."[5]

Setting boundaries for research in aging, then and now, was problematic. Particularly in the field's initial phases, circulating ideas mattered as much as building structures. According to scholars who have studied successful innovations in higher education, greater cross-fertilization occurs if ideas from different perspectives early on inform the ways that research problems are defined, executed, and resolved. Multidisciplinary ideas and new methods of inquiry often result from the exchange.[6] A commitment to the breadth, however, becomes difficult to sustain once specialized networks develop and disciplinary-specific interests diverge. In the history of gerontology, uneasy relationships among medical and biological scientists who did research on aging frustrated efforts to build bridges.

"Geriatrics," Stieglitz asserted, "is thus but a part, a subdivision of the broader field of gerontology."[7] Why subscore geriatrics under gerontology? Physicians were not the only investigators interested in the elderly's diseases. Psychologist Oscar Kaplan, for instance, edited a collection of essays on *Mental Disorders in Later Life* (1945), which analyzed out "some of the physical and psychological factors involved in aging, and discusses prevention and treatment."[8] Furthermore, physicians did not simply "apply" principles from gerontology and internal medicine; some geriatricians also did "basic" research. Stieglitz's own handbook, *Geriatric Medicine* (1943) acknowledged that "geriatrics is not sufficiently demarcated to be classed

---

4 Edward J. Stieglitz, "Aging as a Problem of Industrial Health," *Southern Medicine and Surgery*, vol. 103 (October 1941): 546. See also idem, "Gerontology Comes of Age," *Scientific Monthly*, vol. 62 (1946): 80–2.

5 Edward J. Stieglitz, ed., *Geriatric Medicine* (Philadelphia: Saunders, 1943), p. 3.

6 Muzafer Sherif and Carolyn W. Sherif, *Interdisciplinary Relationships in the Social Sciences* (Hawthorne, NJ: Aldine, 1969), pp. 69, 104; Terry N. Clark, "Institutionalization of Innovations in Higher Education," *Administrative Science Quarterly*, vol. 13 (1968): 1–25; R. G. A. Dolby, "Sociology of Knowledge in Natural Science," *Science Studies*, vol. 1 (1971): 3–21.

7 Edward J. Stieglitz, "Foundations of Geriatric Medicine," in *Geriatric Medicine*, 3rd ed., (Philadelphia: Lippincott, 1954), p. 4. See also, Robert A. Moore, "The Medical Approach to the Problems of Aging," *Journal of Gerontology*, vol. 4 (April 1949): 91. (Henceforth this journal will be abbreviated *JoG*.)

8 Karl M. Brown, "Introduction" in *Mental Disorders in Later Life*, ed. Oscar J. Kaplan (Stanford, CA: Stanford University Press, 1945), p. 3. Eleven physicians (including one Ph.D.-M.D.), three psychologists, a sociologist, and a statistician contributed to the volume.

as a speciality," but fifty-three of the fifty-five contributing authors had medical degrees and most were affiliated with medical schools.[9] The fifth (1946), "thoroughly revised" edition of Malford W. Thewlis's *The Care of the Aged (Geriatrics)* noted that "the many problems that this field has to offer are a challenge to further research. . . . Geriatrics may outweigh pediatrics in importance.[10] Although Thewlis and other observers deplored the neglect of the chronically ill, geriatrics offered doctors who saw great numbers of elderly patients little by way of payoffs, financial or otherwise, in postwar America.[11] For roughly thirty years, the field languished, despite the efforts of its promoters. Interest in geriatrics was spurred by the founding of the National Institute on Aging (NIA) in 1975. Medical schools slowly began to teach electives and to develop programs. By the early 1990s, internal medicine, family practice, and psychiatry offered board certification in geriatrics.[12] The subspecialty's status in these two scenarios is not so much contradictory as incommensurate. Different ways of classifying geriatric knowledge permit different boundaries to be drawn; the same "parts" can be situated into "wholes" that have little in common.

Discomfiture sometimes occurred when gerontologists met among themselves to share new ideas. Keynoting the 1950 Macy Conference on "problems of aging," Lawrence K. Frank found "himself baffled by the lack of an adequate language to discuss the kind of dynamic circular process that we should try to formulate." The presentation bewildered his audience. "I am a little confused by your language, Mr. Frank," acknowledged the physiologist A. J. Carlson, an admission that Macy Foundation president Frank Fremont-Smith, M.D. found "encouraging." William MacNider, a pharmacologist, was confused by Frank's use of the social science terminology. "What is a frame of reference? You are talking in a language I don't understand very well." Psychiatrist William Malamud, new to the field, suggested that the miscomprehension was deeper: "I think what Mr. Frank was presenting to us was his own soul and his way of looking at things.

9   Stieglitz, ed., *Geriatric Medicine* (1943), p. xii. The collection was published a year after the founding of the American Geriatrics Society.

10 Malford W. Thewlis, *The Case of the Aged (Geriatrics)*, 5th ed. (St. Louis MO: Mosby, 1947), p. 24. The first edition of Thewlis's *Geriatrics* appeared in 1919. It replaced Nascher's *Geriatrics* as the standard text in the 1930s.

11 Louis I. Dublin, Howard T. Karsner, O.H. Perry Pepper, and Barney Brooks, *Medical Problems of Old Age* (Philadelphia: University of Pennsylvania Press, 1941), p. 33. See also, James E. Paullin, "The Relationship of Medical Practice to Gerontology," *JoG*, vol. 1 (July 1946): 297–302.

12 Robert N. Butler, "Geriatrics," in *The Encyclopedia of Aging*, ed. George L. Maddox (New York: Springer, 1987), p. 284. Although many clinicians have spent their careers studying old age and treating the aged, I do not believe that geriatrics should be subsumed under gerontology. Thus readers should not expect this book to do justice to the history of U.S. geriatrics; that is the subject for another monograph. Physicians interested in geriatrics figure here only to the extent that they helped to shape biological and clinical research on aging and other institutional arrangements under the aegis of gerontology.

When I try to apply this clinically, I am a bit lost."[13] Why such misunderstanding? Long-time colleagues knew that Frank took values questions seriously; like Dewey, he urged greater reflexivity in combining scientific and philosophical approaches. Frank's endorsement of a "dynamic circular process" for doing gerontology was disturbing precisely because it was so personal. His listeners were not willing to stretch as far as Frank insisted. So even among the cognoscenti, different vocabularies, theories, and methods created communication difficulties, confounded efforts to define gerontology.[14]

This chapter highlights four distinctive intellectual orientations and organizational constellations that emerged after Cowdry's *Problems of Ageing* was published in 1939. It focuses on research developments in Baltimore, at a government research facility directed by a biologist, and at the University of Chicago, where sociologists and psychologists collaborated in studying human development. The analysis ends with accounts of the creation of gerontology centers at the University of Southern California (USC), by a psychologist who had worked at Baltimore and Chicago, and at Duke, where a psychiatrist recruited social scientists to work in a medical school. The research priorities and aging-related activities at these four sites do not fully encompass the range of interests that were articulated earlier in the century. Nor do these case studies begin to tell us much about the grants activities and publication records that are so essential to understanding the range of gerontological *science*. Nonetheless, the survey does show that investigators were committed to doing empirical research, that they invested in longitudinal data sets, and that they exploited disciplinary-specific traditions as they fashioned a broader gerontologic mission.

The federal government advances biological investigations of aging[15]

The Macy Foundation prompted the federal government's initial involvement in research on aging. Having convinced Surgeon General Thomas Parran to authorize a Unit on Gerontology within the National Institute of

---

13 Dialog from the Josiah Macy, Jr. Foundation, *Transactions of the Twelfth Conference*. Quotation from Frank, p. 17; Carlson and Frank Fremont-Smith, p. 37; MacNider, p. 38; Malamud, p. 44.

14 See for instance, Lawrence K. Frank, "Gerontology," JoG, vol. 1 (January 1946): 1–11; Frank Hinman, "The Dawn of Gerontology," JoG, vol. 1 (July 1946): 416–7; Clark Tibbitts, ed., *Living Through the Older Years* (Ann Arbor: University of Michigan Press, 1951), p. 44; Albert I. Lansing, "What Is Aging?," JoG, vol. 7 (July 1952): 452–63; Edward L. Bortz, "New Goals for Maturity," JoG, vol. 9 (January 1954): 67–73. For more on this, see W. Andrew Achenbaum and Jeffrey Levin, "What Does *Gerontology* Mean?," *The Gerontologist*, vol. 29 (June 1989): 393–400. (Henceforth this journal will be abbreviated *TG*.)

15 I will tell only part of the history of what would become NIA here. For later developments, see Chapter 6.

Health (NIH), Macy officials in January 1940 granted $10,000 to support a specialist in aging at the U.S. Public Health Service for one year. Edward J. Stieglitz, a 1921 graduate of Rush Medical College, who served on the University of Chicago faculty from 1923 to 1938, was appointed to the post. Through the Baltimore Department of Public Welfare, Stieglitz was given space for a research laboratory in the City Hospitals. One of the attractions of the site was that the hospitals operated an Old People's Home with approximately 1,000 ambulatory patients. (Unlike nineteenth-century French physicians who based their observation of late-life maladies on chronically ill patients, Stieglitz expected to encounter people with a wider range of medical histories.) The National Institutes of Health agreed to cover research expenses in return for space. Stieglitz quickly started a study of uric acid excretion among aged subjects.[16] If his investigations made research on aging more visible, his lab had great potential to become a "centralizing agency."

Even a small NIH unit needed a national advisory board, Stieglitz figured, so he assembled as prestigious a group as possible. Cowdry/Macy connections are reflected in the appointments of Carlson, Crocker, Frank, and Hastings to the panel. Other members included a zoologist, a clinician, NIH physicians and administrators, hospital superintendents, a medical director of Metropolitan Life Insurance, and an industrial physician who worked for General Motors. The board chose as its first order of business to conduct a survey of research on aging that was under way or planned on U.S campuses, "to bring in closer cooperation investigators interested in related problems, especially when widely divergent methods of approach are being utilized."[17] Meanwhile, Stieglitz professed enthusiasm for all types of inquiry in a series of articles in journals aimed at physicians and biologists. But his top priority was to learn more about structural, biochemical, and physiological changes that accompanied senescence. Stieglitz wanted physician-scientists to do etiological and pathogenetic investigations in concert. "The more we know about the biologic mechanisms of

16 Stieglitz biography in Edward J. Stieglitz, "Geriatrics," *JoG*, vol. 1 (April 1946): 154; for his activities, see idem, "Gerontology," *Annals of Internal Medicine*, vol. 14 (October 1940): 739; and Nathan W. Shock, "The United States Public Health Service–Baltimore City Hospitals Research Section in Gerontology," *JoG*, vol. 2 (April 1947): 169-70, and idem, *The International Association of Gerontology* (New York: Springer, 1988), p. 4. For more on arrangements with the Baltimore City Hospitals, see idem, "Historical Development of Gerontology," paper (1981), p. 4, in the Nathan Shock Collection, "Historical Files," at the Bentley Historical Collection (henceforth BHC), University of Michigan, Ann Arbor; and idem, "The Gerontology Branch of the National Heart Institute and the Baltimore City Hospitals," paper (1960), pp. 1-2, at the BHC. For his intellectual debt to his Chicago mentor and colleague, A. J. Carlson, see Edward J. Stieglitz, *The Second Forty Years* (Philadelphia: Lippincott, 1946), p. 313.

17 "Unit on Gerontology in the National Institute of Health," *Public Health Reports*, vol. 55 (November 15, 1940): 2,099–2,100.

the ageing processes, the more effectively can clinical medicine treat the ageing and the aged."[18]

When Stieglitz resigned for personal reasons a year later, A. Baird Hastings recommended that Nathan W. Shock fill the position. Shock had earned a degree in chemical engineering at Purdue before going to the University of Chicago for graduate studies. Finding the registration line for engineering classes too long, on an impulse he switched fields. (This illustrates the importance of chance in a career.) Shock decided to take courses in psychology under L. L. Thurstone, whose research on factor analysis sparked the former's lifelong preoccupation with developing scales of measurement. Besides working with Thurstone, Shock studied biological chemistry under Hastings. In the course of preparing his dissertation, he developed a pipette that could measure several components on the same 0.1 cubic centimeters of blood.[19] Shock then spent nine years at Berkeley, participating in a major longitudinal study of adolescent growth. In California, Shock met Lawrence Frank and received additional training from such eminent developmental psychologists as Harold and Mary Cover Jones and Jean MacFarlane. He became skilled at administering Stanford-Binet intelligence tests and using Terman group intelligence scales. He inferred from his work on the data sets that adolescence was a physiological not a chronological category.[20]

World War II delayed his immersion into gerontology when he moved to Baltimore, but the interlude gave him time to wrap up his studies of "physiological changes in adolescence." Ultimately, Shock published thirty-four chapters and articles for a variety of scholarly journals.[21] Meanwhile,

---

18 Edward J. Stieglitz, "The Social Urgency of Research in Ageing," in *Problems of Ageing*, ed. Edmund Vincent Cowdry 2d ed. (Baltimore: Williams & Wilkins Co., 1942), p. 906. See also, idem, "Gerontology," *Annals of Internal Medicine*, p. 739.

19 For Shock's Chicago years, especially the lessons he learned from Thurstone and Hastings, see George T. Baker III, "Obituary: Nathan's Last Words," *Experimental Gerontology*, vol. 25 (1990): 206; A. Baird Hastings, *Crossing Boundaries* (Grand Rapids, MI: Four Corners Press, 1989), pp. 44–5, 246–9; Louis Wirth, ed., *Eleven Twenty-Six* (1940; New York: Arno Press, 1974), p. 78; Lester R. Kurtz, *Evaluating Chicago Sociology* (Chicago: University of Chicago Press, 1984), p. 88; Leonard D. White, ed., *The State of the Social Sciences* (Chicago: University of Chicago Press, 1956), p. 310. On measurement, see Randall Collins, "Statistics Versus Words," *Sociological Theory*, vol. 2 (1984): 344–7; L. L. Thurstone, *The Vectors of Mind* (Chicago: University of Chicago Press, 1936).

20 Theresa R. Richardson, *The Century of the Child* (Albany: State University of New York Press, 1989), pp. 139–43.

21 For the Berkeley years, see Elizabeth Lomax, "The Laura Spelman Rockefeller Memorial," *Journal of the History of the Behavioral Sciences*, vol. 13 (1977): 286–7; Institute of Human Development, University of California, Berkeley, *The Course of Human Development* (Waltham: Xerox College Publishing, 1971), pp. 71ff, 476. I also rely on a May 1987 interview with Dr. Shock, who mentioned that he met with the Terman group nearby. They were studying longitudinally the relation between genetics and genius. See Josef Brozek, ed., *Explorations in the History of Psychology in the United States* (Lewisburg:

the federal government's role in biomedical research changed in ways that would affect Shock's subsequent career. Scientists and doctors before World War II had been protective of their professional autonomy, wary of bureaucratic intrusions. As military service accelerated the flow of physicians from general practice toward medical specialization,[22] Washington took steps that made it a major partner in medical affairs. In 1943 Surgeon General Parran reorganized the Public Health Service to enable it "to pay for research to be performed by universities, hospitals, laboratories, and other public or private institutions." Three years later the VA signed an arrangement with U.S. medical schools, which resulted in it becoming a major site for training doctors.[23]

In 1948, NIH became the National Institutes of Health; Congress authorized new institutes to focus on specific acute and chronic diseases. Basic research was considered the way to assure breakthroughs. "Discoveries in medicine have often come from the most remote and unexpected fields of science in the past. . . . It is not unlikely that significant progress in the treatment of cardiovascular disease, kidney disease, cancer, and other refractory conditions will be made, perhaps unexpectedly, as a result of fundamental discoveries in fields unrelated to these diseases," declared a federal medical advisory committee, adding that "discovery cannot be achieved by directive."[24] To ensure fairness, "study sections" were convened in the 1950s at NIH to rank in order the scientific merits of the research proposals investigators submitted for funding. Medical schools in the United States were encouraged to hire research scientists, underwrite training fellowships, and engage in construction projects under this arrangement: They garnered roughly half of all NIH dollars, which grew from less than $4 million in 1947 to $1.2 billion two decades later.

The NIH officials acknowledged certain biases in their modus operandi.

Bucknell University Press, 1984), p. 257; Lewis Terman et al., *Genetic Studies of Genius*, 5 vols. (Stanford, CA: Stanford University Press, 1925–59).

22 There were only fifteen speciality boards; the American Board of Surgery was not established until 1937. John Z. Bowers and Elizabeth F. Purcell, eds., *Advances in American Medicine*, vol. 2 (New York: Josiah Macy, Jr. Foundation, 1976), pp. 524, 813, 824; Julius Richmond, *American Medicine* (Cambridge: Harvard University Press, 1969), p. 23; Daniel J. Kevles, "The National Science Foundation and the Debate over Postwar Scientific Policy, 1942–1945," *Isis*, vol. 68 (1977): 3, 11; Vernon W. Lippard, *A Half-Century of American Medical Education* (New York: Josiah Macy, Jr. Foundation, 1974), pp. 90–1.

23 Parran quoted in Stephen P. Strickland, *Politics, Science, and Dread Disease* (Cambridge: Harvard University Press, 1972), p. 18. For more on the VA, see *infra.*, Chapter 7.

24 Quoted in Richard A. Rettig, *Cancer Crusade* (Princeton, NJ: Princeton University Press, 1977), p. 11. See also, Donald C. Swain, "The Line of a Research Empire: NIH, 1930 to 1950," *Science*, vol. 131 (14 December 1962): 1,233–7. Baird Hastings served on this Medical Research Committee. See Stickland, *Politics, Science, and Dread Disease*, p. 15; Roger L. Geiger, *Research and Relevant Knowledge* (New York: Oxford University Press, 1993), pp. 27, 179–85.

Proposals had to be focused, yet be neither narrow nor too diffuse. Initially, NIH was reluctant to allocate large sums to studies of human development. "Knowledge of life processes and of phenomena underlying health and disease is still grossly inadequate," lamented NIH director James Shannon in 1967. Shannon was convinced, despite considerable resistance from those who insisted that conquering disease was NIH's primary mission, that "the hope of major advances lies in sustaining broad and free-ranging inquiry into all aspects of the phenomena, limited only by the criteria of excellence, the scientific importance, and the seriousness and competence of the investigator."[25] Even in affluent postwar America there were not enough funds to support every deserving inquiry into basic biological (much less aging-related) processes and structures.

A similar, if less generous, pattern altered Washington's relationship to social scientists. Wartime priorities set the stage for America's "military-industrial" complex. Sensing potential conflicts between government, universities, and private industry, Vannevar Bush, director of the wartime Office of Scientific Research and Development, commissioned a blue-ribbon panel to study the matter. Implementing the final report, *Science – The Endless Frontier* (1945), which called for a "new social invention – of government sanction and support but professional guidance and administration,"[26] took five years due to fundamental disagreement over scientific boundaries. Some in Congress wanted greater visibility for the social sciences. Bush initially was opposed, but to win votes, he softened his position: "We have to let the social sciences get a nose under the tent." When Harry S Truman established the National Science Foundation (NSF) in 1950, social scientists garnered less support than their peers.[27] Proposals from the natural and physical sciences received preferential treatment. In 1956, NSF announced an interest in funding such "fields of convergence" as mathematical economics and demography. Projects in "psychobiology" and the "sociophysical" arena, however, were relegated to the "other sciences" category; study sections rarely approved money for "applied" research.[28]

---

25 James A. Shannon, M.D., "The Advancement of Medical Research, *The Journal of Medical Education*, vol. 42 (February 1967): 104–5; Thomas B. Turner, "The Medical Schools Twenty Years Afterwards," ibid, p. 110.

26 Quoted in Kevles, "National Science Foundation," p. 22.

27 There was a gap in the production of Ph.D.s in the natural versus social sciences between 1939 and 1948, when 1,975 men and women received Ph.D.s in the natural sciences compared to 681 in the latter category. Fellowship support was greater in the natural sciences. See Samuel Z. Klausner and Victor M. Lidz, eds., *The Naturalization of the Social Sciences* (Philadelphia: University of Pennsylvania Press, 1986), p. 115.

28 John T. Wilson, *Academic Science, Higher Education, and the Federal Government* (Chicago: University of Chicago Press, 1983), pp. 10; James B. Conant quoted on p. 18. For Bush, see Kevles, "National Science Foundation," p. 24. The ubiquitous Hastings played a role in NSF; see Milton Lomask, *A Minor Miracle* (Washington, DC: National Science

At first gerontology was not greatly affected by changes in Big Government's ties to Big Science. Few, after all, did research on aging in 1945. Six years later, according to figures reported in the *Journal of Gerontology* *(JoG)*, less than 1 percent of all U.S. funds from any source went to gerontologists, compared to 20 percent for cancer research, 17 percent for infectious diseases, and another 11 percent for the study of the cardiovascular system. Even so, by 1951, the federal government was contributing 75 percent of all direct costs ($283,075) for aging research. According to estimates made by NIH's Gerontology Advisory Committee, the total was bigger if the half million dollars the Atomic Energy Committee appropriated for aging-related research in its extramural budget were counted, as well as the $2.3 million that the U.S Public Health Service earmarked for studies of diseases that afflicted old people. In addition, seventeen Federal agencies, ranging from the Civil Service Commission to Oak Ridge laboratories, were conducting studies that had a "bearing on the field of gerontology."[29] But by any measure, aging was a low priority in U.S. research circles.

Against this backdrop, Nathan Shock's primary task was to promote research and training in aging. No scientist employed by the federal government after World War II did more in this regard. He directed the Gerontology Research Center (GRC) from 1941 until his mandatory retirement thirty-five years later; he served as a Scientist Emeritus until his death in 1989. Shock (co)authored more than 350 publications mostly dealing with biochemical, behavioral, and physiological aspects of human aging. He trained more than 200 fellows, including three future presidents (Reuben Andres, James Birren, and John Rowe) of the Gerontological Society of America (GSA), a body he served officially and behind the scenes. His cross-disciplinary reach extended to leadership posts in the American Psychological Association (APA), the American Heart Association (AHA), and the Society for Experimental Biology and Medicine.[30] For nearly fifty years Shock's agenda greatly influenced how key scientists studied basic biological processes of aging, and officials in certain federal agencies proceeded to organize research.

Shock's gerontologic orientation changed little over his long career. "In

Foundation, 1976), p. 65. See also Harry Alpert, "Social Science, Social Psychology, and the National Science Foundation," *American Psychologist*, vol. 12 (February 1957): 95–8; idem, "The National Science Foundation and Social Science Research," *American Sociological Review*, vol. 19 (April 1954): 208–11.

29 "Financial Support for Research on Aging," *JoG*, vol. 7 (April 1952): 309; Nathan W. Shock and Annabell Wehrwein, "Government-Conducted Research in Gerontology," JoG, vol. 6 (January 1951): 68–70; Henry S. Simms, "Government-Supported Research in Gerontology in Private Institutions, ibid. 66–7. I recognize that these data reveal nothing about the scientific significance of the research that was funded or its impact on the subsequent development of the field.

30 Baker, "Obituary," pp. 206–7.

the broadest sense, problems of growth, development, and maturation are as much a part of gerontology as are those of atrophy, degeneration, and decline," he wrote in 1951, but his attention was mainly "confined to changes that occur in later maturity and senescence."[31] By 1960, he had organized the GRC's research program into three categories. *The Basic Biology of Aging* focused on molecular biology, biophysics, cellular and comparative physiology, intermediary metabolism, nutritional biochemistry, and morphology. *Human Physiology* assessed age differences in cardiovascular and renal systems, endocrinology and metabolism, and pulmonary physiology and exercise. *Psychological Aspects of Aging* dealt with physiological issues (the role of the nervous system, as well as sensory and motor deficits) and experimental research on changes in learning and memory and alterations in personality characteristics.[32] Like contributors to Cowdry's *Problems of Ageing*, Shock supported cross-disciplinary work, but only to the extent that it advanced experimental, empirical science. Biology reigned supreme, in his opinion; behaviorists should link their basic research to the "hard" sciences; and other endeavors did not much matter. These priorities recur in a list of six tenets for aging research that Shock composed a few months before he died:[33]

1. "Give me a testable hypothesis . It is worth a thousand theories."
   Shock dismissed theories of aging that failed to specify causal relationships. "The goal of gerontologists is to reduce the dimensions of our ignorance," he declared, "by expanding knowledge about the interrelationships between variables and their relationships to the passage of time." Throughout his career, Shock hypothesized that "aging is basically an impairment of cellular processes, which will be found to be the same for all cells."[34]
2. "Formulate questions to address basic mechanisms of aging and design

---

31 Nathan W. Shock, "Gerontology (Later Maturity)," *Annual Review of Psychology*, vol. 11 (1951): 353.
32 Shock, "The Gerontology Branch," pp. 4–8. Note that Shock's tripartite division was not identical to Stieglitz's.
33 George T. Baker III and W. Andrew Achenbaum, "A Historical Perspective of Research on the Biology of Aging from Nathan W. Shock," *Experimental Gerontology*, vol. 27 (1992): 262. I have deleted the exclamation points punctuating Shock's tenets. For the last five years of Shock's life, Baker worked very closely with Shock. I acknowledge with gratitude the willingness of George Baker, also a biologist and administrator, to share much with me about the development and logic of Shock's views.
34 First quotation from George T. Baker III and Nathan W. Shock, "Theoretical Concepts Governing Gerontological Research," in *Potential for Nutritional Modulation of Aging Processes*, ed. D. K. Ingram *et al.* (Westport, CT: Food and Nutritional Press, 1991), pp. 3–15; second quotation from Nathan W. Shock, "Current Concepts of the Aging Process," *Journal of the American Medical Association*, vol. 175 (February 25, 1961): 656. To note the significance that a social scientist placed on "time," see Lawrence Frank, "Structure, Function, and Growth," *Philosophy of Science*, vol. 11 (1935): 210–35.

scientifically rigorous protocols to examine those questions."

Accepting that "the basic biological fact of aging is that the probability of death increases with age in a definite mathematical relationship,"[35] Shock tested the hypothesis that functional capacity was progressively lost over time. Shock measured rates and flows longitudinally, cell by cell, tissue by tissue, system by system, using precise instruments and statistical models.[36]

3. "Focus research on the processes of aging over the entire life span. Studies on older individuals may tell one about diseases in later life but are not likely to yield information about the basic mechanisms of aging!"

"The essence of gerontological research," Shock asserted in the 1950s, "is that comparisons must be made between organisms at least at two points in their life span, after the attainment of maturity."[37] Longitudinal studies showed changes over time. Following in the tradition of Quetelet, Shock stressed *averages* in describing and explaining normative processes: "Examination of average curves brings to light a number of significant generalizations."[38]

4. "Aging and disease are not synonymous. There are processes of aging and etiologies of disease. The relationships between the two are important but not inevitable."

Echoing a theme in Cowdry's *Problems of Ageing*, Shock argued in 1961 that "perhaps one of the most useful contributions of gerontologic research has been the demonstration that aging is not necessarily associated with deterioration and disease."[39]

---

35 Shock, "Current Concepts," p. 654. See also, idem, "Age Changes in Physiological Functions in the Total Animal," in *The Biology of Aging*, ed. Bernard L. Strehler et al. (Washington, DC: American Institute of Biological Sciences, 1960), pp. 258-63.

36 For two early studies along these lines, see Nathan W. Shock and Marvin J. Yiengst, "Experimental Displacement of the Acid Base Equilibrium of the Blood in Aged Males," *Federal Proceedings*, vol. 7 (March 1948): 114-15; Dean F. Davies and Nathan W. Shock, "Age Changes in Glomerular Filtration Rate, Effective Renal Plasma Flow, and Tubular Excretory Capacity in Adult Males," *Journal of Clinical Investigation*, vol. 29 (May 1950): 496–507. For an illustration of Shock thinking out loud about how he did science, see Nathan W. Shock, "The Science of Gerontology," in Duke University Council on Gerontology, *Proceedings of Seminars*, 1959–1961 (Durham, NC,: Duke University, 1962), pp. 123–37.

37 Nathan W. Shock, *Trends in Gerontology*, 2d ed. (Stanford, CA,: Stanford University Press, 1957), p. 116.

38 Shock, "The Role of Research," p. 15. For a criticism of this approach, see Fred L. Bookstein and W. Andrew Achenbaum, "Measurement as Explanation" in *Voices and Visions of Aging*, ed. Thomas R. Cole et al. (New York: Springer, 1993), pp. 20–45. For concurrent affirmations, see Daniel Offer and Melvin Sabshin, "The Concept of Normality," in *The Foundations of Psychiatry*, ed. Pilrano Arieti (New York: Basic, 1974), pp. 202–8ff.

39 Shock, "Current Concepts," p. 16. For more on this, see above in Chapter 1, and Albert Mueller-Deham and S. Milton Rabson, *Internal Medicine in Old Age* (Baltimore: Williams

5. "Aging is a dynamic equilibrium. The rates of aging differ for various systems in any given organism, however, it is the whole organism that ages and dies."

   Shock closely followed research developments in evolutionary and comparative biology. "The individual animal at any age is a result of processes of accumulation and degradation that take place simultaneously."[40] At GRC he maintained a rat colony and kept species of Drosophila, rotifers, Euglena, and Campanularia.

6. "Well-documented observations and good scientific data are timeless. Also, don't overlook studies in other scientific fields. Much of our knowledge of gerontology today is a by-product of non-aging research."

   Over his career, Shock built a library containing more than 1,000 volumes and 27,000 reprints related to aging. With support from the Forest Park Foundation, he compiled *A Classified Bibliography of Gerontology and Geriatrics* (1951). The distribution of the initial 16,036 entries is revealing. References to the biology of aging (items #116 to 3,164) and organ systems (items #3,165 to 11,784) dominate the volume. There were 2,170 entries for geriatrics. Shock included only 4,080 items in the sections covering psychological processes, social and economic aspects, and miscellaneous items.[41]

Shock transformed the federally supported GRC into a highly visible research center and site for training investigators interested in basic "mechanisms involved in aging." When Shock arrived in Baltimore in 1941, he had one lab assistant; when the GRC in 1975 became the Intramural Program of the new NIA, he was overseeing the activities of 175 researchers and visiting scientists. During much of his career Shock reported to scientists for whom gerontology was at best a secondary concern. (His program was assigned to the National Heart Institute [NHI] in 1949, and then, from 1965 to 1975, it was part of the National Institute of Child Health and Human Development [NICHHD].[42]) Early on, Shock had stressed the value of a multipurpose gerontology center. In 1950 he proposed legislation

& Wilkins, 1942), p. 1. The medicalization-of-aging theme is treated in Part II and Chapter 8.

40 Nathan W. Shock, *Trends in Gerontology*, (Stanford, CA: Stanford University Press, 1951), pp. 1–2. See also Baker and Achenbaum, "A Historical Perspective," p. 265; on GRC labs, see Shock, "The Gerontology Branch," p. 3. Shock had an extensive collection of books on botany and articles about molluscs, snails, and tortoises.

41 Nathan W. Shock, *A Classified Bibliography of Gerontology and Geriatrics* (Stanford, CA: Stanford University Press, 1951). Supplements to the bibliography were published as bound volumes in 1957 and 1963; additional entries regularly appeared in the *Journal of Gerontology* until the 1980s.

42 Shock, "The Gerontology Branch," pp. 1–2; Shock, "Historical Development of Gerontology," p. 5. For a sense of the intellectual fallout from administrative decisions to move

to enable the Public Health Service of the Federal Security Agency more effectively to improve the health and general well-being of the older people of the United States through the conduct of researches, investigations, experiments, and demonstrations relating to the processes of aging and their effect on health including genetic, environmental, and climatic influences and related factors which tend to retard or to promote optimum personality development, and the causes, prevention, control, and methods of diagnosis and treatment of diseases and disabilities of later maturity, including the impairments and defects resulting from cumulative effect of diseases and disabilities, and accidents particularly affecting older people, and methods of maintenance of older people at optimum health and usefulness, including methods of restoration and care of older people who are incapacitated; assist and foster such researches and activities by public and private agencies, and promote the coordination of all such resources and activities and the useful application of their results, provide training in matters related . . . [43]

Shock admitted years later that too many compromises laced this statement. Throughout his life he supported clinical-, disease-, and social-oriented programs, but, as we have seen, basic research directed at basic biological mechanisms of aging always mattered most to him. In any case, the 1950 bid failed, as did a similar request emanating out of the 1961 White House Conference on Aging (WHCoA). Finally, in 1968, a new four-story building, with 200,000 square feet of laboratory and office space was formally dedicated. Friends affectionately called it "The House That Nathan Built."

Shock also gave generously to professional organizations for researchers on aging. He was president of the Gerontological Society (GSA) in 1960–1 and served as editor-in-chief of the *JoG* from 1963 to 1968. Shock occasionally absorbed costs that the Society could not meet out of his own pocket or his unit's budget. (The gesture not only reveals much about the man, but it also reveals how low-budget an operation gerontology was a few decades ago.[44]) This same commitment to forging scientific networks influenced Shock's involvement in the International Association of Gerontology. North American investigators, he felt, had to interact with scientists abroad. Europeans, after all, had been doing aging-related research and convening scientific symposia long before the 1937 conference at Woods Hole. By the early 1950s, Britain, not America, set the pace in the inter-

GRC from one branch of NIH to another, see idem, "Biological Aging Research," *Science*, vol. 158 (December 15, 1967): 1,393–4.

43 "Legislative Proposal – Draft November 6, 1950," sect. 3: Research and Training in Shock Files, series I, BHC. Shock was an author of this text. This document was part of the planning surrounding the Federal Security Agency conference on aging in 1950. See also Nathan W. Shock, "Historical Perspectives on Aging," in *Environmental Physiology*, ed. Yousef Horvath (New York: Elsevier North-Holland, 1980), pp. 386–7.

44 Shock told me about subsidizing annual meetings of the Society and some of its publications in an interview in May 1987.

national community: A British Society for Research on Ageing had been founded in 1939; the Oxford Gerontological Research Unit, started in 1945 under the direction of Russian-born, experimental pathologist V. Koren-chevsky, was thriving; Lord Nuffield was a generous benefactor. Thanks to international contacts that Shock helped to forge, gerontologists on this side of the Atlantic, particularly in the "hard" sciences, were spared some of the insularity that characterized other areas of U.S. scholarship in the 1950s.[45]

Perhaps Shock's greatest legacy, as much intellectual as institutional, was the Baltimore Longitudinal Study of Aging (BLSA) begun in 1958 with assistance from Dr. W. W. Peter, a retired medical officer in the Public Health Service. Peter encouraged individuals not suffering from disease who were living independently in the area to submit to a battery of physiological and psychological tests that Shock and his colleagues were developing. Twenty-five years later measurements were being recorded for more than 1,000 male volunteers who were between the ages of seventeen and ninety-six when they entered the study. (Women were not added to the BLSA until 1978, a research-design issue that did not seem terribly serious to Shock or other investigators on the basis of data collected to date.[46]) The BLSA study, admits its current clinical director, Dr. Reuben Andres, did not begin "with all the right questions." Shock himself acknowledged the possibility that cohort effects distorted the sampling design.[47] The first comprehensive report from the BLSA analysis, *Normal Human Aging* (1984), presented results test by test, differentiating longitudinal and cross-sectional analyses of performance scores. Sharing Shock's belief that gerontologic science should be built hypothesis by hypothesis, GRC scientists chose not to gen-

45 V. Korenchevsky, "European Gerontologic Activities," *JoG*, vol. 4 (October 1949): 314–17; "Gerontology in the United Kingdom," *JoG*, vol. 6 (July 1951): 275–9; Nathan W. Shock with George T. Baker III, *The International Association of Gerontology* (New York: Springer, 1988).

46 Nathan W. Shock et al., *Normal Human Aging* (Washington, DC: Government Printing Office, 1984), p. 1. I do not mean to suggest that Shock and his male colleagues were sexist scientists, but it is important to note that, on balance, biomedical investigators typically seem less persuaded than their social-scientific counterparts that sex- and gender-specific variations cause differences in human aging over the life course. The BLSA investigators found that women, like men, develop age-related thickening in the heart wall and lose muscle mass at about the same rate. Changes in taste sensitivity run parallel, though (p. 163) there do appear to be differences in frequency and uses of day dreaming. Issues surrounding gender-specific differential life expectancies, hormones, nutrition, etc., require additional study, most scientists currently acknowledge.

47 Andres quoted in BLSA, *To Understand the Aging Process* (Washington, DC: National Institutes of Health, 1980), p. 19; Shock in Calvin A. Lang and John P. Richie, Jr., "Bio-gerontological Precepts of Nathan Shock Which Influenced Our Aging Research," *Experimental Gerontology*, vol. 21 (1986): 236–7. See also Ralph E. Knutti, "The Youthful Science of Aging," *Today's Health* (June 1964): reprint; Uriel S. Barzel, "Book Reviews," *Journal of the American Geriatrics Society*, vol. 34 (December 1986): 902–3.

eralize on the basis of their results; the editors deemed any "grand theory" premature.

The BLSA project exemplifies the best and worst features of what might be called "purity" in gerontologic science after World War II. In accordance with Shock's tenets for doing research, GRC's team of experts tested well-formulated hypotheses about basic mechanisms. They designed a rigorous protocol and observed healthy adults, measuring increases and decreases in their bodies' functional capacity over time. The BLSA remains the biggest, ongoing data set of its kind. Shock's "functionalist" approach to measuring age-related changes has broadened contemporary understanding of physiological mechanisms over the life span.[48] Not all biological functions diminish with age. The BLSA psychologists have documented significant continuities in personality across adulthood. The flaws in the longitudinal study are also revealing. Critics have noted that *Normal Human Aging* uses keywords such as "normal" and "normative" interchangeably. In their efforts to design protocol that replicated the controls possible in a laboratory setting, BLSA's architects may have been too reductionist. So careful were they to disentangle "aging" from "disease" that researchers may have ignored interactions that naturally occur in the lives of "average" aging adults. Equally revealing is the belated recognition given to possible distortion arising from discounting gender differences or confounding age, cohort, and period efforts. The GRC position suggests too blind a faith in Shock's contention that "well-documented observations and good scientific data are timeless."

That said, Nathan Shock was surely correct on his deathbed when he claimed that "we have achieved some measure of success." Shock admirably fulfilled Baird Hasting's hope that the next generation would advance the Cowdry cohort's commitment to excellence in biogerontology. Shock was a dominant figure, who played an indispensable role in establishing many of the field's prime institutions.[49]

University of Chicago scholars study the psychosocial dimensions of aging

"Compared with the strides in biological and medical research on old age, the amount of progress in social science on the subject is relatively insignificant," declared a 1948 Social Science Research Council (SSRC) report. "The relation between biological and social factors is recognized in that physiological and psychological measures of capacity are necessarily used in studying the relation of declining capacity to problems of individual

48 Caleb G. Finch, "Nathan Shock's Pioneering Analysis of Physiological Mechanisms in Aging," *Experimental Gerontology*, vol. 22 (1987): 305–6.
49 Baker, "Obituary," p. 206.

adjustment in old age."[50] Just as biomedical researchers documented variations in functional capacities, heredity, and "sequelae of disease," some social scientists in the 1940s also were comparing rates of behavioral and physiological change. Most were doing exploratory projects on "recreation," "opinions and sentiments regarding old age and retirement," and "friendship." As a way to organize future work in sociology, social psychology, and cultural anthropology, the SSRC report recommended that "central emphasis" be placed on *Social Adjustment in Old Age*, "a formulation inclusive enough to embrace the questions and research methods involved in the approach of any social scientist."[51]

The next year, Ruth Shonle Cavan with three colleagues from the University of Chicago published *Personal Adjustment in Old Age* (1949), an analysis of patterns and problems encountered by 3,000 white, English-speaking, mentally competent, middle-class people over sixty. Social phenomena affected the elderly's status in society independently of their physical status. Retirees, reported Cavan, had no prescribed roles to perform; transitions in late adulthood tended to be amorphous. These findings didn't fit neatly into a biomedical model. Stieglitz's clinical classification of the human life span, claimed the authors, "can scarcely be justified socially." Nor could biomarkers be used to (re)construct and measure older people's thoughts and behavior.[52] Cavan's analysis indicated that there were considerable limits to how far ideas in biogerontology could be transferred to social science research, and vice versa. Social scientists had to grapple with methodological issues on their own disciplinary terms.[53]

50 Otto Pollak, *Social Adjustment in Old Age* (New York: Social Science Research Council, 1948), pp. 5, 48. Lawrence Frank was instrumental in drafting this report. This was not SSRC's first foray into old-age issues. It supported a panel monitoring Social Security from 1935 to 1943. See Elbridge Sibley, *Social Science Research Council* (New York: Social Science Research Council, 1984), p. 136. On the weaknesses of the social sciences compared to the natural sciences, see Donald Young, "Limiting Factors in the Development of the Social Sciences," *Proceedings of the American Philosophical Society*, vol. 92 (1948): 325–35.

51 Pollack, *Social Adjustment*, p. 10. See also Donald Young, "Memorandum on Suggestions for Research in the Field of Social Adjustment," *American Journal of Sociology*, vol. 46 (May 1941): 873–86; it is worth noting that SSRC's Committee on Social Adjustment in Old Age was formed in 1943 out of its Committee on Social Adjustment. The survey of activities in "Memorandum on Research in Progress on Social Science Aspects of Old Age" (February 1948), in Shock, Historical Files, BHC. The SSRC received thirteen responses, from researchers at Bryn Mawr, Rockford, and Sweet Briar Colleges; Chicago, McGill, Michigan, Ohio State, and Syracuse universities; Shock at the U.S. Public Health Service; Chicago and Rochester councils of Social Agencies, and the Council of Churches of Christ.

52 Ruth Shonle Cavan et al., *Personal Adjustment in Old Age* (Chicago: Science Research Associates, Inc., 1949), p. 1. See also another classic text from the mid-1940s, Leo W. Simmons, *The Role of the Aged in Primitive Societies* (New Haven, CT: Yale University Press, 1945).

53 Cavan described in detail the *Personal Adjustment* survey instrument, the Activities and

Such attention to methods, critical in developing new fields of inquiry, characterized research at the University of Chicago. In 1929, eight of Chicago's departments were ranked the best in the nation; that 52 percent of the faculty had earned their highest degrees on campus fostered collegiality. To counterbalance parochialism, President Robert M. Hutchins imposed a divisional organization on departments in 1931. He also encouraged the growth of "borderland fields of recent research interest" to flourish under the aegis of a few interdepartmental committees, "thus distinguishing, but connecting, discipline and field."[54]

Social science research flourished at the University of Chicago. Eminent political scientists, psychologists, and sociologists served as presidents of professional associations and edited their disciplines' major publications. Besides fostering close ties with business and government, professors and department heads with an entrepreneurial bent cultivated private donors and foundation staff. Some exchanged roles over their careers. As an officer of the Laura Spelman Rockefeller Memorial Fund (LSRM), Beardsley Ruml (a Chicago Ph.D.) channeled funds to political scientist Charles E. Merriam to build a large social science building on the Midway. In 1929 Ruml returned to Chicago to become the first chair of the social sciences division; Merriam took over the LSRM. During the war, both served on the National Resources Planning Board.[55] Such a fortuitous combination of brains,

Attitudes Inventories, which she designed with Ernest W. Burgess and Robert J. Havighurst, two architects of the SSRC report. For the instruments, see appendices A and B in Cavan et al., *Personal Adjustment*. See also, Robert J. Havighurst, "Validity of the Chicago Attitude Inventory as a Measure of Personal Adjustment in Old Age," *Journal of Abnormal and Social Psychology*, vol. 46 (1951): 24–9. A quotation from Lord Kelvin was selected for the entrance way to the Social Science Research Building at Chicago: "When you can measure what you are speaking about and express it in numbers, you know something about it; but when you cannot measure it, when you cannot express it in numbers, your knowledge is of a meagre and unsatisfactory kind." Charles Merriam and William Ogburn were to debate the appropriateness of this statement. See Barry D. Karl, *Charles E. Merriam and the Study of Politics* (Chicago: University of Chicago Press, 1974), p. 155.

54 First phrase from Robert Redfield, *Levels of Integration in Biological and Social Systems* (Lancaster, PA: Jaques Cattell Press, 1942), p. 1; second phrase from *The Idea and Practice of General Education* (Chicago: University of Chicago Press, 1950), p. 178; Harry S. Ashmore, *Unseasonable Truths* (Boston: Little, Brown, 1989), pp. 77, 177. The first interdepartmental Committee on International Relations was established in 1920. For more of the advantages of this structure, see the address of Ralph W. Tyler at a February 9, 1952 Human Development banquet in the files of the Committee on Human Development at the University of Chicago (henceforth CHD). On Hutchins, see Robert M. Hutchins, *The Higher Learning in America* (New Haven, CT: Yale University Press, 1936); Mortimer Adler, " 'The Chicago School,' " *Harper's Magazine* (September 1941): 377–88; Edward Shils, ed., *Remembering the University of Chicago* (Chicago: University of Chicago Press, 1991), pp. 191–4.

55 Karl, *Merriam*, pp. 134–45; William H. McNeill, *Hutchins' University* (Chicago: University of Chicago Press, 1991), p. 12; Ruth Shonle Canvan, "The Chicago School of Sociology," *Urban Life*, vol. 11 (1983): 407–20; Ethel Shanas, "The American Journal of

money, and connections existed at other U.S. universities. What distinguished Chicago's social science faculty was its penchant for cross-disciplinary risk taking. Because of the university's size, collegial mores, and tradition of promoting open if intense competition, those who might have been "cultural outcasts" (including women, Jews, and African Americans) elsewhere found congenial niches on campus. More than elsewhere, social researchers pooled resources to tackle big problems that transcended disciplinary boundaries.[56]

Though not by design, cross-disciplinary work on aging at Chicago before World War II found a home in the university's second oldest interdepartmental unit, the Committee on Child Development (CCD).[57] In 1934, four years after being organized, the CCD faculty of twelve chose not to foreclose their options by becoming an Institute of Child Development similar to those recently established at Berkeley, Columbia, Yale, and Minnesota. The staff's research focused on patterns of physical growth and nutritional requirements, as well as the development of personality, intellect, and behavior among "normal" children and emotionally disturbed students observed at the university's Orthogenic School.[58] Projects undertaken by the fledgling Society for Research in Child Development were sustained by CCD faculty, who held key offices and wrote seven of the Society's first nine monographs.

In 1937 the committee was given authority to grant master's degrees and Ph.D.s. Three years later, the committee's name changed from the Committee of Child Development to the Committee of Human Development (CHD). The redesignation signaled widening research interests and the wishes of new faculty. A Chicago Ph.D., Ralph W. Tyler returned to the University in 1938 because he was interested "in trying to get a much

Sociology Through Fifty Years," *American Journal of Sociology*, vol. 50 (1945): 522–3. For a compelling example of how a Chicago sociologist affected policy, see how William Ogburn's concept of a "cultural lag" shaped the Hoover study, *Recent Social Trends*, in *Behavioral and Social Science–Fifty Years of Discovery* ed. Neil J. Smelser and Dean R. Gerstein (Washington, DC: National Academy Press, 1986), p. 24. For a broader perspective on the link between Chicago social scientists and policy-making, see William H. Kruskal, ed., *The Social Sciences* (Chicago: University of Chicago Press, 1982), p. 108.

56 I develop this notion of social science interdisciplinarity from Jerry G. Gaff and Robert C. Wilson, "Faculty Cultures and Interdisciplinary Studies," *Journal of Higher Education*, vol. 42 (1971): 186–201; Lowell L. Hargens and Warren O. Hagstrom, "Sponsored and Contest Mobility of American Academic Scientists," *Sociology of Education*, vol. 40 (Winter 1967): 24–38; and Gene M. Lyons, *The Uneasy Relationship* (New York: Russell Sage Foundation, 1969), p. 9.

57 See "The History, Present Status, and Future Plans of the Committee on Human Development," CHD. Nathan Shock had one of the first fellowships supervised by the Committee. See letter of F. Woodward to Edwin R. Embree, March 24, 1931, CHD.

58 For the research agenda, see The Committee on Human Development, *25th Anniversary* (Chicago: University of Chicago, 1965), p. 6. For the relationship of CCD to SRCD, see memorandum of Robert J. Havighurst to Bernice Neugarten, dated February 1979, CHD.

broader view of the development of human beings than is afforded by any discipline separately."[59] So was Robert J. Havighurst, a Ph.D in chemistry and former member of the Wisconsin physics department, who came two years later with a joint appointment in education and CHD. In the mid-1930s Havighurst had worked with Lawrence Frank at Rockefeller's General Education Board.[60] Given the diverse backgrounds of these key actors and differences in opportunities in Chicago and Baltimore, CHD, which lacked GRC's resources in the biological sciences, strived to become a major center in social psychology.

Community studies were the focus of CHD's earliest collaborative ventures. In the late 1930s and early 1940s W. Lloyd Warner and his colleagues discussed the relative merits of possible sites for longitudinal studies of human behavior in what became his "Jonesville" and "Yankee City" series. Under Havighurst a group worked with the U.S. Office of Indian Affairs on cross-cultural studies of education. Meanwhile, Allison Davis and Ernest Haggard challenged the validity of giving low-income, minority children standardized intelligence tests. The recruitment and readjustment of U.S. veterans was another major case study undertaken between 1942 and 1947.[61] The CHD's research funds increased, and enrollment grew from 40 to 160 during World War II. The committee attracted outstanding talent, such as Bruno Bettelheim, Helen Koch, David Riesman and Carl Rogers, to its faculty. Two dozen research projects were in progress in the mid-1950s. Part-time jobs were crafted for people like Bernice L. Neugarten, who took a B.A. in French before earning CHD's second Ph.D.[62] After

---

59 Tyler quotation from The University of Chicago, *Human Development*, February 1948, CHD, p. 1. Havighurst biosketch from ibid., p. 3. See also The University of Chicago, The Committee on Human Development, *25th Anniversary*, 1965, CHD. The Committee on Child Development's founding chair, the anatomist Richard E. Scammon, returned to the University of Minnesota in 1931. More than two decades later, the Committee was concerned about the imbalance due to a lack of a biologist. See Robert J. Havighurst, "The Place of a Biologist in the Committee on Human Development," memo dated February 1953, CHD; on Scammon, see *Who Was Who in America*, vol. 7 (Chicago: Marquis Publications, 1981), p. 504. For the "virtue" of social scientists not borrowing from natural scientists, see Ernest W. Burgess, ed., *Personality and the Social Group* (Chicago: University of Chicago Press, 1929), p. 180.

60 Bernice L. Neugarten, "Robert J. Havighurst, a Pioneer in Social Gerontology," *Zeitschrift für Gerontologie* (März/April 1975): 81–6; Richardson, *Century of the Child*, p. 144.

61 See University of Chicago, *Human Development*, April 1949, pp. 1–3; "Minutes of the Meeting, April 28, 1941, of the Research Committee of the Committee on Human Development," CHD, p. 9; "Race, Class and Socialization: Contributions of the Committee on Human Development," mimeo, October 5, 1983, CHD, pp. 3–4. It is worth noting that the first book-length publication by Havighurst and Neugarten, two of gerontology's giants, was *American Indian and White Children: A Sociopsychological Investigation* (Chicago: University of Chicago Press, 1955).

62 "History, Present Status," (1954), pp. 1–2; CHD, *25th Anniversary*, p. 9. For more on Neugarten, see her "The Aging Society and My Academic Life," in *Sociological Lives*, ed. Matilda White Riley (Beverly Hills, CA: Sage, 1988), pp. 91–106.

a few years Neugarten became the first person tenured exclusively in the committee.

The CHD faculty's involvement in "aging" research was an extension of their earlier work on childhood and youth; it also was an offshoot of ongoing community studies. Havighurst in 1943 mentioned his nascent interest in the problems of the elderly to Ernest Burgess, a distinguished colleague in sociology. Shortly after this conversation, both men assumed major roles in writing the SSRC blueprint for studies of aging. Their partnership quickly placed Chicago into the forefront of designing social science curricula that dealt with later maturity. "A study of social adjustment in old age" was listed in CHD's research program in the university's 1946–7 "Announcements." The graduate course that Burgess and Havighurst offered in the spring 1948 was one of the first of its kind, as was the two-day "institute on problems of old age" that CHD sponsored in August 1949.[63] Students in the early 1950s were given a syllabus "to outline what was considered essential for the education of master's and doctor's candidates in the field . . . [that represented] a considerable effort of integration compared to anything that has previously taken place." At the end of the decade Bernice Neugarten, Robert Havighurst, and Claire Ryder published *A Syllabus and Annotated Bibliography on an Interdisciplinary Course in Social Gerontology.* Material, drawn largely from psychology and sociology, stressed developmental concepts and dealt with topics such as age and sex roles, adjustment issues, work, play, and the family. Lest important topics be ignored, readings were also suggested "for students who have had little biological training."[64]

Having relied on university resources and philanthropic support (from the Julius Rosenwald Fund, Carnegie Corporation, and Rockefeller Foundation), CHD applied for federal support for training in gerontology as soon as it became available. Two fellowships were secured in 1958–9 under the National Institute of Mental Health's (NIMH) program in geriatric psychology; the new National Institute of Child Health and Human Development became the chief source of funding after 1964, with additional fellowships underwritten by the U.S. Administration on Aging, an agency

---

63 The University of Chicago, *Announcements: Study in Human Development*, vol. 46 (June 15, 1946): 7; syllabi and announcement of the 1949 Institute in the CHD files. A 1949 syllabus indicates that the course was offered from the Education, Home Economics, Psychology, and Sociology departments; books to be read included Cowdry's *Problems of Ageing* (1942); Oscar J. Kaplan's *Mental Disorders in Later Life* (1945), the first of this genre; and Cavan's *Personal Adjustment in Old Age.*

64 Comments on the syllabus in Tyler (1952), p. 5. See also Bernice L. Neugarten, Robert J. Havighurst, and Claire F. Ryder, *A Syllabus and Annotated Bibliography on an Interdisciplinary Course in Social Gerontology* (Ann Arbor, MI: Institute for Social Gerontology, 1959), p. 1,959. In later years, Neugarten resisted suggesting that CHD was promoting "social gerontology," as the term was developed at the University of Michigan's Institute of Gerontology in the 1950s. See *infra.*, Chapter 5.

established in 1965. Many Chicago Ph.D.s in adult development and aging from the late 1950s to early 1970s – Vern Bengtson, David Chiriboga, Paul Costa, Nancy Datan, David Gutmann, Margaret Huyck, Eva Kahana, Carol LeFevre, Sheldon Tobin, Lillian Troll, and Vivian Wood – went on to make major contributions in the social psychology of aging. (This roster suggests that, compared to the biological sciences, greater opportunities were open to women trained to do social science research on aging.) In recognition of her success in training researchers in aging, Professor Neugarten received the Gerontological Society of America's first Distinguished Mentorship Award.[65]

Biological perspectives were not a major component of graduate training at CHD, but students nonetheless were afforded "laboratory" experiences. "Our goal is to assist the student to focus his activities in the research field, to provide seminars designed to provide special training in research method and theory, and to implement his course work with relevant field work training."[66] In what was emerging as a Chicago style of doing social research, projects related to human development in the 1930s were based on community studies. Pearl Harbor interrupted plans to launch a committee-wide set of longitudinal analyses of child and adult development directed by psychologists, biologists, and social anthropologists. After the war, several CHD faculty wanted "to secure the kind of knowledge which may assist aging persons on such questions as employment, health, civic participation, and the use of leisure time." On the basis of preliminary work in Kansas City by a local research outfit, Community Studies, Inc., Havighurst and Warner (in collaboration with sociologist Everett Hughes, David Riesman, as well as Ethel Shanas, one of CHD's first doctorates) decided to study aging in this Midwest city. Neugarten and William E. Henry, who also had an appointment in psychology, were instrumental in securing funds from the Carnegie Corporation and NIMH. They were charged with overseeing a cross-sectional survey of adults between the ages of forty and seventy. Another panel of people between the ages of forty and eighty-five were interviewed twice yearly. For the rest of the decade, the Kansas City Study of Adult Life served as the committee's major "social science laboratory."[67]

Just because CHD faculty and students generally shared the same goals

65 Information on funding comes from a grant proposal, prepared February 4, 1969, CHD. It should be noted that CHD was not the only unit on campus receiving NIMH support for research and training on aging. See "Aging and the Aged," *University of Chicago Reports*, vol. 12 (November 1961): 1a-18. Neugarten's mentoring has also been saluted by colleagues in the American Psychological Association.

66 "The History, Present Status and Future Plans of the Committee on Human Development," June 1954, p. 8.

67 *Ibid.*, p, 9; "Aging and the Aged," p. 6a; University of Chicago, Office of Press Relations, release, 6–23–52, CHD. An undated memo from Ethel Shanas to Robert Havighurst on the "Kansas City Sample Selection" merits reading.

and often worked with the same data sets does not mean that they wholly agreed with each other's interpretations. Elaine Cumming and William Henry set forth nine postulates about "the process of disengagement" in *Growing Old* (1961). Developing "an inductive theory of aging to fit [their] data," the pair stipulated that "aging is an inevitable, mutual withdrawal or disengagement, resulting in decreased interaction between the aging person and others in the social system he belongs to."[68] That Cumming and Henry's disengagement thesis was the first theory of aging developed by social scientists working in the field earns it a place in any gerontologic history. The proposition made intuitive sense – most people with advancing age do disengage from previous activities – and was acclaimed by Talcott Parsons, who called *Growing Old* "an important book." Like Cavan and her associates, the pair used the language of the SSRC report but they drew different inferences. Whereas Burgess and Havighurst emphasized potentials, Cumming and Henry stressed finitude: Psychogerontology should focus on a person's mental health "until disengagement is complete," for "death is the last logical step in the process of living."[69] In *Growing Old*, Cumming and Henry crafted a social science analogue to Walter Cannon's concept of "homeostasis."

Several teams of CHD researchers, at first privately and later through publications, questioned Cumming and Henry's findings. Psychologists tended to disagree with sociologists over the degree of "inevitability" of rates of disengagement and about the extent of withdrawal over the life course. Havighurst, for instance, relied heavily on Kansas City data he had collected with Martin Loeb between 1952 and 1955 in advancing his "activity theory" of aging. Far from finding that the elderly withdrew from relationships, Havighurst emphasized that most people readjusted their social roles in late life.[70] Neugarten's skepticism is evident in the essays she published in her reader, *Middle Age and Aging* (1968), and elsewhere:

> It has been tempting for students of behavior to draw parallels between biological phenomena and psychological. . . . It has been relatively easy, if not always accurate, first to assume, then to look for ways of

68 Elaine Cumming and William E. Henry, *Growing Old* (New York: Basic, 1961), pp. 227. 14, In an article in *TG*, vol. 34 (1994), "Re-engaging the Disengagement Theory of Aging," written with Vern Bengtson, I have tried to put the disengagement-theory controversy into historical context. I have also learned from Victor Marshall's manuscript, "Sociology, Psychology, and the Theoretical Legacy of the Kansas City Studies."

69 Parson's comment in his "foreword" to Cumming and Henry, *Growing Old*, p. v. Besides relating disengagement to time and death in this quotation (p. 227), Cumming and Henry also related the theory to other "practical" matters such as intergenerational tensions.

70 For the best discussion of the controversy, see Harold L. Orbach, "The Disengagement Theory of Aging," Ph.D. diss., University of Minnesota, 1975. See also Bryan S. Turner, *Medical Power and Social Knowledge* (Beverly Hills, CA,: Sage, 1987), pp. 116–18. I also rely on interviews I had with Havighurst, Neugarten, and Orbach. See also Arlie Russell Hochschild, "Disengagement Theory," *American Sociological Review*, vol. 40 (October 1975): 553–69.

describing sequential and orderly progressions in psychological and social behavior. . . . In our recent investigations we have perceived age norms and the age-status system as forming a backdrop or cultural context against which the behavioral and personality differences of adults should be viewed. . . . At the same time there were sex differences in these perceptions, and differences between members of different social classes.[71]

Long before feminist interpretations were fashionable in gerontology, Neugarten stressed the importance of sex- and gender-based differences in biological and social time clocks. In studying both children and elders, she challenged Cumming and Henry's assumption about invariant continuities in behavioral patterns. On the contrary: Neugarten tried empirically to disentangle age-conditioned developmental patterns from what she called the "socio-adaptational" effects. She was struck by cross-sectional differences in age, race, and class evident in the Kansas City case study. They demonstrated that there were many pathways of aging, not an inevitable, normative, much less ubiquitous, pattern.

"The disengagement controversy" dissipated long before the fundamental issues it raised were fully resolved. Some protagonists actually disengaged from the field. Cumming never offered "further thoughts" after 1963; Henry distanced himself from *Growing Old* a year later.[72] Moving on – together, separately, and with CHD students – Havighurst and Neugarten pursued questions in the social psychology of aging inspired by their own research agenda. Their research agenda complemented, but did not replicate, the approach taken by Shock's biologists and medical scientists. The two camps basically operated in separate spheres. There were similarities: Biomedical researchers and social science investigators sought indications of "normal" aging; both valued empirical, longitudinal analyses. In neither Baltimore nor Chicago by the early 1960s, however, were biological and behavioral analyses in gerontology being conducted by investigators working together as a team. Whereas Shock discounted the value of theory in developing a science of gerontology, Neugarten contended that "over and above problems of method . . . the student of adult personality suffers from the lack of theory."[73] Elsewhere, however, opportunities were arising to create just such a research environment.

71 Bernice L. Neugarten, "Adult Personality," in *Middle Age and Aging*, ed. Bernice L. Neugarten (Chicago: University of Chicago Press, 1968), pp. 141, 144. See also, idem, "Continuities and Discontinuities of Psychological Issues into Adult Life," *Human Development*, vol. 12 (1969): 121–30. See also Charlotte Buhler and Fred Massarik, *The Course of Human Life* (New York: Springer, 1968), p. 51.

72 Orbach, "Disengagement Theory," pp. 90, 116, 203. See William E. Henry, "Disengagement Theory and the Elderly" in *Creating Opportunities for Older Persons* (Washington, DC: Office of Aging, October 1964), pp. 17–20.

73 Bernice L. Neugarten, "Personality Changes During the Adult Years," in *Psychological*

Gerontology takes root at the University of Southern California and Duke

In February 1964 the University of Southern California (USC) signed a contract with the Rossmoor Corporation so that "research concerning the problems of retirement and aging may be conducted in Rossmoor's and the public's behalf by the University . . . in an efficient and integrated manner, for the ultimate benefit of retired and elderly persons throughout the United States and the World."[74] Rossmoor built retirement communities called "Leisure Worlds," which comprised of dwellings, medical care facilities, recreation sites, and shopping centers for people over age 52. The corporation wanted "basic data concerning the physical, psychological, sociological, and other problems of retirement and aging." It agreed to give USC an advance of $50,000 and then contribute $50 for every unit sold in southern California; the arrangement was potentially worth millions, given Leisure World's appeal. The University of Southern California, having relied on its entrepreneurial instincts since its founding in 1880, thought it was a good deal. Senior citizens were migrating to the area, so there was a future for research on aging. All USC officials needed to capitalize on the opportunity to underwrite a gerontology center with corporate support was to find the right leader.

University of Southern California chancellor Norman Topping, the man who hired football coach John McCay, said that recruiting James E. Birren was the second most important appointment of his tenure. Birren found that he enjoyed investigating how "biological and environmental factors modulated behavioral expressions of physiological mechanisms"[75] in his graduate work on seasickness at Northwestern and especially during his wartime duty at the Naval Medical Research Institute, where he collaborated with biological scientists on measuring fatigue. Between 1947 and 1950, Birren worked at the GRC in Baltimore; his wife, Betty, helped Nathan Shock compile his *Classified Bibliography on Gerontology and Geriatrics*. Birren then spent the next three years on leave at the University of Chicago; he was appointed as an assistant professor of anatomy and formed friendships with Robert Havighurst, Bernice Neugarten, and other members of the CHD. Between 1953 and 1964, Birren served as chief of

Backgrounds of Adult Education, ed. Raymond G. Kuhlen (Chicago: Center for the Study of Liberal Education for Adults, 1963), p. 47.

74 A copy of the agreement, dated February, 3, 1964, is in the Andrus Gerontology Center historical files, University of Southern California archives. Other details cited in this paragraph come from this document.

75 Quotation from an interview with James E. Birren, August 13, 1987. Topping quotation from dinner speech by Norman Topping on the occasion of Birren's "retirement" from USC. For more biographical material, see Vern L. Bengtson and K. Warner Schaie, eds., *The Course of Later Life* (New York: Springer, 1989), pp. viii–ix.

the Section on Aging at NIMH. Despite increasing administrative duties, Birren maintained an active lab. He made his reputation publishing studies that documented how the functioning of the nervous system altered with age. A project begun in 1955 that focused on interrelations between cerebral physiological changes, psychological capacities, and psychiatric symptoms expressed with advancing aging culminated in a major project (with Robert N. Butler, among others) published as *Human Aging I: A Biological and Behavioral Study.*[76] Birren was president of the GSA (1961–2) and an editor of the *JoG* from 1956 to 1962. Almost since its creation, he had been active in the American Psychological Association's Division of Adult Development and Aging.

To a virologist like Topping, Birren's research career and administrative experiences clearly demonstrated that he thrived at the interstices of the biomedical and social behavioral sciences. He was a pacesetter in gerontology with a proven track record at NIH.[77] "Research on aging is undergoing a metamorphosis into an experimental field, and as facts about aging increase, more and more attention will be given to method and theory, not only to manage and systematize the increasing data but also to save time in devising more efficient experiments," Birren wrote in the *Handbook of Aging and the Individual* (1959). "The essential ingredient is an investigator who is aware of the problems of the field and is alert for new or different methods for their solution."[78]

Birren remembers that his first year at USC was rough. He and a secretary *were* the Rossmoor-Cortese Institute. Although Topping had guaranteed support for the first three years, Birren quickly discovered that the agreement with Rossmoor raised sticky questions about lines of authority and responsibility. The deal would not generate the income needed to meet the institute's minimum budget.[79] So Birren applied, with success, for train-

76 For more on Birren's early research, see esp. a trio of essays he wrote with Jack Botwinick that appeared in the *JoG*, vol. 10 (1955): 429–40. For a self-assessment of the significance of this work, see James E. Birren, "Toward an Experimental Psychology of Aging," *American Psychologist*, vol. 25 (1970): 133; see also, J. M. A. Munnichs, "A Short History of Psychogerontology," *Human Development, vol.* 9 (1966): 230–45. For the collaborative venture, see James E. Birren et al., *Human Aging I: A Biological and Behavioral Study* (Rockville, MD: NIMH, 1971), p. 2. It is worth noting that Birren left NIMH in 1964 to become the first head of the Division of Aging of the newly founded National Institute of Child Health and Human Development. Thus, for one year, before finally accepting the USC offer, Birren oversaw the work of his old mentor Nathan Shock.

77 In addition, Birren evinced manifest concern for methodological and conceptual rigor, the cross-disciplinary imagination, and the penchant for networking that often exceeded peer expectations. To wit: Over the course of his career, Birren has edited more gerontology handbooks than anyone else in the field.

78 James E. Birren, "Principles of Research on Aging," in *Handbook of Aging and the Individual*, ed. James E. Birren, (Chicago: University of Chicago Press, 1959), p. 2.

79 See, for example, the memorandum for the record Birren wrote on October 4, 1965, after meeting with the medical director of the Leisure World Foundation, the memorandum

ing grants from the U.S. Public Health Service. The funds enabled him to support graduate students and to make shrewd faculty appointments – such as hiring in 1967 a recent Chicago sociologist, Vern Bengtson, whose reputation would over time be closely identified with USC's. That summer Birren sponsored his first Summer Institute for Study in Gerontology and with seed money from NIMH conducted workshops for professionals.

Obtaining research and training grants gave Birren leverage in requesting a regular academic budget. "The University has already moved into a position of recognition and visibility in a field of national priority," he wrote Topping a year after his arrival.[80] Committed to multidisciplinarity, Birren promoted research projects in biology, psychology, sociology, economics, and fields such as urban studies. He also wanted to establish a ten-year longitudinal study covering the entire adult life span. Aware that Shock's GRC had 90,000 square feet of lab space under construction and that Duke University had erected a new building in excess of 50,000 square feet to house its Center on Aging, Birren wanted to raise $5 million for a similar facility at USC. There were advantages to maintaining a regional focus under the aegis of the Rossmoor-Cortese Institute, but Birren wanted to run a flagship research and training center. "Right now planning for the aging is done *without fundamental understanding of the meaning of aging biologically, psychologically, and socially.*"[81] With the help of former USC athletes and other local talent, Birren sought resources to match his dreams.

In 1968 the American Association of Retired Persons (AARP) approached Birren about the possibility of erecting a facility at USC in honor of its founder, Ethel Percy Andrus, an alumna who had been principal of a high school near campus. The AARP agreed to contribute $2 million or to underwrite half the cost (whichever was less) of erecting a "research and training building."[82] Edward Durell Stone was commissioned to design a

from Birren to the Executive Committee of the Rossmoor-Cortese Institute, dated November 4, 1965; and the memorandum from Aili Larson to Birren, dated December, 9, 1965. A memo from Birren to Topping, dated 10/20/65 indicates that USC anticipated getting $4 million from Rossmoor by 1969, but had received only $88,000 in the first eighteen months. All memos are in the USC archives. Interview with James and Betty Birren in August 1987.

80 Birren to Topping, dated October 6, 1966, USC archives. On the biological side, Birren convinced Ruth Weg, a USC faculty member, to embark on research on aging. He also recruited Bernard Strehler from Shock's lab. Strehler's *Time, Cells, and Aging* (New York: Academic Press, 1962), was one of the most respected critiques of cellular aging then available. Strehler's relationship with Shock had been stormy, however, and so too were his years at USC, before he moved to UCLA. In replacing him with Caleb Finch, Birren once again found a rising star who was to prove as much an anchor in the biological sciences as Bengtson did in the social sciences.

81 Birren to Robert R. Dockson, Chairman, University Planning Commission, November 1, 1966, p. 6 in USC archives.

82 See contracts dated September 6, 1968, and June 1, 1970, which cover several key institutional and personnel contracts. (Technically, AARP at the time consisted of *two* bodies,

55,000 square foot building complete with wet labs and multipurpose auditorium. Additional resources were forthcoming during the decade from Leonard Davis (an insurance executive who made millions by collaborating with Ethel Percy Andrus), the Andrew Norman Charitable Trust, and the Armand Hammer Foundation. In addition to NIH support, private bequests permitted Birren and his colleagues to develop the nation's most prestigious programs leading to *degrees* in gerontology and to establish an institute for advanced study.

The Andrus Gerontology Center under Birren's leadership became an extraordinarily successful enterprise on any number of counts. Between 1965 and 1980, USC's net return on its $7.6 million investment exceeded $22 million in research-generated overhead, tuition, and gifts. Birren recruited more than eighty faculty members (including K. Warner Schaie, Caleb Finch, Diana Woodruff, Neal Cutler, Judith Treas, Fernando Torres-Gil, Pauline Ragan, William Lammers, and Margaret Gatz), most of whom held appointments in one of sixteen other schools and departments. During the first fifteen years, Andrus faculty supervised 95 doctoral students. The Leonard Davis School during its first five years graduated 214 individuals, a third of whom earned bachelors degrees or certificates.[83]

Besides these institutional achievements, Birren has contributed various metaphors to conceptualize the state of gerontologic science during the course of his own professional maturation. Looking back "on events during the formative years of my career," Birren affirmed his long-standing conviction "that the problems of aging are in most cases not like the lock-and-key problems of many areas (e.g., poliomyelitis and immunization), in which there is one single solution. They become transformed over time and as our standards and expectations rise, even as the topics seem to remain the same."[84] Like Cowdry, Steiglitz, and Shock, he felt that different scientific viewpoints were needed to solve various puzzles of aging. In his first handbook, Birren differentiated among the biological, psychological, and social "ages of an individual." In his 1990 handbook, he proposed that "dynamic terms be introduced, such as *senescening* to refer to the biological processes of aging, *eldering* to refer to the social processes of aging, and *geronting* to refer to the psychological processes of aging."[85] Different dis-

---

for the National Retired Teachers Association was separate.) Birren recalls that AARP considered two other sites, Washington and Ann Arbor.

83 University of Southern California, *Ethel Percy Andrus Gerontology Center*. (Although undated, this is clearly a recruiting brochure ca. 1980.) Before he retired from USC, Birren would also be instrumental in shaping one of the nation's first Ph.D. degrees in gerontology. The USC's program, like the one at the University of Massachusetts, Boston, focused on policy.

84 James E. Birren, "My Perspectives on Research on Aging," in Bengtson and Schaie, eds., *The Course of Later Life*, p. 137.

85 Birren, "Principles of Research on Aging," in Birren, *Handbook of Aging and the Individual*, p. 18; James E. Birren and Betty A. Birren, "The Concepts, Models, and History of

ciplines pursued different problems, Birren acknowledged. While he could not impose a "unity of science" where none existed, Birren lamented the absence of conceptual linkages. "The scope of the field and, more recently, the degree of its activity and research productivity have resulted in the creation of islands of knowledge with little communication between them."[86]

Birren became one of the field's most distinguished scientists by attaining and then maintaining a position at the vanguard of psychogerontology. Throughout his career, he attended to fundamental issues. He incorporated lessons he learned at NIH, at the University of Chicago, and from other pacesetters in institution building at USC. The story of how Ewald W. Busse built an impressive Center on Aging in the medical school at Duke University is also instructive, for its congruence with Birren's as much as for its twists.

"Bud" Busse earned his M.D. from Washington University in 1942, where he worked closely with Edmund V. Cowdry and Robert A. Moore, a pathologist who served as the first editor of the *JoG*.[87] Busse entered the U.S. Army after completing an internship; he spent most of his military service in the Neuropsychiatric Center and Army School of Neuropsychiatric Nursing at McCloskey General Hospital in Temple, Texas, where he established two electroencephalographic (EEG) laboratories. After his discharge, Busse joined the medical faculty at the University of Colorado, where he began to integrate various intellectual interests in ways to understand the temporal lobe of the brain. From 1946 to 1953, he was director of the Electroencephalography Laboratory. In addition, Busse received psychiatric training (1946–50) at the University of Colorado Medical Center. He became certified in psychiatry by the American Board of Psychiatry and Neurology in 1948, and a year later by the American Board of Clinical Neurophysiology. Busse also served as head of the Division of Psychosomatic Medicine at Colorado General Hospital (1950–3), and as a lecturer in neurophysiology and psychosomatic medicine in the University of Denver's School of Graduate Medicine (1947–53). These various experiences

---

the Psychology of Aging," in *Handbook of the Psychology of Aging*, ed. James E. Birren and K. Warner Schaie, 3rd ed. (New York: Academic Press, 1990), p. 4. Birren first introduced this trinity of gerunds with J. J. F. Schroots in "Steps to an Ontogenetic Psychology, *Academic Psychology Bulletin*, vol. 6 (1984): 177–90.

86 For a fuller biographical sketch, see the entry in *Profiles in Gerontology: A Biographical Dictionary*, ed. W. Andrew Achenbaum and Daniel M. Albert (Westport, CT: Greenwood Press, 1995). For Ewald W. Busse's own view of his career and of aging, see his essay, "A Temporal Odyssey," *TG*, vol. 9 (1969): 1–8; and idem, "The Myth, History, and Science of Aging," in *Geriatric Psychiatry*, ed. Ewald W. Busse and Dan G. Blazer (American Psychiatric Press, 1989), pp. 3–34.

87 See, for instance, his paper with Robert Barnes and Albert J. Silverman, among others, "Factors That Influence the Psyche of Elderly Persons," *American Journal of Psychiatry*, vol. 110 (1954): 897–903.

convinced Busse he would make the most headway if he were to confine his studies to the brain waves of "normal" elderly patients. In 1952, NIMH began to underwrite Busse's research.[88]

In the fall of 1953, Busse and part of his team moved to the Duke University School of Medicine. There he intended (1) to continue evaluating the significance and possible etiology of localized and diffuse EEG changes found in men and women over the age of sixty; (2) to assess the importance of social and cultural factors as they affect the aging process; and (3) to study the psychological and physiological effects of aging on elderly persons. Over the course of the next dozen years, Busse and his colleagues published a series of papers concerned with the temporal lobe foci encountered in the latter part of the life span. They found, among other things, that the anterior lobe disturbance frequently recorded in the elderly's EEG had no prognostic or diagnostic relationship to aphasia, seizures, or alterations in psychological function.[89] Comparisons with younger subjects, however, revealed significant differences in fast brain rhythms by gender and age. This suggested – although Busse was careful to stress the inconclusiveness of evidence and the lack of a firm causal connection between diffuse EEGs and psychological functions – that a slowing of the dominant alpha frequency, while not evidence of intellectual decline, might be a biomarker that predicted deficits that were either developmental or intellectual. Busse remained interested in studying EEGs throughout his scientific career. An instrument, not a big idea, thus sparked Busse's interest in research on aging. As he matured, he became very committed to understanding all factors that shaped senescence.[90] Busse wrote more than 150 scientific papers, 40 chapters for handbooks and professional volumes, and edited or co-edited 10 books.

Shortly after his arrival at Durham, Busse tried to convince Hollis Edens, Duke's president, that the university needed a gerontology center. He and a group of faculty members argued that "the advancement and dissemination of scientific knowledge is dependent upon proper communication.

88 See, for instance, Ewald W. Busse and W. D. Obrist, "Pre-senescent Encephalographic Changes in Normal Subjects," *JoG*, vol. 20 (1965): 315–20; W. D. Obrist, Ewald W. Busse, Carl Eisdorfer, and Robert W. Kleemeier, "Relations of the Electroencephalogram Intellectual Function in Senescence," ibid., vol. 17 (1962): 197–206.

89 See, for instance, an early paper of Busse's, with R. H. Dovenmuehle, "Studies of Processes of Aging–A Review of the Findings of a Multidisciplinary Approach," *British Journal of Physical Medicine*, vol. 19 (1956): 100–3. In "Primary and Secondary Aging," in *The Encyclopedia of Aging*, ed. George L. Maddox (Springer Publishing, 1987), Busse noted the variations and extremes in biological aging, which does not necessarily begin in the end of life. Primary aging in his opinion was determined by heredity and other inherent human factors; secondary aging was caused by hostile factors in the environment, including trauma and acquired diseases.

90 For more on this, see Ewald W. Busse and George L. Maddox, *The Duke Longitudinal Studies of Normal Aging 1955–1980* New York: (Springer, 1982).

Several scientific disciplines to a large extent have developed independent 'languages' which permit satisfactory interchange of ideas within their own ranks. This system of a highly specialized scientific language works relatively satisfactorily within a limited area but becomes a very serious hindrance when a complex problem is encountered which requires the help of other scientific disciplines. Gerontology is such a complex problem whose solution requires the integration and coordination of various sciences." Edens announced the formation of a university-wide Council on Gerontology in April 1955. Once a month, faculty and visitors shared ideas in an ongoing seminar. Coincident with the creation of the gerontology council, though it basically was a continuation of Busse's studies of the aging nervous system, was the Duke Longitudinal Studies. Begun in 1955, the first wave studied were 270 noninstitutionalized African American and white males and females between the ages of sixty and ninety-four. These volunteers were drawn from three central North Carolina counties. A second wave (drawn in 1970) selected 502 panelists from the rolls of a large insurance company and from Duke Hospital records.[91]

In 1957, the National Heart Institute and NIMH made $1.5 million available to Duke University over a five-year period to set up a pilot regional center for research on aging. In announcing the award, Surgeon General E. L. Burney singled out two reasons for making this grant: Duke was a private-sector university, and it promised to conduct interdisciplinary and multidisciplinary work. Busse became the founding director of the center and served at the helm for the next thirteen years. Distinguished members of the Duke faculty, such as biochemist Philip Handler, sociologist John McKinney, and economists Frank de Vyver, Juanita Kreps, and Joseph Spengler, served on advisory panels. Nathan W. Shock took a keen interest in establishing the center; he was instrumental in organizing a three-day conference on Aging and Radiation there in 1958.[92]

Meanwhile Busse's career flourished. He served as president of both the GSA (1967–8) and the American Geriatrics Society (AGS) (1975–6). A president of the American Psychiatric Association (1971–2) and fellow of the American Association for the Advancement of Science, Busse also was president of the International Association of Gerontology (1985–9).

Recounting key intellectual and institutional developments at GRC, CHD, USC, and Duke highlights certain trends during gerontology's first decades.

91 For more, see Duke University Council on Gerontology, *Proceedings of Seminars*, 1955–57 (Duke University Regional Center on Aging, 1959). Busse recruited George Maddox, Dan Blazer, Erdman Palmore, and (later) Linda George to the faculty – all of whom became stars in the field.

92 James E. Birren and Walter R. Cunningham, "Research on the Psychology of Aging: Principles, Concepts and Theory," in *Handbook of the Psychology of Aging*, ed. James E. Birren and K. Warner Schaie, 2d ed. (New York: Van Nostrand Reinhold, 1985), p. 3.

From Nathan Shock's vantage point, research on aging was making great strides:

> By 1960 Gerontology had become visible as a developing science, thanks to the persistent efforts of a few scientists, private philanthropic foundations and the Federal Government. Developments in molecular biology, molecular genetics, and immunology led to the formulation of biological theories which could be applied to aging at the cellular level. Furthermore, these theories could be experimentally tested. Gerontology became respectable in the eyes of scientists.[93]

Shock identified at least three elements – the recruitment of dedicated, smart researchers with financial backing and institutional support; the creation of a solid knowledge base, which was primarily grounded in the biological sciences; and the refinement of multidisciplinary orientations through lab tests and peer review – as essential for advancing gerontology as a scientific field of inquiry. Others shared Shock's sense of how science matured. "The time has come," wrote Berkeley psychologist Egon Brunswik in 1956, "when the unity of science is best served by stressing the thematic differentiation among the sciences within the over-all unity." Lawrence Frank concurred: "This field [of gerontology] may be viewed as we are learning to conceive of other fields, as arising from the patterned transactional relations of *all* the members of the cultural-social field, each of which carries on continual intercourse with other members of the group."[94]

   For all of their accomplishments, researchers on aging by the early 1960s had not yet standardized definitions or issues. Different organizations, including lay groups, competed for control over how scientific knowledge was generated, and gerontologic rewards and prestige were distributed. According to Stephen Fuchs and Jonathan Turner, such diffuseness in managing scientific production sets the stage for uncertainties: "The structures of organizational control will be informal and patrimonial; and the structures of knowledge highly diverse."[95] Applying Fuchs and Turner's insights to gerontology brings to mind what social geographers characterize as a "hollow sanguine frontier": The case for a science of aging still needed to be made; its status, despite Shock's sanguine assessment, remained mar-

---

93 Nathan W. Shock, "The Evolution of Gerontology as a Science," draft of an essay prepared for *Review of Biological Research in Aging*, dated August 8, 1986, p. 12. Copy given to me by Dr. Shock.

94 Egon Brunswik, "Historical and Thematic Relations of Psychology to Other Sciences," *Scientific Monthly*, vol. 83 (September 1956): 160; Lawrence K. Frank, "Social Systems and Culture" in *Toward a Unified Theory of Human Behavior*, ed. Roy R. Grinker (New York: Basic, 1956), p. 201.

95 Stephen Fuchs and Jonathan H. Turner, "What Makes a Science 'Mature?' " *Sociological Theory*, vol. 4 (Fall 1986): 148; see also Andrew Abbott, *The System of Professions* (Chicago: University of Chicago Press, 1988). On "hollow frontier," see Otto N. Larsen, *Milestones and Millstones* (New Brunswick: Transaction Publishers, 1992), p. 261.

ginal. Some pioneers became disillusioned by the lack of progress being made in research on aging.

Albert I. Lansing had worked with E. V. Cowdry in the early 1940s and, after the war, was a rising star at Washington University. He was one of the first to claim that the growing interest in problems of aging indicated that "gerontology has emerged as a discrete discipline." A series of his articles published in the *JoG* about mechanisms of senescence, which probed the connections between aging and arteriosclerosis, were widely cited.[96] Lansing thus seemed an appropriate choice to edit the third edition of Cowdry's *Problems of Ageing* (1952). How surprising, then, that he sounded so pessimistic a note in his preface. "In some fields of research on ageing little has transpired of note in the last decade," Lansing announced. "Research on the biology of ageing is almost at a standstill. There is hardly a handful of workers in this area today."[97] That sociologists and mental health experts were "moving forward briskly" to the field, in Lansing's opinion, was a mixed blessing. Although he continued to pursue the same types of aging-related research issues he had studied earlier, Lansing disengaged from the gerontologic network; citations to his work in *JoG* declined.

Lansing's invisibility, ironically, illuminates a major identity problem for gerontology after World War II. Investigators did not need to share complementary methodologies or to collaborate in developing paradigms, but they were expected to salute the importance of multidisciplinary research. To count as gerontology, work had to focus explicitly on some intellectual or social issues associated with aging. "Good research may have been carried out, but research so tangentially related to aging that the uninformed reviewer might never guess that presumably it had been initiated under a gerontological aegis," declared Robert Kleemeier. "This does not mean that every project in an aging research program must have age as one of its parameters, but it does mean that gerontological programs must focus unambiguously on age and its relation to other variables."[98] As we will see in Part II, even this common denominator would not sufficiently capture all of the various strands of gerontology, much less suffice to give the field conceptual clarity.

96 Albert I. Lansing, "A Transmissible, Cumulative, and Reversible Factor in Aging," *JoG*, vol. 2 (April 1947): 228; Albert I. Lansing, H. T. Blumenthal, and S. H. Gray, "Aging and Calcification of the Human Coronary Artery," *JoG* 3 (April 1948): 87–97.

97 Albert I. Lansing, "Preface to the Third Edition," in Cowdry's *Problems of Ageing* (Baltimore: Williams & Wilkins, 1952), p. vii. Lansing sounded equally sour in an interview with me thirty-six years later.

98 Robert W. Kleemeier, "Gerontology as a Discipline," *TG*, vol. 5 (1965): 238. See also Alex Comfort, "Feasibility in Age Research," *Nature*, vol. 217 (1968): 320–2.

Part II

Gerontology takes shape in the era of Big Science

LIKE MEMBERS OF ALL other scientific communities, researchers on aging "form their divergent individual practices partly through interacting with nature and thinking by themselves, partly by borrowing from and lending to others."[1] Part One of *Crossing Frontiers* stressed that the roots of "modern" gerontology were very diverse. With the proliferation of journals and handbooks, the creation of research centers, the migration of investigators from a growing number of disciplines and professions, and increasing incidences of specialization and boundary-setting disputes, the field acquired the intellectual and institutional hallmarks of an emerging, occasionally fragmenting, scientific collective enterprise.

Even greater intellectual and institutional branching occurred during gerontology's early years than has been indicated so far. To wit:

In 1939, Sidney L. Pressey and Raymond G. Kuhlen issued *Life: A Psychological Survey*. The book placed more emphasis on the importance of cultural and socioeconomic factors on late-life development than did the contributors to Cowdry's *Problems on Ageing*, published the same year. Others thereafter began to advance arguments along the same lines. Leo Simmons's *The Role of the Aged in Primitive Societies* (1945) offered rich ethnographic evidence demonstrating how different types of cultures produced distinctive types of attitudes and expectations about growing old.[2] Seizing on the significance of societal milieu, Kuhlen subsequently called

1 Philip Kitcher, *The Advancement of Science: Science without Legend, Objectivity without Illusions* (New York: Oxford University Press, 1993), p. 303.
2 Leo Simmons, *The Role of the Aged in Primitive Societies* (New Haven, CT: Yale University Press, 1945); recent work by anthropologists such as Christine Fry, Jennie Keith, and Jay Sokolovsky have moved far beyond Simmons's "western" biases, showing the ways that different cultural traditions affect ideas about old age in different ecological settings in advanced industrial as well as Third World societies.

into question most of the existing research on the relationship between intelligence and aging. Cultural change, he claimed in a 1963 article, "contaminates" both cross-sectional and longitudinal studies by not taking account of the effects of "change in cognitive stimulation which will differentially affect different age groups."[3] Kuhlen's research challenged the scientific "purity" of the gerontologic studies that presumed rather than showed that data, however carefully measured, could ever truly be "timeless."

Then, in *Psychological Development Through the Life Span* (1957), Pressey and Kuhlen opened new markets to gerontologists' research. Stressing themes of "personal value to a reader, of relevance in most fields of applied psychology,"[4] Pressey and Kuhlen invited clinical psychologists and social workers to use available findings when dealing with older clients who were lonely, depressed, or frustrated in efforts to remain productive. Their book's clinical applications offered an alternative to those geropsychologists who believed that more research had to be done in cognitive and social psychology before utilizing results in real-life situations. The potential for schism between "basic" and "applied" behavioral research was no small matter: Pressey in the 1950s was training more Ph.D.s in the psychology of aging than any other mentor.[5]

Kuhlen and Pressey once sounded like mavericks; now, they just seem ahead of their times. In due course, social and behavioral scientists refined the pair's ideas about culture and aging.[6] To the social ethnographic data gathered by anthropologists and sociologists have been added major studies by historians, art and literary critics, philosophers, and theologians, which underscore the importance of time, context, and genre in shaping older people's lives. Similarly, clinical gero-psychology is a booming field; opportunities for applied work in disciplines such as psychology and anthropology presently are greater than prospects for teaching jobs and research posts.

Nowadays, most gerontologic research centers are based in universities or run by the National Institutes of Health (NIH). In 1949, however, the laboratory for gerontology and geriatrics poised to become *the* premier research center in America was maintained and operated by the Loyal Or-

---

3 Raymond G. Kuhlen, "Age and Intelligence: The Significance of Cultural Change in Longitudinal vs. Cross-Sectional Findings," *Vita Humana*, vol. 6 (1963): 124.
4 Sidney L. Pressey and Raymond G. Kuhlen, *Psychological Development Through the Life Span* (New York: Harper & Row, 1957), p. xxii.
5 James E. Birren, "History of the Psychology of Aging," *The Gerontologist*, vol. 1 (September 1961): 129.
6 Particularly influential was *Culture and Aging: An Anthropological Study of Older Americans* by Margaret Clark and Barbara Gallatin Anderson (Springfield: C. C. Thomas, 1967). See also Thomas R. Cole, David D. Van Tassel, and Robert Kastenbaum, *Handbook of the Humanities and Aging* (New York: Springer 1992).

der of Moose at Moosehaven, Florida. Scientists saw great possibilities for a site located in a Sunbelt retirement community. Robert W. Kleemeier, a psychologist recruited from Northwestern to direct the center, felt that "group living in congenial surroundings is not repellant to a great segment of our older people."[7] Kleemeier's premature death, however, dashed hopes for Moosehaven's future. Even so, it is worth pointing out that gerontologists felt that excellent research in the field's formative years could be done in nonacademic settings. The Moosehaven facility had been reorganized to fit Kleemeier's needs. A. J. Carlson, Ernest Burgess, Sidney Pressey, and Nathan Shock had agreed to serve on the advisory committee. Researchers on aging did not require vast sums to do good science; work could flourish at sites where supportive administrators and trustees were not versed in the science of gerontology.

Note that these two additional examples, like most of those introduced in Part One, portray scientists as if they were individual thinkers and entrepreneurs who investigated specialized problems rather independently of external influences. "Scientists actually work together in a variety of *establishments*, where they are employed as professional researchers, technical experts, administrators, managers and teachers. These establishments (or 'laboratories,' 'institutes,' 'research stations,' etc.) are answerable, in turn, to larger *organizations* such as industrial firms, government departments, research councils, and universities," John Ziman points out. "This is a relatively new development. Until say, the Second World War, the majority of scientific research was carried out in the traditional 'academic' style, where each researcher was free – at least in principle – to undertake any investigation that he or she thought worth while."[8] Research on aging evolved into a collective enterprise in an environment dominated by a large, highly organized, research system, a milieu which developed in the United States after World War II.

Gerontology emerged as a field of inquiry in an era of Big Science. As the scale of the scientific enterprise increased, researchers on aging defined and organized their work to take advantage of new opportunities. Investigations were undertaken by multidisciplinary teams working in translaboratory networks. Borders between science and technology, and between basic and applied research, have grown fuzzy, sometimes irrelevant. Because public dollars now fund so much research, "scientific knowledge becomes more politicized and more contestable, less autonomous."[9] The

---

7 Kleemeier quoted in Richard B. Calhoun, *In Search of the New Old* (New York: Elsevier, 1978), p. 211. Kleemeier was also impressed by the facilities built by the Rossmoor company. See also "Current Comment," *Journal of Gerontology*, vol. 4 (July 1949): 251–2.

8 John Ziman, *Knowing Everything About Nothing* (New York: Cambridge University Press, 1987), p. 23.

9 Andrew Webster, *Science, Technology, and Society* (New Brunswick, NJ: Rutgers University Press, 1991), p. 123. For more on Big Science, see Derek de Solla Price, *Little Science, Big*

parochialism of much U.S. gerontology has dissolved, moreover, as North Americans forge partnerships in the international scientific community.

The career of Leonard Hayflick dramatically illustrates how the ways of a gerontologic investigator were affected by the new order. After earning degrees in medical microbiology and chemistry from the University of Pennsylvania, Hayflick spent two years as a McLaughlin Research Fellow in Infection and Immunity in the Department of Microbiology at the University of Texas Medical Branch at Galveston. In 1958, he returned home and became an associate at the prestigious Wistar Institute of Anatomy and Biology in Philadelphia. There, Hayflick and Paul S. Moorhead made what some biogerontologists consider one of the field's most important discoveries.

Since the 1920s, researchers on aging who worked with cell cultures had accepted Alexis Carrel's claim that there was an inverse relationship between the growth of embryonic chicken fibroblasts cultivated in plasma clots and the age of the chicken supplying the plasma. Studies by Cowdry volume-contributor Alfred Cohn, among others, suggested that with increasing age there was a longer latent period preceding the appearance of migrating cells. If these findings were true, then it would be reasonable to hypothesize that biological aging was not due to any intrinsic failure within cells. Senescence occurred at the tissue and organ levels.

Hayflick and Moorhead rejected Carrel's notion that cells might live indefinitely. They took inspiration from nineteenth-century cytologists August Weismann and Charles Sedgwick Minot. Using cultured, normal human fibroblasts, the pair found that cells underwent a finite number of population doublings and then lost their capacity to divide. Hayflick and Moorhead first published their findings in *Experimental Cell Research*, because reviewers for more prestigious periodicals at the time expressed reservations about their techniques and findings.[10] Once in print, the importance of Hayflick's work was quickly recognized. Of the more than 2 million biomedical papers published during the 1960s, only sixteen authors had more than one publication on the list of "most-cited articles;" Hayflick had four, including his paper with Moorhead.[11]

Science . . . and Beyond (New York: Columbia University Press, 1986 [1963]); Don K. Price, *The Scientific Estate* (Cambridge: Harvard University Press, 1965); and John Ziman, *Prometheus Bound* (New York: Cambridge University Press, 1994).

10　The formal citation is "The Serial Cultivation of Human Diploid Cell Strains," *Experimental Cell Research*, vol. 25 (1961): 585–621. For more on this, see Leonard Hayflick, "Origins of Longevity," in *Modern Biological Theories of Aging*, ed. H. L. Warner (New York: Raven, 1987). In addition to granting several interviews, Dr. Hayflick has kindly shared with me personal documents.

11　In an interview, Hayflick took special pride in his inclusion in Eugene Garfield, "Current Comments," *Current Contents: Life Sciences*, vol. 23 (February 4, 1980): 5. See also Leonard Hayflick, *How and Why We Age* (New York: Ballantine, 1994), pp. 123–4. Hayflick also won a Career Development Award (1962–70) from the National Cancer Institute. I

In 1968, Hayflick became a professor of medical microbiology at Stanford. He increasingly played the role of a senior-scientist statesman; he served on several editorial boards, NIH blue-ribbon panels, and was an advisor to the 1971 White House Conference on Aging (WHCoA). Because of his scientific achievements and visibility in national networks, Hayflick's name was prominently mentioned as the likely founding director of the National Institute on Aging (NIA). (He was appointed in 1975 to serve on NIA's National Advisory Council.) Before any appointments were formalized, NIH released reports in March 1976 alleging that Hayflick had profited from selling Wistar Institute-38 cells that he originally had obtained through grants. Feeling beleaguered, Hayflick resigned his position at Stanford and brought suit against the government. After six years of litigation, the parties reached an out-of-court settlement.[12]

From 1976 to 1981, Hayflick served as a senior research cell biologist at Children's Hospital in Oakland. For the next six years, he was a professor of zoology, microbiology, and immunology at the University of Florida; he also directed its Center for Gerontological Studies. Since 1988, Hayflick has been a professor in the anatomy, cell biology, and aging section of the School of Medicine at the University of California, San Francisco. Meanwhile, new branches of biotechnology have spun off work originally sponsored by the federal government. During the past decade, Hayflick's fellow scientists and private foundations have honored his contributions. He won the Sandoz Prize in 1991 from the International Association of Gerontology. His recent book, *How and Why We Age*, was featured on the cover of *Parade* magazine.[13]

Few gerontologists will have careers as distinguished *and* as volatile as Hayflick's. But most of those researchers on aging whom we will encounter in Part II, were, like Hayflick, trained to be specialists or professionals in another field and then became attracted to gerontology. Once committed to research on aging, they increasingly collaborated with people from different disciplines, often working in organizations whose fortunes rose or fell on the basis of how peers outside of the field judged their results.

In Part II, I have selected four different institutional hubs as case studies to trace how researchers on aging interacted. The Gerontological Society is the nation's premier association for "the professional who keeps abreast

cannot ascertain how much the latter accomplishment reflects Hayflick's *specific* contributions to research on aging and how much is due to his work in bacteriology.

12 See Nicholas Wade's article in *Science*, vol. 192 (1976): 125; and "Hayflick-NIH Settlement," *Science*, vol. 215 (1982): 240–1. See also Dorothy Nelkin, *Science as Intellectual Property* (New York: Macmillan, 1984), pp. 20–1. Dr. Hayflick also gave me a copy of his paper, "A Novel Technique for Transforming Purloined Human Cells into Acceptable Federal Policy" (1989), which documents the printed record about the controversy and elaborates the support Hayflick received from his peers.

13 Hugh Downs, "Must We Age?" *Parade*, August 21, 1994, pp. 3–7.

of new developments in the aging field;"[14] the University of Michigan's Institute of Gerontology, a highly regarded academic center; several legislative and executive units of the federal government that sponsored, produced, and consumed research; and the agency that became the U.S. Department of Veterans Affairs. Reconstructing the histories of these institutions reveals that certain trends persist. Today's gerontologists remain as committed to scientific excellence as the Cowdry group. Those who cross frontiers still thrive on the tensions that persist between specialization and multidisciplinarity. Balkanized interests and divided loyalties continue to create imbalances and uneven growth in the field.

The most striking change discussed in Part II is structural. The frontiers of aging have been enclosed by Big Science. Especially since the 1960s, government, big business, multiversities, trade associations, and senior citizen interest groups have also set priorities. The field has matured sufficiently to permit critical assessments of what a "science" of gerontology might be; some within and outside the ranks are pointing out that the meaning of "research" and "science" are not synonymous. To understand why gerontology is beginning to move beyond its earlier positivist assumptions requires a survey of broader developments in postwar U.S. science.[15]

14 For many years, this clause was on the cover of one of the Society's major publications, *The Gerontologist.*

15 For more on this issue, see C. Hakfoot, "The Missing Syntheses in the Historiography of Science," *The History of Science,* (1991): 207–16. For an insider's account see *infra,* Chapter 8; for a useful outsider's critique, see Bryan S. Green, *Gerontology and the Construction of Old Age: A Study in Discourse Analysis* (Hawthorne, NY: Aldine, 1993).

4

Organizing the Gerontological Society to promote interdisciplinary research amid disciplinary and professional constrictions

SHORTLY AFTER THEIR landmark 1937 conference, some Woods Hole participants formed a Club for Research on Ageing so they could pursue further possibilities for advancing a science of gerontology. Annual reunions were supported by the Josiah Macy, Jr. Foundation. Club members then decided that they had to publish a journal in order to disseminate their scientific ideas more widely. So in 1945, eleven days after the war in Europe ended, papers were filed in New York City to incorporate a Gerontological Society. Much of the "Certificate of Incorporation" was boilerplate, necessary to attain nonprofit status. This legal proceeding nonetheless constituted an intellectual investment whereby the Society's founders hoped to spread risks and dividends across disciplinary boundaries and professional domains:

> The purposes for which the corporation is to be formed are to promote the scientific study of aging, in order to advance public health and mental hygiene, the science and art of medicine, and the cure of disease: to foster the growth and diffusion of knowledge relating to problems of aging and of the sciences contributing to an understanding thereof; to afford a common meeting ground for representation of the various scientific fields interested in such problems and those responsible for care and treatment of the aged.[1]

This multidisciplinary enterprise was designed to attract a select group of scientific researchers interested in "problems of aging" and appeal to professionals whose work with the elderly gave them a practical stake in prob-

---

1 "Certificate of Incorporation of the Gerontological Society, Inc.," *Journal of Gerontology*, vol. 1 (January 1946): 134–135. (Henceforth in this chapter, this journal will be abbreviated *JoG*.) Three of the five subscribers (Earl Engle, Lawrence Frank, and Jean Oliver) had been at the 1937 Woods Hole Conference and contributed to the 1939 and 1942 editions of Cowdry's *Problems of Ageing*. So had the Society's first president, William deB. MacNider.

lem solving. From the start, bridging the fundamental interests of these constituencies was not easy. The Society's leaders have been reluctant to stray very far from the norms and reward systems of their home disciplines or professions. Rather than dare to be too different from other learned bodies, the Society's development to date has been constricted by its compliance to academic conventions.

Even if the founders hewed to a conservative approach to fulfilling purposes, chances for the Society's long-term success were not great. Thousands of professional associations had been chartered over the past three centuries on both sides of the Atlantic. A few flourished; many struggled; most did not last long. Among that subset of U.S. disciplinary groups existing in 1985, 90 percent were established in the twentieth century; only 38 percent were formed before 1939, when the first edition of Cowdry's *Problems of Ageing* appeared. So although the Gerontological Society of America (GSA) is "young" compared to the American Philosophical Society (1743), American Pediatric Society (1888), American Physical Society (1899), and the American Sociological Society (1905), it has survived to become one of the oldest multidisciplinary organizations in the United States.[2]

To stimulate growth intellectually and institutionally, the Society not only had to establish its own legitimacy but also to facilitate the career advancement of prospective members. It did so by providing rewards, resources, networks, and status for those who met its criteria for membership. Over time, procedures were routinized to involve senior scholars to attract students with an interest in aging and to retain the loyalty of the rank and file. The format of the annual meetings, division of the membership into sections, and allocation of offices, however, also signaled a desire to satisfy more parochial objectives. University-based investigators were concerned about tenure, promotion, and merit raises. Many health-care professionals, social workers, and service providers needed continuing-education credits; others wanted some sort of recognition for their efforts. So cross-disciplinary aims also served disciplinary or professional functions – and vice versa. Because multidisciplinary activities generally have counted for less than accomplishments or service in one's home field, membership in the GSA, except for those truly committed to its purpose, has been a secondary affiliation until very recently.[3]

2 Magali Sarfatti Larson, *The Rise of Professionalism* (Berkeley and Los Angeles: University of California Press, 1977), esp. pp. 17–40, 246; Burton R. Clark, *The Academic Life* (Princeton, NJ: Carnegie Foundation for the Advancement of Teaching, 1987), p. 37. The Gerontological Society changed its name to the Gerontological Society of America in 1981. For consistency's sake, I shall use the abbreviation *GSA* throughout.

3 Roger Geiger, *To Advance Knowledge* (New York: Oxford University Press, 1986), p. 29; F. Reif, "The Competitive World of the Pure Scientists," *Science*, vol. 134 (December 15, 1961), pp. 1, 957–62; David R. Shumway and Ellen Messer-Davidow, "Disciplinarity,"

The Gerontological Society has had to refine its mission and review objectives since 1945. But there was no recipe for success, no single way to attain legitimacy. "We ourselves do not know exactly how we should operate, what we should do, and where we should lead," declared Robert A. Moore, who served both as editor of the *Journal of Gerontology (JoG)* and GSA president in 1951.[4] The Gerontological Society could not slavishly emulate other groups' practices. Neither could it be blind to changing needs and characteristics within the elderly population, nor ignore new federal and state laws and policies altering its mission. The Society's leadership knew that it had to do what seemed necessary to assure survival. "In the United States," Andrew Abbott observes, "legitimating values for professional structures include their collegiality, their democracy, and increasingly their efficiency."[5] The GSA's structural evolution can be traced along these three dimensions.

First, the Society nurtured collegiality by creating opportunities for bona fide members to engage in scholarly exchanges, committee work, and service activities. Respect for different perspectives, claimed GSA's founders, would advance this multidisciplinary science. "Some of the baffling problems in the field of aging may also stimulate further critical, reflective thinking," Lawrence K. Frank declared in the lead article of the first issue of the *JoG*, "and a greater readiness to consider how we can develop the new concepts and new methodologies commensurate with these perplexing and elusive complexities."[6] Besides reiterating his own belief that effective problem solving required disciplined, scientific inquiry, Frank was trying to minimize either/or choices. Concern for the multidimensional aspects of aging should enhance, not diminish, gerontology's appeal to members of established disciplines and professions.

Second, GSA's exercise in democracy often created tensions between members' wish to acquire and maintain control over journals to disseminate sound knowledge and their hope to reach a larger clientele. Not by accident, a feature in the first issue of *JoG* contrasted the aims of the Society with both Ponce de Leon's search for longevity and serialized comic Man-

Poetics Today, vol. 12 (Summer 1991): 207; Struan Jacobs, "Scientific Community," *British Journal of Sociology*, vol. 38 (1987); 266–76.

4 Robert A. Moore, "President's Report for 1951," mimeo., archives of the GSA, Washington, D.C. See also Diane Crane, *Invisible Colleges* (Chicago: University of Chicago Press, 1972), pp. 12–13, 40; Gerald L. Geison, ed. *Professions and Professional Ideologies in America* (Chapel Hill: University of North Carolina Press, 1983), p. 11; William Goode, "Community Within a Community," *American Sociological Review*, vol. 22 (1957): 194–200.

5 Andrew Abbott, *The System of Professions* (Chicago: University of Chicago Press, 1988), p. 193. By "efficiency," Abbott means "less a property of techniques than of service delivery." See also Arthur Stinchcombe, "Origins of Sociology as a Discipline," *Acta Sociologica*, vol. 27 (1984): 51–61.

6 Lawrence K. Frank, "Gerontology," *JoG*, vol. 1 (January 1946): 7. See also Tony Becher, *Academic Tribes and Territories* (Manchester: Open University Press, 1989), p. 104.

drake the Magician's pseudorejuvenation scheme. Gerontology was not for alchemists, charlatans, conartists, or uninformed adventurers. "What kind of fountain of youth are we seeking: a fountain that will miraculously erase the wrinkles of age, or a fountain that will make the later years of life a health [*sic*] and intellectually occupied period?" The article ended by declaring that the Society's motto was "to add life to years, not just years to life."[7] The pursuit of science was open to all, but implicit in the contrast was the assumption that only experts knew how to produce socially beneficial results.

Finally, institutional choices and mechanisms – ranging from decisions concerning the style, format, and content of journals; to the ways that meetings have been orchestrated – reveal much about GSA's "efficiency" in terms of services and markets. The Society's architects hoped that *JoG* would facilitate research on aging:

> The *Journal of Gerontology*, the first journal in the field, will provide a medium of communication and interpretation in our effort to gain more and surer knowledge of human growth and development. For all the problems of aging we must have more research, more explorations in health care, more guidance for the aged, and we must incorporate this knowledge into our various organizations and services to protect and conserve all members of society.[8]

GSA members expected their editors to maintain quality control as they assessed research findings and translated results from scientific laboratories to lay audiences.

To fulfill this gatekeeping function, the GSA exercised care in establishing turf. Boundaries were not drawn by any single discipline. Groups that played a critical role, however, could expect members of other disciplines and professions to respect their concern over rules that violated their sense of scientific standards. Furthermore, even when it demurred, GSA would not settle merely for occupying areas not yet claimed by other professions. In principle, a "big" multifaceted problem like aging required an institutional umbrella that enabled many kinds of experts to connect gerontologic concerns to broader research issues or current policy debates. In practice, the Society's multidisciplinary "stars," for all their claims of breadth, often proved to be as narrowly focused as successful scholars in any other discipline. Nor did the Society's leadership anticipate an interlocking membership across biomedical and sociobehavioral disciplines. According to one 1929 survey, there was little overlap in memberships of social science

---

7 "The Fountain of Youth," *JoG*, vol. 1 (January 1946): 127. For more on the tension between monopolization and popularization of knowledge, see JoAnne Brown, "The Semantics of Profession," Ph.D. diss., University of Wisconsin, 1985.

8 "Abstract," *JoG*, vol. 1 (January 1946): 7. For more on institutional mechanisms, see Pierre Bourdieu, "The Specificity of the Scientific Field and the Social Conditions of the Progress of Reason," *Sociology of Science*, vol. 14 (1975): 34.

societies.[9] Because few scholars and scientists were interested in study-ing "age" in 1945 anyway, a multidisciplinary gerontologic organization seemed doubly disadvantaged in the beginning.

Therein, paradoxically, lay GSA's best chance for institution building. Gerontology needed a structure that capitalized on the field's diversity with-out gratuitously offending various constituencies. The GSA had to respect disciplinary conventions without being coopted by tribal customs as it re-warded risk taking in multidisciplinary collaborations. Its savvy in nego-tiating with members who espouse different ideals and standards for scientific research is a major reason why the Society has survived more than fifty years. Its unwillingness to advance multidisciplinary objectives at the expense of academic and professional concerns, however, has thwarted its potential.

Multidisciplinary collegiality

"Gerontology is an enterprise calling for many and diversified studies, for pooled and concerted investigations, indeed, for the orchestration of all relevant disciplines and professional practices," Lawrence K. Frank af-firmed.[10] Accordingly, GSA considered collegiality a prerequisite for col-laboration and integration, not a license for abandoning specialization or eschewing traditional modes of disciplinary and professional inquiry. Ger-ontology, Frank insisted, "does not imply any need for regimentation of research or any diversion of investigators from pursuing the problems of major interest to their disciplines."[11] The notion of multidisciplinarity im-plied in Frank's statements nonetheless posed a daunting challenge: How could the Society effect the "orchestration" of all relevant disciplines and professionals without itself intruding in the process upon other fields' boundaries or making claims on the rights of competing scientific organi-zations to produce knowledge in certain ways?

A friendly exchange between two members of the Club for Research on Aging in 1941 prefigured some of the difficulties that gerontologists had in delineating a distinctive area of inquiry. Henry Simms of Columbia's Col-lege of Physicians and Surgeons proposed the creation of a Geriatric Society to "aid in arousing interest in the aging problem and in obtaining the ur-

9 Clark, *Academic Life*, pp. 142–4; Stephen Toulmin, *The Return to Cosmology* (Berkeley and Los Angeles: University of California Press, 1982), pp. 229–30; Stuart Rice and Morris Green, "Interlocking Memberships of Social Science Societies," *American Journal of So-ciology*, vol. 35 (1929): 437–44; Seymour B. Sarason, *The Creation of Settings and the Future Societies* (San Francisco: Jossey-Bass, 1972), p. xiii.

10 Frank, "Gerontology," p. 7. For a complementary British view, see "Research on Ageing," *Lancet*, vol. 2 (August 17, 1946): 249–50.

11 Frank, "Gerontology," pp. 7–8.

gently needed financial support for research in this field."[12] Simms was using the term "geriatric" generically; he envisioned a small group that exchanged ideas and underwrote research. Nathan Shock agreed that such an organization was needed, but he feared that Simms's terminology would unduly limit its appeal: "Since the term 'geriatrics' implies a more or less medical, if not clinical, approach, it would probably be wiser to use the title *Society for the Study of Ageing*, so that the biologists, physiologists, biochemists, nutritionists, anatomists, and so on, will recognize that the society is interested in scientific research as well as the development of geriatrics as a clinical branch of medicine."[13] Research on aging needed clinicians, but Simms's geriatric emphasis did not embrace everybody's interests. To underscore his point, Shock thought it desirable to invite representatives from a wide array of disciplines to be charter members. This, he hoped, would encourage faster growth. Differences in the ways that Simms and Shock saw the relationship of parts to the whole helped to clarify the scope of *geriatrics*. The American Geriatrics Society (AGS), founded in 1942, stressed clinical problems of old age, "the importance of preventive and curative treatment of diseases of advancing years."[14] But articulating AGS's mission in and of itself did not put GSA's mission into sharper focus. Any case statement for gerontology would have to be defined on its own terms.

For decades members of the GSA have struggled mightily with the meanings of *gerontology*. Views expressed by presidents, editors, and GSA members have tended to be quite personal, even quirky. A 1952 issue of the *JoG* featured an eleven-page summary of a discussion of "What is Aging?" The eight-member panel knew "that we won't be particularly successful convincing anybody as to what aging is. But people like to express their views," panel chair Edmund V. Cowdry observed, "and this is an opportunity to express views."[15] Seven years later, the society issued a working definition – "Gerontology is that branch of science which is concerned with situations and changes inherent in increments of time, with particular reference to post-maturational stages"[16] – but that statement hardly settled the debate. Little wonder: Even today *gerontology* remains a technical term

12 Henry S. Simms, "Plan for a Geriatric Society," October 27, 1941, in the Nathan W. Shock Papers, box 1, file 1, Bentley Historical Collection (henceforth abbreviated as BHC), University of Michigan.

13 Letter of Nathan W. Shock to Dr. Simms, October 29, 1941, in the Shock Papers, box 1, file 1, BHC.

14 Malford W. Thewlis, M.D., "History of the American Geriatrics Society," *Journal of the American Geriatrics Society*, vol. 1 (January 1953): 3.

15 Albert I. Lansing, "What is Aging?" *JoG*, vol. 7 (1952): 452–63. Cowdry's comments on p. 452.

16 "Report on Gerontology by Subcommittee on Biology and Medicine, Research and Fellowships Committee of the Gerontological Society, Inc.," *JoG*, vol. 14, section C (July 1959): 366.

used by different specialists in specific ways. Roundtable discussions still spark controversy. As biological chemist Richard C. Adelman, who served as GSA's president in 1987, put it, "We do not yet have the foggiest notion of what aging is or why a phenomenon such as apparent maximal life span ever occurs."[17] Consensus among colleagues will not emerge until there is wider agreement about theories of growth, development, and aging.

In the absence of a neatly defined intellectual agenda, the GSA has endeavored to make a virtue out of appearing open-minded. At least two unifying themes recur in GSA publications. First, it is commonplace for researchers in the field of aging to claim that they have always explored continuities and changes over time. Second, the Society declares that it values excellence in basic and applied scientific research within every relevant disciplinary and professional circle.[18] These are important themata, but gerontologists cannot claim them to be exclusively theirs. "Time" and "space" are as integral to domains as diverse as historical sociology and biological chemistry as they are to research on aging.

That a sensitivity to "temporal processes" and appreciation for "multidisciplinarity" fails to delineate fully the scope or limits of gerontology's subject matter should not be taken as an indication of vacuousness. The absence of an acceptable working definition has tactical advantages, according to GSA's leadership. The elusive quality of *gerontology* promotes comity as well as collegiality. "To allow paradigmatic chauvinism to divide the [GSA] would erode the Society's effectiveness and diminish the importance of the field," argued Barbara Silverstone, who succeeded Adelman as president of GSA in 1988. The Society's goal, in Silverstone's opinion, should be "to promote peaceful, creative coexistence among the disciplines."[19] Gerontology's multidisciplinary parameters, in other words, might legitimately be circumscribed by default, by honoring disciplinary boundaries. Silverstone's choice of the word "coexistence" simply did not convey a sense of agency in exercising power to effect multidisciplinary collaboration.

Establishing intramural borders, however, was another matter, quickly politicized. Assessing the "social urgency of research" based on a 1940–1 survey of gerontologic activities, Edward J. Stieglitz pointed out that "present investigations are widely scattered. There is little orchestration of effort."[20] As we learned in the last chapter, Stieglitz with four contributors

17 Richard C. Adelman, "Editorial," *JoG*, vol. 43 (1988): B1-2.

18 For more on this, see W. Andrew Achenbaum and Jeffrey S. Levin, "What Does *Gerontology* Mean?," *The Gerontologist*, vol. 29 (1989): 393–400. (Henceforth in this chapter this journal will be abbreviated *TG*.)

19 Barbara Silverstone, "Aging, the Future, and the Gerontological Society of America," *Gerontology News* (October 1988): S1.

20 Edward J. Stieglitz, "The Social Urgency of Research," in *Problems of Ageing*, ed, Edmund Vincent Cowdry, 2d ed. (Baltimore: Williams & Wilkins, 1942), p. 903; idem, "The Re-

to the first edition of *Problems of Ageing* proposed dividing the field into three areas. This tripartite division took form in the Society's 1945 bylaws that created three sections: medical research, biological research, and general section.[21] Whether GSA's founders really meant to put "social science" research into an "etc." category is impossible to know, but they obviously recognized the preponderance of biomedical scientists in the ranks during the early years. Of the 80 members in 1946, 43 joined the Clinical Medicine section, 9 came from anatomy and pathology, 7 from physiology, 4 from biochemistry, and one from botany; there were 6 psychologists, 5 sociologists, and 2 from social work; only 3 were listed in the "general" category. Six years later, clinicians and medical researchers made up 46 percent of GSA's membership; biological scientists, another 26 percent. Psychologists (8 percent), social workers and institutional administrators (14 percent), sociologists (4 percent), nurses and dietitians (2 each) rounded out the ranks; the remaining 6 percent fell in the general category.[22]

Bylaws amendments in 1952 instituted a four-section configuration, designed to give symmetry to GSA's multidisciplinary collegiality. The section analogous to the "basic research" section in the biological sciences was called Psychological and Social Sciences; the name was changed in 1975 to Behavioral and Social Sciences (BSS). Those who "applied" social science research, like the physicians and nurses who incorporated bench science in Clinical Medicine, were invited to join Social Work and Administration. (Council tinkered with the fourth section's name. They changed it to Social Welfare and Administration in 1956 and to Social Research, Planning, and Practice [SRPP] in 1969, and from "Planning" to "Policy" in 1993.[23]) Thus there were two sections for people doing gerontology along disciplinary lines, and two others for professionals. Two divisions cut across the "natural" sciences and two covered the "social" sciences. There were two basic and two applied sections. Members could choose their section(s).

lation of Gerontology to Clinical Medicine," in *[Twelfth] Conference on Problems of Aging* (New York: Josiah Macy, Jr. Foundation, 1951), p. 113.

21 Article II of "By-Laws of the Gerontological Society, Inc., as adopted June 15, 1945, and revised February 18, 1946," *JoG*, vol. 1 (1946): 266-7. All members of the Club for Research on Aging on June 15, 1945, were made active charter members of the new Society; the Club, however, continued to meet under Macy auspices into the early 1950s. The GSA's Council could also elect to honorary membership "any person who has rendered distinguished services to the sciences of gerontology or geriatrics." These provisions underscore the permeability of boundaries, intellectual and organizational.

22 Membership figures of 1946 from Table II of Nathan W. Shock's report of the Membership Committee (1950), GSA archives; 1952 figures from Table II of the Membership Committee (1952), GSA archives.

23 W. Andrew Achenbaum, "Reconstructing GSA's History," *TG*, vol. 27 (1987): 21–9. Clinical Medicine's sectional name was almost changed to Health Services. See "Organization Section," *JoG*, vol. 14 (January 1959): 96. For the latest SSRP, see *Gerontology News*, December 1993/January 1994, p. 3.

Despite efforts to attract new members to all sections and to achieve parity across disciplinary and professional ranks, GSA membership was not evenly distributed. Clinical Medicine in 1956 remained the largest section, claiming 37 percent of the society's 1,064 members and fellows. That year 18 percent of the membership belonged to Social Work and Administration, 16 percent in Biological Sciences, and 15 percent in Psychological and Social Sciences, and 14 percent in General.[24] The distinction between basic and applied sections was real, but it should not be overdrawn. The commitment to science was underscored in a 1958 survey of GSA's membership, which confirmed "the concept of the Society as a research-oriented organization."[25]

For the next three decades, the Society prided itself on being the nation's premier multidisciplinary, scientifically oriented research organization. "The GSA set the standard for gerontology inquiry as an interdisciplinary endeavor," claimed Carroll Estes.[26] The signifying language changed very little, as is evident in operational goals set forth in 1989:

> The Society's primary mission was to promote the conduct of and to disseminate the results of multi- and interdisciplinary research in aging. Promotion encompassed expanding the quantity of and improving the quality of gerontological research and increasing funding for gerontological research. Dissemination included the transfer of knowledge among researchers, to practitioners and to decision and opinion makers. Further it was understood that effective dissemination of research findings to and interchanges with practitioners are critical to the successful promotion of gerontology.[27]

This statement might have been written by GSA's charter members, but the membership was changing. In 1991, when the Society had 7,000 members, roughly 46 percent of the membership belonged to the BSS section. Clinical Medicine and SSRP each claimed 23 percent of the total. Only 7.3 percent of all members were affiliated with the Biological Sciences section, a statistic to which we shall return. The remaining 71 members-at-large probably had not yet enrolled in a section; it does not imply a none-of-the-above status. Medicine was the profession of choice (15.6 percent), followed by psy-

24 Membership Status Report, 1956, mimeo, GSA archives.

25 Minutes (as distributed) of the Fourteenth Annual Meeting of the Society and Members of the Corporation of the Gerontological Society, Inc., Pittsburgh, November 1959, mimeo, GSA archives.

26 Carroll L. Estes, Elizabeth Binney, and Richard A. Culbertson, "The Gerontological Imagination," *International Journal of Aging and Human Development*, vol. 35 (1992): 52.

27 "Operational goals," green mimeo, distributed to participants at the 1992 GSA executive retreat at Airlie House, Virginia, in the author's possession. What seems "new" is the use of the term "interdisciplinary" and the omission of any reference to "science." Yet in a letter to the author, July 28, 1994, Jack Cornman, who was involved in writing the 1989 statement, is quite "certain that the omission of 'science' from the statement was not done purposefully."

chology (15.4 percent), nursing (14.3 percent), social work (13.1 percent), and sociology (8.9 percent). Nearly half of GSA's membership held university appointments; more than a third declared research to be their primary function, and another sixth considered themselves as teachers.[28] Social scientists and health-care professionals, not bench scientists, now dominate GSA. This shift in orientation, unforeseen in 1945, surely complicates relationships between this multidisciplinary organization and other academic and professional bodies.

Nor did steadfastness of purpose ensure the rapid growth desired at the outset. Starting with 80 members in 1946, the society had increased only to 1,208 members in 1959, and to 1,713 a decade later. Even in good times, at least 10 percent of the membership did not renew their affiliation from one year to the next. "I think it is important that every member of the society be aware of the existing problem," wrote the chair of the Membership Committee in 1965. "The responsibility of the growth of the society, which has been quite sluggish, to say the least, depends entirely upon the individual efforts of the members to advertise the society, its purposes and activities and to invite new members from among their colleagues and associates."[29] Thanks to the public's growing interest in gerontology, estimated Robert Binstock, GSA's president in 1976, demands on the Society's members and staff outstripped by fivefold their capacity to respond. Unless its membership rolls increased or financial resources grew, Binstock warned, the organization would have to become "highly selective and circumscribed in the scope and depth" of its efforts. Council minutes reflect "continuing concern over decline in membership" well into the 1980s.[30] Compared to other organizations, GSA's growth rate was anemic. The American Psychological Association (APA) had over 4,000 members in 1946; four decades later, its membership exceeded 60,000.[31]

During the 1980s, however, GSA's leadership began to talk differently about the slowness of the society's growth. This organization, it was said, would interest only those specialists and professionals who wanted to do *research* in gerontology and apply its fruits. A 1990 report of the Task Force on Long Range Planning stressed that "the Society finds itself at an interesting and critical point in its development. Uncertainties and opportunities abound. The former makes projections difficult. The latter makes

28 "Elections Are Coming: What Are the Voters?" *Gerontology News*, April 1992, p. 4.

29 E. A. Tonna, M.D., "1965 – Report of the Membership Committee Chairman," GSA archives.

30 "Organization Section," *TG*, vol. 16 (1976): 459. See also Virginia C. Little, "1984 Report: Membership/Fellowship Committee," GSA archives.

31 John G. Darley, "Growth and Allocation of Resources Within the APA," *American Psychologist*, vol. 17 (1962): 465; Joseph Lee Rodgers, "Structural Models of the American Psychological Society at Birth," *Psychological Science*, vol. 1 (March 1990): 82.

choosing necessary."[32] Given the organization's narrowly based appeal, the proliferation of other aging-related professional organizations (including the American Society of Aging (ASA), which actually had begun as an affiliate called the Western Gerontological Society), and their nervousness about the economy, GSA's leadership opted for a "small is good" strategy. At the same time that it was giving airline tickets and discounts to those who recruited new members, the Society redoubled its efforts to become a haven for the committed. "GSA provides a warm and nurturing environment for its long-time members who have given so much to GSA and the larger society," observed Paul Kerschner, the Society's late executive director.[33] Multidisciplinary collegiality counted more than ever. Significantly, what Kerschner characterized as that "particular philosophy and activity that pervades the organization" seemed attractive to younger as well as older cohorts of researchers on aging. "It used to be said that GSA members used GSA as a secondary referent, not primary and that is probably true of many older members, "noted Robert M. Morris. This is "perhaps less so for the latest generation which is finding careers in 'Aging.' "[34]

John M. Cornman, who made planning his top priority as the Society's executive director (1983–92), was convinced that the emphasis on multidisciplinary collegiality was sound strategically, but he hardly underestimated the challenges facing GSA:

> As academic organizations go, the Society is a strange animal, with its mixture of researchers and practitioners from different professions. Yet, when one contemplates the nature of problems and challenges facing the world, the Society is more a model for the future than an oddity of the present. . . . Will the Society become an even more effective leader of multidisciplinary approaches to issues, or, as it and the field of gerontology grow, will it evolve into a traditional academic organization primarily serving the narrower interests of the individual disciplines, which happen to come under its banner?[35]

For all its claims of excellence, GSA still had not made significant inroads into two elite and wide-ranging groups of researchers. First, the prestigious National Academy of Sciences (established in 1863) does not list "aging" among its twenty-five sections, though it has convened five different blue-ribbon panels to tackle specific issues in gerontology and geriatrics since

32 Quoted in John M. Cornman, "A Report on the State of the Society," *Gerontology News*, January 1991, p. 1.
33 Paul A. Kerschner, "It Doesn't Get Better Than This," *Gerontology News*, January 1993, p. 7. Not all old-timers agree. Many of them have complained to me that the meetings had become too big.
34 Letter from Robert M. Morris to author, dated March, 30 1987. Morris had served as GSA's president twenty years earlier.
35 Jack Cornman, "A Report on the State of The Gerontological Society," *Gerontology News*, December 1988, p. 5.

1986. Currently, only two dozen of the Academy's 1,650 members identify an interest in aging-related research. Most have made their mark in traditional disciplines or prestigious postwar fields such as computer science. Second, between 1975 and 1991, the annual percentage of GSA members who are recipients of grants from the National Institute on Aging (NIA) always has been less than 5 percent.[36] Apparently multidisciplinarity in and of itself is not valued in established networks in the natural and physical sciences as highly as is disciplinary rigor in doing research.

An excess of democracy?

After its first decade of operation, GSA clearly no longer resembled the Club for Research on Aging. People could hardly "expect Dr. Shock or anyone else to give the quantity of free service the Society had been getting."[37] An inner circle simply could not do all the committee work deemed necessary. According to Carol Schutz, GSA's longest-term employee and current executive director, the Society had already evolved from an august club to an extended "family" by the time she came to work in 1963. On the Society's fortieth anniversary, President Jordan Tobin recalled that the banter and sparring at annual banquets resembled relatives and close friends gathering at a "bar mitzvah."[38] Yet, in his 1962 presidential address, James E. Birren worried about relations between two kinds of gerontologists in the Society:

> One consists of a slow-moving strain, displaying cultivated forbearance in matters of scholarship and research. The other is the faster moving strain, displaying dedication to the improvement of the well-being of the aged through the application of gerontological findings. . . . Some resolution of the tension [is necessary] between the autocracy of the individual investigator to whom insight and hard work are joint privileges and the democracy of group activity. . . . We have to watch that our sectarian approaches, which are vitally important within our own laboratories, do not conflict with the broad orientation of the larger group. While nature may have contrived to produce aging, nature hardly produced the organization of sciences and professions as we now know them.[39]

36 For information on the National Academy of Sciences, I thank Audra R. Garling of the Academy's Office of News and Public Information. My colleague Richard C. Adelman is currently analyzing the relation of NIA grantees to GSA.

37 Minutes of the Annual Meeting, November 7, 1956, p. 8. GSA archives.

38 Interview with Carol A. Schutz, August 7, 1987; Tobin shared the analogy with me at the fortieth annual GSA banquet, 1985. The Society did not have an executive director until 1964, when Harry Rosen assumed responsibilities in a 10 percent appointment. See *TG*, vol. 5 (June 1965): 273.

39 James E. Birren, "Fifteen Annual Meetings Later," *TG*, vol. 2 (1962): 179, 181. Birren underscored the importance of the tension he had identified twenty-three years earlier in a letter to Mildred M. Seltzer, March 6, 1986, in the author's possession.

Birren's doubt that any subset of the membership could represent the entire Society in determining research priorities had wider relevance than his concern over sectarianism. In addition to clashes between basic and applied researchers, different sections and members within the four sections disagreed about GSA's future. Rather than encourage sharp debate over competing ideas and visions, the Society's leadership crafted, and then has been inclined to rely upon, a governing structure that allowed the *process* itself to mediate differences.

The executive committee of the Club on Research on Aging that constituted GSA's first governing council had been unabashedly elitist in defining their philosophy of science. By the early 1950s, however, steps were taken "for what we might call 'liberalization' of the Society."[40] Provision was "made for the Sections . . . to have greater autonomy and initiative in conducting their own affairs" in 1960. This enabled sections to become freestanding and still retain federated status. They could create section awards, obtain funds for their own projects, and still claim the high ground as they tried to bend Society rules. Thus, the section on Psychological and Social Sciences surveyed *Graduate Education in Aging within the Social Sciences* (1967). A decade later, the Society agreed to publish in *The Gerontologist* (*TG*) only the abstracts of papers from the biomedical sciences, because such citations did not "count" in the social sciences.[41] Some like Nathan Shock decried the move, fearing that it would vitiate multidisciplinarity: "I am not at all sure what will be gained. . . . There are too damned many societies now and now you want some more."[42] Others agreed that making too many concessions to disciplinary individuality might dampen the spirit of collegiality. But the threat of schism was a more terrifying prospect to the membership.

Changes in the manner in which top leaders were selected represented another move toward democratic governance. In the early years an "old-boy/old-girl" network nominated a single candidate for president, who was ratified by voice vote. The method favored stars: All but one of GSA's first ten presidents were listed in *Who Was Who*. By the 1950s, the office was being rotated among the four sections. (The order was disrupted in 1960,

40 "Organization Section," *JoG*, vol. 1 (1946): 136; "Minutes of the Fourth Business Meeting of the Gerontological Society," JoG, vol. 7 (1952): 123.

41 Provision in the Minutes of Council, August 1960, GSA archives, reprinted in "Organization Section" *TG*, vol. 14 (1960): 59. Rose E. Kushner and Marion Bunch, eds., *Graduate Education in Aging Within the Social Sciences* (Ann Arbor: Division of Gerontology, University of Michigan, 1967). The project will be discussed in the next chapter. Compare this with the more widely Society-based supervision of the first trilogy of *Handbooks* edited by Tibbitts, Birren, and Burgess. On awards, BSS established one for "distinguished mentorship" and another for "creative contribution to gerontology" in 1988. On the abstracts, see the Minutes of the Executive Committee meeting, February 25-6, 1977, GSA archives.

42 Shock's remarks in transcript of the August 1960 Council meeting, p. 34.

to permit Nathan Shock to serve during the Fifth Congress of the International Association of Gerontology.) In 1963, Gordon Streib suggested that the bylaws be amended to permit a mail-ballot election, a change accomplished during Bernice Neugarten's presidency (1969).[43] With one exception, a nominating committee selects candidates from each section every four years, usually tapping people who had loyally served the society, not necessarily ones who were distinguished researchers in aging.

That one exception was the first mail-ballot election, which revealed that reliance on procedures alone could not placate sectional rivalries. With 755 ballots, Carl Eisdorfer, M.D., Ph.D. clearly won enough votes for the presidency under the new rules. But his election prompted a dispute about the nominating process itself. Eisdorfer was a fellow in Clinical Medicine as well as Psychological and Social Sciences. He ran as Clinical Medicine's candidate without having been officially chosen by that section; someone else was nominated from the floor. Some on the Council felt that Clinical Medicine should have "another crack" at the presidency, because Eisdorfer's candidacy might count as an "extra" one for the social sciences. (Off the record, it was further suggested that psychiatrists like Eisdorfer did not fit the image of clinical researchers like former presidents Joseph Aub, William Kountz, or Joseph Freeman.) To defuse the situation, Council suspended the rotation and ran a candidate from Clinical Medicine the following year.[44] But it proved easier to ensure fairness in competition for GSA's highest offices than to guarantee equal representation in other areas, especially given differences in sectional sizes and philosophies.

Imbalances in membership across sections affected the quality and quantity of Society participation. In 1974, for instance, the leadership of the Psychological and Social Sciences began to complain that larger sections had to reject more papers for annual meetings and found it harder to communicate with their constituency than smaller sections. Thirteen years later, with 40 percent of the Society's total membership, members of the BSS section were demanding a greater share of the total budget and an extra slot in the rotation for officers. Prominent psychologists and sociologists were insisting that the Society be reorganized to achieve greater parity. A Task Force on Long Range Planning, while "extremely mindful" of the tensions, was reluctant to endorse an *automatic* budget allocation or to amend electoral procedures lest the change "blur the Society's statement about the multidisciplinary character of the field and the importance of

43 List of GSA presidents from 1945 to 1986 appears in Achenbaum, "Reconstructing," p. 23; I looked up names of the presidents in *Who Was Who* (Wilmette, IL: Marquis Publications, 1989). For bylaw changes, see "Bylaws of the Gerontological Society," art. V, section 3 (November 2, 1957), *JoG*, vol. 13 (1958): 91; "Organization Section," *TG*, vol. 3 (1963): 185; interview with Bernice Neugarten, October 1989.

44 "Organization Section," *TG*, vol. 11 (1971): 97–8; letter to author from Harold L. Orbach, a witness to the events, February 19, 1987.

each group of disciplines to the field of gerontology."[45] Equity was best served by refusing to privilege any "single discipline," no matter how large, as "the most important to the field."

Coping with a section's declining strength posed a different set of problems. To put it bluntly, the vast majority of biologists doing research on aging simply were not inclined to join GSA. In the past, Edmund Cowdry, Albert Lansing, and Nathan Shock had argued that biologists would only belong to a multidisciplinary group if its *scientific* standards were as rigorous as any constituent group in the American Institute of Biological Sciences. As early as 1960 influential members of the section were acknowledging another problem: "lack of goals, lack of push."[46] The Biological Science section's presidential nominees in the 1980s (Richard Adelman and Vincent Cristofalo) were unapologetic about using their office to bring top-flight biological scientists into the ranks. "Biology is the weakest section of the Society; the 'chain' that holds our disciplines together will only be as strong as its weakest link," Cristofalo declared. "We need to be innovative and flexible in response to the various disciplinary needs. Much of the effort will have to come from the leadership of the individual sections."[47] The statement, taken at face value, was reasonable. But GSA biologists provoked other sections' resentment by the extent to which they seemed to claim that they were the only *true* scientists in the Society.

The GSA's big-section/little-section issues resemble the fights between big states and little states at the Constitutional Convention of 1787. Similarly, the claims of artists, experts in the humanities, and those who advance interpretive social science have parallels to the demands and status of pioneers in the Northwest Territory. The GSA created an Arts and Humanities Committee in 1976 at the request of its widely respected former president, Joseph Freeman. Over the years, this committee has accrued more power, and it stages well-attended scholarly sessions and multidisciplinary events at annual meetings. Yet its membership is determined by sections, not by the people who necessarily know much about the arts and humanities. Nor are the Arts and Humanities members likely to achieve section status, despite their growing numbers. To accord them equal standing in a "scientific" society raises too many disturbing issues about image, power, and parity.

45 "Equity Among sections," Memorandum of the Task Force on Long Range Planning to Council, October 14, 1987, in the author's possession.

46 Leo Gitman, in transcript of the Minutes of the Fifteenth Annual Meeting of Council, August 6, 1960, p. 26, GSA archives.

47 Vincent J. Cristofalo, "State of the Society, 1992," *Gerontology News*, December 1991, pp. 7, 12. See also letter of Cristofalo to Council, March 14, 1991 (in author's possession). The GSA bylaws stipulated that a group lost its section status if its share of the total membership fell below 10 percent. To prevent BS's demise, Council in June 1991 permitted it to retain its status.

The GSA's "democratic" mode of governance thus has been Janus-faced. Depending on the issue, leaders either glossed over sectional differences for the sake of multidisciplinarity or they tried to protect sectarian interests. In most instances, protagonists did not elaborate the intellectual issues at stake, relying instead on procedural finesses and compromises. Ironically, efforts to effect inclusivity made it more and more difficult to make the Society acceptable to "hard" scientists accustomed to the tension between creating democratic mechanisms for self-governance and acknowledging the community's accountability to the public.[48] The scientific status of the Society's publications revealed profound disagreement over whose standards counted.

Three members of the Club on Research on Ageing (Lawrence Frank, Roy Hoskins, and Edward Stieglitz) helped editor Robert A. Moore design the format of the *JoG* in the 1940s. They included not only biomedical articles but also contributions from the social sciences and the humanities "as they relate to the processes of aging and the care of the aged." To reach a broader audience, the steering committee wanted "to attempt a new type of scientific journalism," such as preparing popular abstracts for major articles.[49] Despite their desire for a multidisciplinary journal, Council insisted early on that the nontechnical features "should differ somewhat" from the scientific sections. Reporting research results, which could serve as building blocks for future investigations, was *JoG*'s primary aim.

As people from different disciplinary traditions began to submit papers for consideration, and as the number of coauthored submissions increased, establishing standards for "research" became a sensitive issue. Editor John E. Kirk asked Council in 1959 whether he should accept "papers, which are not research papers" from Social Welfare. He suggested that the Society establish a *Journal of Applied Gerontology* or a *Journal of Social Gerontology*. "If the Social Welfare people have research results that will meet the standards on research, they would go in the *JG*," Nathan Shock opined. "If someone makes a general talk about the implications of biological research for medicine and social science, this kind of what I call hot-air artistry would go in the Bulletin. If someone has a specific study with some numbers and some data it would then go in the *JG*."[50]

So as to make "no change in the present research orientation of the *JoG*,"

---

48 Steve Fuller, "Being There with Thomas Kuhn," *History and Theory*, vol. 31 (October 1992): 259.

49 "Organization Section," *JoG*, vol. 1 (1946): 263; ibid., vol. 2 (1947): 164.

50 Transcript of the Fourteenth Annual Meeting of Council, November 11, 1959. Kirk's remarks on p. 27; Shock, p. 78. Copy in GSA archives. Shock actually was referring to a GSA Newsletter established in January 1954. See "Summary of the Minutes of the Eighth Annual Meeting of Council," *JoG*, vol. 9 (January 1954): 84. See also Ray Over, "Collaborative Research and Publication in Psychology," *American Psychologist*, vol. 37 (September 1982): 996–1,001.

Council approved a second journal, *TG*, "dedicated to improvement in communication between all who labor in behalf of the aging."[51] Oscar J. Kaplan, *TG*'s first editor, recalls being told not to publish experimental results and not to implement peer review. (Subsequent editors did not consider themselves bound by these restrictions.) A 1963 report sharpened the distinction between the focus of *JoG* and the purpose of *TG*:

> The *Journal of Gerontology* is the scholarly journal, which should publish reports of research and scholarly endeavors in each of the major areas represented by the four professional sections of the Society. . . . It should be the medium for publishing review articles in any area of gerontology. . . . *The Gerontologist*, with a multiplicity of publication objectives, is a medium for dissemination of news of gerontology in general.[52]

Five years later, the contrast was magnified: *JoG* was "science oriented," *TG* was "consumer oriented."[53] *The Gerontologist* now "provides a multidisciplinary perspective on human aging through publication of articles on research and analysis in gerontology, including social policy, program development, and service delivery."[54]

Changes in *JoG*'s format underscore the tension over prioritizing "science" across disciplinary lines. For the first ten years, biomedical reports tended to appear first, although a major piece by a social scientist sometimes was selected as the lead article. Beginning in 1955, *JoG*'s contents were divided into three parts. Section A, which usually filled the most pages, contained peer-reviewed articles in Biological Science and Clinical Medicine. Section B was assigned to the other two sections, and section C dealt with organizational matters and a guide to current literature. Nathan Shock at the time "opposed bitterly the segregation of Section B. . . . It seems to me you are splitting off another slice of the Society, you are fragmenting it." Four years later, GSA president Louis Kuplan agreed: "We are ruining the cross-fertilization, the interdisciplinary approach here."[55] The twofold division was discontinued in 1963 – "We should strive to make our *multi*disciplinary organization . . . much more *inter*disciplinary in its mode of communication"[56] – but then lines were redrawn in 1972. Between

51 "Organization Section," *JoG*, vol. 16 (January 1960): 91; Oscar J. Kaplan, "Communication in Gerontology," *TG*, vol. 1 (March 1961): 3.

52 Report of the Publications Committee, October 1, 1963, GSA archives.

53 Draft from Meeting of the Ad Hoc Committee on Publications, October 16, 1968, p. 2, GSA archives.

54 "General Information and Instructions to Authors," *TG* revised February 1993. Conspicuously absent from this description is any reference to "science," despite the fact that *TG*'s last four editors have been quite concerned about the methodological soundness and scientific presentation of *TG*'s contents.

55 Minutes of the Fourteenth Annual Meeting of the Council, November 11, 1959, pp. 30-1.

56 Special Gerontological Society meeting, July 9, 1968, p. 2, GSA archives.

1973 and 1978, a third section, Social Gerontology, was added. From 1979 to 1985, the Biological and Medical sciences shared a unit, with the other two sections going to Social and Psychological Sciences. Between 1985 and 1987, articles by biologists and clinicians were separated.

Members of different sections, GSA's Publications Committee realized, perceived their respective stakes differently. The Society's journals were to keep experts abreast of developments in the field, though probably no one read everything. For most professionals, *JoG* was *a*, not necessarily the best, medium in which to publish their work. Some feared that publishing in *JoG* did not "count," since their disciplinary colleagues either did not know the journal or dismissed it as second-rate. For biogerontologists, the challenge was not so much to sell *JoG* to biologists as it was to make aging research exciting in biology. Yet if the aim were to enhance gerontologic research among biologists, then it was really more important to get aging-relevant research articles into mainstream biological journals than to change the format of *JoG* to accommodate people already committed to the field.

Editors had different concerns. They knew that *JoG*'s multidisciplinary balance would be measured not just in contents, but also in pages and willingness to take account of disciplinary-specific conventions. In the 1960s, there was not enough space allocated to publish in a timely manner all the biomedical articles accepted. As it was, the pages given to biogerontology could not be underwritten solely by biologists' subscriptions. Editors seemed unwilling to raise rejection rates, which ranged from 32 percent, in the Biological Sciences to 40–45 percent in the other sections. (In 1964, there was an 8:1 rejection rate in *TG*.) The same dilemma existed, albeit evident in different quarters, in the 1980s. Members of both BSS and SRPP were submitting more articles than were biomedical researchers. Acceptance rates ranged from 50 percent in Biological sciences to 30 percent in the other sections.[57]

To accommodate disciplinary and professional interests, Council considered splitting *JoG* into four journals in the 1950s and then again in 1973.[58] A 1986 Task Force on Journals saw several advantages to publishing the *Journals of Gerontology* – one each for biological sciences, clinical medicine, behavioral sciences, and social sciences – under one cover. (Interdisciplinary contributions and applied research were to be routed to *TG*.) The

---

57 "Organizational Notes," *JoG*, vol. 13 (January 1958): 98; Report of J. E. Kirk to the Council, 1961; Report of the 1964 Publication Committee, Table 1; Minutes of the Publications Committee Meeting, November 20, 1980, GSA archives, p. 3. See also A. J. Nederhof, "The Validity and Reliability of Evaluation of Scholarly Performance," in *Handbook of Quantitative Studies of Science and Technology*, ed. A. F. J. Raan (New York: Elsevier, 1988), pp. 219ff.

58 Minutes of Council, October 28, 1955, GSA archives. "Minutes," December 16, 1972, *TG*, vol. 13 (1973): 261.

biologists and social scientists were especially keen to adopt the recommendation. The change would increase the number of pages available to each section. That in turn would reduce the lag time between acceptance and publication – essential in every scientific community. Editors would have greater flexibility in allocating pages; truly successful journals could be published separately. Even bound as one issue, each of the four journals would have its own editorial board, able to set rules that hewed more closely to the disciplinary canons of its expected audience.

Council agreed to split the journal. They felt that they could raise subscription rates and increase pages without losing readers to the growing number of disciplinary-specific, aging-related journals and competing gerontologic periodicals. Some demurred. "Gerontologists have rarely defined either interdisciplinary or multidisciplinary, nor have they distinguished between the two," contended Miami of Ohio sociologist Mildred M. Seltzer. "The persistence of a disciplinary status hierarchy often plays havoc with our multidisciplinary activities, no less so today than in the past."[59] Under the format adopted in 1987, the ordering of the four journals changed with each issue. "The intent," editor in chief George Myers stated, "is to stress the multidisciplinary aspects of gerontology and the equal importance that we accord to the various perspectives in the aging field."[60] Once again, the Society expressed its sense of fairness by adopting a procedural change that took account of disciplinary distinctions without admitting the threat to multidisciplinary collegiality. Divisive decisions were tabled whenever possible, a pattern that was also plain to see in other GSA activities.

Increasing – within limits – the array of services to members

Besides making the arrangements for an annual meeting and ensuring that publications were edited in a timely and professional manner, over time the Society provided other benefits to its members. In April 1950, for instance, Nathan Shock took charge of the "Index to Current Periodical Literature." Its format accorded with Shock's *Bibliography of Gerontology and Geriatrics* begun three years earlier. By November 1980, when he ended the project with the hope that computer searches could do the task better, Shock had indexed 71,698 citations. Thus *JoG* literally was the journal of record for aging research in the 1960s and 1970s.[61]

In addition, the Society rewarded personal achievements that advanced its aims. Starting in 1965, a person who had done "outstanding research

59 "Report of Task Force on Journals," April 30, 1986, GSA archives. Mildred M. Seltzer, "Continuity and Change Revisited," *International Journal of Aging and Human Development*, vol. 35 (1992): 74.
60 George C. Myers, "Editor's Note," *JoG*, vol. 42 (March 1987): 129.
61 "Editor's Report for 1950," *JoG*, vol. 6 (January 1951): 49; Nathan W. Shock, "Current Publications in Gerontology and Geriatrics," *JoG*, vol. 35 (November 1980): 960.

in the field of gerontology" received the Robert W. Kleemeier Award, which was named for an outstanding psychologist and GSA president. Eight years later the Donald P. Kent Award was established to recognize someone "exemplifying the highest standards of professional leadership in gerontology through teaching, service, and interpretation of gerontology to the larger society."[62] For a few years the Society helped the Brookdale Foundation, which has generously supported innovative work in gerontology, select recipients for its $25,000 cash prizes, which were announced at GSA conventions. In a less grand but hardly insignificant manner, dissertations were honored and students were given fellowships in applied gerontology. Sections gave prizes: BSS, for instance, instituted awards for "distinguished mentoring," for offering a "creative contribution," and for "innovative publication." The GSA's fellowship program, initially underwritten by the U.S. Administration on Aging, has trained several hundred promising students, enabling them to gain hands-on experiences in gerontologic settings.[63]

Special training opportunities for minorities have been initiated or furthered through GSA's aegis over the years. Arrangements for fellowships have been set up in the Society's offices as well as in partnerships with various universities and the Administration on Aging. In addition, the Society periodically has emphasized the need to do basic research into the conditions and needs of elderly African-Americans, Asian-Americans, and other groups. The University of Michigan's James Jackson chaired its most recent Task Force on Minorities, which placed editorials in all four *Journals of Gerontology* and issued an ambitious set of recommendations for training and education.

The Society also reached out. From the start GSA members served on blue-ribbon panels, which gave advice about the federal government's engagement in research on aging. Eight of the ten members of the Gerontology Study section established by the U.S. Public Health Service in 1946, for example, were GSA charter members. When the section disbanded three years later, it was replaced with the National Institutes of Health's (NIH) Gerontology Advisory Committee, whose membership consisted entirely of GSA stalwarts.[64] By the 1960s, the formal partnership was

---

62 The Kleemeier Award was called the Searle Award in 1964 and 1965. More than half of the recipients of the Kleemeier Award appear in the forty-seventh edition (1992–3) of *Who's Who*. Only a quarter of the Kent Award recipients are so designated. It is tempting to hypothesize that science counts for more than service not only in GSA but also in society at large.

63 Gordon F. Streib, *Programs for Older Americans* (Gainesville: University Presses of Florida, 1981).

64 Nathan W. Shock, "Activities of the Gerontology Study Section of the United States Public Health Service," *JoG*, vol. 2 (July 1947): 257–60; "The Gerontology Advisory Committee of the National Institutes of Health," *JoG*, vol. 5 (January 1950): 72.

institutionalized. Thus, when the Public Health Service wanted to introduce gerontologic materials into the curricula and training of health-care professionals, it sought input from the Society, "which," in its view, "represents the broadest range of scientific, technical, and educational knowledge in the field of aging." President Leo Gitman noted in 1964 that "the Society was being increasingly called upon to assume a leadership role in the formation of research policy in gerontology."[65] With greater opportunities came tough questions about GSA's advocacy role: Should GSA be disinterested in translating ideas into practice, or should it ask up front for funds from the federal government to do the policy-related research certain well-placed members found interesting?

Early on, Council decided that GSA should not engage in political activities. But in 1955 it formed a legislative committee, charged with offering technical advice to government officials, despite misgivings in the academy about the status of policy sciences in the 1950s. The GSA wanted the Social Welfare section to take the lead, yet still "achieve a research orientation,"[66] to conform to other sections. On the eve of the 1961 White House Conference on Aging (WHCoA), Robert J. Havighurst stressed that GSA was "the one organization which has a definitive point of view on the subject of aging"; its input was vital at the WHCoA, "which can become quite a chaotic thing and open to a certain amount of demagogic action."[67]

By the mid-1960s, leaders such as F. Marott Sinex were urging that the Society move from St. Louis to Washington or New York, "close to the seats of political and financial power." Informal efforts were made to identify individuals who could help advise policymakers on how to conquer disease and shape legislation.[68] Some feared that the Society's legitimate stake in shaping *research* policies would be used as a precedent for broadening GSA's policy-making role, one that exceeded both individuals' expertise and the organization's collective wisdom. Nonetheless, Council in 1966 established a Policy Liaison Committee to discuss with relevant members of Congress and the executive branch such issues as the restructuring

---

65 "Minutes of the Interim Meeting of the Council of the Gerontological Society and the Members of the Corporation, April 6–7, 1963," *TG*, vol. 3 (1963): 91. "Minutes of the Annual Business Meeting, October 31, 1964," *TG*, vol. 4 (1964): 227.

66 Minutes of the Annual Business Meeting, October 28, 1955, GSA archives; Transcript of the Fourteenth Annual Meeting of Council, November 11, 1959, pp. 27–31. For Social Welfare's "research objective," see the Minutes of the Ad-Hoc Council Meeting in St. Louis, February 5–6, 1965, in the GSA archives. For the status of policy science in the 1950s – neither "applied social science" nor "political science," policy-relevant analysis "cuts across the existing specializations. . . . In part it is directed towards the policy process, and in part towards the intelligence needs of policy" – see Peter deLeon, *Advice and Consent* (New York: Russell Sage, 1988), pp. 20–4.

67 Minutes of Council, August 6, 1960, p. 7., GSA archives.

68 Sinex's comments in the Minutes of the Ad-Hoc Committee Meeting, February 5, 1965, p. 4. See also ibid., p. 12, for the need to have specialists lend their policy expertise.

of social services for the aged, new social and economic roles for the elderly, and the recruitment and retraining of older workers. Robert Morris and other GSA members met with John Gardner and Wilbur Cohen at the Department of Health, Education, and Welfare (HEW) and the first Commissioner on Aging "to consider how the Society could best function in relation to new developments in government organization and programs."[69]

Lobbying efforts increased once the Society moved to Washington, D.C., in 1969. The GSA's importance grew as federal involvement in aging issues increased. President-elect Jimmy Carter asked the Society to submit names for his two top aging posts.[70] The symbiotic relationship was underlined in Sen. Charles Percy's decision to hold a formal hearing of the U.S. Senate Special Committee on Aging as the opening session of GSA's 1976 meeting. That 2,000 people attended the session, which focused on prospects for enhancing geriatric medicine, gave the sense that "a GSA annual meeting was an important forum." It also bolstered Robert Butler's efforts to launch a key initiative for the National Institute on Aging. It led to subsequent interactions between the Senate committee and GSA.[71]

On balance, GSA has been reluctant to commit itself as an organization to any specific policy posture. On the eve of the 1971 White House Conference on Aging, it endorsed Nathan Shock's opinion that "we must engage in activity that will help to maintain an adequate level of support for research and training in gerontology." Nor did it object to Society members as individuals testifying or advising governmental groups "if they so choose." No formal action was taken, however, on the question of whether GSA should create a separate lobbying unit,[72] which reduced its capacity to lobby for a new unit of NIH for aging-related activities. Jerome Kaplan and Elias Cohen represented the Society's interests in preliminary discussions of what a "National Institute of Gerontology" should do. The GSA prepared a working paper on "Research and Training in Gerontology" for the Senate Special Committee on Aging. Yet no "official" position was issued. When appropriate, scientists such as Marott Sinex and Bernice Neugarten mentioned their GSA connections as they testified on behalf of the Institute. But so did GSA members who disagreed with their colleagues' "formal" positions. As a result, the Society simply was not a major player in establishing NIA.[73] Few members had strong connections on the Hill, and its small professional staff was too new to Washington.

69 "Organization Section," *TG*, vol. 7 (December 1967): 296.
70 Minutes of the Gerontological Society Executive Committee, November 26, 1976.
71 Letter from Robert H. Binstock to Mildred M. Seltzer, March 7, 1985, in the author's possession.
72 "Minutes of the Meeting of the Council . . . , October 26–8, 1971," *TG*, vol. 12 (1972): 99.
73 "Minutes of the Special Meeting of the Council, May 14–14, 1971," *TG*, vol. 11 (August 1971): 272; Betty A. Lockett, *Aging, Research, and Politics* (New York: Springer, 1983).

During the past two decades, the repertoire of policy-relevant activities expanded. The GSA's Public Policy Committee routinely conducted briefings for Congress and the federal executive branch. In 1977, executive director Edwin Kaskowitz cofounded the Washington-based "Leadership Council on Aging" in an effort to coordinate lobbying efforts within the so-called gray lobby. Besides widening its media network, Council created an Information Service, which fielded more than 100 requests a month about research on aging, the availability of nursing-home facilities, and legislation pending on the Hill during the mid-1980s. The Society sponsored a program to place applied researchers in service-delivery agencies. In an attempt to anticipate "emerging issues" and not simply to react to others' positions, GSA issued *Ties That Bind*, which focused on policy choices in an aging society.[74] Communicating research, not politicking with other special-interest groups, thus remained the Society's primary public-policy activity.

Can a multidisciplinary organization balance academic and professional aims?

Recognizing that no single organization could advance gerontology as a field of scientific inquiry, the Society has long facilitated efforts by diverse groups to create disciplinary and professional specialties in aging. Oscar J. Kaplan, Raymond G. Kuhlen, George Lawton, and Walter R. Miles were among those GSA members instrumental in starting a Division on Maturity and Old Age (Division 20) in the American Psychological Association in 1946. Six years later, GSA's annual meeting was held in conjunction with Division 20. Betty Birren, an officer of Division 20 from 1966 to 1981, enabled gero-psychologists to make contributions to both GSA and APA.[75] Similar overtures were made to the American Society for the Study of Arteriosclerosis. Thanks mainly to Nathan Shock, GSA played a vital role in establishing and then sustaining the International Association of Gerontology. Council considered it "inadvisable" to affiliate closely with "one specific society," although it did accept membership in the American Association for the Advancement of Science in 1958. More recently, newly founded groups with an aging-related focus, such as the National Academy

---

74 Eric R. Kingson, Barbara A. Hirshorn, and John M. Cornman, *Ties That Bind* (Washington, DC: Seven Locks Press, 1986). See also, GSA Council Meeting, November 18–19, 1977, p. 1; "The Gerontological Society of America's Objectives, Rationales and Acitions [*sic*], 1983–1991," mimeo, in author's possession. My interpretation also rests on an interview with Carol A. Schutz, April 5, 1992, and the contents of a blue mimeo summary of GSA goals through 1995.

75 Sidney L. Pressey, "The New Division on Maturity and Old Age: Its History and Potential Service," *American Psychologist*, vol. 3 (1948): 107–9; "Annual Meeting of the Division on Maturity and Old Age of the American Psychological Association," *JoG*, vol. 3 (1948): 302; "Program of the Fifth Annual Scientific Meeting of Gerontological Society, Inc.," *JoG*, vol. 7 (July 1952): 464–71; interview with Betty Birren, August 1987.

for Social Insurance and Americans for Generational Equity, have relied on GSA for technical assistance.[76]

To note that other professional organizations turn to GSA for advice is not to claim that the Society has been a model of financial stability. Fund-raising has long been problematic. Despite support from the Macy, Forest Park, and Glendorn foundations as well as the federal agencies, the Society has frequently incurred small deficits, which meant that it could not make long-term commitments to employees. Grants were the major source of salaries for staff during the 1970s.[77] Two decades later, GSA was still trying to increase its unrestricted fund base to $500,000, hardly a substantial reserve. Hence the Society's leadership kept abreast of other organizations' operations to borrow ideas and to consider possible confederations.

Council periodically discussed the modus operandi of the American Heart Association (AHA) and the American Cancer Society (ACS). Two gerontologic pioneers, Walter B. Cannon and Alfred E. Cohn, had been instrumental in organizing AHA. When the American Society for the Study of Arteriosclerosis merged with AHA in 1959, some Council members wondered if GSA should follow suit, since (from their perspective) the aims of the two organizations were so similar. Incorporated in 1924, AHA strove "to develop new lines of research . . . further public health and industrial education, and to develop a sound public opinion." To promote "research concerned with basic problems," AHA expended $9 million in 1960.[78] By launching a "crusade" to fight a public scourge, the ACS also managed to generate big money for research. The ACS supported education and service, but funding research was its chief mission: By 1987, more than $70 million were invested in extramural projects.[79] In both AHA and ACS, scientists and lay people understood their respective roles: The latter raised money so that the former could do their jobs. Real power was wielded by a sci-

76 Nathan W. Shock with George T. Baker III, *The International Association of Gerontology* (New York: Springer, 1988); "Minutes of the Sixth Annual Meeting of Council," *JoG*, vol. 7 (January 1952): 121; interview with Carol A. Schutz, December 1988.

77 For notices of private support, see *JoG*, vol. 1 (April 1946): 262; ibid., vol. 11 (January 1957): 88; ibid., vol. 12 (January 1958): 86, 88, 100. By 1970, the Treasurer reported that "Federal grants continue to provide the primary income to carry out the special projects of the Society and their overhead contributes significantly to the support of this office." See "Minutes of the Special Meeting of Council, June 8, 1970," *TG*, vol. 10 (1970): 252; see also Memorandum from Carol A. Schutz to GSA Council, March 6, 1991; and a memo from Tom Hickey to GSA sections, April 3, 1992, outlining plans through 1994.

78 American Heart Association, *A History of the Scientific Councils of the American Heart Association* (AHA, 1967); Richard Carter, *The Gentle Legions* (New York: Doubleday, 1961).

79 Walter S. Ross, *Crusade* (New York: Arbor House, 1987). Beginning as a grassroots movement in the Progressive era, ACS did not really take off until it was reorganized in 1945.

entific elite. The GSA's General Membership, some felt, might grow in a comparable way.[80]

The GSA's leadership ultimately rejected the analogy to both ACS and AHA. The public readily perceived that fighting cancer and heart disease were major "problems," which might be vanquished with enough money and brainpower. Aging research, alas, did not promise such major breakthroughs or dramatic results. The Society, moreover, hoped to avoid the clashes that occurred between those in ACS and AHA who did "basic" research and those who wanted "practical" results. Other differences mattered. ACS's research initiatives were bolstered by the National Cancer Institute (NCI) established in 1937, the first of NIH's "categorical" disease centers. The NIA's total budget, in contrast, remains smaller than the administrative component of NCI's budget.[81] Furthermore, AHA's leadership worried openly in the 1950s about the interference of fund-raisers, volunteers, and local chapters in their professional society: "We are principally an organization of physicians and scientists who are attempting to learn something about cardiovascular disease. . . . We are not running a friendship club for the idle nor are we trying to solve social problems other than cardiovascular disease."[82] Speaking in Council in 1959, Nathan Shock urged his colleagues to avoid a similar fate: "There isn't a lay person sitting around this table. . . . Membership in the Gerontological Society cannot be simply on the basis that the guy has reached the age of 70 years."[83] The Society was for serious researchers, not for well-heeled amateurs seeking the fountain of youth.

The GSA's sense of the uniqueness of its mission in fostering scientific inquiry reinforced its desire to remain independent of other aging-related societies. Council politely declined the offer of space from the American Association of Retired Persons (AARP) when the Society moved to Washington. The GSA wanted the two groups to "clarify the differing objectives of a scientific society, i.e., the Gerontological Society, and NRTA-AARP" and "consider the goals of their various publications."[84] Similarly, relations with satellite groups changed with the times. To bolster its membership and span interest in aging, GSA once welcomed regional affiliates. Hence, the 250 members in the Western Gerontological Society who joined GSA

---

80 See Council meeting minutes from September 6, 1952, p. 2; November 11, 1959, pp. 80–1; and May 10, 1960, p. 56. See also *JoG*, vol. 8 (October 1953): 501.

81 Richard Rettig, *Cancer Crusade* (Princeton, NJ,: Princeton University Press, 1977); George L. Maddox, "Gerontology and Higher Education," in *Higher Education and an Aging Society* (Washington, DC: GSA, 1989), p. 50.

82 Quoted in William W. Moore, *Fighting for Life* (AHA, 1983), p. 126. See also Carter, *Gentle Legions*, pp. 72, 291.

83 Minutes of the Fourteenth Annual Meeting of Council, November 11, 1959, p. 80.

84 "Minutes of the Special Meeting of the Council, January 25, 1969," in *TG*, vol. 9 (January 1969): 74.

in 1956. Twenty years later, however, noting that "more and more practitioners became involved," the president of the regional group suggested
severing the relationship. Changing its name to appeal to a national constituency, the American Society on Aging (ASA) had a different mission
than did GSA. Now claiming 8,500 members and sponsoring 20 conferences a year in addition to its annual meeting, ASA considers itself a "national, multidisciplinary coalition" of administrators and executives, service
providers, advocates, educators, professionals, and the retired.[85] There is
overlap in purpose and membership. Yet at this point, ASA has more in
common with the National Council on the Aging (NCOA), a federation of
institutions that provide services to the aging, which has considerably more
influence among Washington policymakers, than it has with "elitist" GSA.

The GSA's reluctance to dilute what it considers its primary aim is apparent in dealing with initiatives that emphasize education and advocacy
more than research. A grant from the Administration on Aging in 1972
enabled a group of Training Program directors to discuss plans for establishing regional gerontology centers. Alarmed by Nixon's proposed cutbacks in federal support for gerontologic training, the ad hoc committee
decided that professional educators had to mobilize as a peer group acting
more effectively than was possible through GSA's education committee.
Hence an affiliated but autonomous entity, the Association for Gerontology
in Higher Education (AGHE), was created in 1973. Several months later,
however, when Council stated that "the Society does not sanction use of
its own staff, address, or facilities for carrying on the business of the Association," AGHE began to function on its own as a shoe-string operation,
soliciting *institutional* memberships, holding annual meetings, and publishing its own journal. The AGHE published an annual directory of educational programs and supported periodic assessments of the quality of
gerontologic education.[86] Budget problems and administrative constraints
may yet force AGHE to return to GSA's fold. Arranging a new partnership
between GSA and AGHE would be difficult, however, given the divergent
attitudes among various disciplinary camps about certifying and creden-
tialing "professionals" in aging.[87]

85 See Minutes of Council, November 7, 1956, GSA archives; *TG*, vol. 15 (1975): 95; Current
information on ASA from the cover page of *Generations*, Winter 1991, and interview.
86 Tom Hickey, "Association for Gerontology in Higher Education – A Brief History," in
Gerontology in Higher Education, ed. Mildred M. Seltzer, Harvey Sterns, and Tom Hickey
(Belmont, CA: Wadsworth Publishing Company, 1978), pp. 2–11; *idem.*, "The Tradition
and Commitment of AGHE," paper (1987); Minutes of the Executive Committee, February 1, 1974, p. 3, GSA archives. See also the series of reprints from David Peterson,
Christopher Bolton et al. in *Educational Gerontology* and elsewhere on the quality of
gerontologic instruction.
87 See Marion E. Bunch and Robert J. Havighurst, "Objectives of Ph.D. Programs in Social
Gerontology," in *Graduate Education*, pp. 16–20; Mildred M. Seltzer, "Issues of Accreditation of Academic Gerontology," *Gerontology and Geriatrics Education*, vol. 5 (1985):

Of all the possible matches with an aging-related organization, a partnership with the American Geriatrics Society has been the most likely. Although AGS originally was limited to "all ethical physicians," honorary membership was extended in 1950 to E. V. Cowdry, Clive McCay, Walter R. Miles, Nathan W. Shock, and Henry Simms – all Ph.D.s active in GSA. Council considered affiliation in the 1950s and 1960s, but feared that competition between its Clinical Medicine section and AGS might harm both groups. Chances for merger increased after 1971, when AGS broadened its purposes to "acquire, organize and disseminate, among medical students, physicians, nurses, social service workers, sociologists, biologists, and other interested groups, knowledge about aging and diseases of aging and aged."[88] Given the differences between geriatricians and gerontologists that have been acknowledged since the early 1940s, however, boundaries were respected. The AGS and the GSA now schedule their meetings so that physicians could conveniently attend both, but neither has tried to force broader potentials for multidisciplinarity on the other's constituency.

Just as GSA has been reluctant to join forces with any other aging-related body, so too it has been wary of identifying too closely with organizations that seek funds for narrowly defined gerontologic research. It had no ties to the National Foundation for Anti-Aging Research, Inc., established in 1951 "to foster the new science of gerontotherapeutics, whose emphasis is directed to the deceleration, and even the limited arrest, of those familiar physiological changes that together constitute 'aging.' "[89] The Foundation stressed the importance of studying growth and the role of hormones, vitamins, and the cardiovascular system in senescence, but its emphasis on therapies and certain research approaches seemed too constraining. Over the past decade, new entities have been formed to underwrite research particularly in the biomedical sciences. Former GSA presidents, such as Vincent Cristofalo, Leonard Hayflick, and John Rowe, have joined the American Federation for Aging Research as *individuals*.[90] The GSA's members, moreover, serve on the board of directors and scientific advisory board of the Alliance for Aging Research, which has focused mainly on medical research. Yet unlike AGS, NCOA, ACS, AHA, and fifteen other research-oriented groups, GSA on the advice of its Public Policy Committee has

7–18. For broader perspectives, Randall Collins, *The Credential Society* (New York: Academic Press, 1979); Benjamin Shimberg, Barbara F. Esser, and Daniel H. Kruger, *Occupational Licensing* (Washington, DC: Public Affairs Press, 1973).

88 W. O. Thompson, "Aging Comes of Age," *Journal of the American Geriatrics Society*, vol. 1 (January 1953): 2; Malford W. Thewlis, "History of the American Geriatrics Society," ibid., p. 6; "Proposed Review of the By-Laws," ibid., vol. 19 (1971): 279; Minutes of Council, August 6, 1960, p. 34.

89 The National Foundation for Anti-Aging Research, Inc., "Prospectus," 1951, p. 3.

90 "The Development of Resources for Research on Aging," *Journal of American Geriatrics Society*, vol. 30 (1982): 83-5; *AFAR Newsletter*, no. 13 (Summer 1989).

elected not to participate in the Alliance's Task Force for Aging Research Funding.[91] No trade association, GSA defines its development as closely resembling that of other disciplinary bodies.

Accounts of various national academic associations do indeed have parallels to GSA's history. Groups such as the American Philosophical Association and the American Historical Association have survived nastier intramural conflicts over methods and grievances (real or imagined) and over professional status than have been experienced in GSA. The tension between basic and applied research that besets multidisciplinary organizations certainly exists in disciplinary bodies as well. With an explosion of knowledge inevitably comes a proliferation of subfields. Compared to better known groups, GSA actually has had a pretty placid existence. It seems less afflicted by organizational identity crises than the American Sociological Association: GSA has not faced possible disintegration due to localized sections vying for power against the central office; "applied" interests have not challenged the place of academic researchers in governance. Nor has GSA endured the radical shifts in objectives weathered by the American Public Health Association since its founding in 1872.[92] It has not been drained by the long-standing fights for disciplinary advantage under the banner of "science" that has characterized relations among psychologists, psychiatrists and social workers.

Of all of the disciplinary stories, that of the American Psychological Association seems to correspond most closely to GSA's history. Both organizations from their inception have reached out to those whose research falls into certain "core" areas, ranging from biophysiological research to social science surveys.[93] APA spokespersons, like their GSA counterparts, have

91 The list of participants is attached to a letter from Dan Perry, the Alliance's executive director, to Barbara Greenberg, September 12, 1989, in the author's file.
92 The literature on disciplinary associations is vast. I particularly relied upon Peter Novick, *That Noble Dream* (New York: Cambridge University Press, 1988); Dorothy Ross, *The Origins of American Social Science* (New York: Cambridge University Press, 1991); Gerald N. Grob, *From Asylum to Community* (Princeton, NJ: Princeton University Press, 1991); David M. Ricci, *The Tragedy of Political Science* (New Haven, CT: Yale University Press, 1984); Nancy R. Bernstein, *The First One Hundred Years* (Washington, DC: American Public Health Association, 1972); Daniel Wilson, "Professionalization and Organized Discussion in the American Philosophical Association, 1900–1922," *Journal of the History of Philosophy*, vol. 17 (1979): 53–69; Jonathan H. Turner, "The Disintegration of American Sociology," *Sociological Perspectives*, vol. 32 (1989): 419–33; Randall Collins, "Is 1980s Sociology in the Doldrums?" *American Journal of Sociology*, vol. 91 (1986): 1,336–55; Albert Gollin, "Whither the Profession of Sociology," *American Sociologist*, vol. 21 (Winter 1990): 316–20; Randall Collins, "The Organizational Politics of the ASA," ibid., pp. 311–15.
93 Amedeo Giorgi, *Psychology as a Human Science* (New York: Harper & Row, 1970), p. 65; Leona E. Tyler, "More Stately Mansions," *Annual Review of Psychology*, vol. 32 (1981): 1–20. Allport's speech reprinted in *American Psychology in Historical Perspective*,

claimed (without risking disciplinary chauvinism) that an ability to attain reliable measurements was the sine qua non of building an empirical science. Other similarities exist. Women have become more visible in the rank-and-file membership of both groups over time, and they have served key leadership posts. Both groups lately have wrestled with budget crises.[94] There are obvious differences, of course. APA, with a membership ten times larger than GSA's, has forty-seven sections; it interacts with more than two dozen other psychological associations as well as state and regional affiliates. "The vast *impact* of that discipline on world sensibility" in the twentieth century demonstrates that psychology's impact on "the very texture of living" far exceeds that of gerontology.[95] Yet precisely because it is older, bigger, and more influential, APA's trajectory enables us to re-examine the strains found in a multidisciplinary forum like GSA.

In 1945, its fifty-third year of operation, APA reorganized so it could "advance psychology as a science, a profession, and as a means of promoting human welfare" – without any explicit acknowledgment that those goals may not be complementary. For years, various "specialized subgroups, both scientific and professional," complained that the Association "did not give adequate attention to divergent interests."[96] Proposals were made to simplify the structure by combining sections or reallocating resources. More than has been true in GSA's Council, however, members of APA have been quite blunt in examining the ideological issues behind such maneuvering. "Contemporary psychology is composed of a collection of relatively independent areas of inquiry," declared Janet T. Spence. "Rather than advancing toward substantive unity, the tide is currently moving in the other direction. . . . In my worst nightmares I foresee a decimation of institutional psychology."[97]

ed. Ernest R. Hilgard (Washington, DC: APA, 1978), p. 128. Compare Joseph D. Matarazzo, "There Is Only One Psychology, No Specialties, but Many Applications," *American Psychologist*, vol. 42 (October 1987): 893–903, with Harold R. Johnson et al., "Foundations for Gerontological Education," *TG*, vol. 20, part 2 (June 1980): 1–61.

94 Gary R. VandenBos, "Loosely Organized 'Organized Psychology,' " *American Psychologist*, vol. 44 (July 1989): 979–86; Ann Howard et al., "The Changing Face of American Psychology," ibid., vol. 41 (1986): 1,311–27; Laurel Furumoto, "On the Margins: Women and the Professionalization of Psychology in the United States," in *Psychology in Twentieth-Century Thought and Society*, ed. Mitchell G. Ash and William R. Woodward (New York: Cambridge University Press, 1987), pp. 93–114.

95 Sigmund Koch and David E. Leary, *A Century of Psychology as Science* (New York: McGraw-Hill, 1985), p. 32.

96 Dael Wolfe, "The Reorganized American Psychological Association," *American Psychologist*, vol. 1 (1946): 3. The APA became a multipurpose organization in 1945, the year GSA was incorporated.

97 Janet T. Spence, "Centrifugal Versus Centripetal Tendencies in Psychology," *American Psychologist*, vol. 42 (1987): 1,052–4. For "tinkering" proposals, see John G. Darley and Meredith P. Crawford, "Growth and Allocation of Resources Within APA," *American*

Fragmentation coupled with flights into faddism characterizes postwar psychology no less than gerontology. Analysts report that members of autonomous APA divisions score differently in terms of determinism, objectivism, holism, and creativity. Division 20's nearest neighbor in APA was the clinical group; no other division claimed close affinity, however, to Adult Development and Aging. Some commentators distinguish between "hard" science, "soft" science, and "professional" practice. Others talk in terms of APA's multiple dimensions rather than bipolarities.[98] Arguably the most significant source of friction was compositional, not philosophical. APA's membership since the early 1960s has shifted away from an academic-based research orientation toward a practitioner/professional one focused in the health services. As differences became more pronounced, trend watchers feared that they "could fractionate psychology and polarize science and practice."[99]

After repeated efforts to bridge the concerns of "health care practitioners" and "academic/research" psychologists within APA failed, an American Psychological **Society** (APS) was established in 1988. The split occurred along divisional lines, separating subfields and distancing professions. Interestingly, APS called itself an "independent, multipurpose organization to advance the discipline of psychology, to preserve the scientific base of psychology, to promote public understanding of psychological science and its applications, to enhance the quality of graduate education, and to encourage the 'giving away' of psychology in the public interest."[100] Rhetorically, the competing groups sound similar. From a historical perspective, a more significant pattern should be noted. This was not the first organizational rift between scientists and practitioners in psychology. When APA could not resolve the question of certification and licensing in 1915, an American Association of Clinical Psychologists was started (1917), but soon disbanded. An American Association for Applied Psychology existed between

---

Psychologist, vol. 17 (1962): 465–74; Dorothy Adkins, "The Simple Structure of the American Psychological Association," ibid., vol. 9 (1954): 175–80; idem, "A Simpler Structure of the American Psychological Association," ibid., vol. 28 (1973): 47–54.

98 Urie Bronfenbrenner et al., "Toward a Critical Social History of Developmental Psychology," *American Psychologist*, vol. 41 (1986): 1,218–30; Gregory A. Kimble, "Psychology's Two Cultures," ibid., vol. 39 (1984): 833–9; Joseph Lee Rodgers, "Structural Models of the American Psychological Association in 1986," ibid., vol. 43 (1988): 372–82. For an early jeremiad on faddism, see Grace Adams, *Psychology: Science or Superstition?* (New York: Covici Friede Publishers, 1931).

99 Ann Howard et al., "Membership Opinions About Reorganizing APA," *American Psychologist*, vol. 42 (1987): 763–79; Howard, "Changing Face;" Robert C. Tyron, "Psychology in Flux," *American Psychologist* vol. 18 (1963): 134–43; Albert Gilgen, *American Psychology Since World War II* (Wesport, CT: Greenwood, 1982): pp. 21ff.

100 Preamble appeared in *Psychological Science*, vol. 1 (March 1990): 80; see also, Joseph Lee Rodgers, "Structural Models of the American Psychological Society at Birth," ibid., pp. 81–4.

1938 and 1942.[101] In the 1960s and 1970s, APA tried to reconcile "the scientific and professional aims of psychology" by establishing Psy.D. as a terminal degree in "applied" areas and reserving the Ph.D. for research. Conflicts over APA's policy role in Washington also sparked debates.[102]

Diverse interests and mutual suspicions, psychologists long have recognized, are inherent in any multifaceted enterprise that draws its membership together from within and outside laboratories, classrooms, and offices. John Dewey, after all, in his APA presidential address (1899), investigated "the problem of the relationship of psychology to the social sciences and through them to social practice, to life itself."[103] Dewey and his successors acknowledged the threefold challenge of crossing frontiers from the realm of theory to the world of practice in dealing with "real" people. Different sets of experts tend to dream about different "truths." They go about their business inattentive to the biases and customs embedded in their respective notions of legitimacy. In multidisciplinary contests, they demand not just the right to voice objections but also the right to veto proposed actions. This is no less true of policy analysts than it is for bench scientists and clinicians.

The APA's struggles offer some sobering lessons for a GSA that "could be a model of a professional/academic organization responsive to reality rather than to how higher education happens to be organized." It probably will not matter whether GSA retains its four-section structure, or like APA expands into forty-seven, or even whether the Society dissolves into competing groups. For more than a century, APA has tried in institutional terms to resolve the same tension between scientists and professionals that bedevils GSA. Being straightforward about the organizational issues in conflict, as APA has done, is not necessarily any more efficacious in resolving differences than relying on bureaucratic legerdemain, as GSA has become

101 Irwin Altman, "Centripetal and Centrifugal Trends in Psychology," *American Psychologist*, vol. 42 (1987): 1,058–69; "Affiliation of Psychological Organizations," *Science*, vol. 99 (1944): 74. On licensing, see Hilgard, *American Psychology*, p. 10; G. S. Speer, "Interprofessional Conference on Certification and Licensure," *National Occupational Conference*, vol. 28 (1949): 124–5; Arthur Brayfield, "What Does APA Do?" *American Psychologist*, vol. 19 (1964): 883–95; Steven J. Danish and Michael A. Smyer, "Unintended Consequences of Requiring a License to Help," ibid., vol. 36 (January 1981): 13–21.

102 "The Scientific and Professional Aims of Psychology," *American Psychologist*, vol. 22 (1967): 49–70; "Preliminary Report," ibid., vol. 20 (1965): 95–100; "Professional Psychologists Seek to Change Roles and Rules in the Field," *Science*, vol. 203 (26 January 1979): 338–40. On policy disputes, see "Relevance in Washington," *Science News*, vol. 96 (September 6, 1969): 177–8; "Psychologists Searching for Social Relevance," *Science*, vol. 165 (12 September 1969): 1,101–4; Daniel Goleman, "Will Nick Cummings Shake Up the APA?" *Psychology Today*, vol. 11 (1978): 94–5.

103 Quoted in Seymour B. Sarason, *Psychology Misdirected* (New York: Free Press, 1981), p. 122. Recall that these ideas are echoed in Dewey's preface to Cowdry's *Problems of Ageing* (1939).

accustomed to do. The challenge is to capitalize on "multidisciplinarity" in a way that invites the creation of novel intellectual paradigms, not simply another strategy for organizing rival tribes. "As with most societal problems today, the challenges and problems of an aging society leap across disciplinary and professional boundaries," noted former GSA executive director John Cornman. "If the field of gerontology remains multidisciplinary, rather than evolving into a series of isolated, fragmented, unrelated research enterprises, then the field could be a model of an area of study designed for tomorrow's world . . . [and] the Society could become a, if not the, center for encouraging broad, integrative thinking about an aging society and the future."[104]

Cornman's vision of GSA as a forum for critical thinking, freed from the constraints of disciplinary canons and professional conventions, harks back to John Dewey's 1939 brief for gerontology as a new field of scientific inquiry. By broadening the range of research topics and methods pertinent to gerontology as a research area, the Society has honored its founders' commitment to multidisciplinary approaches to aging. But in its desire to sustain its constituency's sense of its unique role in the absence of enforcing those counterbalancing, cross-sectional goals that transcend disciplinary aims, ironically GSA has forsaken opportunities to become its "own model." In the future, it must summon more courage in defining what "gerontology" means, in staking its intellectual frontiers.

104 Letter from John Cornman to author, June 7, 1989.

5

Risk taking in the modern research university and the fate of multidisciplinary institutes on aging

THE GERONTOLOGICAL SOCIETY (GSA), the previous chapter showed, has had difficulty defining its multidisciplinary aims and developing *modi operandi* in ways not unduly constrained by the competing professional loyalties of its members. This chapter,[1] which reconstructs the history of the University of Michigan's (U-M) Institute of Gerontology (IoG), illustrates how parochial academic interests can exercise a different set of pressures on centers based in universities.[2] However, the increasing role that state and federal agencies have assumed in addressing the needs of older persons in the United States has created unprecedented opportunities for such centers to produce, disseminate, and apply gerontologic knowledge. These opportunities, in turn, have begun to call into question the purposes and organization of research in higher education.

For roughly a century, departments have represented the range of disciplinary interests on campus and have borne primary responsibility for undergraduate education. Free-standing multidisciplinary units, in contrast,

1 Robert Holbrook, Susan Lipschutz, Harold W. Stevenson, and Mary Ann Swain offered constructive suggestions on earlier versions of this essay. Parts of this chapter are based on a working paper, "Risk-Taking in the Modern Research University: The Case of Multidisciplinary Institutes," written with Fred L. Bookstein and John W. Hagen.

2 I have chosen to focus on the history of the Institute of Gerontology (IoG) for two reasons. First, I know its history firsthand. As a graduate student, I used the Institute's library while writing my dissertation; I have maintained an affiliation with the place for nearly two decades. Because proximity pays, I have had greater access to "official" and "confidential" details here than I could gain elsewhere. Second, more than any other center on aging in the United States, the mission of this Institute changed dramatically over time. Wilma Donahue and Richard Adelman both wanted Ann Arbor to be a pacesetter, but they had different ends in mind and they labored under different restraints. I am keenly aware of the dangers of institutional chauvinism, but my choice of IoG as a major case study affirms that very risk taking described in this chapter.

are supposed to embody "diversity of scholarship . . . novelty and venture-someness, [and] imagination and creativity [that rely more upon] synthetic work and the development of new conceptual paradigms and unifying theories than upon specialization and fragmentation of knowledge."[3] Such grand claims notwithstanding, centers on aging actually are expected to survive on their wits. They rise or fall at the margins of the local academic community on their ability to obtain outside funds and extramural recognition. Intended to manage intellectual risks differently than departments, multidisciplinary centers have come to play important if still anomalous roles at research universities like Michigan.

After World War II, chief academic officers began to experiment with ways that research centers might counterbalance the supposedly deadening effects of specialization by stimulating innovation through cross-disciplinary partnerships. As Ralph Sawyer, dean of U-M's graduate school, put it:

> Interdisciplinary research has become prominent of late, largely because modern problems refuse to be confined within single and traditional academic disciplines. Administratively, this kind of research can create difficulties for universities if they attempt to organize such research strictly within existing departments. We have subscribed to a flexible view for the administration of interdisciplinary research and have supported the establishment of centers, institutes, bureaus, and other units either within colleges or schools or, in some cases, spanning several schools. By such a course administrative arrangements can follow academic needs, not vice versa.[4]

In most departmental settings, one phrases questions in a way that inspires publishable answers to colleagues who promise to listen on the basis of having heard a variant on the query before. In contrast, in an interdisciplinary environment, some questions are interesting precisely because they are so vague and "big" as to raise the possibility of generating findings that, in one eventuality, become path-breaking, but in another, equally probable scenario, will defy immediate resolution.

Clearly, many scholars pursuing knowledge in traditional disciplinary confines take risks as they work at the frontiers of knowledge. Serendipitous results occur everywhere. But only when there is a risk of *no* answer

---

3 Billy E. Frye, provost, valedictory address, U-M, reprinted in *University Record*, 1986. For more on the contrast between departments and centers, see Terence C. Halliday and Morris Janowitz, eds., *Sociology and Its Publics* (Chicago: University of Chicago Press, 1992), pp. 272–8.

4 Ralph Sawyer, dean of the Graduate School, in President's Report for 1963–4, U-M, p. 137. See also M. Dogan and R. Pahre, *Creative Marginality* (Boulder, CO: Westview, 1990). The prototype for institutes that operate independently of universities and academics is probably the Kaiser-Wilhelm-Gesellschaft (1911), though, as I suggested in the Introduction, the organizational genesis might be traced back to Francis Bacon. See J. G. Crowther, *The Social Relations of Science* (New York: Macmillan, 1941), pp. 491–2.

can investigators' findings prove more interesting than the original question itself. Indeed, the very process of searching for multifaceted answers, as John Dewey noted in his philosophy of science, ultimately illuminates broader dimensions of the problem-solving context than seemed relevant at the outset. Because multidisciplinary collaborations generate their own syntax in the course of a research project, they begin with, but ultimately cannot depend solely upon, disciplinary-specific canons. Thus centers and institutes appeal to academic renegades, to researchers daring to address questions that often yield frustrating, fruitless results. Rather than accepting prescribed paradigms, centers rightly give priority to the very anomalies and chancy investigations that sit in departments less comfortably. At their best, they function as an "opportunistic entity," taking advantage of the pool of resources and talent in their midst.[5]

Many collective intellectual risks, to be sure, are foolhardy; centers can suffer from hubris. Particularly as they mature, multidisciplinary units tend to become conservative as they seek permanence and security in a research university. Paradoxically, the more freestanding institutes begin to act like departments, the less likely they will fulfill their mandate to tackle large intellectual problems and to handle organizational risks in a distinctive way. The viability of multidisciplinary centers thus rests on their ratio of successes to failures, not on full-time equivalents (FTEs) and budgetary increments. Successes can open vast new vistas of research within the academic community. Centers can die, by virtue of their successes. But as the history of the IoG illustrates, "success" and "failure" are historically relative terms, conditioned by localized circumstances in a university and broader sociointellectual trends in U.S. society at large.

Institute of Gerontology

In 1965, in the same month that LBJ signed Medicare and the Older Americans Act into law, Michigan made history of its own by becoming the first state to underwrite a center on aging with public funds. On the recommendation of his Task Force on Education, Governor George Romney created IoG "for the purpose of developing new and improved programs for helping older people in this state, for the training of persons skilled in working with the problems of the aged, for research related to the needs of our aging population, and for conducting community service programs

---

5 In "The Disciplinary Stake," *Social Studies of Science*, vol. 13 (1983): 344, Alberto Cambrosio and Peter Keating suggest a "juridical analogy" that supports this thesis. Labs and research teams (and, by extension, centers) are "firms"; disciplines are "corporations," with legitimate yet fictional interests in transactions. The phrase "opportunistic entity" appears in Julie Thompson Klein, *Interdisciplinarity* (Detroit: Wayne State University Press, 1990), p. 123.

in the field of aging."[6] With bipartisan support, $200,000 was appropriated to cover IoG's operations during the first year at U-M and Wayne State; most of the funds went to Ann Arbor. "We thought it would take several years to get anything through the state legislature," recalled Stephen Spurr, who was dean of U-M's graduate school at the time. "But, to our surprise, the proposal was enacted into law and funded almost immediately."[7]

Wilma Donahue, IoG's first director, strove to make her center preeminent in the areas of teaching and service, not research. A Specialist in Aging certificate program began in 1967, which, by 1980, had awarded more than 500 certificates. (A Summer Education Program ran in tandem with 1,000 students registered at its peak in 1979.) Another 400 people graduated from the Residential Institute Program, which operated in fourteen-week summer sessions from 1967 to 1976. These figures do not include persons enrolled in options such as IoG's "faculty seminar" for college instructors in Michigan. With support from the state's Office of Services to the Aging, the Institute also provided assistance for professionals working with the elderly.[8] Formal curricular arrangements were made with U-M's schools of Social Work (1968), Architecture (1969), Education (1970), and Public Health (1970). Dr. Donahue's genius for developing educational programs in a period of growth at U-M and in the federal arena had actually been evident in the late 1940s, when conditions were not so auspicious.

University of Michigan's first collective gerontologic venture had been made possible by a million-dollar gift to the graduate school by Mary A. Rackham in 1936 to support rehabilitation projects for "the sick, aged, young, erring, poor, crippling, helpless, handicapped, unfortunate and underprivileged, regardless of race, color, religion or station."[9] To oversee programs underwritten by the Rackham funds, U-M established an Institute for Human Adjustment (IHA) a year later. A speech clinic and a two-person counseling clinic were transferred to IHA as well as responsibility for services provided for various Rackham relatives. In 1938, Clark Tibbitts was appointed IHA's first director. William Ogburn's student at the University of Chicago, Tibbitts had also collaborated with Ernest Burgess on a study of parole violators. After a stint as an instructor of sociology in Ann Arbor

6 State of Michigan, *Public Acts*, no. 245, July 21, 1965.
7 Spurr quoted in Marjorie Cahn Brazer, *Biography of an Endowment* (Ann Arbor: Michigan Historical Collections, 1985), p. 37. That Spurr may not have been altogether pleased is evident in his memo to Members of the University of Michigan Advisory Committee on Gerontology, April 16, 1965, in Rackham Records, Bentley Historical Collection (henceforth referred to as BHC). There, he recounts the activities of various members, "acting as individuals not as representatives of the University Committee," especially those of Harold Orbach, who was "a practicing Democrat" and member of the Gerontology staff that drafted the legislation.
8 Jeanne E. Miller, "Institute of Gerontology: Education/Service Activities," memo to author, June 14, 1985.
9 Brazer, *Biography of an Endowment*, pp. 8–9.

(1932–4), Tibbitts coordinated urban research projects for the Federal Emergency Relief Association (1934–5) and then served as field director of a national survey for the U.S. Public Health Service (1935–7).[10] Although his concern for older people did not become manifest until he returned to Ann Arbor, Tibbitts's new position afforded him the opportunity to establish U-M's reputation in social gerontology and his own career as a savvy administrator in the aging field.

Under a different set of circumstances, Rackham funds originally might have been used to support research on biological aspects of senescence. University of Michigan president Alexander Ruthven, a zoologist by training, was familiar with Cowdry's work. Seventeen faculty members had proposed an "Aging and Human Heredity" project to be housed in IHA "for collecting and interpreting the scattered researches, and for engaging in research on its own." Although interested in hereditary and environmental issues, Ruthven wanted "to begin our studies in those fields in which results could be obtained rather quickly and in which we could, therefore, gain experience."[11] Accordingly, the president asked Tibbitts to survey gerontology's frontiers. Echoing the language of the National Research Committee's 1938 report, which was largely drafted by his former colleagues at Chicago, Tibbitts affirmed that "it is mandatory that research, which has been so successful in prolonging life, be now directed to the objective of showing how the latter years can be employed to the greatest satisfaction of all concerned. . . . The University appears to have an unequalled opportunity for initiating a program for experiment and research that could have great significance for the entire population of the State and of the country as well."[12]

Like contributors to Cowdry's *Problems of Ageing*, Tibbitts recommended a multidisciplinary approach. "Concentrated attack on only one field such as the medical or psychological might easily give rise to serious

---

10 Biographical details on Tibbitts from The Association for Gerontology in Higher Education, "The Clark Tibbitts Award and Tribute" (Atlanta, 1986), and Robert C. Bannister, *Sociology and Scientism* (Chapel Hill: University of North Carolina Press, 1987), p. 179. See also Coleman R. Griffith, *Principles of Systematic Psychology* (Urbana: University of Illinois Press, 1943).

11 The program outline was attached to a memo from C. S. Yoackum to Alexander Ruthven, April 19, 1940, U-M, Horace Rackham Graduate School, Box 5, BHC. Ruthven's own interest is evident in his letter to Bryson D. Horton, January 13, 1940, Box 5, BHC. In an interview on December 11, 1985, Wilma Donahue told me that it was Ruthven who had suggested the aged as a beneficiary of the Rackham largesse.

12 Clark Tibbitts, "A Proposal for Research into Some of the Problems of Old Age," February 9, 1940, U-M, Horace Rackham Collection, Box 5 BHC. Compare with the recommendation – "There should be consideration of further possibilities for adult education and other measures for enhancing the usefulness and increasing the joy of persons in the later middle and last years of life" – in National Resources Committee, *The Problems of a Changing Population* (Washington, DC: Government Printing Office, 1938), p. 8.

lags or inconsistencies in our knowledge and ability to handle all of the problems of the aged," he observed, urging that "knowledge [be] built up from minute contributions emanating from many sources."[13] Tibbitts itemized a dozen topics worth pursuing, which ranged from studies of annuities and ways to retrain workers, to investigations of personality changes and cancer research. Some of his suggestions – such as offering services to older people with hearing losses through the Speech Clinic and, more ambitiously, building a self-contained residential community that might serve as a "research lab" – patently capitalized on the potential he envisioned for IHA. World War II delayed any U-M initiative on aging; Tibbitts directed the University War Board and Veterans Service Bureau in addition to his other tasks.

After the war, as he turned back to developing an aging program, Tibbitts decided to find out what older people themselves thought were their major problems in adjusting to later years. On the basis of three, nondirected interviews with each of seventy-five randomly selected men and women in Ann Arbor over the age of sixty-five, Tibbitts identified seven basic needs in order of importance: (1) financial security, (2) health and physical care, (3) adequate family and living arrangements, (4) recognition and status, (5) emotional relationships, (6) recognized roles providing useful activity, and (7) religion.[14] Concurrently Tibbitts was serving on the Social Science Research Council's committee on Social Adjustment in Old Age, which inspired social-psychological pilot studies at U-M and Chicago.[15] This work made Tibbitts curious about "the development of valid concepts of adjustment, both in terms of the individual's own feelings about whether or not his needs are being adequately met and in terms of his overt responses or external behavior."[16] Tibbitts's emphasis on "social adjust-

13 Tibbitts, "Proposal," pp. 17, 19.
14 Institute for Human Adjustment report, "An Exploratory Investigation of the Socio-Psychological and Sociological Problems of Adjustment of Older People," December 19, 1947, in the Donahue Papers, Box 19, BHC. Tibbitts was to make this seven-part needs assessment the basis for framing issues at the 1950 National Conference on Aging, which he directed. See Chapter 6, *infra.*
15 "Report of the Committee on Social Adjustment in Old Age," April 1948, Donahue Papers, Box 19, BHC. Tibbitts's work with SSRC meant that he interacted regularly with Ernest Burgess, Ruth Shonle Cavan, and Robert Havighurst at the University of Chicago, Nathan Shock in Baltimore, and Sydney Pressey at Ohio State, among others. So while Michigan's program would not spring from the research strengths being harnessed elsewhere, Tibbitts was well aware of intellectual developments across the country.
16 Clark Tibbitts, "Origins, Scope, and Fields of Social Gerontology" in *Handbook of Social Gerontology*, ed. Clark Tibbitts (Chicago: University of Chicago Press, 1960), p. 16. Tibbitts's definition of "adjustment" parallels discussions of the process of maturing at earlier stages of life. See Paul H. Landis, *Adolescence and Youth* (New York: McGraw-Hill, 1945), pp. 26, 448.

ment" was strategic and intellectual: Advancing this broad theme, he thought, fit IHA's mandate.

Because the elderly said they needed help and sought new opportunities as they adjusted to old age, Tibbitts saw a chance to bring together different groups with a stake in late-life adjustment. "Properly selected experts have a good deal of cogent information which they can impart," he felt, "and that some older people will attend an organized class group to obtain guidance."[17] With logistical support from the University Extension Service he and his colleague Wilma Donahue developed a course on "Aging and Living" in 1948 for older residents in Detroit. A year later, the pair taught classes in Detroit, Flint, Traverse City, Bay City, and Windsor, Ontario. Members of an Ann Arbor Senior Citizen Group, which sprung out of the course, met to discuss psychological techniques for staying mentally alert and health-care concerns before enjoying some recreation.[18] Tibbitts and Donahue produced twenty-six radio broadcasts on U-M's radio, which gave their efforts wider impact than most academic initiatives.

The Institute's staff also designed three conferences – "Living Through the Older Years" (1948), "Planning for the Older Years" (1949), and "Growing in the Older Years" (1950) – in which nationally recognized experts, newcomers to the field, and senior citizens themselves could exchange ideas. The common thread running through these and the next twenty-five annual conferences was that the adaptive adjustment of growing numbers of older people to an ever-changing environment was so important as to warrant a wide range of educational activities, especially in public institutions with a tradition of serving their state and nation. "Much emphasis has been put by our committees, organizations, and institutions to develop youth into successful adults," Donahue noted, "and little thought and less action have been put into programs for the development of adults into successful maturity and old age."[19] Making this case

17 Clark Tibbitts, "Aging and Living," *Adult Education Bulletin*, October 1948.

18 The teleconference course's original title was "Problems and Adjustments in Later Maturity and Old Age," thus underscoring Tibbitt's intellectual orientation. Tibbitts and Donahue, in turn, were assisted by Woodrow Hunter and Dorothy Coons, who would play key roles in IoG for the next several decades. Such continuity of leadership was a stabilizing factor. For more on the course and the Ann Arbor Senior Citizen Group, see Tibbitts, "Aging and Living"; and his letter to Edwin T. Connell, June 15, 1949, in the Donahue Papers, Box 15, BHC.

19 Wilma Thompson Donahue, "Changes in Psychological Processes," in *Living Through the Older Years*, ed. Clark Tibbitts (Ann Arbor: University of Michigan Press, 1951), p. 84. Holding summer institutes in Ann Arbor to advance scientific explorations into a new area is a U-M tradition. Since 1928, its annual Summer Symposium in Theoretical Physics provided an ideal setting for interactions. "The important thing . . . was not the formal lectures," recalled one participant, but "the exchange of ideas among creative workers, mostly young men with young ideas, ideas which were only half finished, uncertain, often

repeatedly and persuasively, Donahue and Tibbitts figured, would justify a place for gerontologic training, research, and service at U-M.[20]

When Tibbitts left Michigan in 1949 to coordinate aging-related concerns in the Federal Security Agency (FSA), Wilma Donahue assumed responsibilities for IHA's nascent gerontologic activities. A Michigan Ph.D. in psychology (1937), Donahue had worked in U-M's Student Health Service and IHA's Psychological Clinic before joining forces with Tibbitts in 1944. In addition to maintaining commitments in all three units and caring for her ill husband, Donahue had investigated blindness for the U.S. Office of Vocational Education. Donahue, as chair of the newly reorganized Division of Gerontology, thus had no less diverse a set of experiences than Tibbitts to tap.[21] "A large part of the Division's work is educational in nature," she observed. Hundreds of students enrolled in workshops and training sessions in the state. Others came from all parts of the nation for summer conferences in Ann Arbor.

Donahue was interested not only in disseminating knowledge but also in applying ideas to improve the quality of late life. "Through research and demonstration we conducted projects that had significance in the development and application of new theories and technology."[22] Dr. Donahue and her staff served as consultants to a variety of federal and state agencies. Countless projects were under way, but retirement, mental health, and living arrangements were the major research foci. Woodrow Hunter became the country's leading expert in preretirement education. Dorothy Coons developed techniques in milieu therapy in the early 1960s that she would adapt in her work with Alzheimer's patients three decades later. Donahue promoted low-income housing for the elderly. "It was here in 1952, through the Fifth Annual University of Michigan Conference on Aging, that Wilma Donahue brought together for the first time a wide-ranging group

---

wrong or sterile." Quoted in Paul K. Hoch, "Institutional Versus Intellectual Migrations in the Nucleation of New Scientific Specialties," *Studies in the History and Philosophy of Science*, vol. 18 (1987): 485.

20 There is much debate as to whether the "first" aging course was held at Michigan, Minnesota, or Chicago. Because each place had a different audience in mind, credit doubtless belongs to all. But there was concern about overlap. Thus, Robert Havighurst wrote about his plans to "attract practical workers in the field, mainly social workers, but also a number of researchers. . . . We do not want to try to compete with anything of a similar nature in Michigan such as the institute of last summer." See his letter to Tibbitts, December 22, 1948, in the Donahue Papers, Box 19, BHC.

21 Wilma Thompson Donahue, "A Survivor's Career," in *Lives of Career Women*, ed. Frances M. Carp (New York: Plenum, 1991), pp. 23-41. Gerontology was made a division within IHA in 1951.

22 Donahue, "A Survivor's Career," p. 34. See also Clark Tibbitts and Wilma Thompson Donahue, "Developments in Education for Later Maturity," *Review of Educational Research*, vol. 23 (June 1953): 202–17; Wilma Thompson Donahue, "Gerontology at the University of Michigan," *Geriatrics*, vol. 15 (April 1960): 222–8.

of architects, builders, financial agencies, researchers, and community planners together with representatives of government and of older people themselves and set them the task of developing the guidelines for a national housing program for senior citizens," declared Assistant HEW secretary Wilbur J. Cohen in 1964. "It was here in Ann Arbor, under her farsighted direction, that the movement for retirement housing received its first major impetus."[23]

Doing basic research was *not* the hallmark of early activities at U-M as it was at the gerontology centers in Chicago or Baltimore. "Although the Division of Gerontology did not expect to become deeply involved with academicians," Donahue took charge of a project initiated at the 1955 meeting of the Gerontological Society "for the purpose of furthering the training of more social scientists in the field of aging in order to increase instruction and research in social gerontology."[24] A grant of $204,000 from the National Institutes of Health (NIH) enabled Donahue to coordinate the preparation of three handbooks: James Birren's *Handbook of Aging and the Individual* (1959), Clark Tibbitts's *Handbook of Social Gerontology* (1959), and Ernest Burgess's *Aging in Western Societies* (1960). In addition, she supervised three national inventories of university research and teaching, generated syllabi for five different courses, and planned summer institutes at the universities of Connecticut and California. Under her aegis, *Graduate Education in Aging Within the Social Sciences* was published.[25]

Despite all of these educational programs and outreach ventures, it must be said that gerontology truly was a marginal enterprise at Michigan until the mid-1960s. A small group of dedicated individuals could blaze frontiers as they saw fit in Donahue's freestanding division. But their efforts did not automatically win them allies within the U-M faculty. Efforts to create a University Council on Gerontology in the 1950s languished; Donahue's proposal to create an M.A. in gerontology failed. The chair's own place in U-M's academic community was not secure. "Wilma has never held a professorial appointment, but has established herself as perhaps the most outstanding authority on gerontology in the country," Dean Spurr wrote in

---

23 See Donahue's various commentaries for the U-M President's Reports. The quotation comes from the 1953 report; the trilogy of research foci are noted in 1965; all reports in Donahue Papers, Box 19, BHC. Donahue's interest in housing can be traced back to memo dated June 28, 1948. Cohen's remarks were prepared for the dedication of Lurie Terrace, October 9, 1964. Document in Clark Tibbitts Papers, Box 5, BHC. Notations on the text indicate that Tibbitts drafted the speech. See also the press release of the Housing and Home Finance Agency, July 8, 1964, in the IoG Files, Box 6, BHC.

24 Both quotations in Donahue, "A Survivor's Career," pp. 34–5.

25 Clark Tibbitts, "Introduction. Social Gerontology," *International Social Science Journal*, vol. 15 (1963): 339–54. Both Donahue and Birren indicated in interviews that their relationship was uneasy. Among other things, Birren did not like the notion of "social gerontology." Several other people commented that Donahue could be "difficult."

1965. "I will be glad to recommend her for a distinguished faculty award, but I doubt that she will qualify because of her lack of a professorial appointment."[26]

Funding gerontology at U-M was as precarious as its intellectual standing. Rackham provided only $25,000 of the $191,226 Donahue reported to be at her disposal in her 1961–2 report; the Extension Service contributed another $5,000; U-M's Institute of Labor and Industrial Relations, $1,188. Grants from the federal government (U.S. Office of Vocational Rehabilitation, U.S. Office of Education, and NIH), in contrast, represented more than 67 percent of the budget. Private support varied from year to year.[27] No wonder Donahue wanted Michigan to create the IoG: That recognition plus the prospect of new sources of revenue were bound to enhance the visibility of gerontology on campus, in the state, and across the nation.

The gamble paid off. As a bona fide Institute promoting teaching, research, and service, IoG was well positioned to seek federal support from its ally Clark Tibbitts, now a senior official in the newly created U.S. Administration on Aging (AoA). "To provide a training program in social gerontology," AoA in 1966 announced its intention to give four regional centers between $100,000 and $200,000 for start-up costs. "The Administration on Aging hopes that our Institute will be interested in becoming the mid-west center," Tibbitts wrote Donahue, adding "(I hope so, too)."[28] In March 1967, IoG was awarded $289,866 for four years to train students enrolled in a master's of public administration degree as specialists in aging, with an emphasis on housing, milieu-therapy programming, and multipurpose senior citizen centers. A year later, Donahue reported that fifty-five people had been prepared to work in aging agencies, and another seventeen graduate students were completing courses and beginning field placements. The Institute seemed to have it all – money, contacts, prestige, and depth.[29]

Satisfied as she approached her seventieth birthday that she had nurtured "a mosaic of training in all areas of the state and at all educational lev-

26 Spurr to Herbert Hildebrandt, assistant to (U-M) president, August 9, 1965, in IoG Files, Box 1, BHC.
27 Wilma Donahue to Dean Sawyer, "1961–1962 Annual Report, Division of Gerontology," Donahue Papers, Box 19, BHC. Beginning in 1950, the Ford Foundation considered making sizable grants to Donahue under its program on "Individual Behavior and Human Relations," but it never did so.
28 Tibbitts to Donahue, October 10, 1966, in IoG Files, Box 1, BHC.
29 University of Michigan News Release, March 16, 1967, and Report to Dean Spurr for the 1966–7 President's Report, both in Donahue Papers, Box 19, BHC. See also "Michigan-Wayne State Stress Crash Training for Specialists in Aging," *Geriatrics*, vol. 23 (August 1968): 36, 41, 45, 48. In 1971, Hunter declared that IoG had made a "singular contribution" in professional training, continuing education, milieu therapy, environment and aging, community action, preretirement education, and housing for the elderly. See IoG Files, Box 12, BHC.

els,"[30] Donahue began a "retirement" furlough in Washington. There, she cochaired the 1971 White House Conference on Aging (WHCoA) and, two years later, established an International Center for Social Gerontology. The University of Michigan conducted a national search for her replacement. Nathan Shock declined an offer.[31] The candidacies of two social scientists prominent in the gerontologic research community were scuttled when relevant U-M departments said that they would only offer untenured "courtesy" appointments. So U-M's Woodrow Hunter became acting director for a year, followed by Wayne Vasey (a social worker) who served for three years before he retired.[32] Vasey told his staff that his successor should be a leader with "sensitiveness to the political process" who was "acceptable as a respected member of the academic community." A reputation in aging was "a desirable qualification," but it should not "override considerations of competence in administration and planning."[33] In 1975, Harold R. Johnson was chosen director. Johnson, a Canadian-born black who had played professional football, represented an AFL-CIO union, directed a statewide Office of Youth Services, and then climbed the academic ladder to become a U-M professor of social work, was told by U-M's provost "to develop as broad a base as possible for your programs, including some efforts in the biological and legal aspects of aging."[34]

Elaborating IoG's original mandate and heeding the charge from the central administration, Johnson worked hard to build bridges with the University's departments and professional schools in the areas of research, teaching, and service. Cooperative academic programs were expanded to seventeen different schools and colleges within U-M. As AoA deemphasized university-based training and opted for contract research,[35] Johnson and his chief assistant Carol Hollenshead placed greater emphasis on developing research and demonstration projects. His staff wrote proposals that built on IoG's expertise on older workers, milieu therapy, housing and community programs, and capitalized on successes in curricular development. The U-M faculty and graduate students were invited to use IoG resources to initiate multidisciplinary proposals in new areas. For in-

30 *Report to Legislature*, January 1, 1972, p. 3, in Donahue Papers, Box 12, BHC.
31 Memo from Woodrow Hunter to IoG staff, November 11, 1970, IoG Files, Box 1, BHC.
32 "Director Named to New University Post," *Gerontology at Michigan* (June 1981). Wilbur J. Cohen, who became dean of the School of Education after serving as LBJ's secretary of HEW, chaired IoG's executive board during this transitional period.
33 Memorandum from Wayne Vasey to IoG staff, November 28, 1973, IoG Files, Box 12, BHC.
34 "A Profile of Harold Johnson," *AGHE Exchange*, vol. 14 (December 1900/January 1991): 12. See also letter of Provost Frank H.T. Rhodes to Harold R. Johnson, December 12, 1974, IoG Files, Box 12 BHC.
35 Ray C. Rist, "Federal Funding and Social Science Research: The Emergent Transformation," *Human Organization*, vol. 35 (1976): 265.

stance, when the National Endowment for the Humanities (NEH) said that it would entertain an aging-related proposal, Hollenshead called me at Canisius College in Buffalo to see if I were interested in putting together a project based on my recently completed Ph.D. dissertation in history. The proposal resulted in a two-year project on "Images of Old Age, 1790 to the Present." Supported by NEH, the venture was designed to relay knowledge in public places. "Images" won awards and was exhibited throughout the country under the aegis of the Smithsonian Institution before being displayed at the 1981 WHCoA.[36]

By August 1980, more than fifty U-M professors were listed as IoG Faculty Associates. Johnson and his six administrators within IoG supervised a sixty-member training and program staff and nineteen office workers. Johnson forged partnerships wherever and whenever possible. Nor did he overlook his larger constituency. The Institute responded to requests for assistance from various Michigan state bureaus, Area Agencies on Aging, Health Planning Councils, direct service agencies (such as Retired Senior Volunteer Programs and local nursing homes) and Native American tribes. His leadership style is evident in the way he described IoG's position on campus:

> The totality of gerontological activity here is difficult to quantify. . . . Although the Institute initiates and coordinates University programs in aging, it also encourages instructional and research units to develop such activities independently. Many of its resources are expended in quiet diplomacy intended to assist other units to develop gerontological projects in keeping with their own scholarly priorities. This approach has served to reduce competition and to involve a broader range of professions and disciplines in the field of aging than at any other institution of higher education in the country.[37]

Johnson's low-key, personable approach worked effectively on U-M's sprawling campus, in which a "fairly stable informal network of linkages" was superimposed on official administrative channels. "Michigan is an unusually decentralized institution, especially on academic affairs," recalls Zelda Gamson, who studies trends in higher education. "Whether it is because people know one another across departments or because of the intensive faculty involvement in larger university affairs, it is not too difficult to get interdepartmental programs going."[38] Sustaining those linkages,

---

36 W. Andrew Achenbaum and Peggy Ann Kusnerz, *Images of Old Age in America, 1790 to the Present* (Ann Arbor: Institute of Gerontology, 1978; rev. 1982).

37 Harold R. Johnson, *The Institute of Gerontology at The University of Michigan, 1975–1980* (Ann Arbor: Institute of Gerontology, 1981).

38 Zelda F. Gamson, "Michigan Muddles Through," *in Academic Transformation*, ed. David Riesman and Verne Stadtman (New York: McGraw-Hill, 1973), pp. 188, 193; David A. Hollinger, "Academic Culture at Michigan, 1938–1988," *Rackham Reports* (1988–9): 58–91.

however, proved more difficult. Johnson's staff consisted mainly of young and middle-aged women who did not have Ph.D.s. Having worked together on summer workshops, conferences and special events, and in the delivery of social services, they constituted a remarkably cohesive and dedicated group. Their success rate in grantsmanship was enviable. But the Institute continued to rely on "outsiders," faculty members around campus and friends across the nation, to supply the intellectual capital to fuel IoG's research initiatives.

When Johnson resigned to become dean of U-M's School of Social Work in 1982, the central administration decided to take a hard look at the IoG. A recession was forcing the University to eliminate programs that lacked strong research foci. "Support for individual centers should be steady and predictable but time limited," observed Harold Shapiro, who became U-M's president in 1980. "Research centers that do not support the mission and values of the institution within which they operate will not prosper."[39] Many faculty members on campus, reflecting an opinion expressed elsewhere, felt that gerontology was still an ersatz field of endeavor. Michigan's Tom Hickey, a pioneer in gerontologic education, worried that "the quality of the gerontology curriculum had declined 'in inverse relation' to its growth." Johnson himself, who had chaired a national blue-ribbon panel on the "Foundations of Gerontological Education," acknowledged that "there is not a sufficient 'distinctive' body of knowledge to warrant a separate degree program, nor is there an adequately defined set of skills needed to work with the elderly."[40]

Despite past triumphs, IoG's future suddenly was in jeopardy. Freestanding centers in Michigan's research-rich environment no longer could justify their existence by claiming to be educational pioneers that ably served policymakers. To survive, IoG needed to be recognized as a center where knowledge was generated, not merely conveyed to the larger academic and policy communities. The University's strategists wanted IoG to extend its network beyond "applied" researchers and social scientists. "Developments in science alone will transform the face of all science-related institutions that wish to remain viable in the next decades," President Shapiro predicted, "for science has not only become an instrument of public policy but

39 Harold T. Shapiro, "The National Research Effort," in *idem. Tradition and Change* (Ann Arbor: University of Michigan Press, 1987), p. 45. For a broader discussion of the complementary relationship between "competition" and "local values," see Walter Ruegg, "The Academic Ethos," *Minerva*, vol. 24 (1986): 393–412. For a less flattering critique of Shapiro's view, see Paul Von Blum, *Stillborn Education* (Lanham, MD: University Press of America, 1986).

40 Hickey quoted in R. L. Jacobson, "Gerontology Said to Lack Identity as an Academic Discipline," *The Chronicle of Higher Education*, vol. 26 (March 27, 1980): 4; Harold R. Johnson, et al., "Foundations for Gerontological Education," *The Gerontologist*, vol. 20 (1980), part 2: 1–61. Johnson quote from "Too Many 'Gerontology Specialists' – U Man," *Ann Arbor News*, October 18, 1978.

is advancing at an unprecedented pace."[41] At a time in which members of the GSA were using terms such as "science" and "research" interchangeably, officials at U-M were becoming very adamant about the difference between "hard" science and "soft" research.

To promote the creation of gerontologic science, Johnson had joined with the Interuniversity Consortium for Political and Social Research to create the National Archive of Computerized Data of the Aged, thus linking IoG with U-M's best-known center for methodological rigor. Responding to the central administration's charge that IoG develop a biological component, Johnson in 1976 had initiated talks to stimulate basic aging research in U-M's medical center and biological sciences. But he and his IoG allies were unable to design a plan that won key faculty support or the provost's confidence. "A really worthwhile program cannot be built just by establishing liaisons among such interested parties unless at least a few of them are both centrally interested and of outstanding scientific reputation," the provost wrote Shapiro. "There may be such individuals in the University, but I do not know them."[42] Appointing a new director thus provided an opportunity to redirect IoG. The selection of Richard C. Adelman, a biological chemist from Temple University, indicated that U-M administrators were intent upon transforming IoG's mission: They wanted their center on aging to invest in basic research, especially in the biomedical sciences. Teaching and service mattered, but they were of lesser importance.

Adelman pursued a three-pronged strategy: (1) a multidisciplinary research program that capitalized on opportunities in the health sciences; (2) educational programs aimed not at a mass market but at providing sophisticated predoctoral and postdoctoral research training; and (3) public-service initiatives that communicated and applied research in selected policy/practice communities. "The educational challenge is development of the capability to produce new generations of basic scientists, from all disciplines, who in addition to their traditional training are capable of interacting with the other disciplines that possess at least equally important tools with which to pursue the answer to a particular question."[43] Adelman envisioned an entrepreneurial, multidisciplinary community of basic scientists.

To accomplish his three-pronged agenda, the new director was authorized to make sweeping changes. His actions caused great consternation.

---

41 Harold T. Shapiro, "American Higher Education," in *Tradition and Change*, p. 118.

42 Author's interviews with Billy E. Frye, former U-M provost, and Robert S. Holbrook, Office of the Vice President for Academic Affairs, 1988. Much of the paper trail on this initiative is found in IoG Files, Box 5, BHC. See confidential letter of Provost Frye to President Harold Shapiro, April 25, 1979, IoG Files, Box 5, BHC.

43 Richard C. Adelman, "The Dilemma of Research Training in Gerontology," *Educational Gerontology*, vol. 12 (1986): 579–84; quotation from p. 581. See also, C. H. Townes, "Differentiation and Competition Between University and Other Research Laboratories in the United States," *Daedalus*, vol. 103 (1973): 153–67.

Upon assuming office, Adelman decimated the program staff he inherited. The talented, close-knit group that Johnson and Hollenshead had nurtured was replaced by another cadre of men and women with Ph.D.s or M.D.s, who had a different set of talents and who had already established themselves as independent investigators. "My intent is to shift the balance in favor of research by providing appointments to investigators with the credentials necessary to obtain faculty rank from the academic departments."[44] The head of the local chapter of the American Association of University Professors (AAUP) denounced the move, but Adelman's superiors were not perturbed. "You have made great strides in further strengthening the relationships between the Institute of Gerontology and the academic programs on campus," an associate vice president for academic affairs wrote the new IoG director in 1983. "I would be interested in any advice you might have as to how one really does this successfully.... Perhaps there are lessons in your experience that can be translated to assist others in strengthening their programs."[45]

A decade later, twenty-five IoG research scientists had been jointly recruited with departments and schools giving tenure-line appointments; the two not on the tenure track were honored by the central administration with the title Distinguished Research Scientists. With few exceptions, this faculty identified primarily with IoG, secondarily with their departments. In addition, there were thirteen Faculty Associates, far fewer than before. Significantly, most of the appointments were in U-M's health-related professional schools; only two had tenure in the liberal arts college; no one is currently affiliated with the schools of Business, Education, Law or Social Work. Former IoG directors questioned the strategy. "Gerontological programs that attempt to survive in splendid isolation may not see the dawn of the twenty-first century," warned Harold Johnson, among others. Yet Adelman could take special pride in enabling the Medical School to recruit talented physicians to develop a geriatric program strong enough to become a "Center of Excellence" on campus. Geriatricians now work with gerontologists "to promote innovative cross-disciplinary programs of research and education."[46]

Adelman's insistence that all activities had to be research-driven precip-

---

44 Memo from Dick Adelman to B. Frye and R. Holbrook, November 28, 1982, in current Director's file.

45 Mary Ann Swain to Dr. Richard Adelman, October 20, 1983, in current Director's files.

46 The quotation comes from Johnson's Clark Tibbitts Lecture delivered at the 1991 meeting of the Association for Gerontology in Higher Education. I thank Dean Johnson for the text. Several years later, amid an intellectual property dispute between an IoG research scientist and a postdoctoral trainee, Adelman found that U-M's decentralized approach to problem solving heightened his sense of isolation. It also seemed to diminish institutional support that might have been expected under the circumstances. On the importance of "centers of excellence" to U-M, see Alan W. Steiss, "The Expanding Mission of University Research," *Reporter*, vol. 35 (1988).

itated changes in IoG's programs and workshops, especially those serving nonmatriculated students. Recognizing that laboratory animal science and medicine was an expanding field, Adelman entrusted one of his mentors, Bennett Cohen, to develop facilities for conducting experiments in close proximity to IoG's laboratories. This initiative brought the Institute to the attention of muscle physiologists, exercise specialists, and pathologists who saw new possibilities for doing research relevant to aging.[47] Adelman's decision to phase out IoG's certificate program proved more controversial. "The proposed changes at IoG have caused a fury within the aging network," reported Olivia P. Maynard, a U-M graduate who directed Michigan's Office of Services to the Aging. "We do not wish to see the needs of practitioners and those preparing to enter the field ignored or lost in the process. My sense is that the Institute is turning its back somewhat on those people it has traditionally served in the education arena, including aging network personnel."[48]

It should be noted that this was not the first time the IoG had curtailed a successful educational program. Hunter and Vasey had concluded by the early 1970s that the annual summer conferences should be discontinued because the format had been emulated by so many other competitors that U-M no longer enjoyed a comparative advantage.[49] But Adelman was less willing than his predecessors to temporize, to accommodate various constituencies who were not themselves committed to fostering a rigorous, scientific environment at IoG. Weekly seminar series featured disciplinary-specific and multidisciplinary research. With support mainly from the National Institute on Aging (NIA), trainees came to work with specific IoG mentors. Adelman felt that such laboratory-based opportunities, in which "small groups of mature scientists pursuing a reasonably coherent programme of research side-by-side with advanced students in the same institutional context and engaging in direct, continuous social and intellectual interaction" was the best way to advance gerontologic knowledge in a scientific manner.[50]

"Service" activities were also transformed. During Johnson's tenure, IoG provided an elaborate information-and-referral service; its staff was willing to stretch in order to fulfill requests for help. Adelman wanted IoG re-

---

47 See, for example, Bennett J. Cohen, "Laboratory Animal Medicine: Guidelines for Education and Training." (Washington, DC: National Academy of Sciences, 1978).

48 Olivia P. Maynard to Harold R. Johnson, October 19, 1983, which was copied to Adelman, in current Director's file. Johnson at the time chaired IoG's Executive Board; he resigned several years later over continued policy differences with his successor.

49 Woodrow Hunter to Wayne Vasey, December 7, 1972, in author's files.

50 Gerald L. Geison, "Scientific Change, Emerging Specialties, and Research Schools," *History of Science*, vol. 19 (January 1981): 23; N. C. Mullins, "Invisible Colleges as Science Elites," *Scientometrics*, vol. 7 (1985): 357–68. External reviews of IoG's mission, especially its training programs, in 1985, 1990 (biomedical), and 1991 (social science), all strongly endorsed this mode of training in "invisible colleges."

searchers to interact with professionals in the field and with public officials only to the extent that the exchange enhanced his Institute's research capacities. Significant contributions were still possible under the new order. External reviews suggested that Brant Fries, an operations researcher hired by Adelman, probably has had a greater impact on the lives of older people than any other scientist associated with IoG. Fries's system for matching patient diagnoses with social and health-care needs has altered nursing-home services in the United States and abroad as much as Diagnosis Related Groups affected hospital practice. Adelman himself served as chair of a Veterans Administration advisory committee which gave greater visibility to gerontology and geriatrics.

Finally, without violating the spirit of IoG's initial mandate, Adelman renegotiated the original terms of its charter. Believing "their program is less than productive" scientifically, he severed long tenuous ties with Wayne State and persuaded U-M officials and the Michigan legislature that state appropriations to IoG must become a line in the university budget rather than a separate item. "Politically, the line item was of great significance to the IoG in its past which emphasized activities in the areas of social services and policy," Adelman wrote. "Given our current pattern of growth and accomplishment in the scholarly direction, I prefer to rely on the judgement [*sic*] of UM Administration rather than the original constituency of State-wide network of social service providers."[51] While his predecessors privately questioned his decision, Adelman's gamble reflected not just his distaste for legislative politics but also his faith that U-M valued IoG's research accomplishments and would continue to do so.

Michigan's IoG has always stood for innovative excellence, but in terms of priorities the Institute of the 1990s differs greatly from its earlier manifestations. Its organizational structure, unlike a department's, could be radically transformed. So, in 1982, when U-M invested heavily in enhancing its research mission, the Institute literally was "born-again." The central administration chose to allow a venturesome leader to pursue a new set of gerontologic objectives that bore just enough resemblance to IoG's original mission to justify keeping the center's name as he jettisoned nearly everything else valued by previous regimes.[52]

51 Both quotations from Dick Adelman to IoG Executive Board, "Relation with Wayne State; State Appropriation," January 17, 1986, in current Director's file.
52 Adelman's risk taking in recruitment paid off. The IoG is considered one of the country's top university-based facilities for research on gerontology. Its faculty attained a funding level in excess of $18 million by 1992; no other university had more NIA grants. The 38 research scientists and faculty associates produced more than 300 publications that year. They served on 51 different editorial boards. Honors abounded: 6 editorships, and appointments to 34 national advisory committees, including 7 chairmanships. Over their careers, the group had collectively won 33 of the highest citations and awards by relevant professional bodies, and funding and civic agencies. There has been little turnover so far.

Putting IoG's history into comparative perspective

How does IoG's development compare with the history of other multidisciplinary centers? In the previous chapter, we looked at the history of the American Psychology Association (APA), as well as other professional and disciplinary organizations, to illuminate important aspects of GSA's story. By the same logic, it might make sense to compare the growth of gerontology at Michigan with developments at Brandeis, Chicago, Duke, Penn State, and the University of Southern California, to mention just five of the other "big" centers on aging. Yet because of fundamental differences in the personalities of key figures, shifts in research priorities, and divergent turning points in their institutional histories, such comparisons would end up stressing unique features and anomalies within each place's university setting, rather than stipulate similarities and differences among centers. Providing a Baedeker's guide to smaller gerontologic programs also would result in an anecdotal analysis.

Recent assessments of the development of gerontology, geriatrics, and aging-studies programs in institutions of higher education suggest two reasons why comparisons in the field are hard to make. First, the number of colleges and universities offering gerontology courses has increased from 57 in 1957, to 159 in 1967, to 1,607 in 1976, to 1,335 in 1983 to 1,639 in 1992. Universities with enrollments over 20,000 that offer graduate training are most likely to have centers or institutes. Yet select types of institutions – such as 71 percent of the historically black colleges and universities surveyed – also offer at least one course on aging.[53] Second, although most programs expose students to the biological, psychological, and social sciences, their orientations differ. Some stress a liberal arts approach, others emphasize professional training, and still others prepare trainees for research careers. The core knowledge and skill outcomes stipulated in these tracks do not overlap greatly.[54] Differences in orientation, according to David Peterson and his associates, may be more salient than differences in size of programs or stability of institutional support. If so, Michigan would appear to be an exceptional case, not indicative of future trends in gerontology. The same could be said of nearly every other program.

Accordingly, I have decided to compare IoG with two other centers broadly interested in issues of growth, development, and aging, which were

From a development brochure produced by Adelman and Achenbaum in 1993. See also Marc deMey, *The Cognitive Paradigm* (Dordrecht: Reidel, 1982), pp. 135–6.

53 David A. Peterson, Pamela F. Wendt, and Elizabeth B. Douglass, *Development of Gerontology, Geriatrics, and Aging Studies Programs in Institutions of Higher Education* (Washington, DC: Association for Gerontology in Higher Education, 1994).

54 Pamela F. Wendt, David A. Peterson, and Elizabeth B. Douglass, *Core Principles and Outcomes of Gerontology, Geriatrics and Aging Studies Instruction* (Washington, DC: Association for Gerontology in Higher Education, 1993).

established at U-M in 1963 and 1964. Not only did these three centers start out with much in common, but they all seem to fit the profile of institutes elsewhere, "the first significant organizational alternative to discipline-based departments." According to Stanley Ikenberry, centers proliferated during the postwar period because of the availability of new financial resources, new constituencies, the desire (on the part of administrators and faculty) for status, and a desire to create hospitable niches in the "multiversity." By looking at three centers on the same campus, it will be possible to refine some of these generalizations.[55]

Center for Human Growth and Development (CHGD)

In November, 1964, U-M's regents established CHGD to pursue four objectives:

1. to coordinate, integrate, and conduct research on normal and abnormal human growth and development, including its biological, intellectual, behavioral, and social aspects
2. to identify and generate problems of research which remain unsolved because of the lack of a multidisciplinary approach
3. to provide new types of advanced training programs for developmental scientists: flexible programs exposing trainees from several disciplines to a broader spectrum of knowledge than traditionally is possible
4. to provide for the constant communication of ideas among scientists within the center and to create a means by which knowledge gained from the research activities of the center can be disseminated rapidly for the good of the public[56]

Growth was rapid at first. Disciplines initially represented in the CHGD included psychology, linguistics, orthodontics, otolaryngology, neuroscience, speech, and pediatrics. Unlike a department where faculty operated collegially as individuals, Robert Moyers, the first director, wanted CHGD to be made up of contiguous "labs" run by senior fellows.[57] This novel arrangement proved impracticable. The Senior Fellows CHGD wanted to recruit to Michigan demanded tenure. Departmental ties may have dampened their desire for entrepreneurship.

Shortly, CHGD found itself unable to progress. In an era of stable and then declining availability of funds, CHGD offered neither client-based services nor any welfare-related payoff for its enterprise. By 1980, CHGD was having great difficulty recruiting new faculty. Lack of wet labs pre-

55 Stanley O. Ikenberry, *A Profile of Proliferating Institutes* (University Park, PA: Center for the Study of Higher Education, November 1970), 18.
56 University News Service, "Regents Approve Creation of Center for Human Growth and Development," November 20, 1964.
57 Robert E. Moyers, White Paper to Dr. James Duderstadt, September 4, 1986.

cluded the hiring of biologists. Rather than interact with anthropologists and clinicians in the Center, CHGD's behavioral scientists cooperated with colleagues in psychology, channeling new members into existing departmental networks on "child development" or "learning theory." The Center did not significantly configure itself to encourage multidisciplinary risk taking. Few acted on a 1988 internal report that called for a cross-disciplinary "Advanced Study Program" working in "conceptual clusters" such as mathematical biology.[58] Instead, most members continued to pursue their own projects independently, much as they would if they were housed in the departments that granted them tenure.

Institute for the Study of Mental Retardation and Related Disabilities (ISMRRD)

In December 1963, a steering committee reported that a critical mass of faculty in education, social work, medicine, public health, and psychology were doing research on mental retardation. The Joseph P. Kennedy, Jr. Foundation had already given U-M a $20,000 grant to plan a diagnostic and treatment facility. Furthermore, Public Law 88-164, the Mental Retardation Facilities Construction Act (1963), set aside construction and operating funds for university-affiliated facilities to conduct interdisciplinary training programs for personnel in the region who worked with the young. All this justified the regents' decision to start yet another U-M institute funded mainly with outside support.

A steady infusion of federal dollars encouraged tremendous growth at ISMRRD during the first decade. By 1976, ISMRRD had a staff of ninety. Researchers hailed from fifteen academic units, but few were tenure-track. Given U-M's strong emphasis on public service in the 1970s, ISMRRD director William Cruikshank, an expert on mental retardation and learning disabilities, developed many programs for a wide range of constituencies, but he did not maintain a careful mix among research, teaching, and service. Unfortunately, training had a lower priority than community involvement at ISMRRD; research in turn became tertiary to performing services for clients.

A 1977 internal long-term planning report warned that "research has not been a high priority area with those funders who provide core support."[59] Two years later, a University committee reviewing ISMRRD noted that "we are not convinced that the teaching activity of the Institute is maximally serving its own needs or the needs of departments." The report

58 Alphonse Burdi, "Recommendations on Recruitments" (Ann Arbor: The Center for Human Growth and Development, 1988).
59 *Annual Report.* Institute for Study of Mental Retardation and Related Disabilities, 1977–8, p. 87, ISMRRD Files, Box 2, Michigan Historical Collection (henceforth referred to as MHC).

recommended far greater emphasis on research for its own sake and closer ties with the medical school. "The recruitment and retention of personnel with high academic credentials is seen as a major problem."[60] The mixed review came at a bad time. Cruikshank was on extended sick leave for most of his last eighteen months as director. By 1981, there were vacancies in five of the eleven program directorships. The U.S. Public Health Service withdrew a major portion of ISMRRD's core funding. After the funding cut, staff was reduced to forty, and more programs were eliminated, transferred elsewhere, or cut to a part-time basis. Nevertheless, U-M's central administration demonstrated some support for the center, assigning it space on campus and supplying start-up funds for a new director.[61]

But the salvaging effort proved to be too little, too late. A 1982 committee reviewing the unit not only judged ISMRRD too narrow in terms of disciplines represented but criticized the lack of a critical core of researchers with high professional standing in the areas of mental retardation and developmental disabilities.

> It may be that the original, very broad interdisciplinary training approach is questionable today.... Excellent training cannot take place without ongoing, related, quality research programs. In this regard the Institute has never realized its own or the University's potential.... The service component must exist to provide a basis for training and research, but it may have become the raison d'être at ISMRRD.[62]

Concluding that ISMRRD was not taking those risks necessary to realize its intellectual potential and that service alone did not warrant its continuance, the Regents acceded to a faculty recommendation that the Institute be closed.

The importance of varying local organizational contexts

Three multidisciplinary institutes, financially independent of departments, started on the same campus at roughly the same time. Their charters stipulated a diverse agenda of training, services, and research meant to foster an intellectually vibrant, integrative set of activities that went beyond the bounds of disciplinary training and individual research projects. After two

60 Robert E. Moyers, letter to Dr. Carolyne K. Davis, June 1, 1979, p. 2, ISMRRD Files, Box 4, MHC; *Annual Report*, Institute for Study of Mental Retardation and Related Disabilities, 1978–9, p. 69, ISMRRD Files, Box 2, MHC.

61 *Annual Report*, Institute for Study of Mental Retardation and Related Disabilities, 1980–1, ISMRRD Files, Box 2, MHC. Herbert J. Grossman, M.D., was recruited from UCLA to be director and appointed professor of pediatrics, neurology, and psychiatry.

62 Charlotte Mistretta et al., Report of the Budget Priorities Committee Sub-Committee to Review ISMRRD, June 8, 1982, ISMRRD Files, Box 4, MHC; Informational Materials, March 4, 1982, Institutional Review Committee, ISMRRD Files, Box 4, MHC.

decades, each had deviated significantly from its original charter. The IoG was transformed from an institute emphasizing teaching and service in social gerontology to one pursuing mainly basic biomedical and social scientific research. The psychological wing of CHGD approximates in miniature what its founders envisioned. The ISMRRD closed as "a disintegrating shadow of an institute that existed before."[63] Several factors can account for these different trajectories.

Intramural

Like other research facilities, CHGD, IoG, and ISMRRD extolled the advantages of multidisciplinarity in delineating and executing their broad mission. Consonant with prevailing wisdom, the centers compartmentalized their agendas, organizing their work according to models that suited specialists' own purposes.[64] They affirmed that "scientific criteria, rather than problem or policy relevance, should guide the setting of priorities," but they rarely showed that they could function as producers of scientific knowledge independently of departments. Nor could they readily demonstrate how the fruits of multidisciplinary research fed back into the curriculum.[65]

Paradoxically, institutes in research universities have difficulty articulating a distinctive mission for themselves whenever their leaders are either too eager or too reluctant to impose their vision on their colleagues. "A director has a very limited power to get his colleagues to do good research, but he can easily stop them from doing so."[66] Michigan's center directors generally have the right to act with more autonomy than department chairs; to succeed, academic entrepreneurs try to effect a mission orientation by reaffirming collective goals and facilitating colleagues' endeavors. The founders – Tibbitts, Donahue, Moyers, and Cruikshank – were successful pros-

63 "ISMRRD Slated to Shut Down," *Michigan Daily*, September 23, 1982, p. 5. For a broader survey, see Stanley O. Ikenberry, *A Profile of Proliferating Institutes*, report no. 6 (University Park, TX: Center for the Study of Higher Education, November 1970).

64 Stephen Toulmin, "The Complexity of Scientific Choice," *Minerva*, vol. 2 (1964), 342–57; Alvin M. Weinberg, *Reflections on Big Science* (Cambridge, MA: M.I.T. Press, 1967); Joseph Ben-David, "How to Organize Research in the Social Sciences," *Daedalus*, vol. 102 (1967), 39–51.

65 "Study Project on Social Research and Development," *The Federal Investment in the Knowledge of Social Problems* (Washington, DC: National Academy of Sciences, 1978), p. 5. Aaron Wildavsky, "The Once and Future School of Public Policy," *The Public Interest*, vol. 79 (1985), 25–41; Harry R. Moody, "Toward a Critical Gerontology," in *Emergent Theories of Aging* ed. James E. Birren and Vern L. Bengston, (New York: Springer, 1988).

66 Keith Mellanby, "The Disorganization of Scientific Research," *Minerva*, vol. 12 (1924): 82; see also C. Rand, *Cambridge, U.S.A.* (New York: Oxford University Press, 1964); Harold Orlans, *The Nonprofit Research Institute* (New York: McGraw-Hill, 1972).

elytizers. Their successors generally were strong advocates for their programs who had mixed results in gaining support from fellow faculty and administration. The divergent results go beyond differences in personality and style. Consider their manner of (1) recruiting professorial and professional allies, (2) building bridges to other U-M structures, and (3) ensuring an efficacious adaptation to change.

In retrospect, it appears that Cruikshank relied too heavily on the intellectual resources he brought to Michigan. He did not make links with the Medical School, as did his counterparts at North Carolina, UCLA, and elsewhere. He failed to recruit researchers respected for their status and energy who would make ISMRRD their primary intellectual base. Instead, concentrating on various service projects, few among his faculty managed to gain tenure at U-M. By the time Cruikshank's replacement was chosen, ISMRRD's future was in jeopardy, and its main funding source cut. A new half-time leader simply could not reverse the tide.

CHGD never changed its modus operandi much – and that may have been too bad. The original Fellows provided some breadth across the behavioral and biological sciences. Yet no "labs" developed. With the possible exception of the psychologists, CHGD has never created a "Michigan" approach to its subject area as distinctive as the orientation of developmental institutes at Yale or Minnesota. Intellectually and administratively, it operates like a medium-size department in an elite, liberal arts college. And it has proven impossible to transform a center when powerful, tenured members have veto powers. Their negative action can only be overturned by a central administration willing to micro-manage. This rarely occurs at U-M.

The Institute of Gerontology might have suffered a similar fate had it remained as isolated as ISMRRD or as risk-averse as CHGD. Influential scientists at U-M and elsewhere still consider much research on aging a dubious enterprise. The Institute's current physical marginality may symbolize a certain intellectual isolation. It is neither on central campus nor in the medical center; the third largest concentration of IoG research scientists are housed at the VA Medical Center. Yet the Institute's reputation on campus is as good as its national standing. The Institute's productivity and priorities for the present are in harmony with prevailing university values and changing federal funding trends. Nor has Adelman demanded that his colleagues share all of his vision for the future. In keeping with "normal" U-M procedures, but without trying to operate as a department chair, he has provided a set of incentives, resources, and flexibility that allows a healthy creative tension among scientists who go about their business in distinctive ways but who do not hesitate to collaborate when mutually advantageous.[67]

67 Peter H. Rossi, "Researchers, Scholars, and Policymakers," *Daedalus*, vol. 93 (1964):

University

Key academic officials might have chosen to monitor U-M's centers and institutes more closely. After all, they had a stake – in terms of funds and space – in the success of these ventures all along. Yet most of the time the central administration maintained a laissez-faire posture. "Because of our long tradition of decentralization," Robben Fleming declared in his 1978-9 presidential report, "we think programs are best run, and problems are best solved by those who are closest to the action."[68] Such a decentralized mode of governance has proved effective in large research universities because it promotes the structural flexibility conducive to institutional innovation and scientific advances. Michigan's center directors thus received little management assistance from the central administration, but they were expected to learn from one another. Savvy managers recognized that "the fundamental determinant of long-run viability is a structure of supportive relationships with disciplinary units."[69] Michigan's centers by the 1970s could hardly afford to operate for long in isolation from campus concerns. At the same time they had to prove their uniqueness if they were to remain independent.

Indeed, Fleming upheld U-M's collegial principle of broad faculty input in debates over priorities. According to the review instituted in a 1977 U-M document on the Discontinuance of Academic Programs, "the criteria for determining whether a program should be eliminated place emphasis on the quality of the program involved. In making an assessment of a program, it is recommended that the quality of faculty, the value and particular character of the program, and the performance of its students should be taken into account."[70] Hence another paradox: Michigan's institutes had to become enterprises with a national base of support, but they knew that they were primarily held accountable to peer review by their U-M colleagues. "Under any circumstances, constant reassessment is necessary if we are to enjoy the vitality produced by gradual movement from areas that may have served us well in the past but no longer satisfy our aspirations for excellence."[71]

In the 1980s, as university officials everywhere devised plans for "selective preservation and change," President Shapiro took steps to make ex-

---

1,142–61. Peter Railton, "Interdisciplinarity, Multidisciplinarity, Nondisciplinarity," paper, 1993.

68 The President's Report for 1978–9. U-M, p. 3. Compare with Donna C. Shalala, "Mandate for a New Century," Henry Lecture, University of Illinois, October 21, 1989, p. 14.

69 John Patrick Crecine, "University Centers for the Study of Public Policy: Organizational Viability," *Policy Sciences*, vol. 2 (1971): 7–32; Peter M. Blau, *The Organization of Academic Work* (New York: Wiley, 1973).

70 The President's Report for 1976–7, U-M, p. 11.

71 Ibid., 1980–1, p. 1.

plicit the cost of independence across the University: "Paradoxically, independence is riskier for a center than for an individual investigator."[72] If they should not be formally connected to the departmental structure, how were institutes to "reinforce" faculty loyalty to U-M as a "coherent, interrelated academic community?" By design and by intent, according to Shapiro, centers are impermanent. Because institutes begin to outlive their usefulness almost immediately after being established, their continued existence is permitted only to the extent that they complement the broader mission of the university. This does not mean that survival tactics are enough.

Centers provide stability to the tradition and order existing in the local university community by taking genuine risks that appeal on intellectual grounds to outside funding agencies. When institutes have a good idea, someone somewhere should be willing to fund it. If outsiders invest, and inside evaluators concur that the problems being pursued have merit, then a center can prolong its life expectancy beyond the duration that might have been projected at the outset. This explains why (within limits) extramural resources also have shaped opportunities and choices for multidisciplinary centers.

National funding

Washington only emerged as a prime supporter of university-based research after World War II. Funds were not uniformly distributed. Research centers by 1967 were capturing 36 percent of all federal dollars being granted to universities.[73] Not surprisingly, given U-M's reputation, CHGD, IoG, and ISMRRD were well poised at their inception to capitalize on the new federal largesse. They were expected to be successful in competing for grants in human development financed by Washington. "Engaging the best of our social science resources to meet contemporary social problems requires the establishment of a new kind of institute with the clearly defined purpose of conducting applied social science research on problems of public significance," concluded the Brim Commission to the National Science Foundation, adding that the unit should be "financially and administratively independent of the departmental structure."[74]

72 J. Froomkin, "The Research Universities." *Proceedings of the Academy of Political Science*, vol. 35 (1983): 34–47; Shapiro *Tradition and Change*, pp. 45–6.

73 Harold Orlans, *The Effects of Federal Programs on Higher Education* (Washington, DC: Brookings Institution, 1962); idem, " 'R & D' Allocations in the United States," *Science Studies*, vol. 3 (1973), 119–59.

74 National Science Board, "Knowledge into Action," Report of the Special Commission on the Social Sciences (Washington, DC: NSF, 1969); Behavioral and Social Sciences Survey Committee, *The Behavioral and Social Sciences: Outlook and Needs* (pp. ix–x, 92), published under the auspices of the National Academy of Sciences and Social Science Research

Yet, except in the early 1970s, winning grants was rarely easy. Peer review could be capricious. Keeping federal funding sources decentralized and spreading dollars across congressional districts made good politics as well as sound policy. Funding for programmatic research, projects specifically targeted by sponsors, became more available.[75] Changes in funding affected academic units. As more groups applied for fewer dollars (in real terms), funding support at the three U-M centers fluctuated. According to data reported by U-M's Division of Research Development and Administration, CHGD garnered $476,000 in the 1972–3 academic year, compared to IoG's $536,000, and ISMRRD's $1.5 million. Four years later, the figures stood at $751,000, $1.2 million, and $1.8 million, respectively. By the 1980–1 academic year, the pattern had reversed. The CHGD captured $2.6 million, IoG $884,000 and ISMRRD, having lost federal support, $438,000. By 1991, ISSMRD was gone; IoG has enjoyed a dramatic growth in external funding; CHGD has been in a steady state. None pursued industrial partnerships.[76]

Even this brief overview helps to illuminate why three seemingly similar institutes should have had such divergent experiences during the first twenty-five years of their existence. More than departments, centers such as CHGD, IoG, and ISMRRD depend on the entrepreneurial, risk-accepting instincts of their leaders and senior researchers. Securing external funds is critical, but it is not enough. The ways directors exercise leadership must accommodate changes in university priorities and administrators' management styles. Because the survival of an institute depends on maintaining standards that would be at least minimally acceptable to "tough" internal reviewers, the importance of having good ideas, not just fundable ones, cannot be overstated. But it is possible to remain aloof from U-M politics and bureaucratic maneuvering and still gain the respect of its faculty and administration. This seems to be a central lesson of the history of the Institute for Social Research, arguably one of U-M's crown jewels.

The Institute for Social Research

The Institute for Social Research (ISR) is known, apart from its research achievements, as the one U-M center that controls its own research over-

Council (Englewood Cliffs, NJ: Prentice-Hall, 1969); M. Useem, "Government Patronage of Science and Art in America, *American Behavioral Scientist*, vol. 19 (1976), 785–804.

75 Donald K. Price, *Government and Science* (New York: New York University Press, 1954); Dael L. Wolfle, *The Home of Science* (New York: McGraw-Hill, 1972); Thomas G. Whiston and Roger L. Geiger, eds., *Research and Higher Education* (Buckingham: Open University Press, 1992), pp. 3–7, 163; Richard Corrigan, "Universities Unplugging into Pork," *National Journal*, February 2, 1986, pp. 338–9; Arthur Levine, ed., *Higher Learning in America* (Baltimore: Johns Hopkins University Press, 1993).

76 Some dispute these "official" figures. Adelman, for instance, invariably declares higher amounts of extramural funding than reported by the University. This is because projects cosponsored by IoG and university departments are usually credited only to the latter unit.

head and buildings. These attributes are intimately related. The ISR set itself apart from U-M's departmental structure for the express purpose of optimal risk management. Its founders considered the collective risk associated with financial independence to be reasonable in their hopes for success as a research enterprise.

The organization that was to become ISR originated in the relocation of Rensis Likert's group from the U.S. Department of Agriculture to Ann Arbor in 1946. The move was owed mainly to the impossibility of flourishing under congressional supervision once the war ended. The University of Michigan seemed rich in resources, despite the central administration's lack of support. Indeed, the regents approved the establishment of a Survey Research Center (SRC) only on condition that the unit be entirely self-supporting.[77] Taking no risks itself, the University threw *all* the risks upon Likert and his fellow entrepreneurs. Such a stance was consonant with the Center's declared mission and limited expense: SRC had to maintain a staff for conducting sample surveys; this was hardly the sort of work likely to be viewed favorably in tenure decisions in the 1940s. The ISR's peers, the Bureau of Social Research, the University of Chicago's National Opinion Research Center (NORC), and the remains of the wartime network of technical contracts, also operated outside the usual university ambit. Since the Federal Government was not yet committed to underwriting basic and applied research in the social sciences, however, SRC lived "from hand to mouth," with very little funding stability; it was often forced to tap its overhead fund to pay senior salaries.

In retrospect, the timing of this venture was fortunate; retaining financial independence became the unit's "key advantage." Very quickly, SRC demonstrated its capacity to fulfill its original objective: "To provide a well-trained staff to conduct sample surveys on problems which are scientifically important or which are of major significance to society."[78] Once success and a stable flow of funding became clear, Likert attempted to integrate the ISR into the academic life of the University "intellectually and politically as well as financially." Within five years, Michigan's General Fund paid 4 percent of the Institute budget; shortly thereafter, U-M partly covered the directors' salaries, and the staff eventually came to be offered some of the perquisites of academic prestige eschewed at the outset. Likert and his codirector Angus Campbell functioned as "administrator-scholars," providing intellectual and political leadership, not research guidance per se. Likert was involved in "promoting the institutional and interdisciplinary mission, in raising money for its research, and in acting often as its am-

77 Charles F. Cannell and Robert L. Kahn, "Some Factors in the Origins and Development of the Institute for Social Research, The University of Michigan," *American Psychologist*, vol. 39 (1984), 1,256–6; Jean Converse, *Survey Research in the United States, 1890–1960* (Berkeley and Los Angeles: University of California Press, 1987).

78 Institute for Social Research. *A Quarter Century of Social Research*, 1971.

bassador of external affairs." Campbell was the "realist," "administrator of internal affairs," and strategist of University politics.[79]

One consequence of ISR's self-conscious separation from U-M's dominant culture was the induction of loyalty to the Institute rather than any other units of the University. This arrangement encouraged collaborative more than individual projects, which engendered a *collective* security beyond the personal security of tenure afforded by the alternative structure of the academic department. Note how differently ISR's risk-related problems were handled from the other institutes and centers at Michigan. First, from the start, ISR staked its future on its value as a national resource rather than tying itself to the research mission of this University in any way. Second, ISR negotiated with the University as an equal partner, not beholden to the departments for its hiring decisions, its management style, or its selection of activities to emphasize. Third, in releasing the University of all responsibility, ISR assumed all the risks of the externally directed research thrust in exchange for complete control of the corresponding rewards. The gamble paid off for both ISR and U-M, but the University never allowed any of its other fifty-one centers to keep all of its indirect costs in return for fiscal self-responsibility.

Several conclusions emerge from this analysis of research institutes at Michigan, which may be relevant to the development of centers of aging elsewhere. First, in their efforts to survive, centers usually find it more difficult than departments to delimit their missions. Disciplinary crises tend to enliven departments without disrupting structural arrangements. An institute, in contrast, will find itself vulnerable if funding diminishes or if it stagnates intellectually regardless of how well it is satisfying its original mission. To the extent that centers like ISR prosper and are able to gain some discretionary use over the "soft money" on which they depend, procedures for establishing priorities and allocating resources "are best described by what is customary or typical rather than what is legally mandated."[80]

Second, as avowedly more distant from the center of campus than many other academic units, centers nonetheless are strategically placed to respond to changing institutional priorities on campus or at funding sources. Alternative organizational models are being considered that might draw the units and other U-M scholars into effective working relationships via product-oriented research. In a climate very different from the Great Society era in which they initially were funded, researchers in both IoG and CHGD still regularly consult with state and federal officials on policy matters. Researchers' expertise has not diminished merely because the political cli-

79 Converse, Survey Research, p. 350.
80 Institute for Social Research, *Blue-Book for the Board of Visitors*, 1986. (Courtesy of Prof. F. Thomas Juster)

mate has changed. Ultimately, however, the esteem (and the continuance that presumably goes with it) accorded to any freestanding unit depends on the value, including the "surprise value," of the research done by its individual investigators as evaluated by colleagues within the university and by outside peers.

Third, the comparative advantages that centers enjoy by claiming to be multidisciplinary diminish as they become more risk-averse and as researchers in other departments cross disciplinary boundaries. Institutes will continue to rely on internal resources, talent, flexibility, and imagination to inspire individual achievement and motivate collective ventures. Researchers tend to do what they were trained to do and want to do. But units like IoG should follow the example of ISR. They must be perceived as places where *collective* risk taking, especially by researchers trained in different fields, is explicitly encouraged. Hence, IoG must increasingly pursue *inter*disciplinary goals, that is, sponsor research projects that build on, but ultimately transcend, disciplinary fiefdoms so as to encapsulate a larger intellectual perspective than any single scholar could manage.

To stay viable in a major research university, institutes must be places where experts and trainees engage together in activities that build on a common set of tasks and techniques in the pursuit of intellectual risks. Many centers do not survive long enough to nurture such partnerships. Other models for multidisciplinary networking besides ISR exist. The MacArthur Research Program in Mental Health and Human Development is a "center without walls," which provides "instances of direct collaboration across disciplinary lines, by people whose previous work shows no interest in such crossing of boundaries."[81] Involvement is by invitation; projects are designed by extensive consulting, conceptual translating, and concurrent splicing and integrating of themes. No one expects the MacArthur venture to last indefinitely, but its immediate payoffs are evident.

A strong emphasis on research in multidisciplinary centers leads, in turn, to distinctive teaching and service functions. Research scientists with faculty appointments in various colleges and schools should teach undergraduate and graduate courses as part of departmental responsibilities. Experiences drawn from their research may well enliven their involvement in developing discipline-specific curricula.[82] Pedagogical responsibilities in institutes, however, should be limited to pre- and postdoctoral training for a number of select students. Fulfilling a service function should be a vital component of a center's mission, but it cannot be disconnected from the units' intellectual base. Institutes probably should do only the applied research that aids the-

81 Robert L. Kahn, "The MacArthur Program in Mental Health and Human Development: An Experiment in Scientific Organization," paper, December 1992.
82 Ernest L. Boyer, *Scholarship Reconsidered* (Princeton, NJ: Carnegie Foundation for the Advancement of Teaching, 1991).

ory building, advances methodology, or explicitly serves an external constituency. Centers and institutes also have a responsibility to disseminate information that helps policymakers understand how the latest research affects the scope of public programs. That said, it must be quickly added that very few academics can really serve as effective policymakers. They usually lack the zest for grass roots politics and the talent for translating esoteric ideas into everyday language.

Ironically, though all multidisciplinary institutes are inclined to build on past strengths, their position in academic settings hinges on their success as risk takers. They should build research partnerships that, for however long they endure, are capable of dealing with a pressing intellectual problem in a manner that fully embraces the possibility of complete failure. Only then have they a chance to succeed. Even so, their future may be in jeopardy. In a worst-case scenario, IoG may find some of its best biomedical researchers working more closely with investigators with U-M's geriatrics center, which moves shortly into new research and clinical facilities. The ISR, which already has a large number of researchers funded by NIA, may lure away some of IoG's social scientists under the leadership of David Featherman, who once directed the University of Wisconsin's Institute of Aging and Adult Life. So IoG looks strategically for opportunities in other places, such as the School of Engineering, as it reassesses its research agenda for the twenty-first century.[83]

83 John Ziman, *Knowing Everything About Nothing* (New York: Cambridge University Press, 1987), p. 5.

6

The federal government as sponsor, producer and consumer of research on aging

THE STATE HAS BECOME a major source of funding for scientific knowledge in every advanced industrial nation. "In the Anglo-Saxon countries," observes John Ziman, "it was customary for state support for basic research to be very limited, except in fields such as medicine and agriculture with direct connections to major sectors of governmental responsibility. This custom charged radically in and after the Second World War. Public funds soon became so vital to the advancement of science – especially the academic research carried out in universities and other higher education institutions – that they largely determined its direction and shape."[1]

We have already seen evidence of the increasing reliance upon federal support by gerontologists who tried to build institutions after 1939 to spur and sustain research on aging, especially in centers of higher education. Training grants from the U.S. Administration on Aging, (AoA) and various units of the National Institutes of Health (NIH) made it possible for faculty members and their students to create and disseminate new ideas about senescence and to develop fresh ways to deal with the problems and opportunities associated with late life. The Gerontological Society (GSA) moved from St. Louis to Washington, D.C., so that it could be closer to those who were deciding how to allocate research dollars and debating how much to invest in gerontology. No history of gerontology can stress enough the critical role played by the federal government in shaping the emergence of this scientific field of inquiry.

The U.S. government's commitment to research and development (R&D) is staggering. Spending on basic science, which the National Science Board at the time characterized as "the principal mode for developing the knowl-

---

1 John Ziman, *Prometheus Bound: Science in a Dynamic Steady State* (New York: Cambridge University Press, 1994), p. 93.

edge base necessary for future science and technological breakthroughs," totalled $9 billion in 1981. The amount almost exceeded the combined investments of the nation's Western partners; two thirds of this total came from federal agencies.[2] Long-term trends for supporting science in higher education are no less striking. In 1940, universities had roughly $31 million at their disposal for scientific research. In fiscal year 1979, the National Science Foundation alone allocated $775 million to university-based research; total government support exceeded $3 billion. According to a study by Roy Rosenzweig for the Association of American Universities, funding grew at an annual rate of 12 percent from 1953 to 1960, and at 14 percent from 1960 to 1968. There was a zero growth rate during the Nixon years, but then a 4 percent rise from 1974 to 1978.[3] Since then, despite fluctuations, the federal investment in university-based science has basically been steady state.

Gross statistics, of course, do not convey the whole story. Big Science relies on sophisticated equipment and large research teams. Research projects tend to be better funded than experiments by solitary scientists in "the honest search for truth." Federal policy-making and agenda-building in science, as in other endeavors, has become highly politicized. They are subject to pork barrel maneuvers as the dollars have increased.[4] To be sure, many investments have not yet paid off. There is still no cure for cancer, AIDS, or other diseases; and some ventures, such as Ronald Reagan's Star Wars Initiative, should not have been pursued over experts' objections. But perhaps the point to be underscored is that the state is more than a patron of science.

The U.S. government also is a producer and a consumer of empirical data and scientific research. Many of our Founding Fathers were intellectuals, leaders who appreciated the practical as well as the theoretical sway of ideas applied to every day life. Federal officials underwrote Meriwether Lewis and William Clark, risk takers who literally crossed frontiers, and then debated over the significance of their 1804–6 expedition for the future development of the republic. Their discussion relied on evaluation by the American Philosophical Society that Thomas Jefferson had requested.[5] Roughly a century later, during the Progressive period, "the Wisconsin idea" brought together university faculty and lawmakers to make policies for children and regulating agencies based on "hard" facts. Wisconsin ush-

2 The quotation came from David Dickson, *The New Politics of Science* (New York: Pantheum Books, 1984), p. 20.

3 Robert M. Rosenzweig with Barbara Turlington, *The Research Universities and Their Patrons* (Berkeley and Los Angeles: University of California Press, 1982), pp. 16–17.

4 For early assessments of these trends, see Daniel Greenberg, *The Politics of American Science* (New York: Penguin, 1969); and Donald K. Price, *The Scientific State* (Cambridge: Harvard University Press, 1968).

5 Joseph P. Martino, *Science Funding* (New Brunswick: Transaction Publishers, 1992), p. 45.

ered in the modern era of the government's use of applied research. According to Theodore Roosevelt, it "has become literally a laboratory for wise and experimental legislation aiming to secure the social and political betterment of the people as a whole."[6] Increasingly during the twentieth century, foundations and think tanks advanced scientific management in the political arena. Herbert Hoover and Franklin Delano Roosevelt relied on experts. James B. Conant, the president of Harvard, was asked in 1940 to mobilize the American scientific community for the impending war. World War II and past war affluence heightened Washington's reliance on science. When University of California chancellor Glenn Seaborg and his colleagues produced their report, "Scientific Progress, the Universities and the Federal Government" (1960), lawmakers were committed "simply in terms of economic self-interest . . . to increase our investment in science just as fast as we can, to a limit not yet in sight."[7]

No wonder, then, U.S. policymakers were predisposed to consider ideas set forth by experts on aging. Gerontology was emerging as a field of scientific inquiry at the very time in which America was awestruck by the power of science to ensure progress. Hence this chapter serves to refocus previous accounts of the federal impact. Specialists typically stress the relationship between old-age problems, mass politics, and public policy. Their emphasis is understandable. The elderly, especially since the 1960s, have become a politically powerful segment of the population. They are "entitled" to a dazzling array of benefits; organizations constituting the "gray lobby" know how to advocate on their behalf. There are now more than 1,000 aging-based associations in the country.[8] Yet most narratives miss the role that gerontology research has played in developing a national policy on aging. Nor, in my opinion, do most histories of aging pay sufficient attention to the state as a creator of gerontologic knowledge. Washington-based lawmakers and bureaucrats have been both producers and consumers. They use ideas about aging and the aged as warning signals, as guides in improving current programs, as educational resources, and as a way to

---

6 Theodore Roosevelt, "Introduction," in Charles McCarthy, *The Wisconsin Idea* (New York: Macmillan Company, 1912), p. vii; see also James A. Smith, *The Idea Brokers* (New York: Free Press, 1991); Ellen Condliffe Lagemann, *The Politics of Knowledge* (Middletown, CT: Wesleyan University Press, 1990); Edward T. Silva and Sheila A. Slaughter, *Serving Power* (Westport, CT: Greenwood Press, 1984). It must be noted, however, that Woodrow Wilson, the only university president to serve as president, feared "a government of experts." See John Wells Davidson, *A Crossroads of Freedom* (New Haven, CT: Yale University Press, 1956), p. 83.

7 Quoted in Roger L. Geiger, *Research and Relevant Knowledge* (New York: Oxford University Press, 1993), p. 169.

8 Christine L. Day, *What Older Americans Think* (Princeton, NJ: Princeton University Press, 1990), p. 3. For a valuable early study, see Frank A. Pinner, Paul Jacobs, and Philip Selznick, *Old Age and Political Behavior* (Berkeley and Los Angeles: University of California Press, 1959).

mobilize support for proposals.[9] Government officials know that ideas can serve, when necessary, to obfuscate or oversimplify issues at stake. Indeed, policy-making in aging has become more sophisticated and complicated as Washington came to rely on gerontologic knowledge in their deliberations. Whether the process has become more enlightened is open to question.

Focusing on the elderly

The federal and various state governments were investigating the demographic, economic, and social characteristics of the nation's elderly decades before any federal agency was specifically assigned a gerontologic mission. The 1830 decennial U.S. census reported the number of whites over the age of sixty state by state. J. D. B. DeBow analyzed gender and racial differences within the aged population and between younger and older age groups based on information collected in the seventh (1850) census.[10] Thereafter, each successive census reported ever more elaborate information on senior citizens, emphasizing their geographic distribution and place of birth. New tables and, later, separate volumes were compiled by federal census officials that gave age breakdowns in terms of older people's gainful employment, housing, propensity to crime, incidence of pauperism, and institutionalization.

The U.S. Census Bureau's interest in older people's conditions notwithstanding, the best analyses of the aged prior to the Great Depression were written by scholarly writers, philanthropies, and by state and local agencies. During the last quarter of the nineteenth century, the plight of this nation's elderly paupers began to warrant investigation. Lee Welling Squier's *Old Age Dependency in the United States* (1912) emulated Charles Booth's pathbreaking *Pauperism and the Endowment of Old Age* (1892) and *The Aged Poor in England and Wales* (1894). Alice Willard Solenberger's *One Thousand Homeless Men* and Alexander Johnson's *The Almshouse*, both published by the Charities Publication Committee in 1911, were meticulous examinations of case records.[11] These works, in turn, utilized survey meth-

9 Stephen Brooks and Alain-G. Gagnon, *Social Scientists, Policy, and the State* (New York: Praeger, 1990), pp. 106–7; David R. Cameron, "Toward a Theory of Political Mobilization," *Journal of Politics*, vol. 36 (1974): 138–71.

10 J. B. D. DeBow, *Statistical View of the United States . . . Being a Compendium of the Seventh Census* (Washington, DC: A. O. P. Nicholson, 1854). See also Margo J. Anderson, *The American Census* (New Haven, CT: Yale University Press, 1988).

11 W. Andrew Achenbaum, *Old Age in a New Land* (Baltimore: Johns Hopkins University Press, 1978), ch. 4; Carole Haber, *Beyond Sixty-Five* (New York: Cambridge University Press, 1983), ch. 2. The Charities Publication Committee also published articles by Homer Folks, who was the first to convert a public asylum into an old-age home to reflect its occupancy. See Homer Folks, "Disease and Dependence," *Charities*, vol. 11 (October 3, 1903): 298. For more on the transatlantic connection, see *The Social Survey in Historical Perspective, 1880-1940*, ed. Martin Bulmer, Kevin Bales, and Kathryn Kish Sklar (New

ods developed by record keepers in state capitals. Carroll Wright, director of the Massachusetts Bureau of Labor Statistics, in the late 1870s issued reports that detailed changes in household composition, employment status, and income over the life course. Bay State officials attracted articles in newspapers and journals with their 1910 *Report of the Commission on Old Age Pensions, Annuities and Insurance*.[12] Public and private agencies produced monographs after World War I on older workers and on the causes of old-age indigence. In the first decades of the twentieth century, in contrast, officials in Washington commissioned major works on early, not late, life. Lawrence K. Frank wrote a chapter on "children and youth" for Herbert Hoover's *Recent Social Trends in the United States* (1933); the two-volume document treated old-age pensions in a cursory manner and allotted only a page to state and familial protection of the elderly.[13]

The federal government's first attempt to develop its own analyses of older people's needs and problems was prompted by its efforts to create a social security system. The five Cabinet-level officers, particularly Frances Perkins and Harry Hopkins, who constituted the Committee on Economic Security (CES), were used to applying social science research in creating policy initiatives. These New Dealers appointed a staff that had experience in taking scholarly ideas and turning them into workable programs. Arthur Altmeyer, formerly Wisconsin's chief statistician, headed a twenty-one-member technical board made up of civic, labor, corporate, and academic leaders most of whom had written on aspects of social insurance. Altmeyer's staff was assisted by actuarial consultants and seven different advisory committees consisting of professionals and experts. Edwin Witte, who chaired the University of Wisconsin's Department of Economics, was named executive director of a research staff of eighty-one men and women on leave from universities, business, federal and state agencies, Brookings, and private practice. Within six months, Witte and his staff had issued nine major reports, scores of memoranda and position papers, as well as the fifty-page document that became the basis for the landmark 1935 Social Security Act.[14]

York: Cambridge University Press, 1991). These works would inspire a rising generation of social critics and old-age advocates, including Abraham Epstein and Isaac M. Rubinow.

12 I relied on Wright's data in *Old Age*, as did Brian Gratton in reconstructing *Urban Elders* (Philadelphia: Temple University Press, 1985). The 1910 Massachusetts report was the model for the 1919 *Report of the Pennsylvania Commission on Old Age Pensions*. The first U.S. studies of the institutionalized poor and/or mentally ill that focused on old age were an 1824 report by John N. Yates, reprinted in New York State Board of Charities, *Annual Report for 1900* (Albany: J. B. Lyon, 1901); and Thomas R. Hazard, *Commissioner on Condition of the Poor and Insane* (Providence, RI: John Knowles, 1851).

13 President's Research Committee on Social Trends, *Recent Social Trends in the United States* (New York: McGraw-Hill, 1933).

14 W. Andrew Achenbaum, "The Place of Researchers in Social Security Policy Making," *Journal of Aging Studies*, vol. 2 (Winter 1988): 301–10. Participants are listed in Social

The background research undertaken in preparation to drafting social security legislation was no mere academic exercise. Nor was it intended to be a political cover. "The [CES] staff is convinced," wrote Princeton economist J. Douglas Brown in 1934, "that it should first seek out the most constructive proposals for old age security adapted to American economic and social conditions and then, and only then, test as far as possible whether such proposals can be made effective within our legal system. Since law is a living science, it is reasonable to assume that if a sound program of old age security can be projected, our system of constitutional law will evolve in time to support that program."[15] Brown was a pragmatist whose recommendations drew on his research into industrial relations and his understanding of human nature. His policy-making colleagues also valued research; they searched for ideas likely to be efficacious in developing major, multifaceted pieces of social welfare legislation. Consequently, they took steps to ensure that the government's reliance on experts would not end once Social Security were enacted. The original legislation provided a mechanism for scholarly feedback: Title VII authorized a Social Security Board, charged with "the duty of studying and making recommendations as to the most effective methods of providing economic security through social insurance."[16] *Social Security Bulletin*, a monthly publication begun in 1937, became an invaluable source of information, featuring philosophical essays and technical data. In addition, the personnel employed by Social Security soon were called upon to expand the federal government's responsibilities toward senior citizens. When the Social Security Board was placed with other welfare agencies and the Public Health Service under the new Federal Security Agency (FSA) in 1939, it became possible to coordinate interagency initiatives on behalf of the aged and to defuse demands by "pension pressure groups."[17]

Security Board, *Social Security in America*, pub. no. 20 (Washington, DC: Government Printing Office, 1937), pp. 516–23.

15 Quoted in J. Douglas Brown, *The Genesis of Social Security in America* (Princeton University: Industrial Relations Section, 1969), p. 8. Through discussions with his colleague Barbara Nachtrieb Armstrong, a Berkeley law professor who had studied foreign pension systems, and debates with Edwin Witter and Thomas Eliot (a lawyer on leave from the Department of Labor), Brown refined the logic of what became Title I (a federal–state old-age assistance plan) and Title II (a program in which employers and employees contributed to a workers' retirement fund). Brown subsequently chaired the advisory council that recommended the pivotal 1939 Social Security amendments and continued to serve as an advisor through the 1970s. See W. Andrew Achenbaum, *Social Security* (New York: Cambridge University Press, 1986), pp. 20, 36–9, 70–3, 143.

16 Social Security Act, ch. 523, 49 Stat. 620, sect. 702.

17 Edward Berkowitz and Kim McQuaid, *Creating the Welfare State*, 2d ed. (New York: Praeger, 1988), pp. 139–41; "Threat of Pension Pressure Groups," *Tax Policy*, vol. 7 (1939): 1–7. The Townsend movement, which galvanized in the depths of the Great Depression, is often remembered as the first senior citizen lobby. Actually the origins of the "gray lobby" date back to the 1920s, with the activities of the American Association for

Initial gerontologic initiatives under FSA's aegis were modest. The Public Health Service created a unit in 1939 to study fundamental biological aspects of the mechanisms and pathogenesis of senescence. For years, as we have seen, it was a one man show. A 1942 survey acknowledged the production of "statistical compilations" by the Social Security Board, but went on to deplore the fact that work on "the social and economic problems of the aged was found to be almost nonexistent."[18] Major bureaucratic fights, occasioned by the executive reorganization, and then World War II, diverted the government's attention from senior citizens' plight. Nonetheless, the National Resources Planning Board (NRPB) in 1943 did anticipate America's need to conserve and utilize the resources of those who lived past the age of sixty-five: "We are surviving longer but have not learned *how* to live during old age in health, comfort, and cheerfulness. The tragic waste of these years recently added to life calls for research and bold experimentation in the better care of the aged."[19] The Board's observation resonated with ideas being discussed at Chicago and Michigan, among other universities at the time. The call to reconstruct old age by helping the elderly to adjust was to be sounded often immediately after the war.

In 1948, on the advice of the National Health Assembly, FSA administrator Oscar Ewing directed his deputy, John J. Thurston, to appoint a Working Committee on Aging made up of managers and senior professionals in agencies that dealt with the elderly. Jane M. Hoey chaired the Committee. A social worker by training, Hoey was chief of Social Security's Bureau of Public Assistance, a program that reached more than 2.5 million elderly recipients. "Aging persons themselves," the Committee declared early on, "as well as governmental and voluntary agencies must participate in programs affecting their welfare."[20] Once the Committee decided to

Labor Legislation, Abraham Epstein's American Association for Old Age Security, the Fraternal Order of Eagles, and lobbying by retired federal employees. See Achenbaum, *Old Age*, ch. 7, and Jack L. Walker, *Mobilizing Interest Groups in America* (Ann Arbor: University of Michigan Press, 1991), pp. 29ff.

18 Characterization by Edward J. Stieglitz in a letter to Dr. John T. King, May 21, 1940, in the Nathan W. Shock Papers, Stieglitz File, Box 2, Bentley Historical Collection (henceforth referred to as BHC). Stieglitz also prepared the *Report of a Survey of Active Studies in Gerontology* (United States Public Health Service: Unit on Gerontology, 1942), p. 49. See also Edward J. Stieglitz, *Annals of Internal Medicine*, vol. 14 (October 1940): 737–40.

19 National Resources Planning Board, *Human Conservation* (Washington, DC: Government Printing Office, March 1943), pp. 94–5. Lawrence K. Frank wrote the document. He also had mentioned the elderly in his contribution to an earlier NRPB volume, *Problems of a Changing Population* (1938).

20 "Are the Aging a Social Problem?" a two-page statement prepared by the Working Committee on Aging, January 12, 1949, in Tibbitts Papers, Box 4, BHC. I was alerted to the importance of Jane Hoey's role by Bruce Craig, an aging program specialist in the U.S. Administration on Aging. Mr. Craig kindly let me read his unpublished paper, "The Frontiers of Public Policy-Federal Executive Branch Leadership: The Working Committee on

stage a "conference on the problems of the aged population," Thurston began corresponding with Clark Tibbitts, then at the University of Michigan, about serving as a consultant. The FSA officials were impressed by Tibbitts's ability to communicate ideas about aging to experts and diverse lay audiences. Tibbitts differed from many who came to Washington from academic backgrounds. First, he appreciated the worth of different types of research, ranging from insights into "everyday operatives" to scientific knowledge. Second, Tibbitts truly believed that federal agencies, such as the Works Progress Administration (WPA), "could bring about an overwhelming improvement in certain phases of our research activity."[21] Here was a man, Thurston rightly perceived, who had the disposition and energy necessary to promote social gerontology research in Washington.

Tibbitts brought to FSA in 1949 many ideas and strategies he had developed during his years in Ann Arbor. The issues that he thought truly mattered – population trends, employment patterns, family relations and living arrangements, aging and health, medical services, vocational rehabilitation, education and counseling, and training personnel – had been at the center of his research program at the Institute for Human Adjustment (IHA). Now Tibbitts had an opportunity to set part of the nation's gerontologic agenda:

> The Federal Government should establish a clearing house for studies of and programs for the aging, with broad authority for research and promotion in this field. . . . National planning by public and private agencies and individuals should be comprehensive in scope and participation. The Federal Security Agency should assume major responsibility in this movement to coordinate present resources and activities and to develop and stimulate the development of new and expanded facilities. The basic approach toward the problem of the aging must be a positive one – maintaining the health, social and economic security and general welfare of the aged segment of the population; attitudes should be changed to accept a positive and dynamic role for aging people in society; Nationwide research, and educational and promotional activity are necessary to activate and stimulate interest in and programs in relation to aging.[22]

Aging." See also, John L. Thurston, "First National Conference on Aging," *Industrial and Labor Relations Review*, vol. 4 (January 1951): 164.

21 On the recruitment, see two notes from John Thurston to Clark Tibbitts, April 16 and September 14, 1948, in Wilma Donahue Papers, Box 19, BHC. On Tibbitts's eclectic view on research, see his notes from a seminar presentation at the Institute of Human Adjustment's Speech Clinic, Ann Arbor, Michigan, February 13, 1947. See also his unpublished paper, "The WPA as an Aid to Social Science Research," August 17, 1940, both in Donahue Papers, Box 19, BHC.

22 "Programs for the Aging," November 23, 1949, pp. 6 and 19, in Donahue Papers, Box 19, BHC. Compare this list with the topics in a memo, "Meeting the Needs of Older People" that Tibbitts, still director of the Institute of Human Adjustment, wrote Thurston on June 21, 1949. Tibbitts wrote "to call attention to the urgency of meeting the psycho-

Tibbitts wanted to link research to action in all stages of program development. Like the Social Security Board, FSA "might furnish data to outside groups in order to stimulate them to provide information and to support action."[23] Tibbitts entertained other ideas for innovative policy-making as plans for the Conference unfolded.

The First National Conference on Aging brought 816 delegates to Washington in August 1950 to discuss eleven broad subject areas. Roughly half of the workshops dealt with the issue of older people's productivity in the postwar U.S. economy. The three-day event was designed as a "forum type of exploratory conference . . . not one action was proposed or taken by the delegate body as a whole."[24] Although intended to be primarily an opportunity to exchange ideas, the Conference produced a set of recommendations. Delegates emphasized the need for education programs to counteract a widespread lack of public interest in aging issues and, more broadly, a "cultural lag" that "stranded" the elderly. They urged Congress to draw up a research agenda, to recruit young men and women with talent to the field, and to sustain long-term research. "More facts [are] needed regarding each of the many aspects of the over-all problem."[25] To this end, middle-range theories and empirical data were included in the final Conference report, *Man and His Years*. The fact-filled volume was frequently cited by scholars writing during the 1950s. It also provided a valuable resource for a growing number of nonacademic researchers in government interested in aging.

Gerontologic research leads to federal initiatives for older Americans

In January 1951, a Committee on Aging and Geriatrics headed by Tibbitts was established within FSA to "develop methods for integration of older persons" into society, "to continue the collection of information about the characteristics and potentialities of older people," and "to satisfy the increasing demands" for programs in public and private organizations.[26] Tibbitts and his staff sought to stimulate interest in aging by publishing a news bulletin, *Aging*, and compiling a *Fact Book on Aging*. He prepared exhibits

social-economic-health needs of older people, and specifically, to suggest the next role that should be assumed by the Federal government." Memo in Tibbitts Papers, Box 4, BHC.

23 "Abstract of Discussion: Federal Security Agency Conference on the Aging," April 22, 1949, p. 5, in Donahue Papers, Box 19, BHC.

24 Thurston, "First National Conference," p. 168.

25 Federal Security Agency, *Man and His Years* (Raleigh, NC: Health Publications Institute, Inc., 1951), p. 243. See also Clark Tibbitts, "Conservation of Our Aging Population," *North Carolina Medical Journal*, vol. 12 (October 1951): 481–5; Craig, "Frontiers of Public Policy," p. 14; Ron Johnston and Dave Robbins, "The Development of Specialties in Industrialized Science," *The Sociological Review*, vol. 25 (1977): 87–107.

26 Federal Security Agency press release, January 24, 1951, in Tibbitts Papers, Box 4, BHC.

on aging and wrote pieces for popular journals to make old-age issues more visible in the media. Tibbitts also delivered scores of speeches at professional meetings and public gatherings.[27] To expand gerontology's frontiers, he provided technical assistance to member of Congress, state commissions, nursing-home groups, and other agencies that dealt with the elderly. Tibbitts saw himself offering a blend of "practical leadership," common sense, and expertise: "The first essential for effective leadership in a field as broad and as interrelated as the field of human aging is for coordination and integration of activity among the agencies concerned."[28] Rather than work alone, Tibbitts recruited academics such as Wilma Donahue and Robert Havighurst to assist him in bridging theory and practice.

Tibbitts's efforts did not go unnoticed. In 1956, Wilbur Cohen affirmed that "the most important contribution the Committee can make is the publication, and widespread distribution, of documentary material." More dissemination might have been possible had the Committee on Aging and Geriatrics not felt hampered by "lack of sufficient technical expertness" and paucity of trained personnel.[29] The nation needed more experts on aging, Cohen among others believed, and the U.S. government had to take steps to remedy the situation. Accordingly, Tibbitts assisted a GSA subcommittee trying to meet some of the training needs in psychosocial gerontology and to research the elderly's mental health problems. He obtained funds for the project from the National Institute of Mental Health (NIMH) and gained cooperation from various universities.[30] In assessing "the future of research and training in social gerontology" in 1959, Tibbitts envisioned the need for more of such ventures: "This forecast of expanding research interest, along with the growing numbers of middle-aged and older people and the demands for social action, imply that there will be an increasing demand for training in the field."[31]

27 See, for instance, Clark Tibbitts, "How to Plan for Retirement Now," *Parade*, July 4, 1954, pp. 4–7. See also his speech, "Trends in Gerontology," delivered to the First Southern Regional Conference on Recreation for the Aging," February 22, 1952; idem, "Progress Report of the State and Committee on Aging and Geriatrics for 1951-1952," report, p. 33; and "Committee on Aging and Geriatrics, report," all in Tibbitts Papers, Box 4, BHC.

28 Clark Tibbitts, "A Proposal for Implementing the Conclusions of the Conference on Aging," paper, November 10, 1950, in Tibbitts Papers, Box 5, BHC. A month earlier, Tibbitts floated the idea of establishing a National Institute of Gerontology in the Public Health Service. See Clark Tibbitts, "A Gerontological Unit," paper, October 9, 1950, Tibbitts Papers, Box 4, BHC. Reference to *Man and His Years* as a "handbook" in idem, "Committee on Aging and Geriatrics," draft 1953 (?), in Tibbitts Papers, Box 4, BHC.

29 Cohen's remarks in Minutes of the Committee on Aging, January 11, 1956, p. 1; see also the comment on staff deficiency in 1951–2 report, both in Tibbitts Papers, Box 4, BHC.

30 Robert Kleemeier, "Report on a Conference Held in Palm Beach, Florida, July 25–31, 1956," reprinted in U.S. Senate, Committee on Labor and Public Welfare, *Studies of the Aged and Aging*, vol. 9 (Washington, DC: Government Printing Office, 1957), pp. 27–59.

31 Clark Tibbitts, "The Future of Research and Training in Social Gerontology," p. 11. This paper, presented at a GSA meeting, is in Tibbitts Papers, Box 5, BHC.

Other governmental agencies besides FSA promoted research on aging during the 1950s. As we have seen, scientists working under Nathan Shock's supervision in Baltimore were investigating basic biological mechanisms of aging, measuring the effect of age on physiological and psychological performance, and determining the extent to which disease altered capacity.[32] Governmental units at the state and local levels also generated facts on aging and tried to recruit talented people to the field. New York and Pennsylvania commissioned studies on the economics of aging and the prejudice encountered by older workers. Louis Kuplan in California chaired a Governor's Conference on the Problems of the Aging in 1951 that explored "a situation that calls for evaluation and for remedial action when practicable." Kuplan focused on the mobilization of senior citizens. Academic researchers, notably sociologists, in many parts of the country did research into the aged's health-care needs in their local communities.[33]

Much of this research activity took place in relative isolation. There was no national clearing house that might refer policymakers and social service providers in one area to projects that were being done in another region of the country. Nor was there a central agency that kept track of research being reported in scholarly journals. If gerontology were to have greater influence on the ways that professionals dealt with the elderly's needs, some commentators felt that those who produced and consumed ideas had to develop better lines of communication.

In keeping with President Eisenhower's belief that Washington should be a "helpful partner in many ways" in stimulating state, local, and private initiatives, units such as Social Security's Bureau of Public Assistance worked with the National Social Welfare Assembly in preparing background material to be used in revising standards for institutional care. Once such information was made available, it quickly became cited in changing regulations that affected a significant subset of the needy aged.[34] Perhaps the most significant application of ideas to practice emerged from the 1954 Governor's Conference for the Council of State Governments. Conference participants requested a survey of state programs for the aged so as to "provide a basis for intelligent planning of adequate care, treatment, and rehabilitation facilities to cope with the needs of the foreseeable future."[35] Under the direction of the University of Chicago's Ernest Burgess and Sid-

---

32 See, for instance, the program descriptions in the annual reports for 1952 and 1959 for the Gerontology Branch, in Shock Papers, Box 9, BHC; see *infra.*, Chapter 3.

33 *Proceedings of Governor's Conference on the Problems of Aging* (Sacramento, CA, 1951), p. 9. See also Dana Burr Bradley's dissertation on old-age politics in Pennsylvania, Carnegie Mellon University, Pittsburgh, 1994; and Gordon F. Streib and Harold Orbach, "Aging" in *The Uses of Sociology*, ed. Paul F. Lazarsfeld et al. (New York: Basic, 1967), pp. 632–4.

34 William Oriol, "Twenty-Fifth Anniversary of the United States Senate Special Committee on Aging . . . ," unpub. version, p. 4, in the author's files.

35 The Council of State Governments, *The States and Their Older Citizens* (Chicago: CSG, 1955), p.v.

ney Spector, a report was issued, *The States and Their Older Citizens,* which tried to summarize the problems at hand and offer a program for action. Burgess and Spector stressed the importance of ideas, noting that they were "still incomplete and relatively unorganized" due to a lack of qualified personnel. "Basic research on aging holds the brightest promise for the future happiness and welfare of older persons."[36] A year later, Spector had another opportunity to stress that research had to be a top priority, this time in a federal-state conference on "Mobilizing Resources for Older People." Efforts to promote better communication of ideas at the grass roots level and between state and federal agencies ably prepared him for an assignment in Washington. There, Spector would help to create a political network that relied on research as its medium.[37]

In January 1959, Senator Lister Hill (D-Ala.), who chaired the Committee on Labor and Public Welfare, announced the creation of a Subcommittee on the Problems of the Aging and Aged. Senator Pat McNamara (D-Mich.), who headed the subcommittee, wanted the body to "increase public awareness" by encouraging "all groups" to collaborate. The Subcommittee made explicit the link between gerontologic research and political action. It intended to "establish firm data as to the exact nature of problems of aged and aging" and to recommend "necessary federal programs." Three other Democrats (John F. Kennedy, Joseph S. Clark of Pennsylvania, and Jennings Randolph of West Virginia) and two Republicans (Everett McKinley Dirksen of Illinois and Barry Goldwater of Arizona) were appointed. Sidney Spector was invited to become staff director.[38] Representatives of the American Medical Association (AMA) and key figures in the Eisenhower administration were "cynical," figuring that the Subcommittee "would just write a report, but not accomplish much."[39] The new Subcommittee, despite the critics, quickly demonstrated that gathering research was a central part of its strategy for developing programs at the national level.

---

36 Ibid., pp. 91, 108. That the second paragraph and the ten areas of "A Bill of Objectives for Older People" in *The States and Their Older Citizens* (p. xi) served as the basis for the preamble for establishing the U.S. Senate Special Committee on Aging in 1961 and for the objectives of the 1965 Older Americans Act suggests how one body incorporated the ideas of another for its purposes.

37 See letter from Sidney Spector to John Sweeney, March 13, 1959, in the possession of William Oriol. I appreciate greatly the access to materials that Mr. Oriol gave me in writing this section of the chapter on the Senate Special Committee.

38 Sen. McNamara proposed the idea in a letter to Sen. Hill in a letter, December 16, 1958; a week later, Sen. Kennedy made a similar proposal, requesting that he be named chair. See also two pieces of correspondence between Sen. Hill and Sen. McNamara (January 27, 1959, and March 17, 1959). The four-part agenda appears in a letter from Sen. McNamara to Sen. Kennedy, March 30, 1959; all in William Oriol's files. The committee also gave the elderly a "privileged influence" in Congress. See Sandra Cameron, "The Politics of the Elderly," *Midwest Quarterly* (Winter 1974): 146.

39 Sidney Spector to Sen. Pat McNamara, December 6, 1960, Oriol files.

To study problems of the aging and aged, the Subcommittee brought to the Capitol "recognized authorities in the field" as well as federal officials and representatives of public and private agencies concerned with the elderly. Among those initially invited were Ernest Burgess, Wilbur Cohen, Wilma Donahue, and Louis Kuplan, who at the time was executive secretary of California Citizen's Committee on the Aging and president of the GSA.[40] In addition, the Subcommittee took testimony from senior citizens at hearings around the country; Senators Randolph and McNamara spoke about problems of the aged on the Westinghouse Broadcasting Company's "American Forum." Local newspapers favorably reported on the "mobilization of community resources and brainpower."[41] Just as Tibbitts had valued practical as well as scientific knowledge, so too McNamara relied on "national" and "practising" [sic] experts to try to persuade his colleagues in the Senate to understand that a comprehensive approach to the elderly's needs was the best way to proceed. "We have felt that the unique contribution of this Subcommittee has been its approach to the problems of aging as an inter-related whole."[42]

The Subcommittee "undertook a swift collection of information and opinions" that were then published in three volumes. The set became a model for doing gerontologic investigations in the policy arena. In the first volume, *A Survey of Major Problems and Solutions in the Field of the Aged and the Aging* (1959), opinions about government responsibility for the elderly and issues such as Social Security, financing health care, and social services were taken from several thousand individuals and organizations: "This is the first time that the views of so many were solicited in this manner."[43] *Aging Americans*, the next in the series, gave older people a turn to speak about their living conditions after "the parade of specialists [had] passed." Illustrated with photographs, the publication presented "the problems of the aged as told by the elderly themselves at the town hall sessions and as observed by the subcommittee at the facilities for senior citizens."[44] It is not surprising that health care and income security were

40 U.S. Congress, "Study of Problems of the Aged," 86th Cong., 1st sess., S. Rep. 47, February 4, 1959, pp. 3–4. "Outline of the Subcommittee's Work," May 1959; see also minutes of meetings in Ann Arbor (March 28, 1959) and with Kuplan (May 6, 1959), in Oriol files.

41 Julian Bartolini with Senators Jennings Randolph and Pat McNamara, "Problems of the Aged in the United States," *The American Forum*, vol. 23 (February 23, 1960); see also "Community Viewpoint on Problems of Aging, U.S. Senate Hearings–1959," Oriol files.

42 Sen. McNamara to Sen. Hill, January 12, 1960, p. 7, in Oriol files. See also S. Res. 266.

43 U.S. Congress, Senate, Subcommittee on Problems of the Aged and Aging, *A Survey of Major Problems and Solutions in the Field of the Aged and Aging*, 86th Cong. 1st sess. (Washington, DC: Government Printing Office, 1959), pp. iii, xiv–xv. The phrase "swift collection" appears in a memo from Eli Cohen to William Oriol, November 13, 1984.

44 U.S. Congress, Senate, Subcommittee on Problems of the Aged and Aging, *Aging Americans*, 86th Cong. 2d sess. (Washington, DC: Government Printing Office, 1961), pp. vi, 1–3.

the top legislative priorities in the last volume, *Action for the Aged and Aging*; they were top priorities on everybody's agenda. In retrospect, the emphasis placed on generating and applying facts on aging and the elderly was noteworthy. The report called for the creation of a National Institute of Gerontology, an executive Office on Aging, and a Special Senate Committee on Aging as vehicles for sharing ideas useful in serving older Americans.[45]

Upgrading the quality of aging research and available pool of investigators was high on the federal agenda. "Such knowledge as there is in the field of aging is too narrowly disseminated and inadequately used," the Subcommittee reported, adding that "much so-called research in the field is second rate, carried on by poorly trained and under supervised personnel." The *Action* report proposed that 1 percent of all Federal research dollars be earmarked for aging research, that the Department of Health, Education, and Welfare (HEW) encourage university-based gerontology centers to focus on socioeconomic aspects of growing older, that provisions be made to support investigators willing to make careers in aging and to sustain longitudinal studies, and that the federal government conduct its own basic and applied research in the social sciences.[46] It is worth pointing out that all but one of the fourteen "medico-biological-chemical" and "social science" researchers who served as expert witnesses were prominent members of the GSA. Academics and lawmakers well understood that they could benefit one another in their mutual desire to promote the scientific study of aging.

The timing of the McNamara Subcommittee's three-volume report is as important as its contents. Lawmakers were disparaging the quality of gerontologic research as preparations were being made for several thousand delegates to attend the January 1961 White House Conference on Aging (WHCoA), which was chaired by Arthur S. Flemming, who served as Eisenhower's HEW secretary. When the WHCoA planning began in 1958, many in Congress questioned the value of research in agenda setting. "In spite of the many surveys, books, and conferences on aging," observed Rep. John E. Fogarty (D-R.I.), an early advocate of the elderly, "the greatest accomplishment to date has been the output of words."[47] To get beyond empty rhetoric, likely WHCoA delegates needed to learn how to use ideas. So a National Leadership Training Institute for the WHCoA was held in

45 U.S. Congress, Senate, Subcommittee on Problems of the Aged and Aging, *Action for the Aged and Aging* 87th Cong. 1st sess. (Washington, DC: Government Printing Office, 1961), p. iii.
46 Ibid., pp. 79–80. 102–3. In its report on *Developments in Aging, 1959–1963*, pp. 135–7, the Senate Special Committee on Aging stressed the slow development of research, the inadequacies of current materials, the acute shortage of teaching and research personnel, while underscoring the importance of interdisciplinary studies.
47 Quoted in U.S. Congress, Senate, Special Committee on Aging, *Developments in Aging, 1970* 92d Cong. 1st sess. (Washington, DC: Government Printing Office, 1971), p. ix.

Ann Arbor a year later to enable participants "to meet many of the foremost leaders in aging and to observe and experience a variety of conference techniques and procedures."[48] The WHCoA planners could hardly insulate the proceeding from politics, however. Preparations inevitably become politically charged once health care for the aged became a major issue in the 1960 presidential campaign. The elderly themselves expressed their political demands at state-level preconferences. Pro-Medicare rallies by United Auto Worker retirees in Detroit and needle-trades workers in Madison Square Garden were extensively covered in the media.

These developments actually may have increased appreciation for the power of ideas in the political arena. Besides demanding medical insurance and "the establishment and increase in grants-in-aid to states to promote and expand services to the aged," delegates to the 1961 Conference called for a federal agency to coordinate public responses to the problems of aging. Deploring the lack of public understanding about the elderly's needs and the absence of a national policy on aging, they urged that more funds be set aside for research and training.[49] Such demands bolstered the case that Senator McNamara was making for a U.S. Special Committee on Aging. McNamara noted with pride that the Subcommittee "has amassed a wealth of information on the subject which is unmatched anywhere" and demonstrated that "the problems themselves are highly interrelated, [which] require coordinated review and call for recommendations based on studies in depth of the total problem."[50] Sen. Jacob Javits (D-N.Y.) stressed the need for research that was not "purely of academic interest." Sen. Clark specifically cited the "utmost cooperation and skillful information" he had received from Sidney Spector and his research director, Harold Sheppard. The Senate's Committee on Rules and Administration added that "we must widen the area of our scientific knowledge by investing in basic research which is our brightest promise to eliminate disability and deterioration with age."[51] Accordingly, the Senate on February 13, 1961, voted a Special

---

48 Clark Tibbitts, "The 1961 White House Conference on Aging: Its Rationale, Objectives, and Procedures," 30 March 1959, p. 9 in Tibbitts Papers, Box 5, BHC.
49 The official report is contained in *The Nation and Its Older People* (Washington, DC: Government Printing Office, 1961). See also, Bennett M. Rich and Martha Baum, *Aging: A Guide to Public Policy* (Pittsburgh: University of Pittsburgh Press, 1984); Henry J. Pratt, *The Gray Lobby* (Chicago: University of Chicago Press, 1976), pp. 59–60, 112. Wilma Donahue et al., "Background Paper on Role and Training of Professional Personnel," *White House Conference on Aging*, May 1960. The National Council of Senior Citizens was also formed as a result of the 1961 Conference. See W. Andrew Achenbaum, *Shades of Gray* (Boston: Little, Brown, 1983), p. 119. Five months later, key figures in the 1961 White House Conference on Aging came to Ann Arbor to participate in U-M's Fourteenth Annual Conference. The proceedings appear in *Politics of Age*, ed. Wilma Donahue and Clark Tibbitts (Ann Arbor: University of Michigan Press, 1962).
50 U.S. Congress, Senate, 87th Cong. 1st sess., S. Res. 33 (January 13–February 13, 1961).
51 *Congressional Record*, vol. 107 (February 13, 1961): 1994–7. Sheppard had come to Washington from the Institute of Gerontology at Wayne State University. See also, U.S.

Committee into existence for one year and authorized its chair, Sen. Mc-Namara, to spend up to $150,000.

"If the new Special Committee on Aging does nothing else," McNamara declared, "it should serve to make the entire citizenry conscious of the otherwise unanticipated consequences – social, economic, and cultural – of the recent strides in life expectancy."[52] The statement underscores the reciprocity between ideas and politics. Understanding the dimensions of demographic aging made it possible for lawmakers to develop "better" policies, which subsequently could be evaluated by experts through sound research. McNamara's colleagues may not have accepted the argument, but they did appreciate its political appeal. The Special Committee's membership was quickly expanded from nine to twenty-one, making it the second largest in the Senate. The increase affected the Special Committee's research agenda, which already had partisan undertones. McNamara made clear that "the big issue" was financing medical care for the elderly; his friends in labor organizations hoped the Special Committee could focus attention on the issue; Spector advised the White House that "it is going to be difficult enough to secure passage of a bill for medical care for the aged through social security with a committee like ours in existence."[53] Republicans sought to use the Special Committee to their own advantage. In November 1961, Keith Jaques, the Special Committee's minority staff representative, was fired. He was accused of telling a senior-citizen group that the Special Committee, which he derided as "a tool of the Democratic Senate Campaign Committee," held hearings "good only for political propaganda . . . all other 'purposes' are only subterfuges."[54]

Amid charges and countercharges during the first months of its operation, the Special Committee nonetheless kept its pledge to emphasize research. After weighing a dozen "topics for discussion and action," Senators chose nursing-home reform, retirement financing, housing, and federal-state activities. By December 1961, they had conducted twenty-nine field hear-

Congress, Senate, Committee on Rules and Administration, *Report*, 87th Cong. 1st sess., February 9, 1961, p. 10. On the budget see ibid., p. 1.

52 Sen. Pat McNamara, "Special Committee on Aging Established by U.S. Senate," *Aging*, May 1961, p. 2. Robert Rienow and Leona Rienow claimed in "The Desperate World of the Senior Citizen," *Saturday Review* (January 28, 1961): 11, that "future politics may well turn out to be a power struggle between the average citizenry and the aged." See also William C. Cramer, "Senior Citizens in Politics," *Congressional Record*, vol. 107 (July 20, 1961): 5,554–5.

53 " 'Old Folks Vote' Causes Scramble," *Corpus Christi Times*, April 6, 1961; notes on a Special Committee on Aging, February 6, 1961; letter from Nelson Cruikshank (former leader in AFL-CIO and the aging network, to William Oriol, December 10, 1984; letter from Sidney Spector to Myer Feldman, Deputy Special Counsel to the President, February 2, 1961; all in the Oriol files.

54 "Minority Staff Member Says Hearings Political," *Idaho Daily Statesman*, November 16, 1961; letter from Sen. McNamara to Sen. Dirksen, November 17, 1961; in the Oriol files.

ings and received testimony from more than 800 witnesses. "Many of our colleagues, members of the administration, state legislators, and students of the problems of aging have been kind enough to tell us that they have found [our] reports and studies of considerable value to them in their consideration of legislative proposals."[55] Satisfied with results to date, the Senate extended the Special Committee's life for another year.

Political commentators and social scientists, trying to explain how the Special Committee on Aging managed to acquire a permanent year-to-year lease on life, usually refer to three functions it served successfully enough to justify its existence. The Special Committee was a symbol of the Senate's commitment to its elderly constituency, as a personal vehicle for powerful lawmakers and an effective legislative catalyst. The very diffuseness of its purview, claim analysts, coupled with its statutory limitations – the Special Committee could not draft legislation – enabled members to be selective in picking issues that cut across the domains of several standing committees.[56] This interpretation does not take seriously enough the Senators' contention that they relied on the unit to generate usable information. The historical record suggests that the Special Committee's efforts were critical in 1965, a watershed year in the national politics of aging. The Special Committee's investigations during the heyday of the Great Society provided facts about older Americans that the lawmakers needed. Its hearings provided an arena in which the interests of Blue Cross/Blue Shield, the American Hospital Association, and the AMA could be weighed against the needs expressed by senior citizens. The Special Committee also responded quickly to calls for more credible expert testimony. When it appeared that War on Poverty initiatives were initially giving scant attention to the elderly, the Special Committee conducted a series of studies and hearings that led to policy changes in the Office of Economic Opportunity.

The Special Committee's greatest success in 1965 was the creation of an Administration on Aging under the aegis of the Older Americans Act, an idea that Sidney Spector had first proposed to the Subcommittee on the Problems of the Aging and Aged in 1959. Principal sponsors of the legislation were Sen. McNamara and Rep. Fogarty. The AoA's primary function was "to serve as a clearinghouse on problems of the aged and the aging,"

55 "Meeting of Special Committee on Aging," April 17, 1961. These four topics became the foci of four ad hoc subcommittees; a fifth involved the involuntary relocation of the elderly. See also letter from Sen. McNamara to Sen. Dirksen, January 8, 1962 (in Oriol files) and U.S. Congress, Senate, Special Committee on Aging, *Report*, 87th Cong. 2d sess., January 25, 1962, p. 2.

56 Dale Vinyard, "The Senate Special Committee on the Aging," *The Gerontologist*, vol. 12 (Autumn 1972), part 1: 298–304; Howard Berliner, "Origins of Health Insurance for the Aged," *International Journal of Health Services*, vol. 3 (1973): 465–73; William Oriol, "A Quarter Century of Focus by Senate Aging Committee," *Perspective on Aging* (July 1984): 4–9; T. R. Marmor, *Politics of Medicare* (Chicago: Aldine, 1966); Richard Harris, *A Sacred Trust* (New York: Simon & Schuster, 1967).

including adequate income, employment, housing, health, "pursuit of meaningful activity" as well as "freedom, independence, and the free exercise of individual initiative in planning and managing their own lives."[57] By June 1966, AoA had selected 36 "demonstration projects" from 103 applications. These studies were designed to facilitate reappraisals of existing services and facilities and to implement new and different approaches. Subjects ranged from the effects of retirement on female workers to studies of the isolated elderly; future studies were to focus on nutrition, mobility, and attitudes. The AoA invested primarily in "applied" research. "As public servants in the Office of Aging," Clark Tibbitts noted, "our time and attention are devoted largely to trying to absorb the knowledge created by scientific researchers and translating it into programs aimed at improving the circumstances of older people."[58]

Tibbitts was given responsibility at AoA for ensuring that men and women would be trained to become specialists in aging. He was well aware of other federal initiatives in the mid-1960s: the National Institute of Child Health and Human Development (NICHD) was supporting graduate education in gerontology at twenty-five universities; the NIMH was supporting aging programs in fifteen schools of social work; other places received support from the Public Health Service, the Rehabilitation Services Administration, and the Veterans Administration (VA). Tibbitts sought to train experts in settings that offered exposure to several professional orientations. "The essence of an institute of gerontology is its multidisciplinary character," he declared, noting that " 'aging' does indeed include both a discipline and a practice."[59] In keeping with the recommendations set forth in a volume on *Graduate Education in Aging Within the Social Sciences*, on which he had collaborated with Wilma Donahue, Tibbitts chose to nurture programs with curricula that focused on specific aging-related policy issues, such as recreation and aging, retirement-housing management, and planning and administration. Tibbitts was pro active. Given considerable

57 "Older Americans Act of 1965," U.S., PL 89–73; U.S. Congress, Senate, Special Committee on Aging, *Developments in Aging, 1965* 89th Cong. 2d sess. (Washington, DC: Government Printing Office, 1966), p. 39; U.S. Congress, Senate, Special Committee on Aging, *Developments in Aging, 1966* 90th Cong. 1st sess. (Washington, DC: Government Printing Office, 1967), pp. 97–101; see also notes taken by Sidney Spector at a meeting with Perrin, Sweeny, Reidy, and Kaiser on May 28, 1959, in the Oriol files.

58 Clark Tibbitts, "Social Gerontology: Is It Legitimate?" speech, April 19, 1963, in Tibbitts Papers, Box 5, BHC. Tibbitts at the time was deputy director of the Office of Aging, which became the organizational basis of the U.S. Administration on Aging. See also his "New Directions in Aging and Their Research Implications," July 23, 1964, Tibbitts Papers, Box 5, BHC.

59 Clark Tibbitts, "Regional Institutes of Gerontology," proposal, December 1, 1967 in Tibbitts Papers, Box 4, BHC. See also, idem, "Main Currents in Training in Aging," report, November 7, 1967, in Tibbitts Papers, Box 5, BHC. The "discipline/practice" theme is elaborated in "New Directions in Aging."

discretion in distributing Title V training grants, his approach was consistent with a growing belief in policy-making circles that the U.S. government "should then be willing to look for and deliberately ask for needed research, without waiting for it to come to us."[60]

The high priority federal administrators gave to applied social science studies in the 1960s paralleled its growing commitments to biomedical research. Activities related to "medical problems" of aging were transferred to the NICHD, established in 1963. In addition to coordinating research and training within the NIH, the program then consisted of fifty-three extramural research projects totalling $2.7 million; three-quarters of the funds supported basic biological research.[61] The government's investment in intramural research was underscored in dedicating the new Gerontology Research Center at the Baltimore City Hospitals in 1968. Besides the aging-research work under Nathan Shock's supervision, researchers from other universities were assigned space in the facilities if they were engaged in collaborative projects with NIH scientists. At the suggestion of a large number of biochemists and other scientists that same year, Sen. Harrison A. Williams (D-N.J.), who then chaired the Special Committee on Aging, proposed that an Aging Research Commission be created to establish a five-year plan for coordinating investigations into the aging process. The Nixon administration chose not to allocate a greater proportion of federal dollars for gerontologic research, but Republicans on the Special Committee nonetheless strongly recommended "increased support, financial and otherwise, for immediate expansion of research in the field of aging." Congress, persuaded that "the need for personnel with specialized knowledge in the field of aging is reaching emergency proportions," managed to restore most of Nixon's initial budget cuts.[62]

Toward the end of his first term, the president often outbid the Demo-

---

60 The view, expressed in 1965 by Francis A. J. Ianni, research director of the Office of Education, is quoted in Gene M. Lyons, *An Uneasy Partnership* (New York: Russell Sage, 1969), p. 239. See also Robert H. Binstock, "The Politics of Aging Interest Groups," in *The Aging in Politics*, ed. Robert B. Hudson (Springfield, IL: Charles C. Thomas, 1981), p. 64. See also Michael Useem, "Government Patronage of Science and Art in America," *American Behavioral Scientist*, vol. 19 (July/August 1976): 994.

61 U.S. Congress, Senate, Special Committee on Aging, *Developments in Aging, 1963 and 1964* 89th Cong. 1st sess. (Washington, DC: Government Printing Office, 1965), pp. 85–6; idem, *Developments in Aging, 1966*, p. 68. The NICHD turned its attention to "the retirement revolution" in 1967. See idem, *Developments in Aging, 1967*, 90th Cong. 2d sess., (Washington, DC: Government Printing Office, 1968), p. 111.

62 Annual Report of the Gerontology Research Center, National Institute of Child Health and Human Development, July 1, 1967–June 30, 1968, in Shock Papers, Box 4, BHC; U.S. Congress, Senate, Special Committee on Aging, *Developments in Aging, 1968*, 91st Cong. 1st sess. (Washington, DC: Government Printing Office, 1969), p. 99. On budget problems, see *idem., Developments in Aging, 1969* 91st Cong. 2d sess. (Washington, DC: Government Printing Office, 1970), pp. 139–42. On Minority support for research, see ibid., p. 163.

crats in proposing additional funds for the elderly, including projects that would generate new ideas about aging. He encouraged the AoA and other executive units to arrange 6,000 community forums in preparation for the 1971 White House Conference on Aging. Nixon appointed Arthur Flemming to chair the proceedings, which were to ensure that due attention would be focused on the fourteen "needs areas" identified in 194,000 questionnaires submitted by senior citizens.[63] Over 38,000 people attended the 1971 Conference; seventeen Special Concerns Sessions dealt with such topics as long-term care and the Spanish-speaking elderly. In their final report, delegates issued 663 recommendations. Many proposals emanating from the 1971 WHCoA were enacted into law shortly thereafter. Amendments to the Social Security Act in 1972 gave a substantial boost to older Americans' monthly income and ensured future increases in benefits through cost-of-living-adjustments. The Older Americans Act was substantially changed in 1973 as part of Nixon's New Federalism. States were encouraged to develop "comprehensive and coordinate service systems to serve older persons." To qualify for federal grants, they were required to designate Area Agencies on Aging to arrange for services in the local community.

Guaranteeing some congruence between research and advocacy became a major task of all components in the U.S. aging network. In 1974, as the delegates had proposed, Congress established both the House Select Committee on Aging (which was to "provide extensive information and public service functions to the general public, and Committee Members and their personal staffs") and the National Institute on Aging (NIA), which was to coordinate biomedical and social scientists' conduct of basic and applied research in gerontology. "Researchers frequently feel . . . that research is their responsibility and not the use of such research," observed John B. Martin, a former U.S. Commissioner on Aging testifying on behalf of the American Association of Retired Persons (AARP). "In judging between the many applications certain to follow the provision of research funds by Congress . . . one important criterion for acceptance of such applications [should] be the applicability of potential findings to the real problems that plague us in the aging field."[64] The distinction Martin made between basic

63 Special Committee on Aging, *Developments in Aging, 1970*, pp. ix–xiii; Judith Turner, "White House Report," *National Journal*, September 25, 1971, pp. 1,966–72; Rich and Baum, *Aging*, pp. 28–30; The Senate Special Committee completed two years of hearings by publishing a five-volume report, *Economics of Aging: Toward a Full Share of Abundance*. U.S. Congress, Senate, Special Committee on Aging, *Economics of Aging: Index to Hearings and Report* 93d Cong. 1st sess. (Washington, DC: Government Printing Office, 1973).

64 Achenbaum, *Social Security*, ch. 3; Rich and Baum, *Aging*, pp. 30–1; Robert B. Hudson, "Accounting for Old-Age Policy," *National Forum*, vol. 62 (Fall 1982): 33–5; U.S. Congress, House, *Activities of the Aging Committee in the 101st Congress, First Session*, 101st Cong. 2d sess. (Washington, DC: Government Printing Office, 1990), p. 2. Martin's testimony appears in U.S. Congress, Senate, Special Committee on Aging, *Establishing a*

and applied research was not invidious; he simply was noting that the use of limited funds required discriminating choices.

Ironically, at the very moment in which politicians seemed to be most receptive to utilizing ideas on aging, the basis for federal support for gerontologic research was eroding. Presidential politics, rather than the presentation of compelling academic arguments, explain the 20 percent increase in senior citizen benefits in 1972. Congress increased appropriations under the Older Americans Act more than threefold in 1973, mainly to implement planning by Area Agencies on Aging, but in the same session it slashed funds for research and training, leaving "gerontology programs crippled."[65] The reduction in appropriations was yet another indication of AoA's vulnerable status. A few years earlier, in 1970, training programs had been transferred from Washington to regional offices as part of the Nixon administration's move to reduce the central agency's discretionary power. After AoA lost access to key officials in HEW as a result of several departmental reorganizations, the Senate Special Committee on Aging held hearings to determine whether a new unit were necessary to replace the beleaguered agency.[66]

The AoA's status in Washington improved when former HEW secretary Arthur Flemming agreed, at age 68, to serve as U.S. Commissioner on Aging. During his first year in office, 1974, he negotiated with nearly two dozen various departments and federal agencies, which enhanced AoA's position as a clearinghouse of ideas in the aging field. Flemming considered it essential that his agency had "the basic knowledge required to do sound decision-making, policy formation and policy direction and guidance." In 1975, requests for proposals were aimed at generating ideas about managing AoA's Title III and VI programs effectively. A year later AoA funded twelve Multidisciplinary Gerontology Centers, to provide a new "educational foundation" for training, research, and service in aging.[67] Such steps

National Institute on Aging 93d Cong. 2d sess. (Washington, DC: Government Printing Office, 1975), p. 29; Dale Vinyard, "The House Select Committee on Aging," *Long Term Care and Health Services Administration Quarterly*, vol. 3 (1974): 317–24.

65 U.S. Congress, Senate, Special Committee on Aging, *Training Needs in Gerontology* 93d Cong. 1st sess. (Washington, DC: Government Printing Office, 1973), p. 3.

66 Theodore H. Koff and Richard W. Park, *Aging Public Policy* (Amityville, NY: Baywood Publishing Co., 1993), p. 73; Special Committee on Aging, *Developments in Aging, 1970*, pp. 129–35. U.S. Congress, Senate, Special Committee on Aging, *The Administration on Aging – Or a Successor?*, (Washington, DC: Government Printing Office, October, 1971). When HEW Secretary John Gardner demoted AoA in the chain of command in 1967, the Committee's protests were to no avail. See Dale Vinyard, "The Senate Committee on Aging and the Development of a Policy System," *Michigan Academician*, vol. 5 (1973): 291–2.

67 U.S. Administration on Aging, *Research and Development Strategy, Fiscal Year 1975* (Washington, DC: AoA, 1975), p. 1; Robert H. Binstock, "25 Years of the Older Americans Act," *Generations*, vol. 15 (Summer/Fall 1991): 14; Byron Gold, "The Role of the Federal Government in the Provision of Services to Old People," *Annals of the American*

gave government officials some confidence that applied research would be utilized more effectively in using federal resources on behalf of older Americans.

The limited applicability of gerontologic research in the new politics of aging

Despite hopes that proposals emanating from two White House conferences would stimulate more federal policy initiatives to benefit older Americans, it was evident by the mid-1970s that a more conservative stance toward aging policies was taking shape. Lawmakers' problems with the country's social insurance system, Old-Age, Survivors, Disability and Hospital Insurance (OASDHI), presaged greater and greater difficulties in developing a coherent national policy for the elderly. The Senate Committee on Aging focused on "the multiple hazards of age and race" under OASDHI. The 1975 Quadrennial Advisory Council on Social Security called for universal coverage and more generous benefits. By the end of the decade, HEW issued two task force reports on Social Security's treatment of men and women.[68] A few years earlier such analyses might have served as the intellectual framework for drafting new legislation. Mounting concern over short-term and long-range financing of Social Security, however, took precedence over new proposals for liberalizing Social Security. Congress grappled with technical flaws in the cost-of-living-adjustment formula set in the 1972 amendments. Even more troublesome were the large and unanticipated shortfalls in the disability insurance program and the burden of paying for the "entitlements" promised to current and future generations of retirees. "There are not going to be any more easy votes on social security," declared Rep. Al Ullman (D-Ore.).[69]

To defuse the situation, Jimmy Carter raised FICA taxes in 1977, and established two blue-ribbon panels, The President's Commission on Pension Policy and the National Commission on Social Security, to evaluate U.S. income-maintenance programs. The president, knowing that unpop-

---

Academy of Political and Social Sciences, vol. 415 (September 1974): 55–69. See also Sharon Simpson and Laura Bleiweiss Wilson, "The Performance of Administration on Aging Multidisciplinary Gerontology Centers for Education and Training," *Educational Gerontology*, vol. 7 (1981): 215–29.

68 U.S. Congress, Senate, Special Committee on Aging, *The Multiple Hazards of Age and Race* 92d Cong. 2d sess. (Washington, DC: Government Printing Office, 1971); "Quadrennial Advisory Council on Social Security: Summary of Major Findings and Recommendations, *Social Security Bulletin*, vol. 38 (August 1975): 32; *Report of the HEW Task Force on the Treatment of Women under Social Security* (Washington, DC: n.p., 1978); U.S. Department of Health, Education, and Welfare, *Social Security and the Changing Roles of Men and Women* (Washington, DC: Government Printing Office, 1979).

69 Quoted in Martha Derthick, *Policymaking for Social Security* (Washington, DC: Brookings Institution, 1979), p. 411.

ular choices would have to be made, wanted experts to make policy recommendations that took account of the economic stagnation in the 1970s.
Ideas grounded in the ebullient assumptions of the 1960s no longer had
credibility in an era of fiscal austerity. Neither Commission issued its report
until Ronald Reagan became president, which effectively nullified their political significance. Furthermore, experts' debates over Social Security in the
media tended to confuse policymakers and the public alike. At the one
extreme, conservative economists such as Martin Feldstein and James Buch-
anan challenged the system's redistributive features. They argued that maintaining the status quo or fueling expectations by promising more would
bankrupt the nation. At the other end of the spectrum, liberals invoked
John Rawls and offered bold critiques of "justice," "equity," and "rights"
under Social Security. Radical sociologists and policy analysts invoked neo-
Marxist theories of the political economy; they interpreted the system's
woes as manifestations of a deeply rooted "crisis of legitimacy" gripping
most advanced industrial nations. Meanwhile, congressional staff members
with Ph.D.s in economics and public administration wrote technical analyses on retirement incentives and OASDHI's impact on the labor supply;
they attended scholarly conferences, exchanging papers on how much senior citizens "really" needed in the face of "governmental overload." Good
ideas abounded. In many ways, the debates occasioned precisely the sort
of refinement of information university-based analysts deemed essential to
policy-making. But Congress in the late 1970s was in no mood for esoteric
arguments. Politicians needed ideas that would get them out of what some
considered a zero-sum game. The lesson was clear: Policy-relevant research
must not only be substantive, but also well timed and artfully crafted for
the political moment.[70]

Subsequently, most studies published after the Bicentennial increasingly
tried to make sense of the new politics of aging. They dissected conditions
that had made it possible to establish programs for the elderly, then made
incremental changes, and then justified reforms in an environment less conducive for liberal change. According to the *1978 Catalog of Federal Domestic Assistance*, eighty programs were directly or indirectly providing
services and benefits worth $120 billion for senior citizens. Testifying be-
fore the Senate Special Committee on Aging in 1978, HEW secretary Joseph
Califano observed: "The past four decades have seen a steady growth in
the number of older citizens, a demographic change both large and striking.
This growth – along with recent trends such as inflation, slow growth and

---

70 See Achenbaum, *Social Security*, ch. 3; idem, "The Place of Researchers in Social Security
Policy Making," p. 306; John Myles, *Old Age in the Welfare State* (Boston: Little, Brown,
1984). For the difficulties in translating academic discourse into language useful to policymakers, see Leland Gerson Neuberg, *Conceptual Anomalies in Economics and Statistics*
(New York: Cambridge University Press, 1989).

problems in health care delivery – presents some formidable challenges to programs serving the elderly.[71]

The consequences of societal aging disturbed Califano. That he brought a fresh perspective and that he opposed unrestricted growth of entitlements in the future made him a controversial official. Califano incurred the wrath of Democratic stalwarts when he tried to curb the growth of old-age benefits. Friends of the elderly shared his worry that OASDHI entitlements were consuming a greater proportion of the federal budget, but they feared a "backlash" in Congress and among ordinary Americans. Fears may have been warranted, but not the ones that were drawing the most attention. Contemporary studies in political gerontology indicated that cutbacks would have an uneven impact on the nation's diverse elderly population. Many older, middle-class voters said they felt powerless, but the truly vulnerable, the experts generally agreed, were the very old, the very sick, and the very poor, who would bear the brunt of any "savings."[72]

In addition, social science research at the time indicated that future "discretionary" old-age benefits were in jeopardy. In the past, reforms designed to benefit elderly Americans had been championed by an activist Member of Congress, a powerful legislative committee, or well-placed officials in HEW or Labor. No executive agency had the responsibility or ability to coordinate federal senior citizen programs. The information network that Congress had begun to set in place in the late 1950s did not fulfill the demands being placed on it two decades later. Case studies warned that congressional staff, with fragmented foci and divided loyalties, could not absorb the welter of information about aging available; a 1977 House study reported that Representatives spent only eleven minutes a day reading. Broader political trends, moreover, were eroding both the illusion and the reality of Washington's control over the policy-making agenda. The

---

71 Joseph A. Califano, Jr., "U.S. Policy for the Aging," *National Journal*, September 30, 1978, p. 1,575; U.S. Congress, House, Select Committee on Aging, *Federal Responsibility to the Elderly* 95th Cong. 2d sess. (Washington, DC: Government Printing Office, 1979). According to the Committee, only AoA and NIA were charged with doing research. See also Patricia L. Kasschau, "The Elderly as Their Planners See Them," *Social Policy* (October/November 1976): 13–20.

72 Representative of the literature are Thomas J. Agnello, "Aging and the Sense of Powerlessness," *Political Science Quarterly*, vol. 37 (1973): 251–9; Pauline K. Ragan and James J. Dowd, "The Emerging Political Consciousness of the Aged," *Journal of Social Issues*, vol. 30 (1974): 137–58; Robert H. Binstock, "Aging and the Future of American Politics," *Annals of the American Academy of Political and Social Sciences*, vol. 415 (September 1974): 199–212; Jerry L. Weaver, "The Elderly as a Political Community," *Western Political Quarterly*, vol. 29 (1976): 610–19; Pauline K. Ragan, "Another Look at the Politicizing of Old Age," *Urban and Social Change Review*, vol. 10 (1977): 6–13; Robert B. Hudson, "Emerging Pressures on Public Policies for the Aging," *Society*, vol. 15 (1978): 30–3; Pauline K. Ragan and William J. Davis, "The Diversity of Older Workers," *Society*, vol. 15 (July/August 1978): 50–3; Douglas Dobson and David A. Karns, *Public Policy and Senior Citizens*, final report to AoA, 90-A-1005, ca. 1978.

New Federalism was encouraging a decentralization of resources: Greater decision making at the state and local level justified additional steps to reduce the importance of Washington as a clearinghouse.[73]

Some analysts found the situation far from hopeless. "We are beginning to see evidence that the current cohort of older persons is setting the stage for age consciousness and age-based political action," reported Neal Cutler.[74] The so-called gray lobby invested in ideas as they engaged in political action. National organizations representing the interests of various segments of the U.S. elderly population date back to the 1920s, but senior citizen groups did not wield real clout for decades. Then, in the 1960s, when the civil rights and women's movements transformed tactics for mobilizing political demands, older Americans became a more powerful presence in Washington. Like other organizations under the economic constraints of the late 1970s, associations cut staff, but they also took steps that consolidated their efforts and, in the process, made them more effective. Out of meetings in 1978 with Nelson Cruikshank, counselor to the President on aging, emerged the Ad Hoc Leadership Council of Aging Organizations, consisting of twenty-two bodies representing 15 million older Americans.[75] Groups such as AARP, the National Council on Aging (NCOA), and the National Council of Senior Citizens (NCSC) continued to operate like trade associations. They provided benefits for their members, served as advocates in Washington, and mobilized political action.[76]

73 Carroll L. Estes, *The Aging Enterprise* (San Francisco: Jossey-Bass, 1979); Jack L. Walker, "Setting the Agenda in the U.S. Senate," *British Journal of Political Science*, vol. 7 (1977): 426; Carol H. Weiss, "Congressional Committee Staffs (Do, Do Not) Use Analysis," in *Social Science Research and Government*, ed. Martin Bulmer (New York: Cambridge University Press, 1987), p. 97.

74 Neal E. Cutler, "Demographic, Socio-Psychological, and Political Factors in the Politics of Aging," *American Political Science Review*, vol. 71 (1977): 1,011–25.

75 David C. Crowley and Deborah Cloud, "Aging Advocacy at the National Level," *Aging*, vol. 297 (1979): 13–17; Dale Vinyard, "Public Policies and the Aged," *Social Thought* (Spring 1980): 31–40; Larry Light, "The Organized Elderly," *Congressional Quarterly Weekly Report* (November 28, 1981): 2,345; Henry J. Pratt, "The 'Gray Lobby' Revisited," *National Forum*, vol. 62 (Fall 1982): 31–3; Neal R. Pierce and Peter C. Choharis, "The Elderly as a Political Force," *National Journal*, September 11, 1982: 1,159–62; Henry Pratt, *The New Aging Lobby* (Ann Arbor: University of Michigan Press, 1983).

76 Allan J. Cigler and Burdett A. Loomis, eds., *Interest Group Politics* (Washington, DC: CQ Press, 1983); Henry J. Pratt, "Old Age Associations in National Politics," *Annals of the American Academy of Political and Social Sciences*, vol. 415 (September 1974): 106–19; James E. Trela, "Age Structure of Voluntary Associations and Political Self Interest Among the Aged," *The Sociological Quarterly*, vol. 13 (Spring 1972): 244–52; Dale Vinyard, "Rediscovery of the Aged," *Society* (July/August 1983): 24–9; Jack L. Walker, "The Origins and Maintenance of Interest Groups in America," *American Political Science Review*, vol. 77 (1983): 390–406; Thomas L. Gais, Mark A. Peterson, and Jack L. Walker, "Interest Groups, Iron Triangles, and Representative Institutions in American National Government," *British Journal of Political Science*, vol. 14 (1984): 161–85; John Mark Hansen, "The Political Economy of Group Membership," vol. 79 (1985): 79–96.

Among the "products" they offered their constituents were information-and-referral services.

Unlike most university-based research institutes, old-age organizations prided themselves on offering their gerontologic expertise to lawmakers in ways that sometimes yielded tangible political benefits. Staff on Capitol Hill, for instance, were very impressed by the 1975 and 1981 Louis Harris surveys of the aged commissioned by NCOA. *The Myth and Reality of Aging in America* did more than demonstrate the deep concern for the elderly's well-being on the part of most Americans surveyed by Harris pollsters. The NCOA report also suggested that it might be a strategic mistake to focus solely on the "problems" of the elderly, because men and women over sixty-five seemed more satisfied with their lot than younger people imagined. Similarly, AARP collaborated closely with Rep. Claude Pepper and his House Select Committee on Aging. It marshaled scholarly evidence and identified members who could offer personal testimony exposing the extent of ageism in the marketplace. The AARP rallied its members, which facilitated the passage of the 1977 amendments to the Age Discrimination in Employment Act.[77] "Technical facts and presentations carry a lot more weight (before the committees) than does any emotional display," noted Laurence F. Lane of the American Association of Homes for Aging. This explains why the Gray Panthers, which attracted considerable media attention, did not change many minds in Congress. That said, conventional wisdom paradoxically held that "Congress treats analysis much as it treats gossip, news, constituency mail, the local newspapers, etc. . . . analysis enjoys no preferred position."[78]

Students of the political economy of aging writing in the late 1970s and early 1980s quickly recognized that new types of research were necessary. "There is a dearth of empirical research on the linkage of old age interests to the economic and political structure and on the political organization and consequences of old age interests at the state and local level," contended Carroll Estes, who urged more attention to social constructions of aging, greater skepticism in dealing with questions of redistributing old-age benefits, and analyses of late life that were sensitive to issues of gender.[79]

77 Steven P. Wallace and John B. Williamson, *The Senior Movement* (New York: G. K. Hall & Co., 1992), p. xxii; Henry J. Pratt, "National Interest Groups Among the Elderly," in *Aging and Public Policy*, ed. William P. Browne and Laura Katz Olson (Westport, CT: Greenwood, 1983), pp. 145–80. Compare this with Andrew S. McFarland, *Common Cause: Lobbying in the Public Interest* (Chatham, NJ: Chatham Publishing, 1984).

78 Lane quoted in Demkovich, "New Kick," p. 1388; second quotation in Bulmer, p. 105. For more on the Gray Panthers, see Ruth Harriet Jacobs and Beth Hess, "Panther Power," *Long Term Care and Health Services Administration Quarterly*, vol. 2 (1978): 238–44.

79 Quotation in Carroll L. Estes, James H. Swan, and Lenore E. Gerard, "Dominant and Competing Paradigms in Gerontology," in *Readings in the Political Economy of Aging*, ed. Meredith Minkler and Carroll L. Estes (Farmingdale, NY: Baywood Publishing, 1984), p. 27. See also, Carroll Estes, "Political Gerontology," *Society*, vol. 15 (1978): 43–9.

Few members of Congress probably read Estes's publications, but they acted as she predicted they would. Amid increasing pressure to cut expenses, lawmakers concurred that they needed basic facts about the elderly's place in an aging society. When the Senate considered abolishing the Special Committee on Aging in 1977 as part of a periodic reorganization of its committee structure, Sen. Frank Church (D-Id.) quickly got fifty co-sponsors to give it permanent standing. Supporters emphasized its role in generating ideas. Sen. Hiram Matsunaga (D-Hawaii) stressed its role as an "information-gathering and advocacy unit." Sen. Edward M. Kennedy extolled the "unique contributions which a fact-finding committee exercising over-sight and advocacy roles can make," citing its string of legislative successes – the 1965 Older Americans Act, the 1967 Age Discrimination in Employment Act, and the 1973 American Community Service Employment Act.[80] Only four Senators voted to abolish the unit.

Under Church and then H. John Heinz III (R-Pa.), the Special Committee worked with the gray lobby to make "facts on aging" more accessible. First, as part of its annual report on *Developments in Aging*, and then as a separate publication issued with AARP, the Special Committee issued *Aging America: Trends and Projections*. Heinz and his staff served as idea brokers in forging the compromise that led to the 1983 Social Security amendments. In a series of background reports about the federal budget, the Special Committee stressed the need "to enable those who set national policy to make rational, well-informed decisions about future spending for older Americans."[81] Groups such as NCOA, in turn, broadened their purview by forging coalitions with organizations representing the disabled and children. Exchanging ideas was a way to build networks. Boards spent considerable time making strategic plans based on the right confluence of connections, opportunities, and coalitions.[82]

Just as research on aging intended for governmental use became more targeted, so too these federal agencies that had responsibility for knowledge production became more focused in stipulating what they wanted. Each year, AoA issued requests for proposals that reflected its shifting policy-relevant problem set. The National Institute on Aging (NIA) offered in *Our Future Selves* an "encyclopedic" research plan, which "requires an incred-

80 Quotations in *Congressional Record*, vol. 123, February 1, 1977.

81 U.S. Congress, Senate, Special Committee on Aging, *Older Americans and the Federal Budget* 98th Cong. 2d sess. (Washington, DC: Government Printing Office, 1984), p. iv; Achenbaum, *Social Security*, ch. 4. Four staff members, William Oriol, John Rother, Stephen McConnell, and Lawrence Atkins, eventually took positions as legislative advisors in the gray lobby.

82 Jack Ossofsky, "Connecting the Networks," *Educational Gerontology*, vol. 14 (1988): 397–8; Charles D. Elder and Roger W. Cobb, "Agenda-Building and the Politics of Aging," *Policy Studies Journal*, vol. 13 (1984): 115–30.Similar trends occurred at the grass roots level. See Ken Lawrence and Dick Harger, "Persistence Is the Key," *Southern Exposure*, vol. 13 (1985): 120–4.

ibly diverse range of training, experimental resources, research tactics, and knowledge."[83] Yet NIA's first two directors, Robert N. Butler and T. Franklin Williams, saw advantages to concentrating on a few items lest their priorities seem diffuse. Both focused on the tragedy of Alzheimer's disease as a way to garner more research dollars. The tack worked: Since 1986, NIA has been mandated by Congress to undertake work on the disease; in 1989, it received an extra $20 million appropriation expressly for this purpose. Now, roughly two-thirds of NIA's budget goes for medically defined problems, most of this for research on Alzheimer's. Between 1980 and 1991, the annual percentage increase in funds allocated for Alzheimer's disease and related disorders exceeded the annual percentage increase in the total NIA budget.

The National Institute on Aging's emphasis on studying diseases has been criticized by researchers on aging. "Less than fifty million dollars of the 401 million-dollar NIA budget in 1993 will be spent on research on the basic aging process, about one-half of the NIH budget and less than the price of television advertising during the 1993 Super Bowl," biogerontologist Leonard Hayflick points out. "Resolving geriatric medical problems without understanding the basic biology of aging will not advance our understanding of the aging process."[84] Other critics deplore the "biomedicalization of aging" inherent in the emphasis on Alzheimer's research. They counter that much of the budgetary reallocation has occurred at the expense of NIA's Behavioral and Social Research (BSR) Program.[85]

Starting with a small backlog of NICHD and NIMH research and training grants that were transferred to her new program at NIA, BSR director Matilda White Riley ably established a rigorous scientific agenda in the social and behavioral sciences. A well-known sociologist, Riley conducted her first work in gerontology when she was asked by the Russell Sage Foundation to survey the quality of workers' gerontology with a team of assistants. Riley summarized the state of empirical research on aging in a three-volume study, *Aging and Society* (1968–1972). She also formulated her own social-stratification model of aging. Under her direction, the Program initially tried to spark interest in four areas – the dynamic character of aging, the interrelatedness of (old) age, cultural variability, and the mul-

83 National Institute on Aging, *Our Future Selves* (Bethesda: Public Health Service, 1977), p. 55. See also Bruce M. Craig, "Weighing the Issues and Conferences of Federal Program Termination," *Gerontology and Geriatric Education*, vol. 3 (1982): 129–37.

84 Leonard Hayflick, *How and Why We Age* (New York: Ballantine, 1994), p. 373.

85 Carroll L. Estes and Elizabeth A. Binney, "The Biomedicalization of Aging," in *Critical Perspectives on Aging*, ed. Meredith Minkler and Carroll L. Estes (Amityville, NY: Baywood Publishing, 1991), pp. 117–34; Richard C. Adelman, "The Importance of Basic Biological Science to Gerontology," *Journal of Gerontology*, vol. 43 (1988): B1–2. See also Patrick Fox, "From Senility to Alzheimer's Disease, *Milbank Quarterly*, vol. 67 (1989): 88–102; Table 1, Budget Office, National Institute on Aging, August 26, 1992.

tiple facets of aging. All of these issues, Riley felt, could contribute to building a multidisciplinary, theoretical construct of aging and at the same time yield practical payoffs. Riley's agenda proved durable. During its first decade of operation, BSR collaborated with eighteen governmental agencies, thirty-five public or private associations or foundations, and nine international organizations. Even while directing BSR, Riley maintained an extensive research agenda. Now in her eighties, Riley serves as a Senior Scientist at NIA; she and her husband continue to study the consequences of societal aging. Whereas in the 1950s it would have been hard to recruit an active scientist for a major administrative post in the aging network, Riley made it possible for younger scholars to follow her example.[86]

"The advent of the NIA led to a dramatic increase in the support of aging research and training in the United States, so that the Institute today is recognized as the premier research institute on aging in the world," declared Robert N. Butler, M.D., its first director. "The NIA utilizes the same grant and training mechanisms as do other NIH Institutes but has changed them in a way that uniquely benefits the development of gerontology and geriatrics."[87] By instituting study panels and stringent peer review and by adhering to the reform guidelines for writing proposals that are used in other biomedical and behavioral fields, NIA has set standards for evaluating research on aging that other organizations in the gerontologic network respect and formulate. The agency underwrites Center grants and provides opportunities for junior investigators and senior researchers. The NIA has generated greater interest in gerontology within the scientific community. In its first year of operations twenty years ago, 65.6 percent of NIA's budget supported extramural research programs. The percentage steadily increased. In 1994, roughly 85 percent of NIA's $420 million budget went to MERIT awards, center grants, and other extramural expenditures. According to Richard C. Adelman, whose Institute of Gerontology (IoG) at the University of Michigan depends heavily on NIA support, "the greatest example of gerontology as *science* is the extramural research support of the NIA.[88]

Other federal agencies had less success than NIA in advancing gerontologic knowledge in accordance with prevailing "scientific" practices. Researchers on aging became more sensitive to the unanticipated uses policymakers might make of their findings, but they were unable to control the extent to which those ideas were politicized. The National Commission on Social Security Reform, which negotiated the compromise that became

---

86 National Institute on Aging, *The Behavioral and Social Research Program at the National Institute on Aging*, a working document (Bethesda, MD: NIA, November 1990).

87 Robert N. Butler, "National Institute on Aging," in *Encyclopedia on Aging*, ed. George L. Maddox (New York: Springer, 1987), p. 467.

88 Personal communication from Adelman to author, September 1, 1994. I thank Dr. Manuel Miranda and his associates at NIA for the data on NIA budgets.

the 1983 amendments, marked time before the '82 elections by dutifully listening to academics such as Michael Boskin make proposals that everybody knew stood virtually no chance of being enacted. The Catastrophic Medicare debacle a few years later might have turned out differently if political expediency had not prevailed over the objections of honest analysts. Gerontologists for years had been urging Congress to provide longterm care insurance; they proposed making home care more affordable by providing it under Medicare. But Ronald Reagan put catastrophic coverage at the head of the agenda in his 1986 State of the Union message. Selling the plan as a boon to families was considered smart politics. Making the program budget-neutral by front-loading taxes and phasing in benefits was consonant with the GOP's vision of domestic policy-making. Curiously, strategists did not take sufficient account of people's ignorance about health insurance: "I don't think there are 300 members of the House who could tell you extemporaneously what Medicare benefits are," said Rep. Pete Stark (D-Calif.), one of the architects of the 1988 law. "I don't think that nine of 10 seniors understand their Medicare benefits until they get sick."[89] Congress chose to ignore polls warning that well-to-do senior citizens preferred not to pay for a program that would duplicate benefits already enjoyed through private plans. "Catastrophic coverage" under Medicare was repealed in 1989, after a debate that pitted healthy, wealthy senior citizens against poorer, sicker older Americans. The setback fomented a backlash in Congress against senior citizens and some of their advocates.[90] A new blueprint was needed. Ideas emerged from work by several federal commissions and task forces investigating problems in the U.S. health-care system. A working group of 500 headed by First Lady Hillary Rodham Clinton produced a 1,500-page document to justify restructuring financing and coverage of health care. In an unreceptive political climate, President Clinton's proposal was probably doomed before anyone had read the case statement.

89 Quoted in "Catastrophic-Coverage Law Is Repealed," *1989 CQ Almanac*, p. 150; see also Lawrence J. Haas, "Fiscal Catastrophe," *National Journal*, October 7, 1989, pp. 2,453–6; J. K. Inglehart, "Medicare's New Benefits," *New England Journal of Medicine*, vol. 320 (1989): 329–36. The 1988 Catastrophic Coverage Act, which represented the largest expansion in Medicare since 1965, gave unlimited coverage for short-term care, after fulfillment of one annual $560 deductible; limited expenses for physicians' services; extended Medicare coverage to outpatient prescription drugs; and gave assistance to low-income persons.

90 Stephen Crystal, "Health Economics, Old-Age Politics, and the Catastrophic Medicare Debate," *Journal of Gerontological Social Work*, vol. 15 (1990): 21–31; Susan Dentzer, "A Health Care Debacle," *U.S. News & World Report*, vol. 107 (October 9, 1989): 16–18; G. Lawrence Atkins, "The Politics of Financing Long-Term Care," *Generations*, vol. 14 (1990): 19–22; Julie Kosterlitz, "Year of Commissions," *National Journal*, October 28, 1989, p. 2,634.

"A growing sense of urgency mandates that the time is right to narrow the gap between the needs of an aging society and the scientific data base," claimed former Gerontological Society president John Rowe, M.D. at a 1992 House hearing on *Aging Research: Benefits Outweigh the Costs.* "Building on the existing academic substrate, the medical and scientific community can leverage both new knowledge and tools from other fields to rapidly develop aging research into a mature component of the national scientific portfolio."[91] A year later, the House Select Committee on Aging, which heard Rowe's testimony, went out of existence as part of a reorganization plan demanded by first-term Members of Congress to cut the budget. Had Claude Pepper not died, and had his successor, Committee chair Edward Roybal (D-Calif.), not retired, it is possible that House politics would have played itself out differently. But after the demise of Catastrophic coverage, Congress no longer had as much to fear from the gray lobby. Groups such as AARP exercised greater caution in presenting ideas on the Hill.[92] Other signs were equally inauspicious. Efforts to stage a 1991 WHCoA were delayed. The GSA, mindful of the ugly partisan tenor of the 1981 gathering, urged that the President *not* to call a conference, but instead to craft an intergenerational agenda for an aging society. Despite GSA's recommendation that the future of aging in America be discussed at the state and local levels, plans were begun to hold a meeting in Washington in 1995.[93]

Fernando Torres-Gil, President Clinton's choice for Commissioner on Aging and the nation's first Assistant Secretary for Aging in the Department of Health and Human Services (HHS), may be able to make aging research the priority in federal policy-making circles that Rowe desired. A former White House Fellow with a Ph.D. in aging from Brandeis, Torres-Gil has taught at USC and UCLA and served on the Hill. A member of a Carnegie Corporation project that studied the "promise and paradox" of societal aging, he has set forth his own policy blueprint in *The New Aging*, which focused on what members of his baby-boomer generation must do to accommodate the conflicting pressures inherent in reconciling generational claims in a population that is increasingly multicultural and long-lived:

---

91 John W. Rowe, testimony dated February 21, 1992, in U.S. Congress, House of Representatives, Select Committee on Aging, *Aging Research: Benefits Outweigh the Costs* 102d Cong. 2d sess. (Washington, DC: Government Printing Office, 1992), p. 59. See also Milan J. Dluhy et al., eds., *Approaches to Linking Policy and Research in Aging* (Jerusalem: JDC-Brookdale Institute of Gerontology, June 1988).

92 Paul Kerschner, "House Aging Committee Endangered by Frugal Frenzy," *Gerontology News*, March 1993, p. 1; Julie Kosterlitz, "Golden Silence," *National Journal* (April 3, 1993): 800–4; interview with Manuel Miranda and Jorge Lambrinos, April 18, 1993. The Senate Committee survived a similar test by a 68 to 30 margin; Martha Holstein and Meredith Minkler, "The Short and Painful Death of the Medicine Catastrophic Coverage Act," in Minkler and Estes, *Critical Perspectives*, pp. 189–206.

93 "GSA Calls for Rethinking on WHCOA," *Gerontology News*, May 1993, p. 3.

"We face in the 1990s a proliferation of proposals addressing the demographic revolution. . . . Few political reforms attempt to restructure social policies for the aging by systematically analyzing how we got where we are and how we can best meet the changing circumstances of the next several decades."[94] Convinced that the programmatic strategies of the past quarter-century no longer could respond to changing times, Torres-Gil felt that his mission was to "integrate our aging concerns and interests into every facet of government . . . [to] 'gerontologize' the rest of the Department."[95]

In stressing the power of ideas in politics, Torres-Gil restated the challenge of synthesizing multidisciplinary research for interagency use articulated by Clark Tibbitts four decades earlier. In the intervening years, experts on aging had become more sophisticated about the ways federal agencies consumed gerontologic research. That said, it is not at all clear that they have any better sense of how to proceed. The 101st Congress in 1990 created a Task Force on Aging Research to "coordinate all federally sponsored research on conditions and diseases leading to dependence among the elderly and identifying the most promising areas of research."[96] Officials from HHS, the VA and Social Security, several Members of Congress, and an array of academic experts debated goals and strategies. Participants documented how intraagency barriers frustrated multidisciplinary efforts in gerontology without developing solutions to the impasse. As we shall see in the next chapter, attempts to "gerontologize" federal programs for veterans, which has had an aging constituency since revolutionary war survivors reached old age, have not been easy. Often the most daunting political obstacles are ones caused by the ideas articulated among experts themselves. Professionals conceptualize "problems" of aging differently. In the process, efforts to "gerontologize" Washington may fail not just because of interest group politics, but due to competing research agendas.

94 Fernando M. Torres-Gil, *The New Aging* (New York: Auburn House, 1992), p. 5. See also, *Diversity in Aging*, ed. Scott A. Bass, Elizabeth A. Kutza, and Fernando M. Torres-Gil (Glenview: Scott-Foresman, 1990).
95 "New Assistant Secretary for Aging Outlines His Goals," *Aging Network News*, vol. 11 (July 1993): 1.
96 U.S. Congress, Senate Special Committee on Aging, *Developments in Aging*, 102d Cong. 1st sess., p. 251.

7

Gerontology in the service of America's aging veterans

JUST AS THERE EXIST striking differences in orientation, scope, and longevity among gerontology programs based in universities, so too the uses made of research on aging by federal agencies vary greatly.[1] As the previous chapter documents, there is no consistent pattern in the ways that the legislative and executive branches of the U.S. government sponsor, consume, and produce knowledge. The aims and impact of scientific work underwritten by public funds, which has exploded since the 1960s, have generally been targeted to particular constituencies for specific purposes. Fields and customers do not overlap greatly. Nor is there yet much centralized coordination of research activities – despite the efforts of the Federal Council on Aging, an assistant HHS secretary for aging, and several congressional oversight committees. Each unit tends to define its mission to older Americans its own way and to operate with considerable autonomy. Rarely by design do two or more federal agencies voice the same rank-order list of concerns for aging people and share the same research aims for an extended period of time. Interagency cooperation is as difficult to negotiate as it is to sustain interdisciplinary research teams.

Maintaining intra-agency consistency, as this chapter illustrates, is also a daunting challenge. With few exceptions, institutional memories in federal agencies with a mandate to address the needs of elderly Americans are not long. So as priorities change and staff move on, old issues are revisited as if for the first time. There is little sense of precedents or traditions in weighing "new" solutions to recurring problems. This insti-

---

1 Earlier versions of portions of this chapter were presented as a report to the Geriatrics and Gerontology Advisory Board of the Department of Veterans Affairs in May 1989 and published as "The Politics of Aging: The Geriatric Imperative of the Department of Veterans Affairs," *Journal of Aging & Social Policy*, vol. 3 (1991): 33–50.

tutional amnesia is one reason why the federal government's use of gerontology in the service of the country's aging veterans has been so Janus-like. I do not claim that the Veterans Administration (VA) has been Janus-faced, in the sense of being deceitful. Rather, I mean to suggest that it has been Janus-headed, of two minds, in evaluating the place of gerontology in its operations. In some ways, the agency has been forward looking; at other times, the VA has been too reluctant to look beyond its own recent past.

Reconstructing the evolution of federal benefit programs for aging veterans thus serves a broader purpose in *Crossing Frontiers*. The case study reveals at least three trends worth underscoring in this history of gerontology in the United States. First, it reminds us that there were important, if sporadic, attempts to do "scientific" research on the aged and the aging before the twentieth century – even if those investigations were not construed as gerontologic at the time. Second, even in recent decades, researchers who have studied the needs of elderly veterans have employed at least two conceptual frameworks. Administrators concerned with health-care delivery evaluated veterans' programs in accordance with prevailing medical paradigms. Those advocating compensation for the disabled and widows stressed the impact of demographic aging in their cost:benefit analyses. The VA uses no single model for gerontologic research. As a result, and this is the third trend, the VA draws boundaries between gerontology and geriatrics to fit institutional aims and to take account of its fiscal exigencies. The advancement of science has not been the primary driving force behind investments in gerontologic research.

These three trends, in turn, highlight a paradox that pervades "gerontology" itself. The U.S. government's stake in aging veterans has long been considered a "special" case, which could be safely ignored or at least viewed as orthogonal to other aspects of gerontology's scientific enterprise. Many high-ranking officials within the VA have been loath since World War II to acknowledge their system's geriatric imperative or to capitalize on their potential to be leaders in the field of aging. Yet a case can be made that no other single organization has been committed longer to doing research on aging or has affected as many U.S. senior citizens as the VA through its training of physicians and deployment of institutional resources. Thus the VA's anomalous stance toward its own record in the aging field attests to gerontology's marginality in the late twentieth century America. For several decades, experts inside and outside of Washington have been detailing the challenges and opportunities presented by World War II veterans. That said, translating empirical data about gains in adult longevity into a coherent set of societal-aging policies, much less grafting gerontologic issues into paradigms that hitherto paid little attention to aging-related issues, remains problematic.

The U.S. Government's historical responses to that "Old Gray Line"

Policy-making for veterans, especially older ones, has been riddled with contradictions from the beginning of our nation's history. Successive cohorts of Americans by and large have felt that they owe more than a debt of gratitude to people who took up arms for their country and risked their lives in wars. Such feelings of filiopiety, patriotism, and duty have been counterbalanced, however, by pragmatic assessments by lawmakers and the public alike concerning how much veterans are owed. Thus requests for special post–military service entitlements made by one cohort have not always been extended to survivors of subsequent conflicts. Nor have they automatically been granted to widows and other dependents. While nineteenth century policymakers perceived the plight of aged veterans to be a "problem," they did not express it as such, in gerontologic terms, for many decades.

The earliest Federal intervention for aging veterans occurred after much debate in 1818, when Congress authorized general service pensions for Revolutionary War military personnel. James Monroe, himself wounded in the Battle of Trenton, declared:

> These men have a claim on the gratitude of their country, and it will do honor to their country to provide for them. The lapse of a few years more, and the opportunity will be forever lost; indeed, so long already has been the interval, that the number to be benefited by any provision which may be made, will not be great.[2]

Many members of Congress disagreed with the president. "The merits [of the Revolutionary veterans' case] have been exhibited to view, and we are told, if we discriminate we shall do an injustice, and if we include all, the finances of the country will be exhausted in the undertaking," observed Rep. Goldsborough. Granting pensions, concurred Sen. Nathaniel Macon of North Carolina, would be "like sweet poison on the taste; it pleases at first, but kills at last."[3] By December 1819, more than 28,500 veterans "in reduced circumstances" had applied for monthly pensions worth $20 to former officers and $8 for enlisted personnel.[4] Some were still gainfully employed, as was "the old gentleman [who] has been 42 years a soldier,

---

2 James D. Richardson, *A Compilation of the Messages and Papers of the Presidents*, 11 vols. (Washington, DC: Government Printing Office, 1911), 1: 558.

3 *Annals of Congress, 1817–1818*, 15th Cong., p. 191. Macon quoted in Richard Severo and Lewis Milford, *The Wages of War* (New York: Simon & Schuster, 1989), p. 87.

4 John P. Resch, "Federal Welfare for Revolutionary War Veterans," *Social Service Review*, vol. 56 (June 1982): 173–91; Theodore J. Crackel, "Longitudinal Migration in America, 1780–1840," *Historical Methods*, vol. 14 (Summer 1981): 133. Half of the applicants in 1820 were at least sixty-five; those over seventy with court-assessed property valued under $100 were most likely to be approved.

mostly serving on the frontiers and is now finishing his days in active serv-ice."[5] Eligibility terms were slowly liberalized. Under a 1832 act, anyone who had served for a total of two years in the Continental Army was to receive full pay for life according to rank, not to exceed a captain's pay. Subsequent amendments benefited the widows of Revolutionary veterans, the last of whom died in 1911.[6] States sometimes provided compensation out of their own treasuries. Mississippi, for example, granted Revolutionary soldiers residing in the state a pension of $100 per year if they were not on the Federal rolls.[7]

Antebellum observers recognized that altruism was only one factor de-termining how their contemporaries would respond to aging veterans' needs. Isaac Mickle in 1840 savagely commented on the hypocritical treat-ment of Revolutionary soldiers:

> What a wonderfully grateful people we are! We will see the few old veterans of the Revolution, starve in unhonored poverty before us, nay we will throw them, all hacked and scarred for our benefit, into ig-nominious prison for a paltry debt; but after they are once dead we scratch up their bones, and place them in a coffin, the cost of which would make the declining days of a dozen old soldiers, cheerful and comfortable; and after carrying banners, bury them again, with grand oration, amidst the roar of artillery, the peal of chimes and a discord of all horrible sounds; and a great ado of praying, and psalm singing, and paeans, and all that sort of thing; and finally end the farce . . . with abundance of dancing, and singing, and a superabundance, of course, of rum.[8]

On grounds of fiscal prudence, Congress delayed inaugurating service-connected pensions to survivors of subsequent wars. Veterans of the War of 1812 finally agitated successfully in 1871 for $8 a month for themselves and for widows (who had married before the Treaty of Ghent). Six years later, Congress loosened eligibility criteria, granting benefits to survivors who had served at least two weeks in the war. Mexican War pensions followed the same pattern.[9] Those who had served sixty days in the Mex-

---

5 John Palmer, *On Journey of Travels in the United States of America Performed in 1818* (London: Sherwood, Neeley & Jones, 1818), p. 87. I thank Seth Himelhoch for this ref-erence.

6 William Henry Glasson, *History of Military Pension Legislation in the United States* (New York: Columbia University Press, 1900), pp. 44, 49.

7 Madel Morgan, "Mississippi State Auditor's Warrants Issued to Revolutionary War Pen-sioners," *Journal of Mississippi History*, vol. 32 (February 1970): 75–80.

8 Entry dated November 26, 1840, in Isaac Mickle, *Gentleman of Much Promise*, 2 vols. (Philadelphia: University of Pennsylvania Press, 1977). I thank Keith Arbour for this ref-erence.

9 Glasson, *History of Military Pension*, pp. 61–7; Gustavus A. Weber and Laurence F. Schmeckebier, *The Veterans' Administration* (Washington, DC: The Brookings Institution, 1934), p. 34.

ican War (1846–8) became eligible for $8 a month in 1887. So did surviving widows – if their spouses were at least sixty-two, disabled, or dependent. More lucrative benefits were approved in due course. To the best of my knowledge, none of these decisions were based on surveys assessing the health status or economic resources of the target population.

Sometimes surviving veterans got in-kind benefits, such as land bounties, which were also used as inducements for military enlistments. In 1776, German mercenaries had been offered fifty acres each to leave the British army and join the rebel forces. Disabled Revolutionary soldiers accepted land in lieu of cash. Surviving military personnel from the War of 1812, angered by the generous size of land grants to Mexican War veterans, petitioned Congress for similar treatment retroactively. Sensitive to the potentially explosive generational equity issues at stake, Congress altered its policy: During the 1850s it distributed land grants of 160 acres to regulars, volunteers and rangers of U.S. and state militia (as well as widows and minor children of veterans) of any Indian war and conflict since 1790.[10] The net result was that nearly 73 million acres of public land were conveyed to War of 1812 survivors.

Older veterans also benefited from the creation of special domiciliary and medical facilities, which afforded an alternative to the dreaded almshouse. Congress enacted legislation in 1811 to establish a Naval Home in Philadelphia. Forty years later, Congress authorized U.S. Soldiers' Homes, the first such facility to be built in Washington. Four years later, an act permitted construction of the "Government Hospital for the Insane" (later called St. Elizabeth's), to serve military and civilian populations.[11] Once again, this federal response to the needs of older veterans reflected the prevailing belief that institutions provided solutions to certain types of medial "problems." It does not represent a commitment to deal with the aged qua aged.

The first legislation that made old age per se a criterion in aiding disabled military personnel and aging veterans arose in the course of attending to the needs of surviving members of the Civil War cohort. Abraham Lincoln in his Second Inaugural Address urged his fellow citizens to "strive on to

10 James W. Oberly, "Information Policy in an Era of Illiteracy: The U.S. Pension Bureau Before the Civil War," *Government Publications Review*, vol. 14 (1987): 287–94; Jerry A. O'Callaghan, "The War Veteran and the Public Lands," *Agricultural History*, vol. 28 (October 1954): 163–8.

11 George E. Ijams and Philip B. Matz, "History of the Medical and Domiciliary Care of Veterans," *The Military Surgeon*, vol. 76 (March 1935): 113–33; Eba Anderson Lawton, *History of The "Soldiers' Home"* (New York: Putnam, 1914). See also Carole Haber, *Beyond Sixty-Five* (New York: Cambridge University Press, 1983), and her "Geriatrics: A Specialty in Search of Specialists," in *Old Age in a Bureaucratic Society*, ed. David D. Van Tassel and Peter N. Stearns (Westport, CT: Greenwood, 1986).

finish the work we are in; to bind up the nation's wounds; to care for him who shall have borne the battle, and for his widow, and his orphan."[12] To fulfill this national duty, the National Home for Disabled Volunteer Soldiers (NHDVS), designed for citizen soldiers who had answered the Union's call to arms, was chartered in 1865. The NHDVS board quickly realized that the homes served a broader gerontologic mission that had to take account of the way that needs changed as their intended beneficiaries grew older:

> Time wears on. The family is separated, the supporting parent or child dies, the consequences of the hardships of the campaign or shock of the wound becomes developed in the system. Age increases. . . . Thus our establishment will become more and more necessary in the immediate future. . . . Then it will be that the necessity of this institution will be fully seen, and the benefits of this noble endowment most clearly appreciated.[13]

By the mid-1870s, managers of various NHDVS branches began to acknowledge that older Civil War veterans needed – and expected – to be treated differently from younger residents. Congress broadened the pool of potential beneficiaries in 1884 by permitting the admission of "all honorably discharged soldiers and sailors . . . who are disabled by age, disease or otherwise, and by reason of such disability are incapable of earning a living."[14] Hence, two decades before Homer Folks, New York City's commissioner of public charities, converted the first poorhouse into a Home for the Aged and Infirm to accommodate its changing residential mix, Congress recognized that NHDVS served a geriatric imperative, even if they did not phrase it that way.[15]

Veterans' facilities became de facto old-age homes by the turn of the twentieth century. The federal home in Dayton, Ohio, was the largest such institution in the world – a city of 6,000 complete with its own bank, fire and police departments, and waterworks.[16] In addition, nearly three dozen Union soldiers' homes were erected by various states between 1864 and

12 Abraham Lincoln, *Speeches and Writings, 1859–1865* (New York: Library of America, 1989), p. 687.

13 *Report of the Board of Managers of the National Asylum for Disabled Volunteer Soldiers,* House Misc. Doc. 45, 40th Cong. 1st sess., pp. 3–4.

14 *Statutes at Large* 23, sect. 5, 121 (1884). For a careful analysis of the evolution of the national homes and their significance in the history of old age, see Judith G. Cetina, *A History of Veterans' Homes in the United States, 1811–1930,* Ph.D. diss., Case Western Reserve University, Cleveland, OH, 1977.

15 For more on this, see W. Andrew Achenbaum, *Old Age in the New Land* (Baltimore: Johns Hopkins University Press, 1978), esp. pp. 80–6.

16 Henry M. Hyde, "A Forgotten Army," *The Reader Magazine* 5 (March 1905): 421–7; Henry S. Burrage, "Caring for the Old Soldier," *World To-Day,* vol. 12 (January 1907): 45–50. Eleven branches were established between 1866 and 1930, with an aggregate capacity of roughly 25,000.

1912. Fourteen homes were established in the old Confederacy. (Missouri and Oklahoma maintained separate homes for Union and Confederate veterans.) The distinction between old-age homes and medical infirmaries was blurred because both mainly provided custodial care. As the president of the board of visitors of Virginia's Robert E. Lee Camp Soldiers' Home observed in 1899, "the home is fast becoming a large hospital."[17] As their patients and residents grew older, the nature of the veterans' homes changed. The facilities provided opportunities for attempting to initiate clinical advances to ameliorate conditions for the elderly.

Although this was not their original purpose, asylums for U.S. veterans became laboratories for applied research on aging. To wit: Administrators increasingly worried about alcohol abuse among their oldest residents. "The members of the board of managers and the officers of the several branches are men (need it be said?) who desire the highest welfare of the old soldiers," declared the Rev. Henry Burrage, chaplain of the Togus, Maine, facility in 1907. "It is not to be forgotten that these are old men. Most of them are between sixty-five and eighty years of age. I have a large amount of pity for those upon whom the drink habit has so strongly fastened its chains."[18] Few commentators at the time shared Rev. Burrage's view that drunkenness among the old was really a major "problem." Orthodox medical opinions about the relationship between age and alcoholism were divided. Intrigued by the possibility that alcohol abuse became more prevalent – and deleterious – in late life, officials combed their medical records and disciplinary reports to see if age-specific patterns actually confirmed their impressions. On the basis of their data, managers of veterans' homes concluded that different standards should be applied to alcohol consumption over the life course. Officers fined and imprisoned men in their thirties and forties who drank excessively, but they encouraged elderly inmates to have an occasional drink to stimulate vitality in their later years. Without intending to do basic, empirical research on aging, the willingness of NHDVS administrators to manage old-soldiers' homes in accordance with the most authoritative "scientific" guidelines available constitutes one of the earliest U.S. forays into a research frontier that shortly would be claimed for gerontology.[19] A real-life problem prompted research that re-

---

17 Quoted in Emily J. Williams, "A Home . . . for the Old Boys," *Virginia Cavalcade*, vol. 29 (1979): 44; Tommy J. Lashley, "Oklahoma's Confederate Veterans Home," *Chronicles of Oklahoma*, vol. 55 (Spring 1977): 34-45. In 1864, Benjamin Fitch opened his home to victims of the war who needed medical care and support services. The Connecticut legislature made Fitch's Home for Soldiers a state agency in 1887; a year later, the federal government authorized per diem grants to State Homes. See *Proceedings of the Commission on the Future Structure of Veterans Health Care* (Washington, DC: Government Printing Office, 1991), part 2: 1,457.

18 Burrage, "Caring for the Old Soldier," p. 49.

19 W. Andrew Achenbaum, Joel Howell, and Michael W. Parker, "Patterns of Alcohol Use and Abuse Among Aging Civil War Veterans, 1865-1920," *Bulletin of the Academy of*

sulted in veterans gaining access to better geriatric care than was available to most Americans at the time.

Similarly, demography and politics ensured that Civil War survivors also enjoyed better protection against old-age dependency than most of their peers. The Arrears Act (1879) and Dependent Pension Act (1890) awarded benefits for non-service-related disabilities. A 1907 law (34 Stat. L., 879) for the first time recognized in statute that being old was a handicap. Veterans who had served for ninety days in Civil War received a monthly benefit worth $12 at age sixty-two, $15 at seventy, and $20 at seventy-five.[20] Those covered by previous veterans' laws gradually were transferred to the rolls under this act. More generous provisions were granted to widows a year later. Congress liberalized terms in 1912, 1913, 1916, 1918, and 1920. Survivors of the Confederacy, of course, were not eligible for federal pensions. To compensate, Southern states provided pensions representing roughly 20 percent of their total expenditures by the first decade of this century.[21]

The federal government spent over $5.2 billion in veterans' benefits, not including the value of land bounties, between 1790 and 1917. It cost the Union military $4 billion to fight the Civil War; the price of war-related pensions demanded by interest groups such as the Grand Army of the Republic (GAR) eventually exceeded $8 billion.[22] Veterans' expenditures for the Spanish-American War ultimately cost more than eight times the military outlay. "In the face of these fabulous figures the assertion that our pension system is a worthy monument of the generous gratitude of the

Medicine of New York, vol. 69 (January–February 1993): 69–85. The incidence of alcoholism among geriatric patients continues to be a major concern of VA researchers. See Kathryn Magruder-Habib, Constance Corley Saltz, and Patricia M. Barron, "Age-Related Patterns of Alcoholism Among Veterans in Ambulatory Care," *Hospital and Community Psychiatry*, vol. 37 (December 1986): 1,251–5; Howard P. Parette, Jr. et. al., "The Aging War Veteran and Alcohol Abuse," *Perceptual and Motor Skills*, vol. 68 (1989): 985–6; Frederic C. Blow et al., "Age-Related Psychiatric Comorbidities and Level of Functioning in Alcoholic Veterans Seeking Outpatient Treatment," *Hospital and Community Psychiatry*, vol. 43 (October 1992): 990–5.

20 The first bills to propose age-and-service pensions for Civil War veterans were introduced in 1889. The Pensions Bureau administered the 1890 measure to a certain extent as an age-based entitlement. Executive Order no. 78 (1904) declared old age to be an infirmity in adjudicating claims. See William H. Glasson, *Federal Military Pensions in the United States* (New York: Oxford University Press, 1918), pp. 231–3, 243–50; Weber and Schmeckebier, *Veterans' Administration*, 44–6.

21 Elizabeth Wisner, *Social Welfare in the South* (Baton Rouge: Louisiana State University Press, 1970); James R. Young, "Confederate Pensions in Georgia," *Georgia Historical Quarterly*, vol. 66 (Spring 1982): 47–52; Jill Quadagno, *The Transformation of Old Age Security* (Chicago: University of Chicago Press, 1988).

22 Glasson, *Federal Military Pensions*, p. 272. The President's Commission on Veterans' Pensions, *Veterans' Benefits in the United States* (Washington, DC: Government Printing Office, April 1956), p. 110–11.

American people sounds like a fiendish mockery," exclaimed reformer Carl Schurz. "No people have ever been more shamelessly victimized than the American people have been in this shameless pension business."[23] Schurz blamed the situation on politicians hungry for votes, attorneys hungry for fees, and greedy veterans hungry for more and more.

Derided and damned as a boon to an "especially worthy" subset of the American population, veterans' pensions were also praised by contemporaries as an important precedent for establishing welfare measures in the U.S. Social reformer Edward Devine in 1917 hailed the Civil War pensions as "a main national provision for old age." He was not alone. Charles Henderson believed that they "acted in great measure as a workingmen's pension system." Isaac M. Rubinow, one of the architects of U.S. social insurance, claimed that "we are clearly dealing here with an economic measure which aims to solve the problem of dependent old age and widowhood."[24] Catering to veterans' old-age interests, in turn, advanced broader societal concerns. Blacks, for example, often were able to petition successfully for veterans' pensions, thereby gaining benefits denied them in other arenas. "Civil war benefits," argues Theda Skocpol among others, "signalled the potential for honorable, cross-class and cross-racial social provision to flourish in American democracy."[25]

Skocpol is correct in noting that veterans' programs provided an important precedent for establishing Social Security on the basis of social-insurance principles in the United States. But Federal officials themselves rarely made the case for old-age pensions by extolling the benefits of Civil War pensions. The next developments in veterans' programs actually were bureaucratic in nature. They tended to isolate veterans' affairs from other domestic issues, rather than build bridges for welfare reform. Various benefits programs for older soldiers and sailors and their dependents were brought together under a single organizational umbrella. The U.S. Veterans Bureau was formed in 1921 by removing hospitals from the Public Health Service and the War Risk Insurance program from Treasury. The Bureau became the U.S. Veterans Administration nine years later by taking the Pension Office out of the Department of Interior and adding the Homes for Disabled Volunteer Soldiers, which had been semiautonomous. Con-

23 Carl Schurz, "The Pension Scandal," *Harper's Weekly*, vol. 38 (May 5, 1894): 410.
24 Quotes from Ann Shola Orloff, "The Political Origins of America's Belated Welfare State," in *The Politics of Social Policy in the United States*, ed. Margaret Weir et al. (Princeton, NJ: Princeton University Press, 1988), pp. 38–9. See also Lee Welling Squier, *Old Age Dependency in the United States* (New York: Macmillan, 1912); and Quadagno, *Transformation of Old Age Security*.
25 Norman R. Peters, "The Civil War Pension File of Lewis Cox and His Wife Lucretia Evans," *Journal of the Afro-American Historical and Genealogical Society*, vol. 6 (1985): 31–3. Theda Skocpol, *Protecting Soldiers and Mothers* (Cambridge: Harvard University Press, 1992), p. 531.

gress, consolidating activities for the sake of efficiency, segregated veterans' programs from those for other deserving groups. These administrative changes did not establish a single modus operandi for the new bureaucracy. Nor did they prompt officials to think of elderly veterans along geriatric lines.

In the medical section, for example, the existing hospital service and district medical service subdivisions were abolished. Put in their place were a general medical division, a tuberculosis division, and a neuropsychiatric division.[26] This arrangement was presumed to meet the needs of the VA's clientele in the 1920s and 1930s; it conformed to prevailing views of how best to deliver medical care to patients with chronic ailments. The model took little account of the ages of veterans; it classified them in terms of diseases. It is highly improbable that the VA would have organized services around anything but a disease-oriented model. That was how many other civilian and military hospitals were arranged. Still, given the demographic profile of the VA's constituency, it is striking that no attention was paid to the special needs of older veterans beyond the need to provide custodial care.

The next surge of interest in caring for aged veterans followed in the wake of World War II. In 1943, convinced "that the time to prepare for peace is at the height of war," F.D.R. ordered the National Planning Resource Board to develop educational, employment, and housing benefits for veterans that would simultaneously serve broader societal needs. The VA kept a low profile at first; key players in Interior, Agriculture, Labor, Selective Service, and the National Housing Agency viewed the VA purely as a service agency.[27] Between July 1, 1945, and June 30, 1946, 1,880 bills pertaining to veterans' benefits were introduced in Congress, and 400 reports were prepared for its legislative committees. When Gen. Omar Bradley took charge of operations, he sought to enhance the VA's reputation. Dr. Paul Magnuson, whom Bradley chose to oversee medical facilities, was appalled by the current state of affairs:

26 *Annual Report of the Director, United States Veterans' Bureau* (Washington, DC: Government Printing Office, 1922), pp. 5, 7; E. O. Crossman, "U.S. Veterans' Bureau Hospitals," *Modern Hospital*, vol. 26 (January 1926): 30–2; Frank T. Hines, "Organization and Function of the U.S. Veterans' Bureau Medical Service," *Medical Bulletin*, vol. 1 (July 1925): 43–8.

27 This was the first time that planning preceded rather than followed veterans' readjustment to civilian life. Franklin Delano Roosevelt, "Message to Congress on Education of War Veterans," October 27, 1943, in *Roosevelt Public Papers, 1943*, ed. Samuel Rosenman (New York: Harper & Row, 1950), pp. 449–55; Davis R. B. Ross, *Preparing for Ulysses* (New York: Columbia University Press, 1969); Dixon Wecter, *When Johnny Comes Marching Home* (Boston: Houghton Mifflin, 1944), pp. 549ff; *Annual Report of the Administrator of Veterans' Affairs for the Fiscal Year Ended June 30, 1945* (Washington, DC: Government Printing Office, 1945), p. 2.

This situation was a perfect example of bureaucracy at its worst. . . . There was not a single veterans hospital that was accredited by the American Medical Association for residencies or internships. No teaching was permitted in those hospitals. They were not even called hospitals—the official name for them was "Veterans Administration facilities." The doctors in those places were the most dispirited, downtrodden bunch you ever saw.[28]

The war hero demanded top quality and efficiency. Hence, the Department of Medicine and Surgery was reorganized to foster better ties between medical schools and VA hospitals. Within four years, centers were handling 85 percent more patients with only 44 percent more beds. In 1948, fifty-eight medical schools were operating residency programs in sixty-eight VA hospitals. By 1965, all forty-six VA hospitals had affiliations with medical schools nearby, which benefited from their training sites.[29]

Economic and administrative efficiency in serving a new cohort of veterans was the primary incentive for fostering new institutional partnerships in the postwar era. "If we are to make the best use of our limited governmental resources . . . it seems appropriate . . . that the activities of these separate systems be somehow co-ordinated, correlated or integrated into governmental medical centers for the care of patients entitled by law to governmental medical aid," urged Gen. R. W. Bliss, Deputy Surgeon of the Army. "Perhaps we should establish specialty centers, transfer patients accordingly and assign our specialists not in terms of the service to which they belong but to the hospital designated for their specialty at the same time utilizing to the full the staffs and facilities of the civilian teaching institutions."[30] In time, the new arrangement made it possible for VA officials to accord a higher priority to research as a way to improve clinical services. Reorganizing medical care to facilitate a team approach, it appears in retrospect, set the stage for the VA to pursue geriatric initiatives. That was not its original intent, however. The immediate aim of rearranging VA facilities was to expedite efforts by young men returning from the European and Pacific theaters to readjust to civilian life. Under Public Law 79-293 (1946), massive construction of hospitals and rehabilitation centers began. To upgrade quality, the hiring, promoting, and firing of VA physicians and dentists were exempted from Civil Service rules and entrusted to medical review boards.

28 Paul B. Magnuson, *Ring the Night Bell* (Boston: Little, Brown, 1960), pp. 268–9.

29 William Rothstein, *American Medical Schools and the Practice of Medicine* (New York: Oxford University Press, 1987), p. 278; John C. Nunemaker, "The Veterans Administration–Medical School Relationship," *Journal of Medical Education*, vol. 34 (February 1959): 77–83. A Carnegie Corporation panel envisioned VA hospitals becoming hubs for regional health-care centers. See Carnegie Commission on Higher Education, *Higher Education and the Nation's Health* (New York: McGraw-Hill, 1970), pp. 56–9.

30 R. W. Bliss, "Modern Governmental Medical Problems," March 19, 1946.

Serving World War II veterans was the top priority, but the VA could not, and did not, overlook elderly veterans. Over 90 percent of those who occupied the complement of 17,600 beds in 1950 were veterans of World War I and earlier periods of military service.[31] Eager to utilize the latest clinical advances in medicine and surgery, including nascent fields, officials started to keep abreast of developments in geriatrics and gerontology. Dr. William S. Middleton, the VA's Chief Medical Director from 1955 to 1963, was particularly committed to making clients' added years useful and worthwhile. "Clearly any good ideas that come of this must be implemented by the interested research and professional personnel of the Veterans Administration," the Advisory Committee on the Problems of Aging noted in its *VA Prospectus on Research in Aging* (1959). "Therefore, those doing research in it, and those only thinking about it were warmly invited to make available their ideas of what should be done and information on what they themselves would like to do."[32] Gerontological Society members Albert Lansing, Jack Weinberg, and James Birren played major roles in setting the VA's aging-related agenda. Martin Cumming, M.D., who directed the VA's Research Service, stressed the importance of an "orderly organization of aging, e.g., molecules, cells, organs, individuals, and groups."[33]

By the late 1950s, the VA was underwriting research in gerontology and geriatrics that not only served its constituency but also contributed to the emerging sciences. In 1958, the VA launched a study of Spanish-American War veterans, which complemented the aims of Duke University's Longitudinal Study of Aging (begun in 1954) and the Baltimore Longitudinal Study of Aging undertaken by the federal Gerontology Research Center (in 1958). A Normative Aging Study began five years later as a comprehensive, interdisciplinary survey in the VA Outpatient Clinic in Boston. On the basis of this project, VA researchers took the lead in efforts to develop biomarkers of "functional" age independent of chronological age.[34] In the clinical sphere, intermediate services were established at certain sites to care for

31 Paul B. Magnuson, "Medical Care for Veterans," *Annals of the American Academy of Political and Social Science*, vol. 271 (January 1951): 82.
32 Veterans Administration, *VA Prospectus: Research in Aging* (Washington, DC: Government Printing Office, 1959), p. 3; see also, *Care of the Aged: Selected Bibliography, 1940–1950* (Washington, DC, 1950), prepared by the VA's Medical and General Reference Library at the request of the Division of Psychiatry and Neurology; and John H. Mather and Robert W. Abel, "Medical Care of Veterans," *Journal of the American Geriatrics Society*, vol. 34 (October 1986): 759.
33 Marin M. Cummings, "Postscript," *VA Prospectus*, p. 125. The VA was supporting ninety research projects in 1960.
34 N. W. Coppinger, "The Psychological Aspects of Aging: A Prospectus for Research in the Veterans Administration," *The Gerontologist*, vol. 7 (April 1967), part 2: 1. For more on NAS, see Benjamin Bell et al., "The Normative Aging Study," *Aging and Human Development*, vol. 3 (1972): 5–17.

older patients who did not need intensive hospitalization but could not qualify for domiciliary care. A Residential Care Home Program, started quietly in 1953, expanded as administrators gained experience in dealing with older clients with psychiatric diagnoses. Personal attendants were provided for the disabled in 1958; veterans with non-service-connected ills gained access to a greater array of outpatient services two years later.[35]

In a 1963 Executive Order, John F. Kennedy set into motion a chain of events that made geriatric patient care an even greater priority than many VA physicians and administrators had intended. The President decreed that the VA would operate 2,000 nursing-home beds. A year later, in Public Law 88-450, Congress doubled that number. This was not the direction that the VA wanted to go. Taking cues increasingly from their medical school colleagues, the VA's Central Office considered improving acute care rather than expanding long-term care to be its primary concern. Administrators saw the construction of new nursing-home facilities as a way to relocate chronic (typically older) patients crowding VA hospitals and to free beds for new (often younger) patients. Concurrently, the VA resisted the Bureau of Budget's proposal to convert its domiciliary program into a nursing-home program, citing its need to continue treatment of minimal care patients in the domiciliary units *and* for nursing care in nursing homes.[36] Despite its recent advances into the frontiers of gerontologic and geriatric knowledge, the VA preferred to position itself at the center of mainstream medicine. In the process, VA officials proved quite effective in parrying other agencies' ideas about how to manage older veterans' programs. They initially did not want to use this opportunity to develop coherent strategies of their own. In the absence of a plan that acknowledged differences in their constituency from the U.S. population at large, VA officials melded gerontologic and geriatric principles in an ad hoc manner with mixed success.

The challenge of providing care for elderly veterans was daunting. Since no new nursing-home construction was permitted at first, officials had to carve out space for 4,000 beds in its own facilities. Geriatrics typically got less-than-desirable space from hospital directors. Pressed to do more, the VA initiated community contract nursing-home care and aided state veterans' programs in the construction and operation of facilities. Key officials in the Central Office, such as Dr. Paul Haber, *were* able to create a niche for gerontological research in the system. Haber capitalized on the VA's new mandate by recruiting a cadre of physicians and nurses interested in

---

35 U.S. Congress, House, Committee on Veterans' Affairs, *Medical Care of Veterans*, House Comm. print no. 4 (Washington, DC: Government Printing Office, 1967), p. 267; Paul A. L. Haber, "The Veterans Administration Community Care Setting," *Psychiatric Quarterly*, vol. 55 (Summer/Fall 1983): 187–91; see also, P.L. 86–639 (1960).

36 Letter to author from Dr. Paul Haber, an architect of the VA's geriatric initiatives, dated April 13, 1989.

developing better ways to deliver services to older patients and in promoting research on aging. "The decision to continue the domiciliary program and to initiate the new nursing home program," contends Haber, "heralded a desire to develop a complete spectrum of care for patients who needed long term care."[37] A broad array of services required a multidisciplinary approach. Investing in research served veterans if a more efficient delivery of services resulted.

Thus, before Congress had enacted measures that would increase research on aging in the health-care area, the VA already was investing in R&D to effect a balanced mix in the continuum of long-term care. Other projects demonstrated the VA's increasing capacity for, and commitment to, research on aging, particularly those dealing with older veterans' health problems and maintenance. "Because of the increasing number of war veterans and their dependents advancing into the older age groups each year, the VA is particularly interested in finding answers to many of the problems of older people," reported VA Administrator William J. Driver in 1968.[38] To increase the talent at its disposal, the VA in 1964 established a "satellite laboratory aging program." The VA invited outstanding non-VA senior researchers to collaborate with VA investigators near their facilities. Albert Lansing and Nobel laureate Linus Pauling participated in the venture.

The establishment of Geriatric Research, Education and Clinical Centers (GRECCs), approved by Congress in 1973, enabled the VA to extend the frontiers of geriatric training and research. The GRECCs were "(1) to provide for the rapidly increasing demand for geriatric and extended health care and medical services being placed upon the VA hospital system by the nation's veterans; and (2) to make the VA hospital system the leader in geriatric research, the training of medical and paramedical personnel in care of the elderly and the delivery of health care to the aged, and to make such system the repository of medical knowledge of the science of gerontology (dealing with the emotional and psychological aspects of aging)."[39] Univer-

---

37 Paul A. L. Haber, M.D., "Geriatric Continuum of Care: The VA's Experience," paper, December 21, 1984, p. 4; Veterans Administration, *Twenty Years of Outreach, 1967-1987* (Washington, DC: VA, 1992), p. 8.

38 Driver's comment appeared in a cover letter dated December 2, 1968 reprinted in U.S. Congress, Senate, Special Committee on Aging, *Developments in Aging, 1968*, 91st Cong. 1st sess. (Washington, DC: Government Printing Office, 1969), p. 174. Research status in 1960 in Robert F. Martin, *The Aging American Veteran and the National Economy* (Washington, DC: VA, 1960), p. 16. See also reports in the 1967 and 1969 issues of U.S. Congress, Senate, Special Committee on Aging, *Developments on Aging, 1967*, 90th Cong. 2d sess., and *ibid.*, 1969, 91st Cong. 1st sess. It is not clear how many of the VA's principal investigators were tied into the community of researchers on aging. Only ten of the forty-four VA scientists mentioned in the VA's 1966 report, reprinted in *ibid.*, 1966, pp. 77–82, were also listed on the rolls of the Gerontological Society that year, reprinted in *The Gerontologist*, vol. 6, no. 3 (September 1966): 1–26.

39 H.R. 4015, 96th Cong. 1st sess., May 9, 1979. The first geriatric residency was established

sity medical schools close to VA centers had a real incentive to establish GRECCs. The program gave salary support for professional salaries. Centers also were to be rewarded to designing multilevel care systems, though early evaluations indicate that the VA's own administrative structure impeded the extent of coordination and integration that might have been effected.[40]

The VA put special emphasis on efforts to coordinate clinical and long-term care programs, educational activities, and research, as the experiences at two GRECCs attest. At the John L. McClellan Memorial Veterans Hospital in Little Rock, Arkansas, Owen Beard and Eugene Towbin developed the nation's prototypical twenty-bed Geriatric Evaluation Unit (GEU), a first step in developing comprehensive long-term-care programs for elderly veterans. A team of physicians, nurses, social workers; physical, occupational, speech, and correctional therapists; dieticians, audiologists, and pharmacologists; and psychologists and psychiatrists met with interns, residents and allied-health specialists to assess patients' conditions. The GRECC's associate director, Sam Goldstein, headed a renowned center for research into the mechanisms of cellular aging, which illuminated variables in the regulation of normal aging and age-dependent diseases. At the Sepulveda VA Center in California, the number of research projects focusing on aging grew from two in 1959 to more than twenty by 1986; scientists were investigating areas of memory, endocrinology, causes of sexual dysfunction, and nutrition and were doing health-services research. Pioneering studies by Phillip Scarpace focused on the effects of aging on the beta-adrenergic receptor. Ten different clinical geriatric programs (including three geropsychiatry services) were affiliated with the Sepulveda GRECC. The Center cosponsored with the VA Central Office ten national training conferences. It developed the Cascade Method, a multidimensional field approach for training trainers, which reduced the costs incurred under traditional methods.[41]

Within a decade of their establishment, the GRECCs had demonstrated that aging-related research could be applied in several ways. Besides reductions in training costs and improvements in the delivery of health serv-

at Mt. Sinai Hospital in New York City in 1972. Presciently, the VA was authorized under P.L. 93–257 to study the *Needs of Veterans and Widows, 72 Years of Age or Older*. See its July 1975 report, which was one of the first to focus on the old-old.

40 See Evan Calkins, M.D., "Role of Veterans Administration Hospitals as Bases for Academic Units in Geriatric Medicine – A Historical Perspective," in *Geriatric Education*, ed. Knight Steel, pp. 54–7. GRECC sites are chosen by peer review. See *Congressional Record*, October 5, 1992, H. 11686.

41 For more on the Little Rock and Sepulveda programs, see "GRECCs: Centers of Excellence," *VA Practitioner* (October 1985): 100–8, and (February 1986): 82–8, respectively. See also Owen Beard, M.D., "The Veterans Administration Hospitals in Resources for Geriatric Education – The Experience at the University of Arkansas, in *Geriatric Education*, ed. Knight Steel (Lexington, MA: Collamore Press, 1981), pp. 49–57.

ices, the VA claimed that "the program has successfully advanced the body of scientific knowledge regarding the medical, psychological, and social needs of older veterans. . . . The focus of each GRECC was determined by the skills, qualifications, and resources of the researchers at the host VAMC [Veterans Administration Medical Center]. This foundation is used to recruit additional researchers and to compete for research funding from both the VA and non-VA sources."[42] The recruitment strategy worked. The first *VA Geriatric Faculty Resource Directory* (1990) listed more than 250 investigators in areas ranging from "aging and cultural attitudes" to "urinary incontinence."

Over time, under the GRECC umbrella, the VA Central Office took additional steps to improve the quality of gerontology and geriatric research in the system. It established a special review group for "Innovative Research on the Biology of Aging" and created merit review panels analogous to National Institutes of Health (NIH) study sections. By fiscal year 1990, more than $214 million was appropriated for studies of chronic heart disease, practical applications of prosthetics, as well as continued improvements in the delivery of geriatric care. According to evaluators from the American College of Physicians, "one of the program's major achievements has been the development of geriatric evaluation units that provide intensive interdisciplinary team assessments to improve the problem identification, treatment and placement of older patients who have remediable impairments, multiple chronic diseases, and interacting psychosocial problems."[43]

The VA changed its organizational structure to coordinate health care and social services for older veterans. The first Assistant Chief Medical Director for Geriatrics and Extended Care was named in 1975. Day-care programs for older veterans began in five VA medical centers between 1979 and 1981. By the early 1980s, VA centers across the nation were following Little Rock's example and creating Geriatric Evaluation Units to assess older patients' medical, functional, psychological, and socioeconomic status. Intramural studies and external review report that GEUs demonstrably improved diagnoses and treatment of older patients. Veterans assigned to GEUs were likely to be transferred to nursing homes and had much lower mortality rates than older subjects in the control group. At the same time, by linking "teaching nursing homes" to GEUs, the functional

---

42 Office of Program Analysis and Evaluation, *Geriatric Research, Education, and Clinical Centers: A Program Evaluation* (Washington, DC: VA, February 1986): pp. ii, 27; Department of Veterans Affairs, *VA Geriatric Faculty Resource Directory* (October 1990).

43 American College of Physicians, "The Role of the Department of Veterans Affairs in Geriatric Care," *Annals of Internal Medicine*, vol. 115 (December 1991): 897. Richard C. Adelman, who has chaired the VA's Geriatrics and Gerontology Advisory Committee, also supplied information for this paragraph.

status of patients living in institutional settings and residing at home improved.[44]

The Department of Veterans Affairs (DVA) currently is at the vanguard in promoting geriatric research. In fiscal 1988, it funded more than $2 million in dementia-related research alone. Outside support for GRECC research has exceeded internal funding for more than a decade. The percentage of GRECC research funding from non-VA sources rose to 79 percent of the total in 1991, which attests to the quality of VA proposals.[45] Some of VA's reports, such as *The Aging Veteran – Present, Future Medical Needs* (1977) and *Caring for the Older Veteran* (1984), not only critiqued clinical aspects of geriatric medicine in the United States, but also emphasized how biomedical and health-services research might ameliorate extended care. A Geriatrics and Gerontology Advisory Committee, formed in 1980, ensures objective counsel from outside experts in the field. The DVA also has been quite willing to join with other researchers in addressing complex problems. A project with Harvard University's Division of Health Policy Research and Education assessed ways to improve integration of VA and community resources to serve the elderly.[46] Other research collaborations have been undertaken with the National Institute on Aging (NIA), the Administration on Aging (AoA), and NASA.

Research *training* in aging remains a high priority at GRECCs. The VA's Geriatric Fellowship Program predates the Accreditation Council for Graduate Medical Education approval of geriatric medicine as an area of special competence. More geriatricians have received training in VA facilities than any other medical site. As of 1991, 275 men and women had completed geriatric fellowships. Roughly 90 percent of this group have elected to continue to specialize in geriatrics; half have obtained academic appointments, which should ensure that their medical schools will pay greater attention to the needs of older patients. In part, the success is a consequence of the

44 Mather and Abel, "Medical Care of Veterans," 757–60; Laurence Z. Rubenstein et. al., "The Sepulveda VA Geriatric Evaluation Unit," *Journal of the American Geriatrics Society*, vol. 32 (July 1984): 503–10; Rubenstein et al., "Effectiveness of a Geriatric Evaluation Unit," *New England Journal of Medicine*, vol 311 (December 27, 1984): 1,664–70; Rubenstein et al., "Growth of the Teaching Nursing Home," *Journal of the American Geriatrics Society*, vol. 38 (January 1990): 73–8; Walter A. Forred et al., "An Educational Report," *Military Medicine*, vol. 157 (November 1992): 586–90.

45 Veterans Administration, *Geriatric Research, Education, and Clinical Centers: FY 1985 Summary of Program Activities* (Washington, DC: VA, 1986); John A. Gronvall, "VA Cabinet Status More than Gesture," *U.S. Medicine* (January 1989): 13. Marsha Goodwin and John E. Morley, "Geriatrics Research, Education, and Clinical Centers: Their Impact in the Development of American Geriatrics," *Journal of the American Geriatrics Society*, vol. 42 (1994): 1,012–19.

46 Terrie Wetle and John W. Rowe, *Older Veterans: Linking VA and Community Resources* (Cambridge: Harvard University Press, 1984).

system's extraordinary role in training physicians and nurses. From roughly 16,000 medical residents in 1960, DVA's program has expanded to 105,000 trainees from 1,000 professional schools by the 1987–8 academic year.[47] The VA network now includes nearly 1,000 medical, dental, and associated health centers, including some, like Louisiana State University's clinical program in Shreveport, initially encompassed entirely by the local VA hospital.

In sum, because of its mandate to care for elderly veterans, the federal government has been a pioneer in gerontology and geriatrics. For veterans and their widows, the system's pensions and in-kind benefits constituted a de facto welfare state before the New Deal.[48] The VA's accomplishments in the health-care sphere are equally impressive. Most experts within and outside of the VA, however, do not value the significance of veterans' programs in the historical context of U.S. social-welfare and health-care policy-making. Nor do they appreciate that the VA often has been a pacesetter by default, its achievements resulting from happenstance more than design. This myopia is regrettable, because DVA's capacity to meet its geriatric imperative is now in jeopardy. The predicament results as much from incipient organizational gridlock and lingering confusion over the VA's commitment to aging research and training as it does from agency rivalries, interest group politics, and budgetary constraints.

The current policy problem

On March 15, 1989, the Department of Veterans Affairs became the fourteenth cabinet, a "promotion" that should be increasing its visibility and resources. Actually, DVA's share of the federal budget has fallen dramatically during the twentieth century. Veterans' pensions accounted for roughly 40 percent of all federal dollars spent during the Progressive period. By 1946, even with the GI bill, the VA received only 7.5 percent of all federal allocations; now less than 2 percent of the national budget is ear-

---

47 John A. Gronvall, "The VA's Affiliation with Academic Medicine," *Academic Medicine* (February 1989): 63; J. William Hollingsworth and Philip K. Bondy, "The Role of Veterans Affairs Hospitals in the Health Care System," *New England Journal of Medicine*, vol. 322 (June 28, 1990): 1,851-7; *Proceedings of the Commission on the Future Structure of Veterans Health Care*, part 1: 385; U.S. Congress, Senate, Special Committee on Aging, *Developments on Aging, 1991*, (Washington, DC: Government Printing Office, 1992), pp. 407–10.
48 In 1929, 82.3 percent of all aged men and women who qualified for any sort of public or private pensions were getting war-related disability and survivor benefits. Roughly four-fifths of the dollars distributed through pensions came from the VA. See Achenbaum, *Old Age in the New Land*, p. 124.

marked for veterans' affairs.[49] Much of this change reflects the fact that the federal budget has expanded greatly since World War II, reducing the veterans' share commensurately. Part of the decline resulted from the deaths of the last Civil War veterans. But some of the reduction is due to budgetary politics. For the past decade, Washington has opted to reduce costs rather than to expand DVA services.[50] In the face of cutbacks and demands for cost containment, the House Committee on Veterans' Affairs routinely requested funds to make up part of DVA's deficit and to allocate more resources to cover services for older veterans.[51] Other lawmakers recognize the seriousness of the problem:

> The VA system offers a more comprehensive array of health, social and economic services to veteran beneficiaries than do other federal programs. However, it is yet to be seen whether the current level and scope of the VA's long term care services will be adequate to meet the growing demand for this type of care. . . . In the short term, veterans and non-veterans alike are likely to feel the pinch of cost containment on all sides.[52]

Senior DVA officials disagree over the most appropriate course of action. Some urge that extended care become congressionally mandated or, at minimum, that higher priority be given to older, sicker, poorer segments of the aged population. "If we are a mature organization, we should opt for the tactic of emphasizing a small piece of the market," contends Marjorie Quandt, the director of strategic planning in the Veterans Health Service and Research Administration (VHS&RA). "Population data indicates this is the population 65 plus, even 75 plus. . . . It means greatly increased investment in gerontology."[53] The DVA's recent chief medical directors, how-

49 Figures from memorandum to members of Geriatrics and Gerontology Advisory Committee from Frederico Juarbe, Veterans of Foreign Wars, May 16, 1988.

50 Linda E. Demkovich, "Taking on the VA," *National Journal* 17 (March 2, 1985): 496; Steve Blakely, "President Proposes Increase for Research, Development," *Congressional Quarterly*, vol. 44 (February 8, 1986): 244; Paralyzed Veterans of America, *Federal Health Budgets and Health Care for Veterans* (Washington, DC: Paralyzed Veterans of America, 1988), p. 16; Juarbe to Geriatrics and Gerontology Advisory Committee, p. 4, in Adelman's personal files.

51 Eli Ginzberg, "The VA Health Care System: The Budget Crunch and the Challenges Ahead," Issue Brief no. 515, 1989, pp. 2–3.

52 U.S. Congress, House, Select Committee on Aging, *Aging Veterans in an Aging Society*, 99th Cong. 1st sess., comm. pub. 99–555 (1986), pp. 4–5. See also Eli Ginzberg, "The Destablization of Health Care," *New England Journal of Medicine*, vol. 315 (September 18, 1986): 757–60; Robert L. Dickman et al., "An End to Patchwork Reform of Health Care," ibid., vol. 317 (October 22, 1987): 1,086–9.

53 Marjorie R. Quandt, "Strategic Planning in DM&S," remarks to the Conference of the American College of Health Care Executives, February 13, 1989, p. 5. Ms. Quandt elaborated: "This does not mean a return to old soldiers' homes. It means shared residencies for acute care in lesser numbers than 1990. . . . It will require more GEUs, expanded

ever, have been disinclined to earmark additional funds for research and training in geriatrics. "The VA has significantly expanded its capacity to deliver medical care on the basis of stable appropriation support," Dr. John Gronvall testified, begging the issue. Nor is Gronvall's assertion merely a rhetorical ploy.[54] Strategic planning projections make little reference to gerontology, geriatrics, or research in aging in setting forth VHS&RA's basic goals, mission, and activities.[55] Despite a steady decline in the number of acute care beds since 1973, only 325 of the 13,000 beds closed in fiscal years 1987 and 1988 were converted to long-term care.[56] Such ambivalence impedes VA policy-making as officials prepare to care for a smaller, but older, population. But uncertainty about the relative status of geriatrics and extended care in DVA's mission is hardly limited to its top executives. Dubiety grips congressional committees and veterans' organizations that have forged close ties with VA bureaucrats since World War II.

Like the gray lobby, veterans' groups operate in different spheres and embrace divergent aims. Various elements of the veterans' lobby interact like "an extended family, with many members of the family constantly feuding about how to reach a common goal: better treatment of the nation's veterans."[57] For much of the postwar period, Rep. Olin E. "Tiger" Teague (D-Texas), a highly decorated veteran, chaired the House Committee on Veterans Affairs, created under the Legislative Reorganization Act of 1946. The establishment of the Senate Veterans Affairs Committee twenty-five years later sparked competition on the Hill, fueled by the VA, over which could deliver the best legislative package.[58] A similar rivalry

GRECCs, and more staff for EENT, urology, orthopedics, neurology, psychiatry, and pharmacy than today."

54 Statement of John A. Gronvall before Subcommittee on Hospitals and Health Care, U.S. Congress, House, Committee on Veterans Affairs, September 7, 1988, pp. 3, 7. His unit had just won an award from the President's Council on Management Improvement.

55 Department of Medicine and Surgery, *Strategic Planning Projections, Fiscal Years 1988– 1992* (Washington, DC: VA, 1988), pp. 9–10. Chief Medical Director's Task Force Report on Fiscal Year 1989 Budget, *Final Report* (Washington, DC: VA, 1988), pp. 14, 17.

56 Congressional Budget Office, *Veterans Administration Health Care: Planning for Future Years* (April 1984), p. 10. See also letter from Cong. G. V. Montgomery to R. C. Adelman, April 17, 1989. Between August 1988 and February 1989, there actually was a 25 percent decline in contract community nursing home beds.

57 Timothy B. Clark, "The President Takes On The 'Iron Triangles' and So Far Holds His Own," *National Journal*, vol. 13 (March 28, 1981): 518; Hugh Heclo, "The Executive Establishment," in *The New American Political System*, ed. Anthony King (Washington, DC: American Enterprise Institute for Public Policy Research, 1978), pp. 88, 102–3. Thus far, the executive branch has had a less decisive role in selecting policy influentials, because it makes relatively fewer appointments to the VA's central administration than it does in other agencies. See Joel Havemann, "Carter Is Taking Pains in Picking His Plums," *National Journal*, vol. 8 (November 20, 1976): 1,652.

58 William H. Harader, *The Committee on Veterans Affairs*, (Ph.D. diss., Johns Hopkins University, Baltimore, 1968).

flourishes among veterans' organizations. By the mid-1980s, there were seventeen autonomous veterans' organizations chartered by Congress as well as fifteen other groups (not including bodies recognized by various states' departments of veterans' affairs). And just as there was a changing of the guard in 1946, when GAR commander Hiram R. Gale, aged 100, finally entrusted his organization's patriotic vocation to the American Legion, so too organizations lobbying for veterans of the two world wars have had to placate associations representing Vietnam-era personnel, who often pit the interests of older veterans against those of younger ones.[59] All these groups duly acknowledge the importance of research, but they pay only lip service to the scientific aims of gerontology and geriatrics. As a result, aging veterans become one, but only one, client; their demands often get lost as the VA with limited resources tries to serve several consumer groups at once.

To this network must be added university-based medical researchers and government health administrators who in their own distinctive way have both advanced and diverted DVA's geriatric mission. Policy Memorandum No. 2, an agreement signed in 1946 between medical school deans and the VA, reduced understaffing and improved the practice of VA clinical care while affording medical professors and residents greater research and training opportunities.[60] Complaints nonetheless persisted. The American Medical Association in the 1950s feared that the VA was going to usher in socialized medicine. Horror stories about misdiagnoses and the mishandled treatment of mental patients appeared in respected periodicals.[61] Despite the high marks given GRECCs, the overall quality of VA patient care remains in dispute. The National Academy of Science and the General Accounting Office have given facilities poor ratings in the areas of outpatient

59 On the GAR, see Wallace E. Davies, *Patriotism on Parade* (Cambridge: Harvard University Press, 1955); C. Joseph Pusateri, "Public Quarrels and Private Plans," *Missouri Historical Review*, vol. 62 (Fall 1967): 1–13. On the American Legion, John Lax and William Pencak, "Creating the American Legion," *The Southern Atlantic Quarterly*, vol. 81 (Winter 1982): 43–55; Roger Burlingame, "Embattled Veterans," *The Atlantic Monthly*, vol. 152 (October 1953): 385–96; Mary R. Dearing, *Veterans in Politics* (Baton Rouge: Louisiana State University Press, 1952), p. 497; Arnold Bortz, "American Legion's Influence Wanes on Capitol Hill," *National Journal*, vol. 2 (June 20, 1970): 1,308–14. On other groups, Charles G. Bolte, *The New Veteran* (New York: Reynal & Hitchcock, 1945); Office of the Administrator, *1984 Directory of Veterans Organizations* (Washington, DC: VA, 1984).

60 Sar A. Levitan and Karen A. Cleary, *Old Wars Remain Unfinished* (Baltimore: Johns Hopkins University Press, 1973), pp. 80–1; D. Mahony, "The Doctor and the Veterans Administration," *Modern Medicine*, vol. 14 (May 1946): 153–9.

61 William B. Walsh, "Who's Right–the A.M.A. or the Legion," *Medical Economics*, vol. 32 (January 1955): 150–5; Wallace Croatman, "That Veterans' Lobby," ibid., vol. 31 (November 1053): 128–34; E. J. Kahn, "Reporter at Large," *New Yorker*, vol. 28 (September 13, 1952): 82ff; Anon., "Veterans in a Snake Pit," *American Mercury*, vol. 83 (December 1956): 107–16.

services, performance of certain types of operations, supervision of residents, and handling of medical records.[62]

In retrospect, Policy Memorandum No. 2's language – "the purpose of both parties being unselfish, and there being no conflict of objectives, there can be no serious disagreement over methods" – sounds naive. Institutional priorities *do* diverge, given differences in orientations and objectives. "Health policy for veterans . . . sought to interrelate two organizational cultures – the university medical center and a large, complex federal bureaucracy. Neither of the organizations had experience with such a formal interrelationship, and neither attempted to understand the other's culture."[63] Thus it is not surprising that the president of the Association of American Medical Colleges should object "to the practice of some medical schools using the VA as a farm club." The DVA's medical administrators and researchers too often accept informal rewards or defer unduly to views enunciated by powerful medical schools deans and chairs. Or, they try to change DVA's internal politics by promoting research initiatives in medical schools that will loop back and alter VHS&RA priorities.[64]

A 1947 report to the House Committee on Veterans' Affairs prophetically had warned about such possible conflicts of interest. The VA "should see to it that the hospital does not become a training ground for medical students rather than a veterans' hospital with the veterans receiving proper treatment."[65] Officials concede that prevailing trends in academic medicine diminish the VA's ability to fulfill its geriatric mission. "The 'graying' of our population," John Gronvall (himself a former medical school dean) noted, "in the short run has probably weakened the partnership between the VA and academic medicine, while in the long run I believe that it can remarkably strengthen the partnership."[66] Specialized care for the elderly remains a fledgling venture in the medical school hierarchy: There are only a few geriatrics departments in America, and the first board certifications have just occurred. The prevailing reward system puts a premium on biomedical research that utilizes the latest technology and promises powerful

62 U.S. General Accounting Office, *Financial Management: An Assessment of the VA's Major Processes* (Washington, DC: Government Printing Office, 1986). See also, "VA, HUD, Independent Agencies Provisions, *Congressional Quarterly Almanac* (1991): 521. For a more sanguine view, see Charles B. Smith and Mark Wolcott, "Veterans Health Care: Lessons for a National Health Care System," *Annals of Internal Medicine*, vol. 115 (December 1, 1991): 907–9.

63 Quoted in Rothstein, *American Medical Schools*, p. 280.

64 Robert G. Petersdorf, "The VA – Medical School Partnership: The Medical School Perspective," *Journal of Medical Education*, vol. 62 (March 1987): 154; Harvey M. Sapolsky, "America's Socialized Medicine," *Public Policy*, vol. 25 (Summer 1977): 259–382.

65 Quoted in Robert Klein, *Wounded Men, Broken Promises* (New York: Macmillan, 1981), p. 48.

66 John A. Gronvall, "The VA–Medical School Partnership," *Journal of Medical Education*, vol. 62 (March 1987): 161.

interventions in acute-care delivery.[67] This is fine for VA scientists doing biogerontology, but not for those doing "home and environment assessment" or investigating "patient and caregiver education and counseling."

Thus the relative neglect of geriatrics and extended care within the VA is reinforced by views held by its respected partners on the outside. Congress receives conflicting expert advice about how to handle graying veterans. Service organizations are aware of aging issues, but they have other special interests to defend. Medical officials in DVA embrace the biases of an academic medical establishment just beginning to take geriatrics seriously. One other element is worth noting: Old-age entitlements rest on a shakier foundation than, say, combat-related disabilities.

"Benefits," in DVA's language, take the form either of "compensation" or "pensions." During the past century, as was the case with other federal welfare policies, age-specific criteria came to be used in deciding who was eligible for veterans' benefits and entitlements.[68] Many veterans and their dependents before the 1880s *happened* to be old when they first received pensions or land bounties, but it was not their age that made them eligible. Civil War pensions, as we have seen, did base entitlements on old age per se. Spanish-American War veterans only had to be fifty-five to qualify for pensions after 1933. Between 1971 and 1986, all veterans over sixty-five were eligible for free VA medical care regardless of financial need. So, for much of this century, the fact that benefits were age-based and the average age of beneficiaries was increasing would have seemed to have set the stage for VA officials to commit more and more funds to age-based research problems.

This did not occur, because veterans' programs differ from other entitlement programs in two key respects. First, veterans' benefits, unlike Social Security checks, have been reduced. The first cut occurred two years after the first non-service-connected Revolutionary War pension was granted; Congress in 1820 imposed a stringent test to reduce the pool of potential recipients. Older pensioners living in Confederate states, moreover, were dropped from the federal rolls in 1862. Under an Act to Maintain the Credit of the U.S. Government (1933), Franklin Delano Roosevelt slashed the budget of VA hospitals by 23 percent and of domiciliary units

---

67 Kenneth M. Ludmerer, *Learning to Heal* (New York: Basic, 1985); Paul Starr, *The Transformation of American Medicine* (New York: Basic, 1983).

68 "Compensation" consists of payments to veterans and their families for disabilities and deaths related to military service. "Pensions" are payments for disabilities unrelated to military service. For more on entitlements, see W. Andrew Achenbaum, "The Meaning of Risk, Right, and Responsibility in Aging America," in *What Does It Mean to Grow Old?* ed. Thomas R. Cole and Sally Gadow (Durham, NC: Duke University Press, 1986), pp. 63–98; idem, *Social Security: Visions and Revisions* (New York: Cambridge University Press, 1986), pp. 220–1. See also "Health Care Funding Tops Veterans Agenda," *Congressional Quarterly*, vol. 47 (Feburary 4, 1989): 218.

by 40 percent. Nor have cuts been made only in times of national emergency. Lyndon Baines Johnson in 1965 tried to save $25 million by eliminating eleven VA hospitals, seventeen regional offices and four nursing homes; he settled for half of the package.[69] Second, DVA in the face of fiscal constraints has contracted its geriatric mandate by substituting stricter eligibility criteria than chronological age. The Veterans' Health-Care Amendments of 1986 (P.L. 99-272), for instance, established three categories of hospital eligibility based on need. Older veterans no longer are automatically entitled to extended care.[70] That two-thirds of the current elderly veterans still meet eligibility requirements despite the elimination of the sixty-five-year-old baseline underscores the connection between poverty and ill health in late life among DVA's target population at risk. But so far there has been little willingness to seek new funds from Congress to increase DVA's capacity to meet the needs of *all* the veterans who require nursing-home care.[71] This trend tends to diminish the focus on chronological age even as the VA beneficiary pool grows older.

Should Congress increase DVA budgets and facilities to accommodate aging veterans? Does "veteranship" nowadays still carry moral legitimacy? Has the political clout of "that old gray line" diminished? There is no consensus about the future of aging veterans' entitlements, nor much thinking about the issues at stake.[72] A persuasive case can be made for according older veterans' special treatment. "Our country has a long-standing policy of compensating veterans for their past contributions by providing them with numerous advantages," opined Chief Justice William H. Rehnquist in 1983. "This policy has always been deemed to be legitimate"[73] Yet no DVA hospital was ever designed to be as grand as Les Invalides or Chelsea. Preferential treatment in employment can no longer

69 William Pyrle Dillingham, *Federal Aid to Veterans, 1917-1941* (Gainesville: University of Florida Press, 1952); Byron Stinson, "Paying the Debt," *Civil War Times Illustrated*, vol. 9 (July 1970): 20–9; Donald J. Lisio, "The United States," in *The War Generation*, ed. Stephen R. Ward (Port Washington: Kennikat Press, 1975), 38–58; John D. Weaver, "Bonus March," *American Heritage*, vol. 14 (June 1963): 18–23, 92–3.

70 For the rules from the consumers' perspective, see Veterans Administration, *Federal Benefits for Veterans and Dependents* (Washington, DC: Government Printing Office, 1987).

71 As a working goal, Secretary Edward Derwinski said, the VA planners have tried to reach roughly 15 percent of the population eligible for care since the early 1980s. See U.S. Congress, House, Committee on Veterans' Affairs, *Health Care Services for Aging Veterans*, Serial 101-8, April 13, 1989, p. 99.

72 For good starting places, see Morris Janowitz, "Military Institutions and Citizenship in Western Societies," *Armed Forces and Society*, vol 2 (February 1976): 185–204; James B. Jacobs, *Socio-Legal Foundations of Civil-Military Relations* (New Brunswick: Transaction Books, 1986).

73 Rehnquist quoted in *Proceedings of the Commission on the Future Structure of Veterans Health Care*, Part 1: 435. For a more elastic view of "veteranship," see Douglas W. Nelson, "Alternative Images of Old Age as the Bases for Policy," in *Age or Need?* ed. Bernice L. Neugarten (Beverly Hills, CA: Sage, 1982), p. 157.

be justified, some analysts claim, since those veterans who need it least benefit the most. Successive surveys of World War II survivors have found veterans healthier and more economically secure on average than their male peers who did not serve. Many are eligible for old-age benefits from Social Security, private pensions, and health-care plans in addition to VA assistance.[74] Other kinds of questions arise. Should elderly veterans be entitled to better care and greater benefits than Vietnam-era veterans? Does the Agent Orange controversy show, as Vietnam-era victims of this tragic form of chemical warfare claim, that the VA's mission is to "limit the liability of Government for the wages of war?"[75] Is the clinical care provided by the VA for the elderly less costly than that in the private sector? If the aged veteran does not deserve special status, should the VA rely on others besides its own research faculty to do gerontologic research?

"The least justifiable pension," wrote Willard Waller in 1944, "is that which goes to all war veterans who have attained a certain age, their physical condition and financial standing being disregarded."[76] Such a sentiment doubtless would be widely supported today. Indeed, only service-connected pensions have really enjoyed solid support since World War II. A 1954 Roper poll found 86 percent of veterans favored medical care for service-connected disabilities, but only 22 percent could justify non-service-connected care and a mere 13 percent supported broad eligibility for pensions. A 1971 Harris survey of Vietnam-era veterans detected little change in views.[77] Yet, in weighing future options, policymakers must acknowledge

74 Isser Woloch, *The French Veteran* (Chapel Hill: University of North Carolina Press, 1979); Marcus Cunliffe, *Soldiers & Civilians* (Boston: Little, Brown, 1968); A. O. Genung, "The Much-Abused War Pensioner," *Arena*, vol. 20 (September 1898): 404–16; Gregory B. Lewis and Mark A. Emmert, "Who Pays for Veterans' Preference?" *Administration & Society*, vol. 16 (November 1984): 328–45. For surveys, see Robert J. Havighurst, *The American Veteran Back Home* (New York: Longmans, Green, 1951); John E. Booth, "Veterans: Our Biggest Privileged Class," *Harper's Magazine*, vol. 217 (July 1958): 19–25; Veterans Administration, *The Veteran Age 65 and Over* (Washington, DC: VA, March 1968); J. Peter Mattila, "G.I. Bill Benefits and Enrollments," *Social Science Quarterly*, vol. 59 (December 1978): 535–45; Jere Cohen et al., "Military Service Was an Educational Disadvantage to Vietnam-Era Personnel," *Sociology and Social Research*, vol. 70 (January 1986): 206–8.

75 Severo and Milford, *Wages of War*, p. 422; James B. Jacobs and Dennis McNamara, "Vietnam Veterans and the Agent Orange Controversy," *Armed Forces & Society*, vol. 13 (Fall 1986): 57–79. That the VA uses different evaluating criteria from other agencies such as the Health Care Financing Administration (HCFA) adds to difficulties in establishing a basis for comparison. See Hollingsworth and Bondy, "VA's Affiliation," p. 1854.

76 Willard Waller, *The Veteran Comes Back* (New York: Dryden Press, 1944).

77 Holman Harvey, "Must We Follow the VA Route to Socialized Medicine?" *Reader's Digest*, vol. 64 (March 1954): 47–51; Paul Starr, "The $12 Billion Misunderstanding," *Washington Monthly*, vol. 5 (November 1973): 56. No references in these surveys were made to the priority to be accorded geriatric and gerontologic research in the VA.

the ephemeral nature of public opinion. After all, in 1979, 75 percent of all veterans did not realize they were at the time eligible to free nursing-home care: If they were in a medical crisis, rediscovering their veteran status would have been advantageous. A 1983 Harris survey reported, moreover, that current utilization rates of VA hospitals probably underrepresent future demands. Most aging veterans say that they have a positive attitude about VA care and expect to end up there when necessary. But few World War II survivors have yet entered a facility, and the situation is too fluid to predict with any certainty.[78]

The VA's gerontologic and geriatric imperative

By the turn of the century, more than a third of all U.S. veterans will be at least sixty-five.[79] Of the 38 million men and women who ever served in the Armed Forces, 28 million are still alive. Almost two-thirds of all American males sixty-five and over will be veterans in 2000. The number of veterans surviving past seventy-five, that subset of the elderly population most likely to require financial and medical assistance, has tripled in the past two decades.[80] The needs of these older veterans are diverse. Paralyzed and disabled veterans and their advocates focus on late-life vicissitudes as their constituencies age. Many members of minority groups, who compose roughly a quarter of the VA user population, receive minimal or no Social Security and Medicare benefits; some are ineligible for Medicaid due to program cutbacks.[81] Almost 45 percent of the veterans using DVA medical

---

78 Veterans Administration, *Survey of Aging Veterans* (Washington, DC: Office of Reports and Statistics, 1984); Phil Keisling, "Soldiers of Good Fortune," *Washington Monthly*, vol. 15 (May 1983): 21–8.

79 This is not the largest proportion in U.S. history. Sixty-three percent of all veterans were over sixty-five in 1910, as men who had fought in the Civil War reached old age. Calculated from data in U.S. Department of Commerce, *Historical Statistics of the United States, Colonial Times to 1970* (Washington, DC: Government Printing Office, 1975), part 2, p. 1,144. The median age of all veterans is fifty-four years, two decades greater than the median age of the population as a whole.

80 Veterans Administration, *The VA Today: Meeting Tomorrow's Challenges* (1988); Allan L. Damon, "Veterans' Benefits," *American Heritage*, vol. 27 (June 1976): 49; Veterans Administration, Office of Strategic Planning, "Update of the 'Demographics'", December 1988, pp. 14, 18. A historical comparison underscores the significance of these recent trends. Civil War survivors dominated the veterans' ranks in 1910, but that group still made up only 31.1 percent of the U.S. male population over sixty-five and 44.8 percent of its native-born subset.

81 William Frank Page, "Why Veterans Choose Veterans Administration Hospitalization," *Medical Care*, vol. 20 (March 1982): 308–20. U.S. Veterans Administration, *Caring for the Older Veteran* (Washington, DC: Government Printing Office, 1984), part 2, p. 14. Women veterans, however, use facilities less than their male counterparts because of lower awareness of benefit programs. See Linda DePauw Grant, "Harris Survey Provides Data on Women Vets," *Minerva*, vol. 3 (Winter 1985): 25–9.

facilities have no insurance coverage of any kind.[82] Lots of other groups have a stake in veterans' affairs. The DVA currently serves a third of all American families, including households with veterans' widows and dependents who historically have received old-age pensions and benefits.[83]

The DVA's cumulative successes and failures in delivering coordinated, comprehensive health-care services to large numbers of eligible, elderly veterans should provide valuable lessons as policymakers refine strategies and principles for allocating limited resources in an equitable, efficient manner. With 172 medical centers, 126 hospital-based nursing-home units, 35 domiciliaries (including 10 for the homeless), and 340 outpatient clinics, the VA operates America's largest medical complex. Its reach extends to contract care in non-VA hospitals and community nursing homes, and support care by 67 State Veterans Homes in 40 states among other arrangements.[84] Annually, the VA treats more than 1.1 million inpatients and handles more than 21.4 million outpatient visits and 27,000 nursing-home admissions.

Asked how DVA would respond to the needs of growing numbers of aging veterans, former Secretary Edward Derwinski declared: "I told our people to make sure they've dusted off all their plans and . . . to be ready for it. We don't need to study it. . . . We don't need to go back to the drawing board for new plans. They'd better have some good ones ready to go. If they don't, they've been derelict in their duties."[85] Basically, the plans recommended by various groups in recent years cluster around four options: (1) maintain the status quo; (2) strengthen the VA's internal capabilities to promote geriatrics and extended care; (3) create a National Geriatric Service; (4) transfer the VA's geriatric mission to other public or private agencies.[86]

Of these options, probably only one will survive negotiations. Embracing a reactive posture under option 1 is a surefire recipe for ensuring greater long-term costs. Such a strategy, after all, was adopted by nineteenth-

82 John A. Gronvall, "Low Insurance Veterans in the VA Health Care System," *Health Affairs*, vol. 6 (Spring 1987): 167–75.

83 Richard Cowan, "Senate OKs Cabinet Status, Judicial Review for Vets," *Congressional Quarterly*, vol. 46 (July 16, 1988): 1,977.

84 "Report of the VA's Activities on Behalf of Older Persons," Mimeo prepared for U.S. Senate Special Committee on Aging, 1988, p. 2; see also, Thomas T. Yoshikawa, "United States Department of Veterans Affairs Health Care for Aging Veterans," *Facts and Research in Gerontology* (1992): 432; Special Committee on Aging, *Developments in Aging, 1991*, p. 398. By way of comparison: The VA operated 171 hospitals, 209 outpatient clinics, 18 domiciliaries, and 84 nursing care units in 1975. See Herald Stringer, *The Older American Veteran* (Los Angeles: National Senior Citizens Law Center, 1975), p. 8.

85 Quoted in statement of Hon. Lane Evans, chairman of House Veterans Affairs Subcommittee on Oversight and Investigations, in hearings on health-care services for aging veterans, April 13, 1989, pp. 5–6.

86 W. Andrew Achenbaum, "The Politics of Aging: The Geriatric Imperative of the Department of Veterans Affairs," *Journal of Aging & Social Policy*, vol. 3 (1991): 33–50.

century Congresses in responding to veterans' demands for service-connected pensions and benefits. Adopting option 3 seems premature, because DVA does not yet have the relevant experience to assume a role as senior partner in forming a National Geriatrics Service. Critics of DVA will argue, moreover, that the agency has been insensitive to gender-specific issues.[87] The proposal to dismantle DVA (option 4) has a distinguished pedigree dating back to the Hoover Commission on reorganizing the federal bureaucracy (1949) and embellished by conservative groups such as the Heritage Foundation, which want veterans placed into "more efficient" private hospitals.[88] But neither the public nor the private sector has the capacity to absorb an unexpected and large number of elderly patients. For instance, despite evidence that the VA's geriatric-evaluation units have been effective in reducing costs and speeding recovery, few hospitals have facilities to assess patients' physical, social, and emotional problems. According to a recent study, such units are closing at roughly the same rate that new ones open. A significant number of acute-care hospitals have decided against creating a GEU.[89]

In contrast, option 2 – strengthening DVA's capacity to serve aging veterans – presumes that gerontologic research and geriatric care can be "provided in a variety of institutional and noninstitutional settings and includes acute, ambulatory and chronic care services which are both medically and socially oriented."[90] It acknowledges the need for targeting in an era of limited resources. A VA task force report, *Caring for the Older Veteran* (1983), for example, proposed setting eligibility at age seventy-five for comprehensive services. The report also voted that the VA "has given strong support to research in the biological, clinical, psychosocial, rehabilitative, and health service delivery aspects of aging. . . . By understanding the net-

---

87 L. Rossi, *Report of the Veterans Administration Advisory Committee on Women Veterans* (Washington, DC: Veterans Administration, July 1984); Maureen P. Schuler et al., "Psychological Services Offered to Female Veterans," *Journal of Clinical Psychology*, vol. 42 (July 1986): 668–75.

88 National Academy of Sciences, *Study of Health Care for American Veterans* (Washington, DC: Government Printing Office, 1977), p. 279; Keisling, "Old Soldiers," p. 27. Even those friendly to the VA have noted some advantages to treating chronically ill, older patients in general hospitals. See J. F. Casey, "The Care and Treatment of the Elderly, Chronically Ill Neuropsychiatric Patient in the Veterans Administration," *Southern Medical Journal*, vol. 51 (January 1958): 31–4.

89 "Hospitals in Stall on Geriatric Evaluation Units," *Productive Aging News*, issue 72 (June 1993), p. 8.

90 Veterans Administration, *Caring for the Older Veteran*, Report of the Special Medical Advisory Group Task Force on the VA Geriatric Plan (July 18, 1983), p. i. See also, idem, *Health Care of the Aging Veteran*, Report of the Geriatrics and Gerontology Advisory Committee (April 1983), pp. 3, 54. See also the recommendations made by Veterans of Foreign Wars' Dennis Cullinan before the Subcommittee on Oversight and Investigations, H.R. Committee on Veterans' Affairs, April 13, 1989, p. 6.

works of causality in aging, it may be possible to identify a limited number of major events or common denominators of changes which establish the preconditions for various age-related diseases."[91] Encouraging the VA to focus its gerontology agenda on major priorities – biomedical research, rehabilitation, and health-services delivery – might also improve integration within the system. The House Select Committee on Aging in 1984 gave priority to research focused on the needs of minorities and ethnics. The option reaffirms the view of the National Research Council (1977), which urged vigorous support of DVA research as a way to promote excellence overall.

There is bound to be sharp resistance from physicians, nurses, surgeons, and planners who do not want to give geriatrics greater visibility within DVA. The specter of generational inequity will be raised. Managers and care givers may be directed to oversee geriatrics services with nothing but a title as a reward. If DVA's budget remains tight, then new funds for aging veterans will have to come from other departmental accounts. This guarantees sharp disputes among experts, possibly struggles between medical and lay management. Even a budget-neutral arrangement is likely to end up costing more, as veterans survive longer.

Despite such obstacles, what makes option 2 so compelling is that DVA "provides the opportunity to test the impact of an array of services under a single administrative auspices. Because program control is vested in a single organization it is possible for various VAs to make modifications and observe their effect."[92] The DVA can serve as a laboratory for geriatrics and extended care in the nation at large. With the VA's Geriatrics and Gerontology Advisory Committee and several service organizations urging the best geriatric care possible, with growing interest for geriatrics in medical schools, and some support in DVA and Congress for this mandate, the moment appears propitious.

An analysis of the four-volume *Proceedings of the Commission on the Future Structure of Veterans Health Care* (1991), however, suggests that VA decision makers are not ready to put an aging policy in place. "Our customers – our veterans – have high expectations. . . . Frankly, they're getting older. That seems to be the major challenge we face," declared DVA Secretary Edward Derwinski in his opening statement. "We're barely keeping up with the challenges and responsibilities we have to an aging veteran population." Yet five paragraphs later, Derwinski amended his assessment. He identified "three very major challenges in the patient population," add-

91 Veterans Administration, *Caring for the Older Veteran*, p. ii; Select Committee on Aging, *Aging Veterans in an Aging Society*, p. 13.
92 Robert L. Kane and Rosalie A. Kane, "The Extent and Nature of Public Responsibility for Long Term Care," in *Policy Options in Long Term Care*, ed. J. Meltzer et al. (Chicago: University of Chicago Press, 1981).

ing disabled and mentally ill veterans to older ones.[93] Derwinski's deputy, Anthony Principi, testified that the VA's agenda consisted of patient care, education, research, and backup for the Department of Defense's health system.[94] Jesse Brown, who became Clinton's DVA secretary, declared that "the VA should be *THE* national model for rehabilitation medicine in specialties including amputations, orthotic/prosthetic evaluations and training, spinal cord injury, head injury, independent living training, housing, and employment evaluation, training and placement in coordination with VA's Vocational Rehabilitation Service."[95] No wonder former GSA president John Rowe detected "tension or disagreement . . . between two scenarios . . . one in which the VA provides primary care and expert care in particular populations, be they geriatrics, spinal damage, alcohol, drug addition, et cetera, so that it has certain comparative advantages, and a second scenario in which the VA maintains a freestanding, full thickness, competitive, high quality health care system."[96]

The two models for integrating VA health care are at odds. One, a *geriatric* paradigm set forth by a subcommittee headed by Rowe, calls for implementing an interdisciplinary, vertically integrated, acute and long-term system of geriatric care, in which GRECCs link training and research in clinical programs. This model seems to be the one Secretary Brown had in mind when he decided to convert 5,000 acute-care beds by 1998 and to build additional nursing-home facilities.[97] The alternative is an *ambulatory* model, which promises to provide comprehensive care outside of a hospital environment. A notion discussed in VA circles for more than two decades, the ambulatory approach stresses epidemiology, decision analysis, technology assessment, and cost-effective utilization of resources. Advocates liked its presumed cost-saving features.[98] The debate over these two models is reminiscent of the discussions prompted in 1978, when one set of experts claimed that "the VA is in a position to provide care for the elderly outside institutions and can be a forerunner in development programs as models for other government agencies and voluntary associations," and another

---

93 Edward Derwinski in *Proceedings of the Commission on the Future Structure of Veterans Health Care*, part 1, pp. 10–11.

94 Ibid., p. 535.

95 Ibid., p. 466. Brown at the time was executive director of Disabled American Veterans.

96 Ibid., p. 666.

97 Ibid., part IV. The model appears in Appendix 1; see Rowe's commentary, ibid., part 3, p. 2,571ff. See also Peter H. Stone, "At Their Service," *National Journal*, vol. 25 (June 19, 1993): 1,562–4.

98 For an early statement, see the VA report in U.S. Congress, Senate, Special Committee on Aging, *Developments on Aging, 1970* (Washington, DC: Government Printing Office, 1971), p. 304; see also *Proceedings of the Commission on the Future of Veterans Health*, part 1: 376, and the American Legion's criticism, ibid., part 2: 2,150. Aging veterans were estimated to represent 32 percent of all users of the ambulatory system.

group of experts who predicted that such recommendations would be ignored.[99]

For years, DVA has sincerely tried to honor its commitments to aging veterans, but it has been reluctant to expand its noninstitutional care programs, highlight its geriatric mission, or convert hospital beds to nursing-home beds. "An insulated protectorate," the VA thus far has been a "political afterthought" in health-care policy talks. Claiming that the system's very survival is now at stake, Rep. G. V. "Sonny" Montgomery, who chairs the House Committee on Veterans Affairs, excoriates the "VA's failure for more than a decade to position itself to effectively care for aging veterans."[100] Groups such as the Paralyzed Veterans of America also chide DVA for its "lag in preparing for the impact of veterans' aging," noting the continuing relevance of its comprehensive study published in 1984.[101] The DVA's unwillingness to rearrange its priorities along geriatric lines partly results from blindness to the implication of the health-services and rehabilitation research it has supported. But the agency's ambivalence about the role that gerontology can play in the service of aging veterans might also reveal a broader cultural current – a failure of imagination whenever scientists and experts think about the future of aging research and try to communicate their specific ideas to lay audiences.

99 See the three commentaries by Arnold Relman, S. J. Farber, and Eli Ginzberg in *New England Journal of Medicine*, vol. 298 (March 16, 1978): 623–8.

100 G. V. Montgomery, "The VA's Sickbed," *Washington Post*, vol. 115, July 2, 1992: A21. The phrase "insulated protectorate" comes from John K. Iglehart, "The VA Medical Care System and the Private Sector," *New England Journal of Medicine*, vol. 313 (December 12, 1985): 1,552–6.

101 Paralyzed Veterans of America, *The VA Responsibility in Tomorrow's National Health Care System* (Washington, DC: PVA, 1992), p. 75.

Conclusion

The current state of the field

There never was a golden age in gerontology's past. "Gerontologists who have lived long enough to represent their subject matter will recall the days when our field was all but invisible within the panoply of established scientific disciplines," recollects Robert Kastenbaum. "We often described ourselves as a____with a special interest in aging and the aged. (This blank would be filled variously by 'psychologist,' 'biologist,' 'economist,' etc.)."[1] Still, many U.S. researchers in the early 1960s expressed high hopes for the field's future. Clark Tibbitts pointed out that "half our scientific knowledge has been gained since 1950." Investigators were excited by the opportunities for combining basic and applied research on aging. As Leonard Cain put it, "This new and burgeoning field represents a peculiar amalgam of scientific research and reformist commitment with the attributes of a major social movement."[2] By the end of the decade, other prominent gerontologists spoke more guardedly. "In spite of the enormous increase in research output and in spite of our pride in the advancement of knowledge, superficially seen as the result of this increase," declared two Gerontological Society (GSA) presidents, Carl Eisdorfer and Powell Lawton, "our concepts of research and theory have not advanced beyond viewpoints of the nineteenth century."[3]

1 Robert Kastenbaum, "Visiting Hours in Shadowland," *The Gerontologist*, vol. 32 (February 1992): 133. Kastenbaum has been a trailblazer in gerontology and thanatology.
2 Clark Tibbitts, "Social Aspects of Aging," *Journal of the American Geriatrics Society*, vol. 11 (December 1963): 1,134; Leonard D. Cain, Jr., "Review" in *American Sociological Review*, vol. 29 (June 1964): 459.
3 Carl Eisdorfer and M. Powell Lawton, eds., *The Psychology of Adult Development and Aging* (Washington, DC: American Psychological Association, 1973), p. 55. Eisdorfer and Lawton's observation is ambiguous because they do not make clear their frame of reference.

Gerontology did not become a Big Science, but it grew more scientistic. "After a while," continues Kastenbaum, "there were enough of us blankety-blanks to persuade at least each other that we now had something resembling a coherent field of research, service, and education."[4] Leaders extolled "partnerships among the disciplines and professions."[5] A recent National Institute on Aging (NIA) Task Force on Aging Research identified eleven major topical areas on aging on the basis of a review of seventy-one different blue-ribbon reports and recommendations from 2,500 experts.[6] Geometrical increases in research affected all aspects of "the aging enterprise," without necessarily advancing gerontology as a science. Before World War II, Walter Pitkin and Lillien J. Martin had had to rely mainly on anecdotal evidence in studying people's capacity to "salvage" old age. In contrast, Barbara Silverstone and Elaine Brody in the early 1970s had at their disposal large bodies of scientific data as they began to write practical guides on elder care, which were not intended primarily to be contributions to the scientific literature. In anticipation of 1999, designated the "International Year of Older Persons," the International Federation on Ageing promotes cross-cultural analyses of social welfare and health care, but it does not offer a model for analyzing societal aging.[7] Higher demand for skilled personnel and greater sensitivity to the needs of a diverse population, in turn, have expanded career "lattices" and raised professional standards for delivering and evaluating services. David Peterson and associates at the University of Southern California, among others, indicate that many who work with older people lack basic training in specific knowledge areas.[8] Certi-

On the one hand, they may be bemoaning the lack of theory building in this twentieth-century field. On the other hand, they may be clinging to an Enlightenment hope that "total knowledge" is possible. For a more sanguine assessment, yet one that also notes the paucity of theoretical grounding, see Gordon F. Streib and Harold L. Orbach, "Aging," in *The Uses of Sociology*, ed. Paul F. Lazarsfeld, William H. Sewell, and Harold L. Wilensky (New York: Basic, 1967), pp. 612–40.

4 Kastenbaum, "Visiting Hours," p. 133.

5 J. Richard Connelly, "Partnerships Among the Disciplines and Professions," *AGHE Exchange*, vol. 15 (September/October 1991): 1; George Maddox, "Duke University Center for the Study of Aging and Human Development," in *Gerontology: The Next Generation* (Atlanta: Southern Regional Educational Board, 1992), pp. 5–7; Ajith Silva and Priyanthi Silva, "Is Gerontology Not a Discipline?" seminar paper, University of Massachusetts, Boston, Fall 1992.

6 Interim Report of the Task Force on Aging Research, December 1992, pp. 2–3.

7 Marcia G. Ory and Kathleen Bond, eds., *Aging and Health Care* (New York: Routledge, 1989); Bennett N. Rich and Martha Baum, *The Aging* (Pittsburgh: University of Pittsburgh Press, 1985); Barbara Silverstone and Helen Kandel Hyman, *You & Your Aging Parent* (New York: Pantheon, 1976); Elaine Brody, *Mental and Physical Health Practices of Older People: A Guide for Health Professionals* (New York: Springer, 1985); "Ten Years After the World Assembly on Aging," *Ageing International*, vol. 19 (December 1992): 10; on Pitkin and Martin, see W. Andrew Achenbaum, *Old Age in the New Land* (Baltimore: Johns Hopkins University Press, 1978), pp. 118, 227.

8 David A. Peterson and Pamela F. Wendt, "The Certification of Professionals in Gerontol-

fying professionals may not remedy the situation as much as advocates hope: Shortages are anticipated among health-care professionals who deal with aged patients and physician-scientists who do geriatric research.[9]

Thus, by the end of the twentieth century, gerontology has emerged as a field, not a scientific specialty. Indeed, some researchers on aging have begun to subvert the assumption that gerontology should be classified primarily as a "science." Experts trained in the humanities (among others, Thomas Cole, Carole Haber, H. R. Moody, and Kathleen Woodward) have utilized ways of thinking about aging in a rigorous, empirical manner – historical methods, Continental modes of philosophical inquiry, and psycho-linguistic criticism – to enrich our current understanding of the meanings and experiences of old age. Social scientists using ethnographic approaches and qualitative data have also called for a "critical gerontology" that challenges much of the field's epistemological girding.[10] "Gerontology remains a kind of shadowland today, despite all the studies, courses, conferences, publications, and service programs," Kastenbaum asserts. "Still looking for a home, gerontology is highly dependent on the whims of the academic/governmental complex. And here, with some charmed and legendary exceptions, we are flitting shadows indeed."[11] Bern-

ogy," *AGHE Exchange*, vol. 16 (November/December 1992): 1; David A. Peterson, Pamela F. Wendt, and Elizabeth B. Douglass, *Determining the Impact of Gerontology Preparation on Personnel in the Aging Network* (Washington, DC: Association for Gerontology in Higher Education, 1991).

9 As late as 1956, fifty of the nation's top sixty medical schools were opposed to creating a separate Department of Geriatrics. According to the Alliance for Aging Research, we currently are producing only a quarter of the geriatrics-trained physicians that we need; the gap is expected to widen until at least 2030. See Edmund Vincent Cowdry, "Preliminary Report of the Committee to Investigate Post-graduate Educational Opportunities and Residencies in Geriatrics and Gerontology," July 1956, GSA archives; Association of American Medical Colleges, "Physicians for the Twenty-First Century," *Journal of Medical Education* (November 1984), part 2. Current data in "Geriatrics – The Urgent Need for Investment," *Productive Aging*, issue 64 (June 1992): 1.

10 See, for instance, Thomas R. Cole et al., *Critical Voices and Visions* (New York: Springer, 1993); Mark R. Lubinsky and Andrea Sankar, "Extending the Critical Gerontology Prospective," *The Gerontologist*, vol. 33 (1993): 440–4. For non-U.S. examples, see Peter B. Stafford, "Towards a Semiotics of Old Age," in *The Semiotic Web 1988*, ed. Thomas A. Sebeok and Jean Umiker-Sebeock (Berlin: Mouton de Gruyter, 1989), pp. 271–99; Alfons Marcoen, "The Search for Meaning: Some Reflections from a Psychogerontological Perspective," *Ultimate Reality and Meaning*, vol. 16 (1994): 228-39; and Bryan S. Green, *Gerontology and the Construction of Old Age* (Hawthorne, NY: Aldine, 1993). *The Journal of Aging Studies*, edited by Jaber Gubrium, is becoming the major vehicle for disseminating this approach.

11 Kastenbaum, "Visiting Hours," p. 133. Gerontologists, of course, are not the only multidisciplinary group of researchers whose existence seems shadowy. Social psychologists once shared problems and citations; limited funds, modest advances in theory building, and turf battles with psychology and sociology departments have fragmented the field. Urban studies also languishes, in part because it tends to borrow rather than create intellectual capital. See William Sewell, "Some Reflections on the Golden Age of Interdiscipli-

ice L. Neugarten goes a step further, predicting "the end of gerontology" in a few decades. Chronological age, she asserts, is "not a useful concept" for research, education, or service delivery: "The study of aging as it is presently defined will become less and less viable as age becomes less a criterion of anything."[12]

Crossing Frontiers suggests two "internal" reasons why gerontologists' "claims to truth" have "little or no impact on the development of community-based knowledge."[13] The field's research partnerships and "tribal" networks are fragile. Researchers on aging do not yet possess distinctive models and methods; colleagues do not employ the same vehicles for evaluating and communicating results.[14] Big Science impedes consensus building in two other ways. Competition for resources has stiffened in recent decades. Faced with budget deficits and painful choices about priorities, officials typically deem "interdisciplinary programs" to be less "rigorous" than the "source" disciplines. "Programs that include policy studies" raise "an additional problem" in the minds of administrators, which explains why some gerontology centers have been cut or eliminated on campuses.[15]

nary Social Psychology," *Social Psychology Quarterly*, vol. 52 (1989): 88–97; James S. House, "The Three Faces of Social Psychology," *Sociometry*, vol. 40 (1977): 161–77; and Daniel Rich and Robert Warren, "The Intellectual Future of Urban Affairs," *The Social Science Journal*, vol. 17 (1980): 53–66. Some members of mainstream social science departments question whether their respective departments are truly enclosed by theories and methods. See Jack Amariglio, Stephen Resnick, and Richard Wolff, "Division and Difference in the 'Discipline' of Economics," *Critical Inquiry*, vol. 17 (August 1990): 108–37; Irving Louis Horowitz, *The Decomposition of Sociology* (New York: Oxford University Press, 1993); and David Ricci, *The Tragedy of Political Science* (New Haven, CT: Yale University Press, 1984).

12 Bernice L. Neugarten, "The End of Gerontology," [Northwestern University] *Center on Aging*, vol. 10 (Spring 1994): 1.

13 Stephen Cole, *Making Science* (Cambridge: Harvard University Press, 1992), p. 16; Thomas Gieryn, "Boundary-Work and the Demarcation of Science from Non-Science," *American Sociological Review*, vol.48 (December 1983): 781–95; Craig Calhoun, Edward LiPuma, and Moishe Postone, eds., *Bourdieu: Critical Perspectives* (Chicago: University of Chicago Press, 1993).

14 Tony Becher, "The Counter-Culture of Specialisation," *European Journal of Education*, vol. 25 (1990): 333–45; Paul J. DiMaggio and Walter Powell, "The Iron Cage Revisited," *American Sociological Review*, vol. 48 (1983): 147–60; Stephen Turner, "Paradigms and Productivity," *Social Studies of Science*, vol. 17 (1987): 35–58; Steve Smith, ed., *International Relations* (Oxford: Blackwell Publisher, 1985), p. 9; Donald T. Campbell, "A Tribal Model of the Social System Vehicle for Carrying Scientific Knowledge," *Knowledge*, vol. 2 (1979): 181–201.

15 Donald Kennedy, "Making Choices in the Research University," *Daedalus*, vol. 122 (Fall 1993): 132–6; Richard M. Freeland, *Academia's Golden Age* (New York: Oxford University Press, 1992), p. 11; William Bechtel, ed., *Integrating Scientific Disciplines* (The Hague: Nijhoff, 1986), p. 3. On the allocation of resources, see Roger Geiger, *Research and Relevant Knowledge* (New York: Oxford University Press, 1993); Joseph Martino, *Science Funding* (New Brunswick: Transaction Publishers, 1992); National Academy of Sciences, *The Behavioral and Social Sciences* (New York: Prentice-Hall, 1969); and D. L. Krantz

Meanwhile, new inquiries into hermeneutical discourse, which define alternative ways of interpreting Science, substantiate the value of (still tenuous) efforts to establish critical gerontology. Lately, philosophers distinguish between *understanding* and *explaining* phenomena across domains; they pay greater attention to gendered patterns of data and to incommensurate ways of interpreting ideas within biomedical, behavioral, and social domains.[16]

With a nod to C. Wright Mills and others who have stressed the importance of sustaining a self-conscious "scientific spirit," Carroll Estes and associates worry about the current state of "the gerontological imagination":

> The very strength of the field is also its weakness. We lack age disciplinary perspective or stronghold, while we also lack the models and support for truly interdisciplinary work. . . . The lack of a disciplinary stronghold means that both the theory and practice of gerontology is often fragmented among multiple disciplines, each with its own body of knowledge, traditions, theories, methods, and disciplinary prerogatives and parochialisms. There is little agreement as to what "gerontology" is, or, for that matter, what a "gerontologist" is.[17]

and Lynda Wiggins, "Personal and Impersonal Channels of Recruitment in the Growth of Theory," *Human Development*, vol. 16 (1973): 133–56.

16 On the hermeneutics of scientific discourse, see Fritz Maclup, "Are the Social Sciences Inferior?" *Society* (May/June 1988): 57–66; Nicholas Rescher, *The Limits of Science* (Berkeley and Los Angeles: University of California Press, 1984); Thomas Kuhn, "Panel Discussion on Specialization and Professionalization Within the University," *American Council on Learned Societies Newsletter*, vol. 36 (1985): 18–31; David R. Hiley, James F. Bohman, and Richard Shusterman, eds. *The Interpretive Turn* (Ithaca, NY: Cornell University Press, 1991); Richard Rorty, *Consequences of Pragmatism* (Minneapolis: University of Minnesota Press, 1979); and Pauline Marie Rosenau, *Post-Modernism and the Social Sciences* (Princeton, NJ: Princeton University Press, 1992); W. J. T. Mitchell, ed., *The Politics of Interpretation* (Chicago: University of Chicago Press, 1983); and Abraham Kaplan, *The Conduct of Inquiry* (San Francisco: Chandler Publishing, 1964). The literature on "gendered" science is growing. See Harriet Zuckerman, Jonathon R. Cole, and John T. Bruer, *The Outer Circle* (New York: Norton, 1991); and Joan E. Hartman and Ellen Messer-Davidow, eds., *(En)Gendering Knowledge* (Knoxville: University of Tennessee Press, 1991) for an introduction. For the ideas of two leading researchers on aging, see Bernice L. Neugarten, "The Aging Society and My Academic Life," in *Sociological Lives*, ed. Matilda White Riley (Newbury Pk., CA: Sage Publications, 1988), pp. 91–106; and Alice S. Rossi, *Seasons of a Woman's Life* (Amherst: University of Massachusetts: Social and Demographic Research Institute, July 1983).

17 Carroll L. Estes, Elizabeth A. Binney, and Richard Culbertson, "The Gerontological Imagination," *International Journal of Aging and Human Development*, vol. 50 (1992): 50. See also C. Wright Mills, *The Sociological Imagination* (New York: Oxford University Press, 1959); Warren Weaver, "Science and Complexity," *American Scientist*, vol. 36 (1948): 536–44; Rockefeller University, *Beyond Tomorrow*, a 75th Anniversary Conference (New York, March 8, 1976), pp. 31–2, 111; Edward Shils, "Science in the Public Arena," *American Scholar*, vol. 56 (Spring 1987): 196.

Many specialists in aging impose narrow boundaries on their subject. All sorts of "interdisciplinary amalgams" have been designated, ranging from anthropological gerontology (1976), applied gerontology (1963), critical gerontology (1988), cytogerontology (1974), dialectical gerontology (1975), experimental gerontology (1963), gerontotherapy (1949), hermeneutical gerontology (1988) to social gerontology (1958).[18] This proliferation of subfields attests to the lack of a shared agenda that cuts across, and is distinguishable from, other disciplines and specialties. It may reflect some practitioners' modest scientific sophistication. The technical complexity achieved by researchers on aging has not been matched by an accumulation of theoretical insights. Historical memories are short. E. V. Cowdry's 1939 handbook, I claim, heralded the "modern" era of gerontology. Yet *Problems of Ageing* is not mentioned in George Maddox's *The Encyclopedia of Aging* or many other contemporary references.[19] The low priority accorded to preserving the founders' papers or to maintaining libraries and collections, moreover, underlines a certain indifference about the foundations of gerontology.[20]

Some investigators have been willing to examine the field's myths and traditions in a critical way. In my opinion, Robert N. Butler's *Why Survive?: Being Old in America* (1975) conveyed the gerontologic imagination better than any "insider" writing on the subject. "An emotional appeal is not my primary intention," Butler declared. "I am concerned, rather, with an appeal to rationality and an examination of public policy toward the elderly." Choosing to make "heavy use of statistics rather than to rely on generalized case illustrations," Butler, a psychiatrist by training, showed how *ageism* (a term he coined in the late 1960s) made old age a tragedy and the waste of social services and human resources an "absurdity, all but

18 W. Andrew Achenbaum and Jeffrey S. Levin, "What Does *Gerontology* Mean?" *The Gerontologist*, vol. 29 (June 1989): 393–400. Since writing that essay, I should add two more subfields: "financial gerontology" (1976) traced in *Aging, Money and Life Satisfaction*, ed. Neal E. Cutler, Davis W. Gregg, and M. Powell Lawton (New York: Springer, 1991); and "qualitative gerontology," in a book by that title edited by Shulamit Reinhart and Graham Rowles (New York: Springer, 1988).

19 Nor is Cowdry or his work mentioned in the 1990 editions of the *Handbook of Biology and Aging* or the *Handbook of Aging and the Social Sciences*, though Lawrence Frank's contribution to the second edition of the Cowdry volume (1942) is quoted in the *Handbook of the Psychology of Aging*, p. 11. Alex Comfort cites an article from the third edition in *Biology of Senescence*; Finch includes Cowdry's name in the index but does not cite him in the text of *Longevity, Senescence, and the Genome*. Leonard Hayflick, on the other hand, emphasizes Cowdry in his *How and Why We Age*, pp. 3–4.

20 Ellen Messer-Davidow, David R. Shumway, David J. Sylvan, eds., *Knowledges* (Charlottesville: University Presses of Virginia, 1993), p. 45; Joyce A. Post, *Gerontology and Geriatrics Libraries and Collections in the United States and Canada* (Westport, CT: Greenwood, 1992); Sture Allen, ed., *Possible Worlds in Humanities, Arts and Sciences* (Hawthorne, NY: de Gruyter, 1989), pp. 33, 50.

inevitable."[21] *Why Survive?* won a Pulitzer prize; it has remained in print far longer than most books on aging.

No other academic researcher on aging, physician scientist, or social service practitioner has popularized gerontology to the public as effectively as "outsiders" writing on the subject. Betty Friedan intended *The Fountain of Age* (1993) to have the same impact on attitudes toward age as did her *Feminine Mystique* (1963). In the course of her decade-long project, Friedan incurred many debts from such "eminent gerontologists" as James Birren, Robert Butler, Margaret Clark, David Gutmann, Myrna Lewis, and John Rowe. But she did not list "gerontology" in the index. And in several places, Friedan expressed her "suspicion that the science of gerontology itself was perpetuating the fear and dread of age."[22] *The Fountain of Age* celebrates late-life wisdom and vitality to counterbalance "this strange predilection of gerontological experts for dealing with age only in terms of pathology, and what appeared to be a serious discomfort with any view of positive aspects of aging."[23] Ken Dychtwald also accentuates the potentials of human aging. Dychtwald was a twenty-three-year-old instructor at the Esalen Institute when he began to "practice yoga and share feelings with septuagenarians." Sixteen years later, the press was calling him "America's most visible expert on aging."[24] Dychtwald's major work, *Age Wave* (1987), had an initial printing of 150,000 copies and a $100,000 promotional budget. Full of facts, *Age Wave* was a "page turner" that conveyed an optimistic message: "The Age Wave will give us not merely the opportunity to live well and to live long, drawing much from life, but will also provide us with the time and energy to give more back, enriching society with special quality and deep experiences."[25] The message sold – by 1988 Dychtwald was charging $15,000 an appearance and had an impressive list of corporate clients.

Friedan and Dychtwald do not pretend to be scientists. Nor do they desire to capitalize on people's desire to be young. Yet there are latter-day charlatans and alchemists who do prey on people's fears of aging. A mere 7,000 GSA members receive *The Gerontologist* compared to the 300,000 who buy *Longevity* magazine, which features antiaging strategies. Durk Pearson and Sandy Shaw's *Life Extension – A Practical Scientific Approach* has sold more than 1.7 million copies since 1982; the pair now run a clinic

21 Robert N. Butler, M.D., *Why Survive? Being Old in America* (New York: Harper & Row, 1975), pp. xii–xiii, 420.

22 Betty Friedan, *The Fountain of Age* (New York: Simon & Schuster, 1993), pp. 71–2.

23 Ibid., p. 24.

24 Adelle-Marie Stan, "Young Guru of Aging," *New Choices*, vol. 28 (December 1988): 10–12.

25 Ken Dychtwald, *Age Wave: The Challenges and Opportunities of an Aging America* (Los Angeles: Jeremy P. Tarcher, Inc., 1987), p. 350. The publishing information came from the front material of the "uncorrected proof" copy.

and mail-order business offering concoctions such as Power Maker II, which promises to "fire up your brain." In 1990 alone, Americans spent an estimated $3–4 billion on cosmetic surgery and another billion dollars on moisturizers, far more than is earmarked by federal agencies for aging-related research.[26]

Lawrence K. Frank, one of gerontology's principal U.S. architects, recognized as early as the 1950s that the field needed a new orientation. "In all research it is becoming clear that the often unrecognized concepts and assumptions, the unspoken preconceptions dictate which questions will be asked, what observations and measurements will be made, and how the findings will be interpreted," Frank wrote his friend, Clark Tibbitts. "We await more imaginative thinking and a new conception of the aging process."[27] To amplify this point, Frank revisited "field" theory, which he first had borrowed from the physical sciences:

> To develop a field theory, we must apparently give up the concept of specific entities with rigidly defined boundaries, and recognize that we are dealing with a total field in which we can distinguish continually fluctuating components. If I understand correctly, this is what happened in physics where an earlier conception of an electron as a specific entity has been replaced by the idea of an electron as indicating only a high probability that certain kinds of electrical charges will be present in a given location. . . . We are attempting to get away from fixed boundaries since they create a difficult problem of how to get across those boundaries. Thus, if we are faced by boundaries which are created by our own conceptual formulations, we then have to create another set of entities or processes to transcend the boundaries we have imposed on the situation.[28]

The metaphorical phrase "gerontology as a field" has become hackneyed. Gerontology's multidisciplinarity enriches analyses of specific problems, but researchers with necessary expertise are still deterred from entering into

26 Rochelle Green, "Can You Live Longer?," *Consumer Reports* (January 1992): 7–15. See also U.S. Congress, Senate, Special Committee on Aging, *Developments on Aging, 1991*, 101st Cong. 2d sess. (Washington, DC: Government Printing Office, 1992), vol. 1: 250–1. The National Academy of Science's Institute of Medicine hoped to persuade officials to increase the budget to $1 billion annually. At a time when the U.S. spent an estimated $616 billion on health care, the government's investment represented only 1.6 percent of the health budget. This does represent an improvement. See Institute on Medicine, "Aging and Medical Education," mimeo, September 1978, pp. 29–31. See also testimony by Richard C. Adelman before the Senate Committee on Appropriations, April 17, 1991. Researchers on aging have not yet figured out how to capitalize on this market for their knowledge.

27 Lawrence Frank to Clark Tibbitts, undated, handwritten letter (ca. 1959, based on internal evidence), in Tibbitts Papers, Box 5, Correspondence 1958–60, Bentley Historical Collection (henceforth abbreviated as BHC).

28 Lawrence K. Frank, "Analysis of Various Types of Boundaries," in *Toward a Unified Theory of Human Behavior*, ed. Roy R. Grinker (New York: Basic, 1956), pp. 354, 357.

aging-related conversations. The sort of paradigm shift that Frank envisioned for gerontology in the 1950s has occurred in such different domains as the geosciences and anthropology in the 1960s, psychiatry in the 1970s, and bioethics and genetic engineering in the 1980s.[29] Research on aging, I believe, would benefit from reassessing the field's metaphors and themes, including those that lately have received minimal attention.

Reconstructing gerontology

Scholars since Aristotle have extolled metaphors that stir human imagination. They provide, in I. A. Richards's phrase, "a transaction between contexts."[30] Lively metaphors prompt fitting comparisons; outmoded ones stultify thinking. One way to evaluate gerontology's intellectual growth is to go back to the primary sources, recover investigators' original intent, and determine if their present (dis)use seems appropriate in light of current knowledge. "The power of metaphor," according to Paul Ricoeur, is "to break an old categorization, in order to establish new logical frontiers on the ruins of their forerunners."[31] In operational terms, the challenge is to make "latent paradigms explicit" and to discard assumptions of depreciating value.[32]

29 On the geosciences, see John A. Stewart, *Drifting Continents & Colliding Paradigms* (Bloomington: Indiana University Press, 1990); and John McPhee, *Assembling California* (New York: Farrar, Straus & Giroux, 1993). On anthropology, Renato Rosaldo, *Culture & Truth* (Boston: Beacon, 1993), p. xvii. On psychiatry, Avram Mack, "The Remedicalization of Psychiatry," senior honors essay, University of Michigan, 1994. On genetic engineering, see Susan Wright, "The Social Warp of Science," *Science, Technology & Human Values*, vol. 18 (Winter 1993): 79–101; and idem, "Molecular Biology or Molecular Politics," *Social Studies of Science*, vol. 16 (1986): 593–620. On bioethics, see Leon Kass, *Toward a More Natural Science* (New York: Free Press, 1985); David J. Rothman, *Strangers at the Bedside* (New York: Basic, 1991); and Laurence J. O'Connell et al., eds., *Beyond Principles* (Valley Forge: Trinity Press, 1993). See also, Thomas Kuhn, "The Histories of Science," *Academe*, vol. 72 (1986): 29–33.

30 I. A. Richards, *The Philosophy of Rhetoric* (New York: Oxford University Press, 1965), p. 94. For Aristotle, see the 1954 Modern Library editions of his *Rhetoric*, pp. 168–89, and his *Poetics*, p. 255. See also, Andrew Ortony, ed., *Metaphor and Thought* (New York: Cambridge University Press, 1979), pp. 31–7; Nancy J. Nersessian, "How Do Scientists Think?" in *Minnesota Studies in the Philosophy of Science*, vol. 15: Ronald N. Giere, ed., *Cognitive Models of Science*, (Minneapolis: University of Minnesota Press, 1992), pp. 2–8.

31 Paul Ricoeur, *The Rule of Metaphor* (Toronto: University of Toronto Press, 1975), p. 197. See also, Paul Hoyningen-Huene, *Reconstructing Scientific Revolutions* (Chicago: University of Chicago Press, 1993), p. 163; P. B. Medawar, *The Threat and the Glory* (New York: HarperCollins, 1990), p. 4.

32 The phrase "latent paradigms" comes from Richard M. Lerner, ed., *Developmental Psychology: Historical and Philosophical Perspectives* (Hillsdale, NJ: Lawrence Erlbaum, 1983), pp. 165–6. Psychologist and computer scientist John Holland stressed the notion

Multidisciplinarity fosters the historical search for similarities amid dissimilarities in research on aging. To wit: When trailblazers such as Leonard Cain first presented their models of social gerontology, they stressed that "biological characteristics of man at various stages of the life course be recognized as limiting factors in the construction of age status patterns." Interdisciplinary research on aging, conversely, "has had a salutary effect on sociology by strengthening awareness of the importance of biology and other disciplines concerned with human behavior," according to Matilda White Riley.[33] Another example illustrates why gerontologists should look again at work done by "outsiders." Few now take seriously Leo Szilard's hypothesis of somatic mutation; the biophysicist failed to prove that exposure to radiation accelerated the aging process in certain species of wasps. "It may be a wrong theory," declared Szilard, "but it is a theory – in the sense that it has made hard and fast predictions."[34] In gerontology, where "hard and fast" explanations and predictions are not common, Szilard's ideas, like theories by nineteenth-century biologists Charles Sedgwick Minot and Edmund B. Wilson, may yet spark imaginations.

The theory of somatic mutation is only one of many multidisciplinary approaches that analyzes anatomical, metabolic, neurological, endocrinal, genetic, and pathological changes as well as environmental insults that occur at the (sub)cellular, molecular, organic, and systemic levels over an organism's life cycle. Biogerontologists have proposed, tested, and scrapped many hypotheses that fall under homeostatic, cell loss, catastrophic, cancer-related, circadian, free-radical, adduct formation, metabolic, nutritional, growth-limitation, and wear-and-tear theories of aging.[35]

Whereas many biogerontologists ground their research on aging in biochemistry, another (smaller) group subscribes to evolutionary theories of

of the "depreciating value" of ideas in an Institute of Gerontology seminar, December 9, 1993.

33 Leonard D. Cain, Jr., "Life Course and Social Structure," in *Handbook of Modern Sociology*, ed. Robert E. L. Faris (Skokie, IL: Rand McNally, 1964), p. 273. Cain devoted three pages to the topic. See also Matilda White Riley's memo, October 24, 1978, to Bernice Neugarten, in Neugarten's possession. Interestingly, while acknowledging the pioneering work of Cain and Norman Ryder, Riley does not say much about the importance of biology in her essay, "Sociology of Age," co-authored with Anne Foner and Joan Waring in *Handbook of Sociology*, ed. Neil J. Smelser (Newbury Pk., CA: Sage, 1988).

34 Editors of *International Science and Technology*, eds., *The Way of the Scientist* (New York: Simon & Schuster, 1966), p. 29; see also Gina Kolata, "Theory on Aging Is Tested, Adding 30% to Flies' Lives," *New York Times*, February 25, 1994.

35 See, for instance, Bernard L. Strehler, *The Biology of Aging* (Washington, DC: American Institute of Biological Sciences, 1960); Alex Comfort, *Ageing: The Biology of Senescence*, 2d ed. (New York: Holt, Rinehart & Winston, 1964); George A. Sacher, "Theory in Gerontology, Part I" in *Annual Review of Gerontology & Geriatrics*, ed., Carl Eisdorfer, vol. 1 (New York: Springer, 1980), pp. 3-25. I also used Vincent J. Cristofalo's paper, "The Future of Research on the Biology of Aging," presented at the twenty-fifth anniversary of the IoG.

senescence. In "The Duration of Life" (1889), August Weismann distinguished evolutionary causes from physiological approaches to senescence. Longevity, claimed Weismann, "is really dependent upon adaptation to external conditions . . . governed by the needs of the species."[36] The classic restatement of the evolutionary position was articulated in 1957 by George C. Williams, who deduced that "rapid morphogenesis should be associated with rapid senescence, that senescence should always be a generalized deterioration of many organs and systems, and that post-reproductive periods be short and infrequent in any wild population."[37] If Williams were correct, the force of natural selection simply declines with age: People adjust to their environment, but senescence is nonadaptive. Such methodological reductionism, according to Ernest Mayr, shows why "the theory of evolution is quite rightly called the greatest unifying theory in biology."[38]

"Death may not be related to aging," counters Edward Masoro, who points to "the enormous role that genetics play in the aging process."[39] Evolutionists acknowledge that widening gene pools may contribute to our survival, but insist that senescence reflects increased vulnerability to environmental insults. In the *Journal of Gerontology: Biological Sciences*, evolutionary biologist Michael Rose wrote, " 'Physiological aging' and related terms or concepts are of no significance for population genetics theory." And so the battle lines are drawn, but rarely crossed. As Richard Alexander observed, "it is curious that Williams' (1957) evolutionary theory of senescence, involving one of our most inexorable and disturbing characteristics, has not been adequately tested and has occupied very little research time and effort, despite its obvious explanatory potential and the expenditure of millions each year on gerontology."[40]

36 August Weismann, *Essays upon Heredity and Kindred Biological Problems* (Oxford: Oxford University Press, 1889), p. 9. See also Michael R. Rose, *Evolutionary Biology of Aging* (New York: Oxford University Press, 1991). The earliest Darwinian explanation of aging was advanced in the 1860s by Alfred Russel Wallace, a codiscoverer of natural selection.

37 George C. Williams, "Pleiotropy, Natural Selection, and the Evolution of Senescence," *Evolution*, vol. 11 (December 1957): 398–411; quotation on last page. I thank Paul W. Turke for introducing me to this literature and for sharing his 1992 paper, "Evolution of the 100 Year Lifespan – and Beyond," IoG.

38 Robert E. Kohler, *From Medical Chemistry to Biochemistry* (New York: Cambridge University Press, 1982); Vasiliki B. Smocovitis, "Unifying Biology," *Journal of the History of Biology*, vol. 25 (1992): 1–65; Alexander Rosenberg, *Sociobiology and the Preemption of Social Science* (Baltimore: Johns Hopkins University Press, 1980), p. 151.

39 For "facts" that support an evolutionary theory, see S. Jay Olshansky, Bruce A. Carnes, and Christine K. Cassel, "The Aging of the Human Species," *Scientific American*, vol. 268 (April 1993): 46–52; R. Floud, K. W. Wachter, and A. Gregory, *Height, Health and History* (New York: Cambridge University Press, 1990); and H. Th. Waaler, "Height, Weight, and Mortality," *Acta Medica Scandinavia*, supplement 679 (1983): 1–56. For a succinct gerontologic refutation, see Edward J. Masoro, "Biology of Aging," *Archives of Internal Medicine*, vol. 147 (January 1987): 166–9.

40 Michael R. Rose and Joseph L. Graves, Jr., "What Evolutionary Biology Can Do for

Since then, Caleb E. Finch's *Longevity, Senescence, and the Genome* (1990) tried to extend "gerontological thought beyond its usual focus on biological, medical, and social phenomena of late-in-life involution to basic issues that are central to developmental, evolutionary, and reproductive biology."[41] Finch compared species with different developmental patterns and adult life histories to formulate a typology of senescence that ranges from "rapid" to negligible. Eschewing a monocausal model, he hypothesized that different genomic influences vary according to the evolutionary history of each organism. His model lends some support to both evolutionists and physiologists.

Social scientists sometimes take advantage of new biological perspectives on senescence. "In the biological sciences, long-term, naturalistic field studies provided an impetus for fresh perspectives on parenthood and the life span," Jane Lancaster and associates observed. "New theoretical models transformed evolutionary biology as behavioral ecology advanced the concept of life history strategies and tactics and sociobiology modeled parent investment theory."[42] Similarly, Alice Rossi and Peter Rossi analyze parent–child relations over the life course in bioevolutionary terms. They consider their work an advance over "earlier deterministic models of adult development and of aging as programmed senescence," and they offer a fruitful method for charting "biopsychological processes of individual development and aging or institutional patterns that affect the timing, duration, and sequencing of statuses along the life line."[43]

An issue that interests the Rossis – whether continuities over the life cycle are more important than changes – has long fascinated gerontologists. "The same questions are involved in a study of ageing and senescence, as in the study of child growth and development," Lawrence K. Frank announced in 1940. "Maturity is a progressive change characterized by the capacity

Gerontology," *Journal of Gerontology*, vol. 44 (1989): B27–9. In "Evolutionary and Critical Gerontology," in *Voices and Visions of Aging*, ed. Thomas R. Cole et al. (New York: Springer, 1993), p. 71, Rose restated the argument positively: "The status of aging as a biological research problem will be transformed from marginal respectability to mainstream acceptance. All of the working parts of successful science will be in place, hard theory and hard experimentation. It would remain only to inform the rest of the scientific community of the new state of affairs." See also Richard D. Alexander, *The Biology of Moral Systems* (Hawthorne, NY: Aldine, 1987), p. 42; and Thomas B. L. Kirkwood, "Comparative and Evolutionary Aspects of Longevity," in *Handbook of the Biology of Aging*, ed., Caleb E. Finch and Edward L. Schneider, 2d ed. (New York: Van Nostrand Reinhold, 1985), pp. 36–8.

41 Caleb E. Finch, *Longevity, Senescence, and the Genome* (Chicago: University of Chicago Press, 1990), p. 646.

42 Jane B. Lancaster et al., eds., *Parenting Across the Life Span: Biosocial Dimensions* (Hawthorne, NY: Aldine, 1987), p. 3.

43 Alice S. Rossi and Peter H. Rossi, *Of Human Bonding* (Hawthorne, NY: Aldine, 1990), p. 12. See also Alice S. Rossi, "Sex and Gender in an Aging Society," in *Our Aging Society*, ed. Alan Pifer and Lydia Bronte (New York: Norton, 1986), pp. 111–39.

to function more or less adequately in accordance with the development needs and activities of the organism at each stage of growth."[44] Frank represented the stages of growth in a curvilinear manner, with adult maturity at the apex. "As in early childhood phases of life, there may, in later life, be a gradient of ageing which arises because of this intra-organic, functional interdependence, wherein the involution of one organ system and process evokes a series of changes in every other organ system and process. . . . Cell replacement, often with less differentiated forms, may offer an excellent clue to this process."[45] Frank deliberately was attempting to integrate environmental, biological, and behavioral factors, but he remained open to "the possibilities for refining . . . our conceptual formulations with which we order and interpret our data. This seems to be especially important in the study of ageing where both individual *variations* and the pattern of individual *variability* . . . [reveal] trends or progressive alterations revealed through a wide variety of observations made upon a single individual organism."[46] Gerontologists, according to Frank, should take a developmental perspective to multidisciplinary research.

Most postwar gerontologists ignored Frank's plea. They focused on the later years, probing the dynamics of "successful aging" and measuring morale, life satisfaction, and well-being. Their longitudinal studies rarely included children.[47] Conversely, most clinicians do not have much interest in gero-psychology. In a 1980 survey, 70 percent of all practitioners claimed that they never worked with the aged; only 0.4 percent of all clinicians devoted at least 51 percent of the practice on older patients. "We need to revitalize and redirect teaching, research and practice; we need to introduce psychologists to the hidden majority of American elders, the hardy survivors," declared David Gutmann recently. "Similar paradigm shifts are required to thaw our frozen, biased conception of the aging population."[48]

---

44 Lawrence K. Frank, "Comments on the Problems of Ageing Presented to the Meeting of the Club for Research on Ageing," January 12–13, 1940, mss. in the Nathan Shock Papers, Box 2, BHC.

45 Ibid., p. 9. The "curve with an upward and downward inflection" is on p. 10.

46 Ibid., p. 14. See also Lawrence Frank, "Time Perspectives," *Journal of Social Philosophy*, vol. 4 (July 1939): 293–312.

47 Linda K. George, "Social Structure, Social Processes, and Social-Psychological States," in *Handbook of Aging and the Social Sciences*, 3d ed., ed. Robert H. Binstock and Linda K. George (San Diego, CA: Academic, 1990), p. 188; George E. Vaillant and Caroline O. Vaillant, "Natural History of Male Psychological Health, XII," *American Journal of Psychiatry*, vol. 147 (January 1990): 31–7; Scientific Directorate, *Vitality for Life* (Washington, DC: American Psychological Association, July 1993). The APA represented the collective efforts of twenty-three organizations, including GSA and NIA.

48 David Gutmann, "The Disappearing Geropsychologist," *[Northwestern] Center on Aging*, vol. 8 (Fall 1992): 2, is a professor of Psychiatry and Education as well as director of the Older Adult Program (Psychology) at Northwestern. See also Klaus F. Riegel, "History as a Nomothetic Science," *Journal of Social Issues*, vol. 25 (1969): 99–127; John F. Santos

The intellectual framework for such a paradigm shift has already been laid. Paul Baltes and other life-span developmentalists study constancy and change, gain and loss, from conception to death; they look for multidirectional similarities and variations in individual plasticity through "a family of perspectives [that] characterizes the life-span approach."[49] Existing social-support and social-integration models complement this perspective. A life-span approach promotes qualitative gerontology. As Nancy Datan observed, "With the graying of America has come increased attention to the older population, manifest through a greater appreciation of the individual as active in the construction of knowledge, in the creation of consistency in personality development, and in the shaping of the life course."[50]

This approach also lends itself to work in the biomedical sciences. For more than two decades, the Seattle Longitudinal Prospective Study on Alcohol and Pregnancy has been assessing the long-term effects of moderate levels of prenatal alcohol exposure.[51] The Seattle team employed sophisticated biometric techniques for modeling latent variables through partial least squares to link physiological features and behavioral traits and to trace causal interactions over time. Methodologically, this alcohol study may expedite the search for "bio-markers" of aging "to measure senescence in a variety of physiological subsystems."[52]

Some researchers on aging will bristle at my proposal that a study of

and Gary R. VandenBos, *Psychology and the Older Adult* (Washington, DC: American Psychological Association, 1982).

49 Paul B. Baltes, "Theoretical Propositions of Life-Span Developmental Psychology," *Developmental Psychology*, vol. 23 (1987): 612.

50 Nancy Datan, Dean Rodeheaver, and Fergus Hughes, "Adult Development and Aging," *Annual Review of Psychology*, vol. 38 (1987): 176–7. See also Toni C. Antonucci, "Social Supports and Relationships," in *Handbook of Aging and the Social Sciences*, ed. Binstock and George, 3rd ed., pp. 218–9. See also the attempt to integrate a life-span approach in teaching in Iris A. Parham, Leonard W. Poon, and Ilene C. Siegler, *Access: Aging Curriculum Content for Education in the Social-Behavioral Sciences* (New York: Springer, 1990).

51 Among other things, the Seattle study shows that prenatal drinking is not "safe," but binge drinking has more serious consequences than "moderate" consumption in mid-pregnancy. Children suffering from fetal-alcohol syndrome encounter learning problems in arithmetic, and have difficulty with self-regulation and interpersonal conduct. See Ann P. Streissguth et al, *The Enduring Effects of Prenatal Alcohol Exposure on Child Development* (Ann Arbor: University of Michigan, 1993), pp. 13–14; Streissguth et al., "Neurobehavioral Effects of Prenatal Alcohol," *Neurotoxicology and Teratology*, vol. 11 (1989): 461–76.

52 One of the most ambitious postwar projects, the VA's Normative Aging Study, sought "a unifying concept which would enable the measurement of aging in its various aspects, and the relative rates of age change, both across areas and over the lifespan." Constructing biomarkers has proven a quixotic venture. In adopting Quetelet's ideas and methods about "social physics," researchers on aging failed to heed warnings about the misuse of "averages [that] projected themselves as laws in the future." For more on this, see Fred Bookstein and W. Andrew Achenbaum, "Aging and Explanation," in *Voices and Visions*, ed. Cole et al., pp. 20–45.

fetal alcoholism is relevant to understanding "normal" processes of senescence. Their objection conforms to a gerontologic tradition, for the historical record shows that few gerontologists have explored interactions between health *and* disease. At the same time U.S. Surgeon General Thomas Parran created a Public Health Service unit to study aging, he invoked the language of the 1937 Cancer Act "to make grants in aid to universities, hospitals, laboratories, and other public institutions" to study cancer and "other diseases." A. Baird Hastings had "qualms" about the scheme, "which left medical science in one compartment, biological science in another, and [made] little provision for bringing to bear the concentrated efforts . . . of physicists, chemists and the like."[53] Notions of "growth" and "development" as ongoing processes were at odds with the static ontology of clinicians' disease categories long before the "modern" era of gerontology. And, as we have seen, researchers still talk about "aging" and "disease" as if they exist in separate realms.[54] According to James Birren, overstating the distinction points to "the tensions in our explanatory systems, the gaps in our explanations and what past metaphors do not do for us in describing the characteristic pathways to old age."[55]

One reason that gerontologists have difficulty reconciling scientific images of aging and disease is that the relationship between morbidity and mortality has changed greatly. Nearly 90 percent of all Americans who died in 1850 were under the age of sixty-five compared to less than 40 percent in 1970; chronic diseases have replaced acute illness as the principal object of physicians' concern. Many diseases of late life are preventable or controllable, but with advancing age, risks increase: Only an eighth of all Americans over age sixty-five suffer from Alzheimer's disease, but nearly half of the population over age eighty-five are afflicted with the malady.[56] The AIDS epidemic, however, has forced the scientific community and the public at large to rethink the relationship between age and disease. The

53 Quotations in Daniel M. Fox, "The Politics of the NIH Extramural Program," *Journal of the History of Medicine and Allied Sciences*, vol. 42 (October 1987): 454, 460.

54 British medical scientists interested in pediatrics faced a comparable dilemma. See David Armstrong, "Child Development and Medical Ontology," *Social Science and Medicine*, vol. 13 (1975): 9–12. See also Daniel M. Fox, "The Segregation of Medical Ethics," *Journal of Medicine and Philosophy*, vol. 4 (1979): 81–97. For contemporary views, see John Rowe and Robert L. Kahn, "Human Aging," *Science*, vol. 237 (10 July 1987): esp. 148–9; and a paper, "Future of Aging Research," by Harvey J. Cohen delivered in Ann Arbor, October 11, 1990.

55 James E. Birren and Jackie C. Lanum, "Metaphors of Psychology and Aging," in *Metaphors of Aging in Science and the Humanities*, ed. Gary M. Kenyon, James E. Birren, and Johannes J. F. Schroots (New York: Springer, 1991), pp. 115, 126.

56 Howard Spierer, *Major Transitions in the Human Life Cycle* (U.S.A.: Academy for Educational Development, June 1977), p. 11 and fig. 4; David Armstrong, *Political Anatomy of the Body* (New York: Cambridge University Press, 1983), p. 87; Public Service, *Healthy People 2000* (Washington, DC: Government Printing Office, 1991); seminar by Carl Cottman, Institute of Gerontology, February 17, 1994.

acquired immune deficiency syndrome is a multifactorial, synergistic disease; no cure is in sight, but it can be managed under a propitious set of genetic, physical, and environmental conditions. Like Alzheimer's patients, victims of AIDS suffer chronic debilities and risk deadly infections from day to day. Such realities challenge the gerontologic wisdom of separating disease and illness from aging.[57] They invite us to seek historical precedents for studying them together.

The first group of U.S. researchers on aging, including two contributors to *Problems of Ageing* (Alfred E. Cohn and Louis Dublin), paid far more attention to chronicity than later cohorts. "Senescence is characterized by two outstanding manifestations – debility and increasing death rate," observed Henry S. Simms, a GSA charter member. "Of the two, debility seems to cause the greater concern to the average individual."[58] The federal government seemed willing to respond to the concern. "As the country's health workers speed their attack on vital problems, particularly those related to chronic diseases of old age, wide public support may be anticipated," opined Thomas Parran. "Never before has there been such keen and widespread interest in health matters throughout the land."[59] By the 1950s, however, research in aging rarely dovetailed with work on chronicity, and vice versa. Medical researchers focused on "their" disease or mechanism. Disability provisions were added to Social Security in the 1950s, yet those who advocated greater disability benefits soon perceived members of the gray lobby as competitors, not allies. The face of disability changed: In 1974, older people dominated the Supplemental Security Income (SSI) rolls; by 1994, most beneficiaries were children or the disabled.[60]

A convergence of interests between age and disabilities may be imminent, thanks to policy initiatives at the federal level. The short-lived Catastrophic Coverage Act (1988) amended Medicare to accommodate those with chronic illnesses by eliminating the requirement that hospitalization precede

57 Robert S. Root-Bernstein, *Rethinking AIDS* (New York: Free Press, 1993), p. 338; Bryan S. Turner, *Medical Power and Social Knowledge* (Newbury Pk., CA: Sage, 1987), p. 17.

58 Henry S. Simms, "Physiological Alterations as a Cause of Senile Debility and Senile Mortality," *Science*, vol. 91 (January 5, 1940): 4. Five years later, Simms, a Columbia medical professor, contended that 90 percent of all deaths in the United States resulted from the progressive loss of resistance to disease with advancing age. See also William I. Laurence, "Tomorrow You May Be Younger," *Ladies Home Journal*, vol. 62 (1945): 22; Ernst P. Boas, *Treatment of the Patient Past Fifty* (Chicago: Year Book Publications, 1941); Daniel M. Fox, *Power and Illness* (Berkeley and Los Angeles: University of California Press, 1993), pp. 42–5.

59 Quoted in Donald C. Swain, "The Rise of a Research Empire, NIH, 1930 to 1950," *Science*, vol. 138 (14 December 1962): 1,234–7.

60 Mental illness now represents the primary diagnosis of a quarter of those getting Disability or SSI checks, compared to 10 percent twenty years ago. See National Academy of Social Insurance, *News Link*, vol. 1 (December 1993): 2; Edward D. Berkowitz, *Disabled Policy* (New York: Cambridge University Press, 1988) and seminar, Institute of Gerontology, February 7, 1994.

coverage of nursing-home expenses. The Americans with Disabilities Act (1990) forbids "discrimination against a qualified individual because of the disability of such individual in regard to job application procedures; the hiring, advancement, or discharge of employees: employee compensation; job training; and other terms, conditions, and privileges of employment," language that parallels the intent of the Age Discrimination in Employment Act and the elimination of mandatory-retirement provisions. Any health-care reform in the 1990s doubtless will combine programs once intended for just the elderly or just the disabled.[61]

A rising cohort of investigators, moreover, has done the conceptual spadework necessary to recombine research on disability and aging in fresh ways. "In the Disablement Process," Lois Verbrugge and Alan Jette excoriate "a bedlam vocabulary" and "research protocols that combine items from different concepts." The pair focus on the onset and duration of chronic illnesses over the life span, analyzing acute conditions, brief episodes of impairment, lifelong disabilities, and youth-onset conditions: "The concept of disability is given no sociological heft. We stretch its scope to all activity domains, defend the metric of difficulty over dependency, introduce the notions of intrinsic and actual disability, and discuss the virtue and verity of a person–environment perspective."[62] Meanwhile, Fernando Torres-Gil told a meeting of Disabled American Veterans in 1993 that "the issues currently facing us – disability, aging, and the need for health care and long-term care – are all part of the same agenda." There is bound to be resistance to the message of the nation's first Assistant Secretary of Health and Human Services for Aging. Congress authorized an Arthritis Institute at the National Institutes of Health in 1984, but President Reagan vetoed it as too costly. Some gerontologists may see the emphasis on disability as further evidence of the "medicalization" of aging; they fear that it is a ploy that will backfire, increasing stereotypes of the elderly. Those who represent disability groups will be reluctant to erode their new-found visibility.[63]

"When should we abandon our metaphors?" wondered James Birren, who understands that metaphors do not inexorably yield to scientific hypotheses. Answering his own question, Birren noted that gerontologists had to look beyond their empirical data for broader implications: "There seem to

---

61 See section 102 of the Americans with Disabilities Act. See also Daniel M. Fox, "Policy and Epidemiology," *The Milbank Quarterly*, vol. 67 (1989): 279.

62 Lois M. Verbrugge and Alan M. Jette, "The Disablement Process," *Social Science Medicine*, vol. 38 (1994): 12.

63 W. Andrew Achenbaum, "View from Academe," *Aging Network News*, vol. 11 (February 1994): 9; Joseph P. Martino, *Science Funding* (New Brunswick: Transaction Publishers, 1992), p. 91. See also Bruce C. Blaney, "Adulthood or Oldness," paper presented at the Connecticut Council on Developmental Disabilities, November 1993.

be some large questions that shift in focus but never seem to be answered as more data accumulates."[64] Gerontology has come a long way from Metchnikoff's phagocytic theory. Given our current state of knowledge, it seems unlikely that future researchers will end up in Ponce de Leon's swamp or that their work will go up in smoke like the experiments and potions concocted by Tenier's alchemist. Nonetheless, there is still too little science in this multidisciplinary endeavor, and the power of gerontology's metaphors are now largely rhetorical. Comprehending the mysteries and problems of aging, as Bacon envisioned and Dewey warned, requires a combination of metaphors, facts, theories, networks, methods, and dreams.

Research on aging probably will remain at the borders of disciplinary enclaves and professional cultures. But gerontology is not obsolescent. Bolstered by changes in Big Science and federal policy-making, gerontologists enjoy opportunities for risk taking comparable to those that attracted eminent scholars to the field more than a half-century ago. Only self-reliant scholars (and, it must be admitted, foolhardy ones) dare to collaborate in multidisciplinary investigations in order to tackle a "big," multifaceted problem. Therein lies the excitement. This analysis suggests ways to proceed. In future interactions, I recommend that investigators take a life-span developmental approach to aging. They should also consider a fuller repertoire of ideas about aging, including promising theories outside their specialties. Metaphors and themata emanating out of "the disablement process," in my opinion, point the way to imaginative theory building, which can yield practical outcomes. Gerontology will continue to open new frontiers of knowledge as long as highly trained scholars are willing to cross the boundaries of their own scientific training and appreciate the rewards of broadening their fields of vision.

64 Birren and Lanum, "Metaphors," p. 124. See also Klaus Riegel, *Psychology mon amour* (Boston: Houghton-Mifflin, 1978).

Index